AN AQUEOUS TERRITORY

AN AQUEOUS TERRITORY

Sailor Geographies and New Granada's

Transimperial Greater Caribbean World

ERNESTO BASSI

DUKE UNIVERSITY PRESS

Durham and London

2016

Library of Congress Cataloging-in-Publication Data
Names: Bassi, Ernesto, [date] author.
Title: An aqueous territory : sailor geographies and New Granada's
transimperial greater Caribbean world / Ernesto Bassi.
Description: Durham : Duke University Press, 2017. | Includes
bibliographical references and index.
Identifiers: LCCN 2016023570 (print)
LCCN 2016024535 (ebook)
ISBN 9780822362203 (hardcover : alk. paper)
ISBN 9780822362401 (pbk. : alk. paper)
ISBN 9780822373735 (ebook)
Subjects: LCSH: Geopolitics—Caribbean Area. | Caribbean
Area—Boundaries. | Caribbean Area—Commerce. | Caribbean
Area—History. | Caribbean Area—Politics and government. |
Imperialism.
Classification: LCC F2175.B37 2017 (print) | LCC F2175 (ebook) |
DDC 320.1/2—dc23
LC record available at https://lccn.loc.gov/2016023570

Cover art: Detail of Juan Álvarez de Veriñas's map of the southern portion of the
transimperial Greater Caribbean. Image courtesy of Archivo General de Indias,
Seville, Spain (MP-Panama, 262).

TO

CLAU, SANTI, AND ELISA,

mis compañeros de viaje

CONTENTS

ACKNOWLEDGMENTS

Writing about border crossers and the transimperial milieu they inhabited requires lots of international travel. Like Antonio Machado's (and Joan Manuel Serrat's) *caminante*, I have walked along many roads in the process of writing this book. And while I have not sailed a hundred seas, researching the lives of many who actually did has taken me to multiple archives and libraries on both sides of the Atlantic. In the process I have acquired many debts, met lots of wonderful people, and turned several libraries into my personal office.

Cornell University and the University of California, Irvine (UCI), the two institutions that I consider my academic homes, provided most of the financial support that made this book possible. Funds from Cornell's History Department and the Society for the Humanities covered a postdissertation trip to Colombia's National Archives in 2013. Cornell's Institute for the Social Sciences gave me the physical space and time I needed to finish the revision process. Grants and fellowships from UCI's Humanities Center, the School of Humanities, the Center in Law, Society and Culture, and the All-UC Group in Economic History allowed me to conduct archival research in Colombia, Spain, and the United Kingdom. A residency scholarship from the Escuela de Estudios Hispanoamericanos made research in Seville's Archivo General de Indias (AGI) possible.

Archival research cannot be conducted without those who retrieve the documents from their hidden underground repositories. The staff of London's National Archives and the friendly and collaborative employees of Seville's AGI provided invaluable help. In Colombia's Archivo General de la Nación, I benefited from the expertise of research room director Mauricio Tovar and the whole staff. I am particularly grateful to Ana López, Fabio Castro, Rovir Gómez, Anhjy Meneses, Zenaida López, Fredy Duque, Enrique Rodríguez, and Doris Contreras for guiding me when I had little idea of how to find what I was looking for.

My intellectual debts are many. Since 2012, I have been part of a superb academic community where I have found many friends and even more critical readers. Cornell's history department has not only given me the space and time needed to revise the dissertation on which this book is based but also offered a captive audience of fantastic colleagues, most of whom read substantial portions of this book and offered valuable feedback. Ray Craib has been the best senior colleague one could ask for. He read many full versions of the manuscript, and our numerous conversations clearly made this a better book while also making me a better historian. Robert Travers and Jon Parmenter also read the whole manuscript and made insightful comments that helped me better pitch the book to non–Latin Americanists. Most of my department colleagues read parts of my work for two lively and productive meetings of the Comparative History Colloquium. I am particularly grateful to Durba Ghosh, Derek Chang, and Eric Tagliacozzo for reading several chapters and offering useful advice, criticism, and bibliographical suggestions. Aaron Sachs, Camille Robcis, Margaret Washington, Rachel Weil, Mary Beth Norton, Judi Byfield, and María Cristina García also read portions of the manuscript and offered fruitful thoughts. Julilly Kohler-Haussman and Mostafa Minawi not only read large chunks of the manuscript but, most importantly, were cosufferers in the process of writing our first books. As department chair, Barry Strauss showed his full support of my career advancement by becoming a dear protector of my writing time. The administrative, technical, and logistical aid Katie Kristof, Barb Donnell, Judy Yonkin, and Kay Stickane provided allowed me to navigate Cornell and made many additional writing hours possible. Outside the history department, my fellow Cornell colonialist Ananda Cohen-Suárez has been one of the best interlocutors one could wish for. Some of the most stimulating conversations that greatly helped me frame and reframe my arguments took place during the first time I taught the graduate seminar on entangled histories of the Americas and the Atlantic. I thank Josh Savala, Kyle Harvey, Molly Reed, Esmeralda Arrizon-Palomera, and Elise Amfreville for their careful reading, thought-provoking questions, and provocative papers.

Before Cornell, I acquired my intellectual debts at UCI. My dissertation supervisor, Jaime Rodríguez, provided constant encouragement, read and reread every dissertation chapter, always offering precious feedback, and made sure to let me know that he expected much of me. I hope that I am fulfilling his expectations. In Rachel O'Toole I found the best mentor a grad student could hope for. Countless conversations with Rachel during and after my UCI years decisively influenced and continue to influence my approach to history, the historical profession, and life in academia. Steve Topik is a historian worth imitating. I certainly take from him the interest in locating Latin America and

Latin Americans in a larger global setting. Steve's office was always open, and sitting by his fair trade cups I participated in some of the most intellectually inspiring and exciting conversations of my graduate student years. Winston James paid careful attention to my initial attempts to define the Caribbean, and, despite not always agreeing on the matter, he took seriously my answers to the question, What is the Caribbean? Laura Mitchell introduced me to world history, an approach that decisively permeates my arguments and writing. Her Approaches to World History seminar greatly contributed to turning my initial idea of writing a local history of Caribbean Colombia into a much more stimulating project concerned with transimperial connections. David Igler, Pat Seed, Dan McClure, Eric Steiger, Alberto Barrera, Annette Rubado, Heidi Tinsman, Aubrey Adams, Tina Shull, Annessa Stagner, David Fouser, and Young Hee Kim read aspects of my graduate work that, in hindsight, I now see as my initial attempts to approach the transimperial Greater Caribbean from New Granada's shores. Raúl Fernández provided unconditional support and *sabor* throughout my Irvine years.

Beyond my two intellectual homes, many people and venues have made research, writing, and spreading my work a highly stimulating experience. In Bogotá, workdays at the archives often included lunch, coffee, and after-hours historical conversation with Daniel Gutiérrez, Jesse Cromwell, Sergio Mejía, and Carlos Camacho. In Seville, the midmorning breaks to get a timely *cafelillo con leche* provided both physical energy and mental stimulation to continue plowing through documents. I thank Ramón Aizpurúa, Luis Miguel Glave, Esther González, and Cameron Jones for the many great conversations we had over coffee. During my stay in London, my friend Bill Booth provided much-needed research assistance that made my short visit to Kew extremely productive.

As graduate student and assistant professor, I have benefited from participation in multiple seminars and conferences where I have met peers and mentors, many of whom later became friends. My participation in the annual meetings of the American Historical Association, the Gran Colombia Studies panels of the Conference on Latin American History, and the Forum on European Expansion and Global Interaction allowed me to share and receive valuable feedback on my work and to become part of an exciting community of historians whose work and ideas greatly influence my own. In particular, these venues allowed me to meet and share ideas with Alex Borucki, Marcela Echeverri, Pablo Gómez, Fabricio Prado, Linda Rupert, Elena Schneider, Madalina Veres, Molly Warsh, and David Wheat. Numerous invitations to present aspects of my work were also critical in refining my arguments and ideas. I thank the organizers of the New York State Latin American History Workshop (Bridget Chesterton), the Colloquium of the Omohundro Institute of Early American History and Culture (Elena Schneider), the conference "Placing History, Historicizing Geography" (Bertie Mandelblatt and Dean Bond), the conference "Rethinking Space in Latin American History" (Stuart Schwartz, Gil Joseph, Santiago Muñoz, and Adrián Lerner), the workshop "Entangled Histories of the Early Modern British and Iberian Empires and Their Successor Republics" (Jorge Cañizares-Esguerra, Bradley Dixon, Christopher Heaney, and Mark Sheaves), and the conference "Rethinking Historical Space/Area in Historical Study" (Martin Klimke, David Ludden, Lauren Minsky, and Mark Swislocki) for putting together outstanding venues for intellectual exchange. I also thank the attendants at these events for pushing me to think harder about regions, geography, the sea, and more. Invitations by Johanna von Grafenstein (Instituto Mora), Jonathan Ablard (Ithaca College), Francisco Scarano (University of Wisconsin, Madison), and Nancy Appelbaum (Binghamton University) forced me to organize my thoughts and further refine my arguments. Many conversations and e-mail exchanges with Anne Eller on the Greater Caribbean during the Age of Revolutions shaped my thinking. I also thank her for close readings of the introduction and the conclusion. Nancy Appelbaum, Lina del Castillo, and Andrea Wulf taught me a great deal about Colombia's politician-geographers and the Bolívar-Humboldt connection. Anne McPherson's comments on an early version of chapter 3 helped me present the story of maritime Indians better. Before I decided to become a professional historian, Linda Newson and Alberto Abello introduced me to the history of colonial Latin America and to the serious study of Caribbean Colombia that, in the long term, resulted in this book.

At Duke University Press, Gisela Fosado has provided fantastic guidance to this neophyte of book publishing. She liked what I presented at a conference, asked for more, and continued to like the succeeding versions. Art editor Christine Riggio drew beautiful maps and helped me prepare all the illustrations. Lydia Rose Rappoport-Haskins guided me through the final stages of manuscript preparation. I am deeply thankful to the two anonymous readers whose wise comments, critiques, and suggestions pushed me to revise, reorganize, and rewrite important portions of the manuscript. Both readers demonstrated an enthusiasm for the book that greatly encouraged me to work hard on the revision process.

Throughout the research and writing process I was lucky to count on supportive friends and family who made research and writing possible. In Bogotá, Mauricio Calderón and Isabella Gardeazábal and my aunt Carmen Arévalo made their homes my home. Staying with them not only allowed me to stretch my meager financial resources but, most importantly, gave me companionship during lonely weekends when I missed my family the most. In London, María Isabel Irurita, Juan Camilo Cock, and Martina were the best hosts one could ask for. Staying with them not only resulted in a free-of-charge London but also gave me the great joy of meeting old friends again.

The help of my immediate family has been simply immeasurable. My parents, Chila and Rafa, have always supported my historical endeavors and have actually been pretty interested in my research and writing. My interest in the Caribbean, in fact, I owe in great part to them. *Muchas gracias mami y papi!* Claudia Roselló and Santiago Bassi have been my fellow travelers along this historical road. When I was abroad doing research, they held the fort back in California. When I was home, they encouraged me and created regenerative distractions that helped me think better and pushed me to keep writing. Elisa Bassi joined us later in the journey. For most of her life, Ithaca has been home, which means that she has had to put up with less research-related absence than Clau and Santi. But, like Clau and Santi, Elisa has caught me (several times) thinking about the book at moments when I should have been giving my undivided attention to my playful daughter. Even before this book was in the makings, Clau, in the words of Serrat, *cerró su puerta y echó andar.* Today, three countries and more than a decade later, she is still here and, with Santi and Elisa, continues to hold the home fort when I am away.

Clau, Santi, and Elisa, I thank you for joining me in creating our own geography and envisioning a wild variety of potential futures. This book is for you. It is what it is, in part, because of you. I am the historian that I am, in large part, because of you. The flaws, though, are solely mine.

Uncovering Other Possible Worlds

Geography's discursive attachment to stasis and physicality, the idea that space "just is," and that space and place are merely containers for human complexities and social relations, is terribly seductive. . . . If space and place *appear* to be safely secure and unwavering, then what space and place make possible, outside and beyond tangible stabilities . . . can potentially fade away. Geography is not, however, secure and unwavering; *we produce space, we produce its meanings, and we work very hard to make geography what it is.*

—KATHERINE MCKITTRICK, *Demonic Grounds*

On October 13, 1815, the legislature of the young republic of Cartagena approved a proposal to put the city under the protection of the British Crown. Swearing allegiance to His Britannic Majesty, Cartagena's governor Juan de Dios Amador believed, constituted "the only measure capable of saving this city." Besieged since mid-August by a strong Spanish contingent under field marshal Pablo Morillo, Cartagena, independent since November 1811, was targeted for favoring political autonomy over allegiance to King Ferdinand VII after the French invaded the Spanish Peninsula in 1808. "Let us," Governor Amador said, "offer the province [of Cartagena] to a wise and powerful Nation, capable of saving . . . and governing us. Let us put [the province] under the shelter and direction of the Monarch of Great Britain." Cartagena's legislature did not need much time to reach a decision. Persuaded that "under the circumstances manifested" the governor's proposal was "the only one capable of saving the State," the legislature unanimously approved Amador's measure and granted him power to contact the British authorities of Jamaica.[1] On the next day, Amador dispatched a commission to inform the authorities of Jamaica of the decision. That same day (October 14, 1815), Gustavo Bell Lemus tells us, "the British flag was raised in the city [of Cartagena]."[2] In Jamaica, reasserting their recent commitment to remain neutral in Spain's conflict with its American territories, British authorities refused to provide any help to Cartagena's delegates. Without external support, Cartagena, unable to resist the Spanish siege, surrendered to Spanish forces on December 6, 1815.[3]

The siege of Cartagena is a well-known piece of Colombia's patriotic narrative.[4] Because of its tenacious resistance during the siege, the city is known to all Colombians as "the heroic city." The request of Cartagena's legislature to offer the province to the British Crown is less known. Historians of Colombia, especially those specializing in the local history of Caribbean Colombia, are familiar with the declaration but have not delved into its analytical possibilities, simply regarding it as a desperate measure taken under desperate circumstances. Since the proposal was ultimately rejected, it has been considered inconsequential, a mere anecdote with little value to understand Colombia's nation-making process.

While this book is not about Cartagena (although Cartagena figures prominently in its pages), the city's 1815 siege and, in particular, the request of its legislative body serve as a good introduction to the book's approach. Instead of a history concerned with explaining origins (i.e., a genealogy of what ended up happening), this book advances a history that rescues the notion that for any given historical outcome there were many alternatives. These alternatives, many of which, as Peter Linebaugh and Marcus Rediker put it, "have . . . been denied, ignored, or simply not seen," offer us a window to understand that what ended up happening was not bound to happen.[5] Read in this light, the request of Cartagena's legislature emerges as a telling example that "another world *was* possible," one in which, as Cartagena's legislators unsuccessfully hoped, the wars of independence that resulted in the creation of the Republic of Colombia could have resulted in the establishment of a British colony in the Caribbean coast of the Viceroyalty of New Granada.[6] This study does not depict that unrealized future (i.e., it does not pursue the counterfactual question of what might have happened if the British authorities had accepted the request of Cartagena's legislature). It does, however, take seriously the notion that a British Cartagena was a constitutive part of the "horizon of expectation" of the city's legislators.[7] It was part of what, in her analysis of colonial internationalisms in the twentieth-century interwar era, Manu Goswami called the "open-ended constellation of contending political futures" that informed what Cartagena's legislators and other city residents considered a plausible world.[8]

The implications of this approach for our understanding of Caribbean and Colombian history are considerable. To think of what the subjects we study considered plausible forces us out of entrenched habits of narration that naturalize a definition of the Caribbean region as consisting only of the Caribbean islands and an understanding of Colombia as a country lacking strong historical connections with its Caribbean neighbors. By stressing the thick connections linking New Granada's coasts with Jamaica, Curaçao, Hispaniola, Saint Thomas, and the coastal cities of the United States (chapters 1 and 2), and by explaining the "decaribbeanization" process through which early Colombia's nation makers chose to erase these connections (chapter 6), this book uncovers ways of inhabiting the world that are not captive to anachronistic world-regionalization schemes and, thus, allows us to understand how the historical subjects we study developed a sense of place—how they located themselves in the larger world—and envisioned potential futures for themselves and those whom they claimed to represent.

An Aqueous Territory: Sailor Geographies and New Granada's Transimperial Greater Caribbean World traces the configuration of a geographic space—the transimperial Greater Caribbean—and the multiple projects its inhabitants developed to envision their future, their geopolitical imagination.[9] It approaches these two processes from the perspective of the Caribbean coast of northwestern South America—from Cape Gracias a Dios to the Guajira Peninsula, or what during the eighteenth and early nineteenth centuries was referred to in Spanish sources as the northern provinces of the Viceroyalty of New Granada and in British sources as the Spanish Main. From this geographical vantage point, the study of the configuration of a transimperial Greater Caribbean and its inhabitants' geopolitical imagination turns into a study of the creation of a transimperial geography that connected Caribbean New Granada with the "British" Caribbean (especially Jamaica), the "French" Caribbean (especially Saint-Domingue or Haiti), the "Dutch" Caribbean (especially Curaçao), and, under specific circumstances explained in chapter 1, "Danish" Saint Thomas and the United States.[10]

The geographical vantage point of the analysis is important because it allows for the transimperial Greater Caribbean—a regional space that in chapter 2 I define as malleable and flexible—to look different, to cover a different area depending on the vantage point taken. While from the vantage point of New Granada's Caribbean coast, Neogranadan ports like Portobelo, Cartagena, Santa Marta, and Riohacha and ports that face the southern Caribbean Sea (Kingston, Les Cayes, Curaçao) appear prominently, the use of a different vantage point results in other ports taking center stage. Studies of New Orleans as commercial center of a geographic space similarly evolving from transimperial or transnational connections, for example, make ports like

Havana and Cap Français (later Cap Haïtien) more visible. Something similar happens when Florida becomes the vantage point. When studying commercial connections between New Spain (Mexico) and the Caribbean, Veracruz, Havana, Puerto Rico, Spanish Florida, Spanish Louisiana, and Santo Domingo, all of which received *situados* (financial transfers to cover defense expenditures) from the Viceroyalty of New Spain, appear as the key nodal points of the Greater Caribbean.[11]

The geographical vantage point also highlights the extent to which key economic and social institutions spread unevenly through space. Slavery, for the purposes of this book, provides the best example. While from the vantage point of Cuba the demand for more slaves that emerged immediately after the outbreak of the Haitian Revolution ushered in the island's sugar revolution and its concomitant loyal adherence to the Spanish Crown, similar cries voiced from New Granada's Caribbean shores were initially ignored or not heard by imperial authorities and then completely silenced by the turmoil and diplomatic imperatives of the wars of independence. From Cuban shores, thus, slavery and enslaved people were among the most visible elements of a transimperial Greater Caribbean.[12] The view from New Granada was quite different. Because *An Aqueous Territory* embraces the Greater Caribbean from New Granada's shores, slavery appears in this book more as a project in the minds of bureaucrats and local elites who aspired to become wealthy planters than as a reality experienced in the flesh by a large group of the region's inhabitants. This is not to say that there were no slaves on New Granada's Caribbean shores but that the northern provinces of the viceroyalty were, like Cuba before its sugar revolution, "more a society with slaves than a slave society."[13]

An Aqueous Territory advances two central arguments: first, that in the decades between the end of the Seven Years' War and the final years of the wars that led to the emergence of the Republic of Colombia, sailors frequently crisscrossing political borders in Caribbean and Atlantic waters and gathering and spreading information obtained at ports and on the high seas constructed the space of social interaction, or region, that I call the transimperial Greater Caribbean; second, that, like sailors, many other less mobile subjects used this transimperial geographical framework as a chalkboard on which they conceived analyses of their present and visions of potential futures. While many of these visions never came to fruition, those who envisioned them certainly intended to turn them into reality. Because both mobile sailors and less mobile coastal and island denizens influenced and were influenced by the development of this transimperial geography, it can be asserted that the actors of this book lived in what Jesse Hoffnung-Garskof has called "a transnational [or transimperial] social field." Life in this transimperial milieu led them to develop what Micol Seigel called "transnational [or transimperial] mental maps" that allowed them to make sense of the world they inhabited.[14]

Given the agitated geopolitical environment of the second half of the eighteenth and the first half of the nineteenth centuries, the circumstances under which Caribbean dwellers created spaces and envisioned futures were complex and full of contradictions. During the Age of Revolutions the political map of the Atlantic as well as its commercial codes and legal cultures were greatly transformed. New republics began to emerge where there had previously been colonies and European overseas territories. Imperial reformers successfully pushed for less stringent commercial restrictions, and European powers began to view interimperial trade in more favorable terms while remaining wary of the smuggling practices associated with these commercial transactions.[15] Slavery and the slave trade became targets of criticism—from below and from above—that led several empires and emerging republics to abolish one or the other during the first decade of the nineteenth century. At the same time, however, the period witnessed the biggest increase in slave imports to the Americas, a trend that was particularly marked in Spanish America, which, in the century between the outbreak of the American Revolution and 1866, imported 60 percent of the slaves it imported since the beginning of the slave trade.[16] As Greg Grandin forcefully argued, the Age of Revolutions, sometimes characterized as the Age of Liberty, was also the Age of Slavery. From Spanish American shores the calls for "*más libertad*" were accompanied by cries for "*más comercio de negros*—more liberty, more free trade of blacks."[17] These dramatic transformations and contradictions nourished Caribbean inhabitants' sense of what was possible, sharpening their awareness of what geographer Doreen Massey has called "contemporaneous plurality" and, most likely, emboldening many to pursue chimeric projects conceived within the Greater Caribbean's transimperial geography.[18]

This book uncovers other worlds by making visible a geographic space that was lived and experienced but not necessarily filled with the patriotic sentiment of nation-states or the geopolitically charged justifications of area-studies divisions. Additionally, because most of the projects pursued by the subjects who populate this work did not reach fruition, *An Aqueous Territory* uncovers other worlds in the sense that it complicates standard narratives of the Age of Revolutions that see this period as one of violent, but straightforward, transition from colony to nation. By contrast, taking seriously the conception of these projects and the belief that they constituted plausible scenarios, this book reveals the existence of "structures of feeling" that crossed imperial borders and determined transimperial "ways of being in the world," many of which have remained silenced by the historiographical weight of national states, nation-making projects, and nationalisms.[19]

Border-Crossing and the Creation of a Transimperial Greater Caribbean

The process of creating spaces is associated with one of two key terms that constitute the conceptual foundations of this study: spatial configurations. Following Edward Soja and other scholars of space, I argue against the existence of "an already-made geography [that] sets the stage" for history to happen.[20] Instead, with Doreen Massey, I take space "as always in process," "as always under construction."[21] The recognition of this dynamic and constructed nature of space is crucial in two respects. First, it forces us to ask questions about the nature of the construction process. Who is constructing the space? Through what processes? Under what circumstances? Second, it requires us to interrogate the outcome of the process. What is the shape of the space that is being created? To whom is this space meaningful and how? How does this space enable a better understanding of the world, peoples, and period we are studying? While these questions are empirically answered in chapters 1 and 2, it is worth laying out some of the theoretical and methodological sources that inform my approach to these spatial questions. The idea of region is a good place to begin.

Region, like nation, is a commonly used term. Unlike nation and nationalism, however, region and regionalism have not been subjected to acute historical scrutiny. The fact that region is used to describe both subnational and supranational geographic spaces reveals the degree to which the term remains undertheorized.[22] In fact, as historian Michael Goebel put it, it seems that the most common way to define a region is "through what it is not: a nation."[23] Despite this sharp distinction, regions and nations (or, more precisely, the territorialized versions of nations: nation-states) have many things in common.

Like nation-states (and empires), regions occupy space and, because of that, can be located on maps. Unlike nation-states (and empires), however, regions' precise locations tend to be difficult to determine. Even for regions with denominations commonly used (e.g., the South East in the United Kingdom, the South in the United States, the Bajío in Mexico, Southeast Asia, Latin

America, the Atlantic), "it is very difficult to say precisely where [a region's] edges" are or when a particular region constitutes a coherent geographic unit of analysis.[24] Regions, historians tend to agree, are "elusive" and characterized by their "fuzziness."[25] Should the elusiveness and fuzziness of regions be regarded as a problem to be solved? Should historians aim to establish criteria that make it possible to define regions as clearly bounded spatial units? In other words, how should historians conceptualize regions and what, ultimately, is the trouble with regions?

Following geographers John Allen, Doreen Massey, and Allan Cochrane and critical theorist Michel de Certeau, I contend that regions should be conceptualized as fluidly bounded and amorphously demarcated spatial units shaped and reshaped through everyday social interactions.[26] This approach calls for understanding regions as meaningful geographic spaces that make sense to those who experience them on a daily basis. While what is meaningful and makes sense appears to be intangible and difficult to measure, it allows me to point to a crucial element of regions: "they are," as Eric van Young put it, "difficult to describe but we know them when we see them."[27]

Thinking of regions in these terms, in turn, creates another set of problems associated with the need to make regions comprehensible and visible to scholars accustomed (and even trained) to see spatial units in close connection to political geographies, most of which are constructed based on what Neil Smith and Ann Godlewska called a "European planetary consciousness" that privileges empires, republics, and other clearly bounded spaces over equally cohesive (at least to those who experienced them) but less clearly demarcated spatial units.[28] The problem, as Fernando Coronil argued, is that we "lack . . . an alternative taxonomy" that allows us to identify and name spatial units that might have been lived realities but that did not benefit from the elaborated apparatus that enabled empires and nation-states to occupy central stage in the historical imagination.[29] After all, regions, unlike empires and nation-states, are not generally backed up by administrative bureaucracies, nationalist ideologies and discourses, political agendas, and other propagandistic devices that grant political geographies archival visibility and the ability to endure in collective memory.[30] How, given their lack of this elaborated apparatus that, taught to those who learn to feel national pride and nationalist fervor, works as the glue that holds nations together, can regions—especially those constructed from below—be imagined and made visible? My contention is that taking mobility as a defining criterion has the potential to illuminate regional configurations and communities that escape the eyes trained or coerced to look for "imagined communities" that cohere around linguistic, religious, or ethnic units, the weight of imperial bureaucracies, and the printed trail left behind by patriotic narratives, cartographic representations, and other cultural artifacts of nation making.[31]

Mobility, Tim Cresswell and Peter Merriman claim, "create[s] spaces and stories."[32] Through mobility individuals fill space with meaning; they develop "a sense of place"; they "endow . . . significance to space."[33] During the Age of Sail, sailors were the mobile actors par excellence. Frequently moving across political borders in a constant circulation between ports, islands, and coasts, individual sailors traced personal paths that gave shape to their very own lived geographies. The aggregation of innumerable lived geographies makes it possible to see the contours of what in chapter 2 I call the aqueous territory that constitutes the transimperial Greater Caribbean. The region that emerges of the sum of individual sailors' mobilities is one that can be characterized as amorphously bounded, flexible, malleable, multicultural, geopolitically unstable, and both personally threatening and liberating. In this transimperial space, in addition, the sea, far from being "just . . . a space that facilitates movement between a region's nodes," emerges as a central component of the regional configuration.[34] "Rather than an interval between places," it becomes "a place."[35]

Unearthing the transimperial Greater Caribbean that emerges from the aggregation of sailors' personal geographies, I argue, contributes to a better understanding of the world that sailors and the other characters of this book inhabited. Rescuing this aqueous territory as a constructed and evolving lived geography constitutes an important antidote to historical narratives that take nation-states, area-studies divisions, and empires as geographic units of analysis that remain fixed through time. Fixing geography—or, as Patrick Manning put it in his critique of the "parochialism and exceptionalism" characteristic of area studies, limiting the geographic unit of analysis ex ante—creates the fiction that history unfolds within clearly bounded, previously determined, and historically static areas.[36] In doing so, the demarcation of an area silences many lived experiences and hinders our understanding of the world, peoples, and times we study. In other words, historians working within previously defined geographic units of analysis projected backward onto a past for which these units lack explanatory power run the risk of misinterpreting the lives of the subjects they study. As Walter Johnson argued in his reframing of the history of the Mississippi Valley's Cotton Kingdom and the U.S. Civil War, framing the stories we tell "according to a set of anachronistic spatial frames and teleological narratives" hinders our ability to understand where the subjects that we study "thought they were going and how they thought they could pull it off."[37]

In the specific context of this book, the implication of uncovering the transimperial Greater Caribbean as seen from New Granada's shores is that it represents an explicit acknowledgment that the subjects under study did not live lives bounded by the political geographies of the time nor were their lived experiences circumscribed by geographical frameworks defined after their own time. Their lives, in short, make evident the extant, but limited, value of using geographical labels like Colombia, Caribbean, Latin America, and Atlantic to encapsulate their lived experiences and understand how they interpreted their place in the world. This book's subjects inhabited a space that comprised islands, continental coasts, and open waters, a space that was not exclusively Spanish, British, or French but simultaneously Spanish, British, and French, as well as Dutch, Danish, Anglo-American, African—or, more specifically, Cocolí, Bran, Biafada, Zape, Kimbanda, and more—and indigenous, or, more precisely, Wayuu, Cuna, Miskito, Carib, Creek, and more. Theirs, as a historian of Curaçao's place in the early modern Atlantic has put it, was a world of "connections that extended across political, geographic, legal, socioeconomic, and ethnic boundaries, beyond a single colony or empire."[38] It was an "entangled" world.[39] The transimperial Greater Caribbean brings these entanglements to the analytical center stage and, because of this, constitutes an alternative framework that, like other ocean- or sea-based world regionalization schemes, "allow[s] us to see some things clearly, while making others difficult to detect."[40] The implication here is not that a transimperial Greater Caribbean framework is inherently better than other geographical frameworks but that uncovering it brings to life human interactions occluded by conventional definitions of the Caribbean that tend to create an artificial barrier between the continent's coasts and the Caribbean islands.

Like many other geographical labels, "Caribbean" constitutes an example of the type of "summary statements" that, Ann Stoler believes, need to be further scrutinized.[41] The term must be recognized as an "inaccurate but convenient label," whose uncritical use can result in the production of historical narratives that unconsciously silence key aspects of the lived experiences of the subjects we study and, unconsciously or not, tend to transform history into a teleological narrative that forecloses the possibility of thinking geographical spaces (and history) otherwise.[42]

Defining the Caribbean constitutes a sort of rite of passage for Caribbeanists. Following and expanding the tracks laid down by Sidney Mintz, innumerable Caribbeanists have given us a variety of answers to the question, What is the Caribbean?[43] Emphasizing the role of the Plantation (with a capital P) as unifying factor, Mintz, Antonio Benítez-Rojo, Franklin Knight, and many others have defined the Caribbean as a "societal area" characterized by its "lowland, subtropical, insular economy," a history of European colonialism that featured the swift extirpation of the region's native population, the development of export-oriented agricultural productive units, the massive introduction of foreign populations (mostly African slaves but also Asian coolies), a persistence of colonialism, and the emergence of what Knight called a "fragmented nationalism."[44] The outcome of this characterization, when visualized on a map, is a geographic space that encompasses Cuba, Hispaniola (Haiti and the Dominican Republic), Jamaica, Puerto Rico, the Bahamas, the Lesser Antilles, Belize, and the Guianas. The continent's Caribbean coasts, thus, are mostly denied their belonging to the Caribbean.

Efforts to understand the Caribbean beyond the Plantation have allowed historians to visualize the region as a larger geographic space, as a Greater Caribbean.[45] Emphasizing environmental factors, Matthew Mulcahy, Sherry Johnson, and Stuart Schwartz have demonstrated that hurricanes can be region makers. In their studies, a natural phenomenon—hurricanes—gives coherence to a geographic space that forces us to reconsider the size and limits of the Caribbean. Their Greater Caribbean is a region defined by nature—it is there. Humans do not create it; they adapt to it.[46] Allowing more room for humans in the creation of the Greater Caribbean, J. R. McNeill combines ecological contexts with human activity to show how humans, in their capacity as agents of environmental change, turned what was already an ideal site for the incubation of the mosquitoes that carry malaria and yellow fever into an improved breeding and feeding ground where these mosquitoes could thrive. In McNeill's approach, thus, the malaria- and yellow fever–carrying mosquitoes, aided by the deforestation and soil depletion humans produced, gave meaning to a geographic space comprising "the Atlantic coastal regions of South, Central, and North America, as well as the Caribbean islands themselves, that in the course of the seventeenth and eighteenth centuries became plantation zones: from Surinam to the Chesapeake."[47] This Greater Caribbean was not just there for humans to adapt to it, as that of Schwartz, Mulcahy, and Johnson. Instead, it emerged as an unintended consequence of human activity on an area that shared a set of ecological traits.

An Aqueous Territory proposes another approach: one that stresses the human-made nature of regional configurations, the role of social interactions in the creation of regions, and the dangers associated with projecting twentieth-century world regionalization schemes back onto a past for which they lack explanatory power. While not inherently better than other approaches to the region, the Greater Caribbean of this book offers a historically sensitive way of understanding how the sea captains and sailors, military adventurers, indigenous peoples, imperial bureaucrats, insurgent leaders, and nation makers that populate this book's pages produced, used, and transformed a geographic space. A transimperial Greater Caribbean framework enables a better understanding of the ways in which these mobile and not-so-mobile subjects "order[ed] their knowledge [and experience] of the world."[48] Paraphrasing Karl Marx, it is possible to assert that just as "men [and women] make their own history," people make their own geography. Neither history nor geography are made "under self-selected circumstances, but under circumstances existing already, given and transmitted from the past" and, it must be added, the present.[49]

Envisioning Futures in a Transimperial Greater Caribbean Milieu

The second key term that provides conceptual coherence to this book is geopolitical imagination. By geopolitical imagination, I understand, following geographers John Agnew and Gearóid Ó Tuathail, the ways in which individuals and groups "visualiz[e] global space" and conceive and present arguments about "the future direction of world affairs" and "the coming shape of the world political map."[50] This definition allows for every person to be a geopolitical analyst—it democratizes geopolitics and the geopolitical imagination—thus taking the exclusive rights to a geopolitical imagination away from "major actors and commentators" to put geopolitics within the reach of subalterns and other *minor* actors.[51]

As used in this book, the concept is closely related to imagined communities, the term Benedict Anderson popularized as a way to define a nation and the nationalist pride of belonging to such a political community.[52] While Anderson's origins inquiry—he was interested in explaining "the origins and spread of nationalism"—allowed him to develop a compelling explanation of why and how the nation-state became the hegemonic way of envisioning and organizing global space, it made him blind to the existence of what Akhil Gupta called "other forms of imagining community" or "structures of feelings that bind people to geographical units larger than nations or that crosscut national borders."[53] Like Gupta, as well as Partha Chatterjee and Arjun Appadurai, I seek to uncover visions of community that ended up being "overwhelmed and swamped by the history of the postcolonial [national] state."[54] That the nation-state ended up being the hegemonic "imagined political community" does not mean that it was destined to be.[55]

The notion of geopolitical imagination is also associated with the concept of "mental maps." Defined as "the ways in which people build up images of other places," mental maps invite us to approach the world of those we study in their own subjective terms, which is to say, to imagine the "imaginary worlds" they imagined.[56] Mental maps usually result in the production of geographical distortions that transform absolute space (i.e., space that can be "measured by distance: inches, feet, meters, miles, etc.") into a mental construction in which other variables become consciously or unconsciously chosen tools to measure and experience proximity.[57] Mental maps allow us to understand that distance, as Sylvia Sellers-García put it, is "less a question of measurement and more a question of perspective."[58] Remoteness and proximity are in the eye of the beholder. In the transimperial Greater Caribbean, as this book shows, the sense of distance or proximity could be measured through—among many other variables—fear of invasion, availability and affordability of goods, access to news and information, desire for revenge, the threat of economic decline, racial prejudice, and intellectual formation. Rather than imposing on the subjects I study anachronistic ways of seeing, experiencing, and envisioning the world, thinking about their mental maps allows me to frame their actions within their own frameworks of interpretation. In this sense, instead of limiting their field of vision by forcing their imagination to fit within predetermined geographical compartments that forcefully separate what was actually connected, I let those whose lives I study define their world and show us the potential futures they envisioned and the projects through which they sought to implement them.

For the inhabitants of New Granada who participated in the creation of the transimperial Greater Caribbean and took part (or intended to take part) in projects conceived within this transimperial milieu, a future as members of a political community we now know as the Colombian nation was only one of many imagined possibilities. That the imagined political community called Colombia ended up prevailing should not discourage the study of the multiple alternative communities to which New Granada's inhabitants imagined they could belong. In terms of geographical extension, the communities envisioned ranged in size from tiny independent city- and island-states like the ephemeral republics established in Caracas, Cartagena, and Florida

(Muskogee and Amelia Island) to the ambitious continental project of creating a vast, hemispheric confederation of independent republics.[59] Regarding the political model best suited to these nascent political entities, the visions included dreams of establishing an independent, constitutional monarchy preceded by a European prince, debates about the type of republicanism—federalist or centralist—that needed to be established, and even projects to paint northern South America imperial pink and incorporate it into the British Empire.[60] In the transimperial Greater Caribbean of the Age of Revolutions, people literally lived between a variety of imperial projects and national dreams.

Their projects, associated as they indeed were with particular mental maps or with what, following Thongchai Winichakul, can be called an imagined "geo-body," allow us to visualize in cartographic ways the potential futures that they envisioned.[61] Thus, while maritime Indians (chapter 3) envisioned a future of continued political autonomy through enduring connections with non-Spanish Europeans, Jamaica planters and merchants visualized a future map of the Americas in which northern South America would be incorporated into a refashioned British Empire (chapter 4). Meanwhile, Simón Bolívar (chapter 5) and early Colombia's nation makers (chapter 6) envisioned an emerging Colombian nation either fully incorporated or at least fullheartedly accepted (by its European and North American brethren) into the Euro-Atlantic community of civilized nations. Evidently, these visions offer only a limited scope of the projects that transimperial Greater Caribbean dwellers imagined. They are intended to illustrate rather than to exhaust the analytical possibilities of using the transimperial Greater Caribbean as geographic unit of analysis.

Worthy of mention here, given their notoriety in Caribbean history and their conspicuous presence in the transimperial Greater Caribbean, is the absence of specific analysis of the geopolitical imagination of sailors, slaves, and free people of color. Their absence should not be taken as indication that they lacked a geopolitical imagination or that the projects and futures they envisioned were less important than those included in this study. Sailors, for instance, were not merely creators of spaces that others used to develop projects and visions for the future. Sailors, as Marcus Rediker has amply demonstrated, also "imagined and sometimes actually built subversive alternatives" to imperial regimes and "autonomous zones" that they ruled through their own unwritten codes.[62] Like them (sometimes with and almost always because of them) the slaves and free people of color who experienced the transimperial

Greater Caribbean from New Granada's shores envisioned plausible futures based on the news and information they gathered in port cities like Cartagena, Santa Marta, and Riohacha. As the work of Marixa Lasso and Aline Helg has demonstrated, the enslaved and free colored populations, just like those whose projects and visions I analyze in this book, used the transimperial Greater Caribbean that sailors created to envision the future direction of the events that were shaking the world they inhabited.[63] For all of them, the transimperial Greater Caribbean offered a canvas on which they could conceive and develop visions of potential futures. *An Aqueous Territory* should be taken as an invitation to continue to explore the numerous visions that the existence of a transimperial Greater Caribbean made possible.

Toward a More Balanced Atlantic

While primarily conceived as a study of spatial configurations and geopolitical imagination, *An Aqueous Territory* is at the crossroads of a number of historiographical traditions. Its analysis of communication networks in the Greater Caribbean inserts New Granada into ongoing conversations about the role of sailors as carriers of information and about the growth of interimperial trade in the western Atlantic in the aftermath of the Seven Years' War and the American Revolution.[64] The case studies of the Greater Caribbean's geopolitics and geopolitical imagination explore the possibilities of using Caribbean New Granada as a testing ground for indigenous-European encounters (with an emphasis on indigenous perspectives and ability to maintain their political autonomy), British imperial history, Haitian revolutionary studies, and the Atlantic nature of Spanish America's nation-making process.[65] But above all, this study situates New Granada (and by extension Latin America) at the heart of an Atlantic historiography that, despite, the recent surge in studies that pursue transnational or transimperial connections, continues to reproduce the fiction of the existence of what David Hancock self-critically called an "Age of Imperial Self-Sufficiency."[66]

Like Hancock, Jorge Cañizares-Esguerra and Benjamin Breen have lamented the tendency of "scholarship on British, Dutch, French, Spanish, and Portuguese Atlantics" to follow "separate trajectories." This compartmentalization of Atlantic history, they rightly claim, produces "the unhappy result that twenty-first-century scholars sometimes fail to notice influences that would have been obvious to early modern individuals."[67] By depicting a world of actions and imaginations that refuse categorization within neatly defined national or imperial compartments, *An Aqueous Territory* has the potential to correct a historiographical map of the Atlantic in which, as Allan Greer noted, "the phrase 'Atlantic history' frequently serves as shorthand for the history of the *British* Atlantic in the early modern period."[68] This book, in short, contributes to what Roquinaldo Ferreira—in his study of the transoceanic connections that created a Brazilian-Angolan "social and cultural continuum"—called the need to "rebalanc[e] Atlantic history."[69] In addition, my work contributes to the rebalancing effort by responding to the increased "global awareness" of U.S. colonial historians who have created what a historian of New France called "the brave new borderless world of colonial history."[70]

An Aqueous Territory is not alone in its effort to uncover lived experiences that allow us to see Atlantic empires and their borders as "entangled," "hybrid," "porous," "fluid," and "permeable" and the Caribbean as a hub of transimperial interactions.[71] Transimperial interactions were, of course, experienced by those who frequently crossed political borders. But physical mobility was not the only way to experience transimperialism. As James Epstein has demonstrated, sharing an island with a large French population and living under British control while maintaining a Spanish legal and judicial system, the residents of Trinidad during the first decade of the nineteenth century did not need to move to live in a transimperial milieu.[72] Similarly, as Cuba made its transition from society with slaves to slave society (1790s–1820s), Cuban residents experienced the transimperial forces shaping the present and future of the Spanish island. While in the immediate aftermath of the outbreak of the Haitian Revolution the emerging Cuban planter class rushed to import sugar-making machinery and to welcome French sugar planters and technicians, the island's slaves and free people of color demonstrated familiarity with transimperial currents of thought and information when they used British and French abolitionist ideas and news from Haiti to argue for an expansion of their rights.[73] Like them, slaves, free people of color, and indigenous groups in Florida formulated and implemented strategies of resistance based on their acquaintance with U.S., British, and Spanish legal systems. Their familiarity with the legal pluralism of Florida demonstrates their understanding of themselves as inhabitants of a transimperial world.[74]

Like many inhabitants of Anglo North America, Trinidad, Cuba, and Florida, the people who inhabited New Granada's Caribbean provinces lived in an entangled world. Transimperial interactions allowed them to experience and imagine a Greater Caribbean and the Atlantic from New Granada's shores. The sailors, royal authorities, maritime Indians, slaves, merchants, and free people of color who directly or indirectly embraced the transimperial Greater Caribbean from New Granada's shores were part of and, indeed, constructed a world in which indigenous-European encounters, British imperial history, Haitian revolutionary studies, and Spanish American independence and nation making could comfortably fit in a single, larger narrative of revolutionary transformations in a transimperial, multilingual, cosmopolitan, and entangled Atlantic world.

Organization of the Book

The book is organized in two parts. Part I, Spatial Configurations, traces the process of configuration of the region I call the transimperial Greater Caribbean, emphasizing the role of commercial policies and following ships and their captains and crews as they crisscrossed Caribbean and Atlantic waters. Taken together, the two chapters that make up part I advance an argument for the quotidian nature of border crossing in the late eighteenth- and early nineteenth-century Greater Caribbean. Based largely on shipping returns for the ports of Caribbean New Granada (particularly Cartagena and Santa Marta) and Jamaica (especially Kingston), these two chapters also uncover the role of mobility and communication networks in the configuration of transimperial geographies and contribute to historians' ongoing efforts to challenge assumptions regarding the existence of isolated spheres of self-sufficient empires.

Chapter 1, "Vessels: Routes, Size, and Frequency," studies interimperial trade from the vantage point of New Granada's Caribbean ports from the effective instauration of *comercio libre y protegido* (free and protected trade) in the mid-1780s to the final years of the independence wars that led to the creation of the Republic of Colombia. While not new, these commercial exchanges across political borders grew in intensity during the second half of the eighteenth century. Following the paths of ships that frequently crisscrossed imperial political boundaries connecting New Granada's Caribbean coasts to foreign colonies, this chapter argues that from the 1760s, and with more intensity after the American Revolution, the Caribbean was turning into a de facto free trade area largely, but not exclusively, controlled by Great Britain from the Caribbean commercial center of Kingston, Jamaica.

In chapter 2, "Sailors: Border Crossers and Region Makers," I shift from ships to people. Focusing on the navigational trajectories of captains and sailors who, between the 1780s and the 1810s, connected New Granada's ports with other Caribbean and Atlantic ports, this chapter argues that the circulation of people and information made possible the emergence and consolidation of the aqueous territory I call the transimperial Greater Caribbean. Sea captains and the crews they commanded were the creators of this transimperial region. Their circulation and the information they spread resulted in the creation of what Michel de Certeau called a "theater of actions," whose configuration challenges preconceived notions about the existence of isolated Spanish, British, and French imperial spheres.[75]

Part II, Geopolitics and Geopolitical Imagination, focuses on how the transimperial region made possible by the communication networks detailed in part I facilitated the development of geopolitical projects that included, among many others, a persistent autonomy in the face of European encroachments (chapter 3), a vision of a British Empire in New Granada's Caribbean coast (chapter 4), Simón Bolívar's failed dream of a British-sponsored independent South American republic (chapter 5), and the imagined construction of an Andean republic that mirrored the North Atlantic bastions of civilization (chapter 6). The four chapters present case studies conceptually glued together by the key notion of the geopolitical imagination. While broad enough to provide a good idea of the sense of possibilities that characterized life in the transimperial Greater Caribbean during the Age of Revolutions, these case studies are far from exhausting the multiplicity of projects through which those experiencing this aqueous territory from New Granada's shores interpreted their present and envisioned potential futures. If these case studies demonstrate that other worlds were possible, they also imply that these other worlds were not limited to those analyzed in these chapters.

Chapter 3, "Maritime Indians, Cosmopolitan Indians," studies the connections that allowed Cunas and Wayuu to become cosmopolitan. It also emphasizes how the interactions associated with cosmopolitanism put these indigenous groups on an equal footing with European allies and rivals and allowed them to sustain their challenge to Spanish authorities and remain unconquered. In the process, by emphasizing indigenous mobility, multilingualism, technological capacity, and political autonomy, the chapter challenges geographical fictions of territorial control embedded in European-drawn maps of the Caribbean and sheds light on European perceptions of indigenous peoples (and what these perceptions actually say about the maritime Indians). In short, this chapter argues that the maritime Indians, like the people Ira Berlin and Jane Landers called "Atlantic creoles," were "cosmopolitan in the fullest sense." Like Atlantic creoles, maritime Indians were "familiar with the commerce of the Atlantic, fluent in its new languages, and intimate with its trade and cultures."[76]

In chapter 4, "Turning South before Swinging East," I use the stretch of coast from Central America's Mosquito Coast to the port city of Cartagena in the Viceroyalty of New Granada as a window to the geopolitical imagination of Caribbean merchants and planters, royal officers, and military adventurers. This coastal territory, largely populated by independent indigenous groups dexterous in using the Anglo-Spanish rivalry to their own advantage, served as a chalkboard for these different groups to draw their visions of the future. Jamaican planters and merchants struggling with the scarcities generated by the prohibition on trade with the newly independent United States sought alternative sources from which to obtain foodstuffs, wood, and cattle to feed the island's plantation economy. Military adventurers—especially British loyalists eager to avenge British defeat in the American Revolution—and merchants with interests in Central and northern South America looked to turn this area into a territory formally or informally dominated by Britain. New Granada's authorities sought to establish effective control of the area—an achievement that, Viceroy Antonio Caballero y Góngora believed, required promoting trade and developing the region's productive capacity through the promotion of cotton cultivation. This chapter brings together the visions of these three groups to argue that, in the aftermath of the American Revolution, their disparate interests converged around the idea and necessity of keeping the British Empire Atlantic centered (at a time when India's appeal to British imperial authorities was on the rise).

Chapter 5, "Simón Bolívar's Caribbean Adventures," follows Bolívar's route of Caribbean exile from mid-1815 to early 1817 to explain the role of Jamaica and Haiti in Spanish America's wars of independence. Locating Bolívar within a larger group of creole military adventurers who used their Caribbean exile to plot projects to return to the mainland and revive the war for independence, this chapter advances four arguments that shed light on the geopolitical imagination of creole adventurers, British and Spanish imperial officials, and independent Haiti's government authorities. First, I argue that Haitian president Alexandre Pétion's pro-insurgent diplomacy and Jamaican authorities' adherence to British neutrality allowed Haiti to emerge as an international revolutionary center actively exporting revolution. Second, the gradual success of British military campaigns against Napoleon and Caribbean-wide fears of the spread of Haitian revolutionary ideals deterred Jamaican authorities from supporting Spanish American insurgents. Third, guaranteeing British neutrality policy and attempting to hold Pétion true to his promise of neutrality required policing and diplomatic pressure from Spanish officials in New

Granada, Venezuela, and the Spanish Caribbean islands. Finally, that a combination of news about developments in Europe, personal fears of the Haitian Revolution, and Enlightenment ideas about race and civilization informed Bolívar's expectations for support and strategy during his Caribbean journey.

In chapter 6, "An Andean-Atlantic Nation," I trace the nineteenth-century process of imagining and constructing Colombia as what I call an Andean-Atlantic nation. Shifting the geographical vantage point from New Granada's Caribbean coast to its Andean capital, this chapter studies the process through which two groups of Colombian nation makers—*criollos ilustrados* (enlightened creoles) and politician-geographers—endeavored to decaribbeanize the nascent republic and to create an Andean-Atlantic republic that was to resemble civilized Europe and the United States. Their efforts illustrate key elements of enlightened creoles' geopolitical imagination and make it possible to understand why the transimperial Greater Caribbean did not find its way into Colombia's nation-making narrative.

Uncovering other worlds or acknowledging that other worlds were and continue to be possible, in my approach, takes the form of an interest in articulating regions otherwise, in articulating lived geographies that do not respond to contemporary or anachronistic world regionalization schemes excessively respectful of political geographies. The challenge is to develop ways that allow us to see beyond political geographies and imposed world regionalization schemes that clearly informed but never fully reproduced the many ways in which groups and individuals created, experienced, imagined, and envisioned their world.[77] In taking up this challenge, *An Aqueous Territory* should work as a reminder that for any given historical outcome there were "other possibilities, other ways of being in the world, and other opportunities that were figuratively and literally foreclosed."[78] That these alternatives were unsuccessful and—perhaps because of this—forgotten should not be taken as sign that they were unimportant and unworthy subjects of historical inquiry.[79] The British Cartagena that never was, just like the postindependence Cartagena that ended up being, has a history worth uncovering.

I

—————

Spatial Configurations

—————

CHAPTER I

Vessels

Routes, Size, and Frequency

De La Habana a Portobelo,
de Jamaica a Trinidad,
anda y anda el barco barco,
sin capitán.

—NICOLÁS GUILLÉN, "Un son para niños antillanos"

On October 19, 1806, after a long and eventful journey, the Spanish brig *Concepción* entered the port of Maracaibo in the captaincy general of Venezuela. Scheduled to travel from Veracruz to Maracaibo, the *Concepción* reached its final destination after unplanned stopovers in Sabanilla (sixty miles northeast of Cartagena) and Jamaica. According to its captain, Domingo Negrón, the brig was forced off its original route in the first days of August, when it was "captured off the coast of Cartagena by the *Veteran*, [a] British ship of seventy canons, and two Spanish merchant schooners, [which the *Veteran*] was convoying." After spending three days in Sabanilla, the *Concepción* was taken to Jamaica, where Negrón and his crew "were detained [for] thirty-five days." Negrón's description of British commercial relations with Sabanilla—during his stay in Jamaica he witnessed the departure of "eight Spanish ships to said Sabanilla"—greatly alarmed Spanish authorities, for whom commercial exchanges with a warring foreign power taking place at an unauthorized port were, even in a climate of increased openness to interimperial trade, still illegal.[1]

In sharp contrast with the *Concepción*, the Spanish schooner *Esperanza* (captains Domingo Pisco and Josef Borregio) enjoyed nothing but calm and friendly seas during the multiple times in 1814 that it sailed between Kingston and the minor port of Riohacha—a port benefiting from royal permits authorizing it to trade with foreign neutrals.[2] Neither enemies nor the oft-cited "winds and currents" seemed to have affected any of the seven recorded Kingston-Riohacha round trips that the *Esperanza* completed that year. Its pattern of navigation, based on what can be gathered from Kingston's shipping returns, was pretty regular: After entering Kingston, the *Esperanza* stayed in port between five and eleven days before sailing back to Riohacha; between three and four weeks later it once again appeared entering Kingston. Relatively short stays in port were followed by short navigations to a nearby port. Since no shipping returns are available for Riohacha, however, it is impossible to know with certainty the path the *Esperanza* took in those three- to four-week intervals between departure from and arrival to Kingston.[3]

The eventful journey of the *Concepción* and the apparently eventless one of the *Esperanza* contain key elements to understanding the commercial networks that linked New Granada to the wider world. Both the *Concepción* and the *Esperanza* were among the myriad brigs, schooners, and sloops that, like the ship of Nicolás Guillén's poem (see epigraph), "roam[ed] and roam[ed]" Caribbean waters connecting imperial spheres often thought of as disconnected.[4] Their journeys speak of both the dangers and promise of interimperial trade in a period marked by almost constant warfare in Atlantic coasts and waters. Their journeys also make visible two of a handful of Neogranadan ports that, despite their commercial dynamism, have generally remained at the margins of historical accounts of New Granada's foreign trade.

For captains and sailors sailing the Caribbean and for Spanish authorities following the movement of vessels from the Caribbean coast of New Granada, neither Sabanilla nor Riohacha were invisible. Nor were they the only hidden ports trading with Jamaica in a manner that defied straightforward classification as licit or illicit. In a report submitted to New Granada's viceroy in November 1803, Manuel Hernández, the Spanish Crown's royal treasurer at Portobelo, described the commercial dynamism of the western Caribbean island of San Andrés (120 miles off Nicaragua's coast). At this island, Hernández explained, Spanish and foreign vessels docked to exchange "our colonial produce" for "all the clothes and [other] effects needed for the consumption of the Viceroyalty [of New Granada] and . . . that of Peru through Panama." Concealed coves and tiny islands in the Guajira Peninsula (e.g., Bahia Honda and Portete) and the vicinities of Santa Marta (e.g., Gayra), Portobelo (e.g., Chagres and San Blas), and Cartagena completed Hernández's inventory of hidden ports ideally suited "for the undertaking of such [illegal] negotiations."[5]

Despite their recurrent appearances in the historical record, these hidden ports have not been able to secure a place in the historiography of New Granada's trade during the late colonial period. Making these ports visible and illustrating the ways in which they participated in interimperial commercial networks challenges two long-standing assumptions about trade relations in New Granada and the Atlantic world. First, that the major port of Cartagena dominated New Granada's trade with both Spain and foreign colonies.[6] Second, that by the end of the eighteenth century European empires, as dictated by mercantilist principles, continued to operate "within autarkic commercial systems" that deemed illegal any commercial interaction with foreigners.[7] My interpretation, largely based on the inclusion of New Granada's minor and hidden ports in the Caribbean and Atlantic commercial landscape, brings to life a Caribbean world of everyday transimperial interactions made possible by the increased willingness of Atlantic empires to legalize (and regulate) interimperial commercial exchanges. In this transformed commercial landscape, contraband ceased to be statically defined by the mere fact of commercial contact with foreigners and acquired a more dynamic definition in which a combination of goods traded, ports of origins and destination, and geopolitical circumstances determined the legality of commercial transactions.[8]

The term "hidden ports" requires further clarification. Spanish commercial legislation ranked American ports according to their centrality to the Spanish transatlantic commercial system. In New Granada, Cartagena was the only major port. The ports of Santa Marta, Riohacha, and Portobelo were classified as minor ports. To these two official terms I add a third one—hidden ports—to refer to ports frequently mentioned in Spanish reports as sites used by Spanish, British, Dutch, French, and Danish subjects to engage in illicit commercial exchanges. In British reports and port records, hidden ports like Sabanilla, San Andrés, and Chagres were not hidden at all. Given the fragmentary nature of shipping returns for New Granada's Caribbean ports (information on arrivals and departures is only available for Cartagena and Santa Marta for selected years), British records make visible not only hidden ports but also minor ports like Riohacha and Portobelo.[9] Thus, while minor ports also tend to be hidden in the Spanish archives (no shipping returns are available for Riohacha and Portobelo), much of the trade conducted in these ports was legal by late eighteenth-century standards. Hidden ports (Sabanilla, San Andrés, and Chagres, among others), on the other hand, are hidden both because their commercial dynamism is hard to see in Spanish archives and because, when they do appear, these ports do so as sites where hidden or illicit activities took place.

In this chapter I study interimperial trade from the vantage point of New Granada's Caribbean ports from the effective instauration of *comercio libre y protegido* (free and protected trade) in the mid-1780s to the final years of the independence wars that led to the creation of the Republic of Colombia.[10] While not new—transimperial exchanges had been a feature of the Caribbean's commercial landscape since the sixteenth century, when British, Dutch, and French buccaneers and privateers first broke Spain's exclusive access to Caribbean waters—these commercial exchanges across political borders grew in intensity during the second half of the eighteenth century.[11] By following the paths of ships that frequently crisscrossed imperial political borders connecting New Granada's Caribbean coasts to foreign colonies, this chapter argues that from the 1760s, and with more intensity after the American Revolution, the Caribbean was turning into a de facto free trade area largely, but not exclusively, controlled by Great Britain from the Caribbean commercial center of Kingston, Jamaica.

Largely based on previously unexplored Jamaican shipping returns, this reconstruction of New Granada's commercial networks presents the main routes, ports, types of vessels (by size and nationality), frequency of travel, modes of trade (legal and illegal), and commodities traded (see map 1.1).[12] The reconstruction, while meticulous, is nonetheless still partial. A more complete picture could only be drawn by using shipping returns from other key Caribbean and Atlantic ports engaged in trade with New Granada. Records of arrivals and departures from Philadelphia, Baltimore, Curaçao, Saint Thomas, Les Cayes, and other ports could add further nuances to the picture presented in this chapter. However, Britain's increasing maritime power during the second half of the eighteenth century constitutes a good justification for the choice of Jamaica. As Jamaica's most important and dynamic port, Kingston appears in this chapter as the commercial center of the transimperial Greater Caribbean. Preceded by a brief historical context of the period leading up to the 1780s, the central section of this chapter demonstrates the eighteenth-century progression toward free trade in Caribbean waters and the ways in which the combined effect of war and innovations in commercial regulations made it possible for Great Britain, through its main Caribbean entrepôt, Kingston, to corner most of the benefits to be obtained from interimperial Caribbean trade.

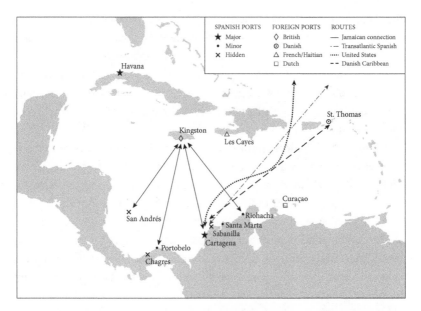

Map 1.1 New Granada's commercial networks. Illustrates the routes that connected New Granada's ports—major, minor, and hidden—with the transimperial Greater Caribbean and the central place of Kingston, Jamaica, in these connections.

How the Seven Years' War and the American Revolution Transformed Caribbean Trade

The eighteenth century, as one historian characterized it, was a period of "total war" between the British Crown and the French and Spanish monarchies united through the Bourbon Family Compact.[13] From the War of Spanish Succession (1701–1714) to the Napoleonic Wars (1799–1815), the eighteenth century rarely witnessed periods of peace lasting more than a decade.[14] Eighteenth-century warfare altered the balance of power, reshaping the world's political map and bringing about dramatic transformations in Caribbean commercial policies and practices.[15] In turn, commercial practices, which in the Caribbean were largely characterized by the violation of mercantilist policies, usually provided valid justifications for a European monarch to declare war against a rival power.

War made it difficult to continue commerce as usual. The scarcities associated with warfare often forced imperial authorities to introduce commercial exceptions that legalized trade with foreigners. During the second half of the eighteenth century, these exceptions gave impetus to new economic ideas that favored free trade over traditional mercantilist policies.[16] Peace treaties signed to end wars often included clauses with commercial concessions and territorial transfers that reshaped the world's political map. In the eighteenth-century Caribbean, the combination of wartime exceptions and concessions made at different peace treaties ultimately resulted in a gradual destruction of the barriers to interimperial trade.

Completely forbidden until the first years of the eighteenth century, interimperial commercial exchanges in the Caribbean were first legalized, under exceptional circumstances, in 1701, when France secured the exclusive right to introduce slaves to Spanish America.[17] At the end of the War of Spanish Succession, however, France lost this privilege to the British Crown, which also obtained from Spain an unprecedented "right to send a trading vessel (the 'Annual Ship') to the Spanish American trade fairs held at Portobelo and Veracruz."[18] This concession notwithstanding, official support by any European Crown to trade with foreigners remained tenuous until the 1760s.[19] Ships in distress, regardless of their nationality, were usually allowed to enter foreign ports, but regular interactions were never officially encouraged.[20] The Seven Years' War, a war fought on a global scale and with equally global consequences, inaugurated a new epoch in terms of governmental attitudes toward trade with foreigners in the Caribbean. In the words of a contemporary observer, the war forced European powers, starting with France, to "resort . . . to the expedient of relaxing [their] colonial monopoly" and to "admit . . . neutral vessels" into their ports.[21]

The British occupation of Havana during the last phase of the Seven Years' War (1762–1763) signaled an immense weakness on the part of Spain to maintain effective control, not only of peripheral areas of its vast empire but, most disturbing to Spanish authorities, of key ports in Spain's transatlantic commercial system. The impact of this traumatic event on Spain went far beyond the cost the Spanish Crown had to pay in order to recover its most valuable Caribbean city: "transfer of west Florida to the English, English control of the Honduras coast and its dyewoods, and abandonment of Spaniards' rights to fish off Newfoundland."[22] Besides transforming the political map of the Americas, the war and the British occupation of Havana greatly influenced the ways in which imperial bureaucrats and ideologues both in Spain and Britain rethought the administration and defense of their overseas territories.[23]

From a Spanish perspective, the problem went beyond the obvious inability to guarantee the defense of Havana and other Caribbean cities from future attacks by Britain or other European rivals. The problem, a group of Spanish policy makers thought, resided in the outdated commercial system— the Cádiz-controlled monopolistic *sistema de flotas* (convoy system)—that still regulated transatlantic trade between Spain and its Spanish American territories.[24] The solution, advanced by a junta (committee) in charge of "review[ing] ways to address the backwardness of Spain's commerce with its colonies and foreign nations," called for opening more ports in Spain to direct trade with the colonies, eliminating the convoy system, and offering incentives for Spanish traders willing to travel to Africa in search of slaves for the Spanish Caribbean.[25] The junta's recommendations, made available in early 1765, were quickly turned into the Reglamento del comercio libre a las Islas de Barlovento (or the First Reglamento, a new commercial code regulating trade between the Spanish peninsula and the Spanish Caribbean), which not only allowed Cuba to trade directly with multiple Spanish ports but also authorized the island's planters to buy slaves directly from foreign depots in the Caribbean.[26] Beyond Cuba the effects of this new policy were limited, but its passing, by signaling the potential direction of trade legislation, raised the hopes of many both in Spain and the colonies who had long complained about the need to overhaul the outdated commercial legislation and practices.

For Britain, victory in the war meant more than the acquisition of Spanish territories. The further acquisition of several French Caribbean islands— Dominica, Grenada, and Saint Vincent—turned Britain into the dominant power in the Caribbean Sea. Victory in the war, however, came at a high cost. To recover financially from the expenditures incurred during the war, the British Parliament proposed a number of legislative acts designed to extract more revenue from its colonies. The passing of the Sugar Act (1764) and the Stamp Act (1765) triggered a crisis in the commercial exchanges between Britain and the North American colonies. The combination of its newly acquired status as main Caribbean power and the North Atlantic commercial crisis provided an opportunity for Kingston's merchants to successfully advance their proposal to legalize (and thus to expand) trade between the British Caribbean and Spanish America. Referred to in Britain as "the Spanish trade," the encouragement of this line of commerce was designed to weather the crisis in North Atlantic trade and, most importantly, to avoid French and Dutch exploitation of the coveted Spanish American markets. Convinced by this argument, the British Parliament passed the first Free Port Act, which received royal consent in June 1766. The act opened four ports in Jamaica and two in Dominica to foreign vessels loaded with bullion and other foreign produce not available in the islands. In exchange, foreigners could buy "all British produce and manufactures . . . excepting only a range of strategic naval supplies and iron from British North America."[27] From this moment, it became legal, in British eyes, for Spanish vessels to enter Kingston and other selected British ports in the Caribbean, even if these trips continued to be outlawed in Spanish legislation.

Despite the initial enthusiasm with which Jamaicans and Cubans received the new commercial legislation, both Spanish comercio libre for its Caribbean islands and the first British Free Port Act failed to substantially alter the Caribbean commercial landscape. In Britain, an opponent of the Free Port Act said in 1773 "that the benefits that had arisen from the free port trade were very much outnumbered by the disadvantages."[28] In the Spanish case, the benefits the new commercial code was producing for Cuba and newly added ports in the Spanish Peninsula (in particular Catalonia) became powerful arguments to expand the geographical scope of the First Reglamento. Convinced by the argument to turn trade with the colonies into the engine of peninsular growth, the Crown expanded comercio libre to Louisiana (in 1768), Yucatán (1770), Santa Marta (1776), Riohacha (1777), and, with the passing of the Reglamento y aranceles reales para el comercio libre de España a Indias (the Second Reglamento) in 1778, to all Spanish America with the exception of New Spain. By increasing to twenty-five the number of Spanish American ports allowed to trade directly with thirteen peninsular ports, the Second Reglamento raised expectations about the prospects for colonial development. The expectations of immediate change, however, were quickly curtailed by Spain's entrance into the American Revolution.[29]

In 1779, when Spain entered the American Revolutionary War as an enemy of Britain and ally of France, both the British free port system and Spain's yet-untested Second Reglamento practically collapsed. With only Dutch and Danish ships eligible to enter the British free ports, the commercial benefits to be obtained were minimal.[30] Spain, on the other hand, instead of witnessing the commercial revival promised by comercio libre, suffered the interruption of its transatlantic trade, which forced it to yield to colonial pressures pushing for a measure that, despite its always contentious nature, became a permanent feature of colonial Spanish America's commercial landscape: legal trade with foreign neutrals.[31] The end of the war, however, brought the necessary conditions for both Spanish comercio libre and the British free port trade to flourish. The British Empire, after losing the thirteen North American colonies, embarked on a process of imperial reorganization that included looking for new commercial partners.[32] Spain was finally able to see what co-mercio libre could do for it. The results were immediate and astonishing. In only one year between 1784 and 1796 did Spain's exports to Spanish America fail to at least triple their 1778 value. Spanish American exports to Spain experienced an even more astounding increase: In the twelve years from 1785 to 1796 only once did they account for less than ten times their value of 1778.[33] New Granada, a young viceroyalty, separated from Jamaica by only five days of navigation and with many development projects to consolidate, seemed a perfect market for what both commercial policies had to offer.

The Caribbean and Atlantic Trade of New Granada's Ports

The "convergence" of British and Spanish commercial policies toward more open trade resulted in the expansion and legalization of transimperial interactions that had previously been deemed illegal.[34] The consolidation of the British free ports after the American Revolution, coupled with Spanish authorities' allowances to trade with foreign neutrals, provided a much-needed boost to an economic future that Kingston merchants perceived as uncertain.[35] European wars of the 1790s and the early nineteenth century, with their consequent territorial reorganizations, basically ruled out Dutch and French competition in Caribbean trade. Benefiting from their neutrality during these wars, other, less traditional powers—the newly independent United States and the Danish Caribbean islands—were able to breach what was increasingly looking like a British monopolistic commercial space. From the 1780s to the 1810s, thus, the combination of relaxation of commercial policies and warfare gave shape to a system of interimperial trade characterized by a revival of Kingston as a major Caribbean commercial center, accompanied by a sporadic boom of the Danish Caribbean islands and an early insinuation of the United States' future commercial power.

From the perspective of New Granada's ports, the workings of this new commercial system can be summarized by four big developments: (1) increased trade with Spain during the 1780s; (2) legalization of trade with foreign neutral colonies accompanied by a redefinition of the modes of conducting contraband trade; (3) diversification of ports engaged in international trade; and (4) higher frequency in terms of contacts with foreign territories. As a whole, the period between 1784 and 1818 was characterized by a consolidation of commercial networks linking several Neogranadan ports (not only

Cartagena) with a variety of Spanish and foreign ports in the Caribbean and the northwestern Atlantic.

Cartagena's centrality in New Granada's commercial relations, both with Spain and with foreign Caribbean colonies, is unquestionable. As one of Spanish America's major ports and as the base of an important group of merchants that until the late 1770s monopolized New Granada's transatlantic trade, Cartagena had been central to the Spanish commercial system since the sixteenth century.[36] However, the excessive focus on Cartagena has created a tendency to ignore other ports and, in the process, to erase important routes communicating New Granada with the Caribbean and Atlantic worlds.[37] In the Cartagena-centered accounts of trade, ports like Santa Marta, Portobelo, and Riohacha—officially classified as New Granada's minor ports—appear as subordinates of Cartagena. Their subordinate status relegates these ports to the condition of local ports almost exclusively connected to the wider world through their local trade with Cartagena. Largely the result of the availability of primary sources (shipping returns for New Granada's ports are available only for Cartagena and Santa Marta), the published accounts of New Granada's commercial relations have ultimately simplified what contemporary actors recognized was a sophisticated commercial system of exchanges. The use of alternative sources (in this case shipping returns from Kingston, Jamaica) should produce a more nuanced reconstruction of the commercial networks connecting New Granada with Caribbean and Atlantic ports.

The Commercial Relations of New Granada's
Major Port: Cartagena

In the half century between the approval of comercio libre in 1778 and the definitive expulsion of Spanish authorities from the newly established Republic of Colombia (1821), vessels entering Cartagena generally did so through a set of model routes, dictated by a combination of Spanish commercial policies and expectations, interimperial rivalries, and local contingencies. Ships usually entered Cartagena following routes that included transatlantic voyages (from the Spanish Peninsula), Caribbean transimperial tours (from one or more foreign Caribbean islands), or coastal journeys (from other ports of New Granada and Venezuela). Some itineraries, like that of the *Nazareno*, which in 1785 sailed from Cádiz to Cartagena and, after five months in that port, returned directly to Cádiz, were fairly uncomplicated.[38] Others, like that of the *Santiago* in 1793, included multiple visits to major and minor ports controlled by different European powers.[39]

Ships navigating the Spanish transatlantic route entered Cartagena either directly from the Spanish Peninsula or via Havana and/or Puerto Rico. Generally, Spanish vessels crossing the Atlantic westward were loaded with *frutos, géneros, caldos,* and *efectos de Castilla.* These generic labels included a variety of commodities ranging from provisions and foodstuffs (soap, flour, rice, dried fish and meat, cheese, and more) to liquors (wine, beer, and *aguardiente*), clothes (linen, wool, and cotton), construction materials (iron), and military and naval equipment (bullets, gunpowder, and rigging).[40] On their way back to Spain, ships transported bullion (silver and gold) and an array of agricultural produce and animal exports, including cotton from Cartagena, cacao from Guayaquil (exported through Portobelo and Cartagena) and Santa Marta, dyewoods (*palo brasilete* or Brazil wood) and hides from Santa Marta and Riohacha, and tortoise shells from Portobelo and Riohacha.[41]

The transatlantic route linking Cartagena to Spain, a key component of the Spanish project to turn Spanish American territories into exporters of raw materials while developing the industrial production of the Spanish Peninsula, went through two major transformations between the late 1770s and the eruption of the Anglo-Spanish War of 1796. On the one hand, the number of ships crossing the Atlantic to enter Cartagena reached unprecedented numbers. On the other hand, more ports both in Spain and New Granada became directly involved in transatlantic commerce. From six in 1784, the number of ships reaching Cartagena from Spain rose to twenty-four in 1785 and thirty-two in 1789.[42] Between 1785 and 1788, the best years of comercio libre, the annual average number of departures from Cartagena directly to Spain was 11.5.[43] In what accounted for one of the few indisputable successes of Spain's new commercial policy, vessels from Barcelona and Málaga disputed Cádiz's commercial hegemony, effectively undermining its monopoly of the Spanish transatlantic trade. Of the seventy-one ships that entered Cartagena from Spain in 1785, 1789, and 1793, thirty-four came from Barcelona and Málaga and thirty-one from Cádiz (see table 1.1). During the 1790s, the return of international hostilities (especially after 1796) produced a dramatic and definitive decline in Spanish–Spanish American trade. The number of ships entering Cartagena from Spain dropped from fifteen in 1793 to zero in 1800. In both 1808 and 1817, two vessels entered Cartagena from Spain. The number of ships sailing from Cartagena to Spain suffered a similar decline.[44]

An analysis of the communications between Santa Marta and Spain reflects a similar trend for the first decade of the nineteenth century. In 1801, 1807, and 1814, only one ship, *El Rayo* (*Lightning*), sailed from Santa Marta "to

TABLE 1.1 Ships Entering Cartagena from Spain, 1785–1793, by Port of Origin

	Cádiz	Barcelona and Málaga	Other ports
1785	13	11	0
1789	14	15	3
1793	4	8	3
Total	31	34	6

Source: AGNC, AA-I, Aduanas, 8, 195–219; AGNC, AA-I, Aduanas, 16, 1099–1042; AGNC, AA-I, Aduanas, 22, 539–569

any port in the [Spanish] Peninsula."[45] Besides *El Rayo* only one other Spanish vessel departed from Santa Marta to Spain in the three years for which information is available.[46]

In the final analysis, therefore, despite the obvious increase in New Granada's trade with Spain and the successful diversification of Spanish ports trading with Cartagena, comercio libre did not deliver what it had promised for this viceroyalty. While interested supporters like José Moñino, count of Floridablanca (prime minister during the 1780s), praised comercio libre because it produced "a fortunate revolution in the trade of Spain and its colonies," dissenting voices in New Granada believed that the results offered no motive for celebration.[47] As John Fisher and Anthony McFarlane have shown, between 1782 and 1796 New Granada's exports to Spain accounted for only 3.2 percent of all Spanish American exports. The viceroyalty's imports, although relatively more important than its exports, accounted for only 8 percent of Spanish exports.[48] This record, for a viceroyalty containing about 10 percent of the Spanish American population, was clearly no cause for celebration.[49] Thus, it is hardly surprising that those who were discontent soon started to voice their disappointment with the results of comercio libre. Viewing trade with foreigners as the only way to alleviate "the great scarcity of clothes" and other goods that affected the viceroyalty, merchants and provincial authorities pushed for a further intensification of commercial reform.[50]

The petitions and complaints of merchants and provincial authorities in New Granada captured the attention of viceroys and metropolitan policy makers and led to the passing of a number of royal orders allowing trade with foreigners.[51] Always regarded as a temporary measure and subject to a number of restrictions, trade with foreigners was, from the 1780s to the late 1810s, a permanent, though highly controversial feature of New Granada's trade.[52] Merchants heavily invested in trade with Spain were strong opponents of the measure; those who saw trade with Jamaica and other Caribbean colonies as an opportunity to make a profit supported the extension of the temporary measures. Viceroys and provincial authorities adopted different approaches to foreign trade depending on the interest groups that managed to capture their attention. Praised by some as "the best recourse to confront contraband" on the grounds that it had been proven that "when licit ways are open, the illicit ones are closed," trade with foreign neutrals also faced criticism from those who argued that it was actually the source of all the contraband undertaken in the Viceroyalty of New Granada.[53] As José Ignacio de Pombo, one of the best-informed and most influential contemporary analysts of commercial matters, put it, trade with foreigners constituted "an addiction, difficult to cure after acquired."[54] Mostly conducted in Spanish vessels, but with a far from negligible participation of British, Danish, Anglo-American, French, and Dutch ships, foreign Caribbean trade was always subject to a set of critiques that linked it to an increase in contraband and the spread of revolutionary ideas.[55]

Between 1785 and 1818, trade with foreigners moved through several stages. Initially promoted based on the necessity to supply the newly established towns in the Darién, by the beginning of the 1790s the need to trade with foreigners, especially to acquire slaves, was invoked as part of a larger strategy to promote agricultural development and exports.[56] As the 1796–1808 Anglo-Spanish War began and its negative effect on the Spanish transatlantic trade was first felt, commercial exchanges with foreigners became the only available means of supplying the Spanish possessions in America. During the 1810s, the scarcities and need for weapons created by the independence wars forced both royalists and republicans to turn to foreigners to maintain the war effort. As a whole, in the four decades between 1780 and 1820, trade with foreigners moved from generally prohibited to absolutely necessary. Initially regarded as both a much-needed complement and a harmful competition to Spanish transatlantic commerce, trade with foreigners became the only means for Neogranadans to obtain flour, liquor, spices, oil, iron, clothes, weapons, and many other commodities not readily available in the viceroyalty.[57] Despite the conditions imposed on it and the debates it sparked, trade with foreigners was a reality that slowly transformed the Caribbean into a de facto free trade area, where an ever-increasing number of vessels legally crossed political borders to buy and sell different types of commodities.

During the 1780s, the argument for the establishment of foreign trade found its highest-ranking supporter in Viceroy Antonio Caballero y Góngora (in office between 1782 and 1789). The viceroy's measures favoring commercial exchanges with foreigners met opposition from both the interior and coastal provinces of New Granada and were accompanied by an increased surveillance of New Granada's coasts to curtail contraband. Caballero y Góngora defended his measures, arguing that the influx of foreign foodstuffs and artillery was required to successfully colonize the Darién—an area where *indios bárbaros* (nomadic groups who had successfully resisted Spanish conquest), aided by British smugglers, lived independently from the Spanish Crown. In his opinion, the scarcity of flour in the new towns of the Darién forced him to allow the import of "foreign flours" as his "only recourse" to "not let his Majesty's vassals perish."[58] Navigating with *passports* (official licenses) granted by Caballero y Góngora, thirty-nine vessels, most of them Spanish, entered Cartagena from foreign territories between January 1786 and April 1787. Jamaica, with sixteen vessels, followed by Saint-Domingue with seven, Curaçao with four, and Charleston (United States) with three, figured as Cartagena's most important commercial partners.[59] From the interior provinces of New Granada, opponents of the measure complained that Caballero y Góngora had sent envoys to New York, Charleston, and Jamaica to buy foodstuffs (mainly flour) under "the deceptive pretext of aiding the misfortunate Darién expedition."[60] This measure, merchants and notables from Santa Fe claimed, resulted in the ruin of the interior provinces of New Granada and constituted a "fountain of wealth for foreigners."[61]

In New Granada's Caribbean coast the most important opponent to Caballero y Góngora's designs was the newly appointed head of the coastguard, Juan Álvarez de Veriñas. Entrusted with the mission of curtailing contraband between the Caribbean islands, mainly Jamaica, and the coast of northern South America from the mouths of the Orinoco River to Panama, Veriñas believed that granting permission to "national and foreign vessels" to take "foodstuffs to the towns in the Darién" provided the best "pretext" for contraband. Moreover, Veriñas argued, permission to trade with foreigners was the reason New Granada's ports were populated "with more foreigners than Spaniards."[62]

Despite the opposition, trade with foreigners, especially with Jamaica, was further legitimized during the early 1790s as a way of promoting the viceroyalty's agricultural production. Perceiving Saint-Domingue's plantation economy as a development model worthy of imitation, leading figures of Santa Marta and Cartagena argued for the need to import slaves en masse.[63] Granted to Cartagena and Riohacha in the first quarter of 1791, the permission to import slaves from foreign colonies faced immediate criticism.[64] Opponents of the measure argued that traveling to foreign colonies to buy slaves was "only

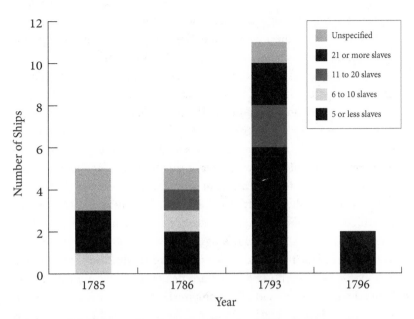

Figure 1.1 Ships transporting slaves from Kingston to New Granada, 1780s–1790s.

a pretext to trade clothes" and claimed that "the ships that went [to foreign colonies] to look for blacks, brought back contraband goods."[65] Despite these well-founded complaints, legal trade with foreigners (and the contraband conducted under its cover) continued unabated during the first half of the 1790s. Shipping returns for Cartagena in 1793 show that twenty-one vessels, all of them Spanish, legally entered Cartagena from Jamaica, while only six entered from other foreign territories (four from Curaçao and two from Saint Eustatius).[66] Of the twenty-one ships that entered from Jamaica, eleven were transporting slaves, seven entered in ballast—a strange occurrence that contemporary observers believed covered stopovers to unload contraband goods before entering Cartagena—and four imported provisions (flour and dried meat) and military and naval equipment.[67] Furthermore, of the eleven ships importing slaves, two carried more than twenty, two more than ten, and six fewer than five slaves, suspiciously low numbers that led to the idea that these vessels were actually conducting a different type of trade (figure 1.1).[68] Similar low numbers imported in 1791 had already led Viceroy Josef Ezpeleta to conclude that this trade in slaves was only "a shadow for contraband."[69] The contraband associated with the trade in slaves was also linked to "the permission to ship *frutos del país* (agricultural produce) to foreign colonies."[70]

Together, the export of agricultural and animal produce (dyewoods, cotton, cattle, and hides) and the import of slaves were considered a unique opportunity for foreigners to acquire the coveted Spanish American gold and silver.[71]

Spanish suspicions about the slave trade working as cover for contraband find support in statistical evidence that demonstrates that New Granada never became the massive importer of slaves envisioned by supporters of the schemes to turn the viceroyalty's northern provinces into a plantation economy à la French Saint-Domingue. Despite sound economic arguments by creole reformers like Antonio Narváez y la Torre, the numbers support Viceroy Ezpeleta's conviction that in Caribbean New Granada there was "little or no need for slaves" or, alternatively, that the region's "*vecinos* and planters lacked the faculties to buy them."[72] As figure 1.1 shows, in a sample of twenty-three vessels entering Cartagena from Kingston between 1785 and 1796 carrying slaves as part of their declared cargo, 52 percent (twelve ships) transported fewer than ten slaves. This evidence clearly demonstrates the dramatic failure of the schemes Narváez and others proposed. The low numbers, moreover, suggest that, as Ezpeleta and his informants claimed, sale in New Granada was not the intended purpose of these slaves' transportation.[73]

The schemes—both to turn northern New Granada into a plantation society and to use the slave trade as cover for contraband trade—also make visible other ways in which slavery and the slave trade were central to the ways in which the transimperial Greater Caribbean was experienced from New Granada's shores. At the height of the slave trade, a place like Caribbean New Granada did not actually need to import massive numbers of slaves nor in fact become a plantation society for slaves, the slave trade, and slavery to be central to its geopolitics, geopolitical imagination, and everyday life.

The previous discussion of trade with foreigners in the period of Anglo-Spanish peace between 1783 and 1796 clearly shows the increasing importance of Jamaica as Cartagena's main commercial partner. Ideally positioned to trade with New Granada and with a long history of illegal commercial exchanges with this Spanish viceroyalty, Jamaica was also legally endowed with the commercial legislation—the free port system—that enabled it to respond to New Granada's call for trade with foreigners. During the 1780s, Jamaica faced competition from Saint-Domingue, the Dutch Caribbean, and the newly independent United States. French traveler François Depons, for instance, not only claimed that until the late 1780s Saint-Domingue was New Granada's most important foreign commercial partner, but also asserted that the availability, quality, and price of French articles in Saint-Domingue "banished every idea of resorting to Jamaica for supplies."[74] While the available shipping returns do not provide sufficient evidence to disprove Depons's assertion, what is clear is that by the mid-1790s the French and Haitian Revolutions had eliminated French competition, and British commercial dominion of Caribbean waters was becoming stronger.

The outbreak of the Anglo-Spanish War in 1796 inaugurated a new phase in interimperial commercial relations in the Caribbean. With Spain and Great Britain at war, the thriving trade between Jamaica and Spanish America became outlawed, and its very existence was altogether threatened. The number of ships entering Cartagena from Jamaica, according to Spanish port records, dropped from twenty-one in 1793 to four in 1800 and five in 1808.[75] Of the nine vessels registered in Cartagena's customs records in 1800 and 1808, five entered after the end of the war, two entered with Spanish soldiers sent from Jamaica as part of negotiated exchanges of prisoners, and one entered after being released by Jamaican authorities following its capture near Curaçao by a British brig.[76] The decline in Santa Marta's trade with Jamaica was equally dramatic, with only one ship, the Danish schooner *Hob*, entering from Jamaica in 1801 and 1807.[77]

In order to avoid shortages during the war, Spanish authorities resorted to trade with neutrals to guarantee the supply of New Granada's ports. Thus, the decline in trade with Jamaica was accompanied by an increase in the number of foreign ships entering Cartagena and Santa Marta from the United States and the Danish Caribbean. In 1800, six U.S. vessels entered Cartagena from U.S. ports, mainly Philadelphia, and three ships (all of them Danish) entered from Saint Thomas.[78] In 1805, an account of the trade of Cartagena reported that five ships entered the port from New York, Philadelphia, and Alexandria. By contrast, during the same year only two ships entered Cartagena from Spain.[79] Trade with neutral foreigners, especially with the Danish Caribbean, also proved important for Santa Marta, which in 1807 received seven vessels (four Spanish and three Danish) from the Danish islands of Saint Thomas and Saint Croix.[80] The increasing appearance of U.S. ships in Cartagena's shipping returns confirms the claim of a British observer who complained that "the merchants of the United States were the first, and by far the most enterprising adventurers in the new field that was opened to neutrals."[81] Similarly, a description of Danish Saint Thomas's trade and navigation as "flourishing" and "increas[ing] every year" and of its harbor and streets as "filled" with "a great many small and large vessels" and "with people of all colours and nations" suggests the important role the island played in commercial networks linking different imperial spheres.[82]

The substitution of U.S. and Danish commerce for British trade, however, was only apparent. As Francis Armytage and Adrian Pearce have shown, trade between the British Caribbean islands and Spanish America, including New Granada, continued, although with less intensity, throughout the Anglo-Spanish wars.[83] Taking advantage of licenses granted by British authorities and benefiting from British naval protection at seas, Spanish vessels, like the eight schooners that Domingo Negrón saw depart from Kingston for Sabanilla in 1806, continued to sail between New Granada and Jamaica. Despite the war, it continued to be legal for these vessels to enter Kingston. Because war against Britain made this trade illegal in Spanish eyes, departing from and returning to New Granada required some legal maneuvering. Contemporary observer William Walton described "the means by which the clandestine intercourse with British islands, under passes granted by the governors, was carried on": "The Spanish vessels cleared out for Guadeloupe, Martinique, and St. Domingo, then in possession of their allies, and when they returned, produced false clearances and fabricated papers. . . . Thus the clearances in the Spanish custom-houses are made nearly all for islands, to which there never existed a trade of the smallest nature."[84]

Similarly, François Depons asserted that during 1801, it was common for "vessels going to Jamaica, Curaçao [then under British control], or Trinidad" to declare that they were sailing "for Guadaloupe."[85] Complementing this trade in Spanish ships was a far from negligible contraband in British vessels.[86] Trade with neutrals under Spanish permits, trade with Jamaica in Spanish vessels under British permits (legal for British, illegal for Spanish authorities), and contraband trade in British vessels continued to be the means of supplying New Granada's ports until the end of the war in 1808.

The end of the war against Britain in 1808 only came as a direct result of the Napoleonic invasion of Spain. Therefore, the peace with Britain did not promise any economic revival for the Spanish transatlantic trade. In fact, Napoleon's invasion of Spain quickly resulted in the eruption of civil war throughout Spanish America.[87] In Caribbean New Granada, the provinces of Cartagena and Santa Marta went to war in 1811, with Santa Marta's government declaring its loyalty to the Spanish king and Cartagena leaning toward declaring independence from Spain.[88] In November 1811, when Cartagena declared its absolute independence from Spain, the emergence of a new political actor—the independent government of Cartagena—further transformed commercial exchanges between New Granada and Jamaica.[89]

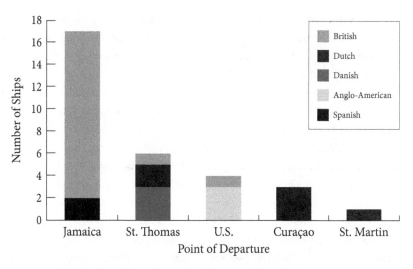

Figure 1.2 Nationality of vessels entering Cartagena from foreign territories, 1817.

For Kingston's merchants, the first half of the 1810s constituted a golden age that witnessed "the height of the free port trade."[90] The British-Spanish alliance against Napoleon and Britain's pledge to remain neutral in the conflict between Spain and its Spanish American territories allowed Kingston's merchants to trade with both Cartagena and Santa Marta.[91] Supplying guns and foodstuffs to the armies fighting in New Granada in exchange for gold, cotton, dyewoods, and hides proved a profitable business that further increased the dynamism of Kingston's commercial activity. In 1814, Santa Marta, then the most important port in Spanish New Granada, received twenty-one vessels (ten British and eleven Spanish) entering from Jamaica.[92] The increasing importance of British vessels in the trade between Santa Marta and Jamaica points to a change in the characteristics of New Granada's foreign trade. This change became clearer by 1817, when, as is evident in figure 1.2, Spanish ships in Cartagena's trade with Jamaica were almost completely replaced with British vessels.[93] Additionally, evidence from New Granada confirms Frances Armytage's conclusion that by 1817, free trade in Caribbean waters reached its zenith.[94] While British ships and Jamaica were dominant as carriers and points of exchange, the role of Dutch, Danish, and U.S. ships and the importance of Saint Thomas, U.S. ports (mainly Philadelphia and Baltimore), and Curaçao were by no means marginal.

The previous analysis, depending as it does on the port records of Cartagena and Santa Marta, naturally highlights the participation of these two ports in New Granada's foreign trade. The absence of records for other ports of New Granada leaves the impression that Cartagena dominated foreign trade. A closer look at Cartagena and Santa Marta's records, however, reveals that many Spanish ships involved in New Granada's foreign trade were also part of a local trade. In 1793, for example, ships like the *Santiago*, the *Esperanza*, and the *Santo Cristo de la Espiración* repeatedly entered Cartagena from Jamaica loaded with slaves or bullion or in ballast and then cleared out for local ports like Riohacha and Sabanilla loaded with provisions (e.g., corn) or in ballast, declaring that they were going to get dyewoods or cotton to export later to foreign colonies. Others, like the schooner *Ana María*, conducted a similar type of local-foreign trade through Portobelo.[95] Similarly, ships like the *Bella Narcisa*, which entered Santa Marta from Saint Thomas several times during 1807, conducted a trade that connected local ports like Cartagena, Santa Marta, and Riohacha with foreign neutral colonies.[96] From the perspective of Cartagena and Santa Marta's port records, the role of minor ports like Santa Marta, and Riohacha and Portobelo even more so, in the networks connecting New Granada with foreign territories appears secondary. However, a turn to alternative sources (in this case Kingston's port records) shows the central role of minor and hidden ports in New Granada's foreign trade.

The Jamaican Connection Revisited: Kingston and New Granada's Minor and Hidden Ports

In 1986, Colombian historian Gustavo Bell Lemus provided a preliminary exploration of the commercial links between New Granada's ports and Jamaica. Bell's "Jamaican connection" emphasizes the commercial intercourse linking Cartagena with Kingston and hypothesizes about potential cultural and political consequences of this trade.[97] Drawing largely on McFarlane's early work on New Granada's commercial relations, Bell reinforces the importance of Cartagena while undermining the key role of the minor and hidden ports in the trade with Jamaica.[98] Based on Jamaican shipping returns available for selected years between 1784 and 1817, the present section revisits the Jamaican connection to provide a more nuanced account of the commercial relations between New Granada and Jamaica.[99]

Between the 1780s and the 1810s, a significant number of foreign ships entered the free ports of Jamaica.[100] From 250 in 1784, the number rose to 474 in 1815.[101] While ports like Montego Bay, Port Antonio, and Savannah la Mar handled some foreign shipping, throughout the period Kingston was by far the most important free port not only in Jamaica but throughout the British

Caribbean.[102] Vessels from the Spanish, French, Dutch, and Danish Caribbean frequently entered the port of Kingston. Trade with foreigners was so important to Kingston's commercial activity that in 1785, more than twenty years before the free port trade reached its height, 33 percent of the ships entering the port were foreign vessels.[103] Foreign ships entering Kingston in the 1780s were mostly French, with Spanish ships accounting for 26 percent out of a total of 237 in 1785.[104] However, with the onset of the Haitian Revolution and the British takeover of several Dutch possessions including the Caribbean entrepôt of Curaçao, the distribution of foreign vessels suffered a drastic change, with the Spanish share rising to 51 percent in 1792 and to 100 percent in 1810 and 1814.[105]

By the 1810s, trade with Spanish America in Spanish vessels had become the "mainstay of [Kingston's] urban economy," and Kingston was regarded as the "emporium of Cuba, Guatimala, . . . Mexico, . . . Carthagena, Santa Martha, and Rio-de-la-Hache . . . ; of Maracaibo and Porto-Cavello."[106] Merchant-turned-novelist Michael Scott, a resident of Kingston between 1810 and 1817, described Kingston as a "superb . . . mercantile haven" that gathered "the whole of the trade of Terra Firma, from Porto Cavello down to Chagres, the greater part of the trade of the islands of Cuba and San Domingo, and even that of Lima and San Blas, and the other ports of the Pacific." During this period, he added, "the island [of Jamaica] was in the hey-day of its prosperity."[107] Another contemporary observer described how Spanish vessels sailed from Kingston loaded with "slaves, flour, [manufactured?] cotton, linens, woollens, chiefly coarse, hardware and all kinds of British manufactures, and lately a good deal of rum. . . . They bring cotton, cocoa, coffee, horned cattle, horses, mules, assess, hides, oil, tallow, corn, fish, poultry, mahogany, nicaragua wood, fustic, logwood, brazilleto and other dyewoods, lignum vita, sarsaparrilla, indigo, money and bullion."[108] The result of this profitable trade, Scott claimed, "was a stream of gold and silver flowing directly into the Bank of England to the extent of three millions of pounds sterling annually."[109] New Granada's participation in Kingston's Spanish American trade was significant and comparable to that of Cuba. During the height of the British free port system in 1814, 30 percent of the 402 vessels that entered Kingston from Spanish America did so from New Granada, which is comparable to the 40 percent that entered Kingston from Cuba and immensely superior to the 5 percent that entered from Venezuela. About a decade earlier, in 1796, New Granada's share had been 32 percent, with Cuba, Venezuela and other Spanish ports accounting for 39 percent, 8 percent, and 21 percent, respectively.[110]

Contrary to what the port records from Colombian archives and Bell's analysis illustrate, Cartagena's position as the most important point of contact between New Granada and Kingston was not unchallenged. New Granada's minor ports (Portobelo, Santa Marta, and Riohacha) and even hidden ports like Sabanilla, San Andrés, and Chagres maintained an important commercial exchange with Jamaica. Between 1784 and 1817, the vessels entering Kingston from New Granada's minor ports always outnumbered those entering from Cartagena. In 1785, of the twelve vessels that entered Kingston from New Granada, ten came from minor ports (five from Riohacha, four from Santa Marta, and one from Portobelo).[111] Throughout the period (with the probable exception of the 1796–1808 war years, for which detailed statistical information on arrivals and departures is not available), the trade between Kingston and Neogranadan ports grew steadily until its collapse at the beginning of the 1820s.[112] In 1810 and 1814, during the height of the free port system, seventy-nine (out of a total of 164) vessels entering Kingston from New Granada did so from minor ports. Cartagena's participation in these two years was 5 percent (two ships) and 27 percent (thirty-two ships), with hidden ports (Chagres, San Andrés, and Sabanilla) accounting for 24 percent (eleven ships) and 29 percent (thirty-five ships), respectively.[113] The increasing participation of minor and hidden ports in trade with Jamaica reveals an undermining of Cartagena's dominance that generated multiple complaints from its merchants about the contraband undertaken in Portobelo and Riohacha.[114]

Bullion, cotton, cattle and hides, woods, and dyewoods were the most important commodities transported from New Granada to Kingston. The ships trading between Kingston and Neogranadan ports generally specialized in a particular geographic area and typically entered Kingston with commodities produced in the vicinities of their port of departure (see table 1.2). An analysis of the itineraries of Spanish vessels that frequently entered Kingston from New Granada's ports forces us to reconsider Cartagena's role as the dominant commercial center of the viceroyalty. Instead, Cartagena appears as the center of one of three routes with similar shares of New Granada's Jamaican connection (see map 1.1). Through this route cotton and bullion reached Kingston, and Cartagena was legally supplied with dry goods, flour, liquors, iron, earthenware, and slaves. A variation of the Cartagena-Kingston route included a stopover in the hidden port of Sabanilla before entering Cartagena from Kingston. This stopover, Cartagena merchants complained in 1795, allowed "almost all ships that sail with licenses to bring slaves from Jamaica" to transport "considerable quantities of clothes which they unload in Sabanilla or the Rosario Islands."[115]

TABLE 1.2 Typical Cargoes of Spanish Vessels Trading between New Granada and Kingston, 1784–1817

	Cargo In	Cargo Out
Cartagena	Bullion and cotton; sometimes in ballast	Dry goods, slaves, flour, liquors, earthenware, and iron
Portobelo	Bullion; sometimes in ballast	Dry goods, slaves, flour, liquors, earthenware, and iron
Santa Marta	Cattle, Nicaraguan wood, and cotton	Dry goods, slaves, flour, liquors, earthenware, and iron
Riohacha	Nicaraguan wood, cattle, and hides	Dry goods, slaves, flour, liquors, earthenware, and iron
Chagres	In ballast	Dry goods, slaves, flour, liquors, earthenware, and iron
San Andrés	Cotton and tortoiseshell	Dry goods, slaves, flour, liquors, earthenware, and iron
Sabanilla	Cotton and fustic	—
Old Providence	Cotton	—
San Blas	Tortoiseshell	Dry goods, slaves, flour, liquors, earthenware, and iron
Spanish Main	Cotton and cattle	Dry goods, slaves, flour, liquors, earthenware, iron, and clothing (handkerchiefs, osnaburg, and blankets)

Source: TNA, CO 142/22–29.

The Cartagena-Kingston route became particularly important during independent Cartagena's war against loyalist Santa Marta. Between 1811 and 1815, when Cartagena was an independent state, it depended almost completely on Jamaica for military supplies and victuals, which were exchanged for Cartagena's cotton. During 1814, at least four schooners—the *Annette*, the *San Josef*, the *Marinero Alegre*, and the *Veterano*—made several round trips between Cartagena-Sabanilla and Kingston.[116]

Riohacha and Santa Marta commanded another route—the eastern route—and Portobelo was the center of western New Granada's route. Nicaraguan wood, cattle, and hides constituted the main commodities exported from New Granada via the eastern route, while bullion and some tortoiseshell from the neighboring San Blas island were the main exports of the western route. Riohacha was home to a small merchant fleet that maintained a particularly strong connection with Kingston. One of the ships of this fleet—the schooner

Esperanza—made at least seven Kingston-Riohacha round-trips in 1814.[117] The Kingston-Riohacha route was one of the most traversed paths between the 1780s and the late 1810s. Complementing the Riohacha-Kingston route was a triangular itinerary that connected Santa Marta and Riohacha with Kingston. Either entering from Riohacha and departing toward Santa Marta (like the *Samaria* in 1814) or entering from Santa Marta and departing toward Riohacha (like the *Providencia*), a number of vessels anchored at Kingston as part of a route that supplied eastern New Granada's ports.[118] Western New Granada's route, for its part, was likewise well traversed by a handful of vessels doing the Kingston-Portobelo round-trip (e.g., the *Alexandre* in 1817) and several ships suspiciously sailing in ballast from Chagres.[119]

In addition, the island of San Andrés, conveniently located in the middle of the Portobelo-Jamaica and Cartagena-Jamaica routes, conducted an important trade with Kingston. Inhabited during the 1790s by a largely British population, though legally part of the Viceroyalty of New Granada, San Andrés's role as a hub for contraband with Jamaica was a permanent concern for Spanish authorities. Its proximity to the British enclaves in Honduras and the Mosquito Coast increased San Andrés's importance as a regional commercial center. Spanish proposals about how to deal with the island went from naturalizing the island's British inhabitants to fomenting its formal colonization and trade through the application of tax exemptions.[120] A particular source of apprehension was the practice of sending bullion and cotton to San Andrés in order to exchange it for all sorts of British goods imported from Kingston.[121] According to Viceroy Antonio Amar y Borbón, a number of vessels, of which Antonio Figueroa's *Santísima Trinidad* constituted a recent example, extracted bullion from Portobelo, which they used "to buy victuals in the islands of San Andrés."[122] The island's connections with Jamaica seemed to have strengthened with the growing success of the British free port system, to the point that in 1814, twelve vessels entered Kingston from San Andrés.[123] Of these, at least three—the *Esperanza*, the *Perla*, and the *Penelope*—did several round trips.

Last, a number of ships engaged in the Kingston–New Granada trade seemed to have been less geographically specialized. Ships like Manuel Bliz's *Soledad* and Gerardo García's *Flor de la Mar* bought and sold merchandise along the different ports of New Granada's Caribbean coast. While in 1785 the *Soledad* conducted businesses in Cartagena, Santa Marta, and Riohacha, in 1817 the *Flor de la Mar* visited Riohacha, Santa Marta, and Portobelo.[124] The *Soledad*, the *Flor de la Mar*, and all the other vessels involved in New Granada's Jamaican connection can be seen as important agents of New Granada's participation in the Caribbean networks of interimperial trade that gave shape to the transimperial Greater Caribbean. Two other characteristics shared by these merchant vessels—their size and the frequency of their trips—further contributed to the strengthening of this interimperial trade system and regional space.

Caribbean Peddler Vessels and the Importance of Frequency

In his 1979 study of global trade, Fernand Braudel proposed a distinction between wholesalers and peddlers as a tool to interpret the workings of Indian Ocean trade. Debating whether the early modern Indian Ocean was "a world of pedlars or of wholesalers," Braudel concluded that he was "more inclined to see [the merchants of the Indian Ocean as] . . . wholesalers."[125] Transferred to the late eighteenth- and early nineteenth-century Atlantic and Caribbean worlds, Braudel's framework leads to an obvious conclusion. While the Atlantic was a world of wholesalers, with a few big vessels carrying huge volumes and values, the Caribbean was a world of peddlers.

Spanish oceangoing vessels engaged in comercio libre weighed on average 182.4 tons.[126] Loaded with the right type of merchandise, a small quantity of such vessels entering Cartagena and Santa Marta once or twice per year (around eleven per year entered Cartagena between 1785 and 1788), coupled with a working network of internal distribution, could have satisfied most of New Granada's demand for imported goods.[127] This ideal scenario constituted the main goal behind the Spanish Crown's policy of comercio libre. However, as has already been shown, a reality plagued by conflicts with other European powers greatly limited the effective impact of comercio libre. In practice, New Granada—and this probably applies for other Spanish American territories in the circum-Caribbean—was supplied through Caribbean networks of interimperial trade little related to Spain's projected commercial policy.

New Granada's Caribbean foreign trade was conducted in small vessels (see figures 1.3 and 1.4) that were unable to carry huge amounts of products but were fast enough to avoid enemies at sea and foreign ports. In order to sell large quantities of merchandise, peddler vessels involved in intercolonial trade relied on frequent trips and relatively short stays in ports, rather than on large cargoes and extended periods of time anchored in ports.[128] Small vessels, multiple round-trips, and short stays in port diffused the risk associated with a trade that many times, as in the trade in clothes conducted under cover of the legal trade in slaves, included an illegal component. This method also allowed for a dynamic exchange of news, ideas, and rumors that, just like contraband trade, greatly concerned Spanish authorities and merchants with an

Figures 1.3 and 1.4 Schooners of the transimperial Greater Caribbean. Top: British schooner *Hornet*. Bottom: Spanish schooner *Esperanza*. Images courtesy of National Maritime Museum, Greenwich, London, UK.

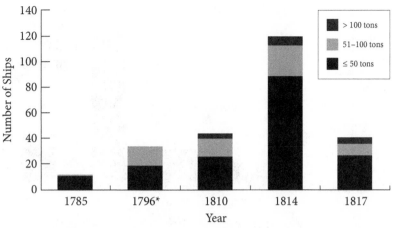

Figure 1.5 Size of Spanish vessels entering Kingston from New Granada, 1785–1817 (by tonnage).

interest in the Spanish transatlantic trade. Like the Bermudian sloops studied by Michael Jarvis, New Granada's peddler vessels, of which Domingo Pisco and Josef Borregio's *Esperanza* is a useful example, countered "what they lacked in size" with "speed and efficiency." Speed and efficiency, measured not only in terms of actual navigation speed but also in their ability to spend "less time in port loading and unloading," to reach ports and semihidden coves that "deep-water ships could not" and to make multiple round trips within a single year, made Jarvis's conclusion that "bigger was not always better" as valid for the southern Caribbean as he found it to be for the Northwestern Atlantic.[129]

Information for selected years on the tonnage and crew size of vessels entering and leaving Kingston from New Granada (see figures 1.5 and 1.6) provides a good sense of the types of vessels engaged in New Granada's Jamaican connection. Mostly classified by customs officers as schooners, Spanish vessels entering Kingston were largely of less than 50 tons (68 percent), with a significant 25 percent weighing between 51 and 100 tons. Large vessels of over 100 tons were a strange occurrence, with the *Lugan*, a 140-ton brig navigating the eastern New Granada route in 1814, standing out as the only frequent visitor of Kingston with these characteristics.[130] Similarly, when measured by number of men, the vast majority of vessels entering Kingston from New Granada were classified as small schooners with crews of ten or fewer men (70 percent), with medium-sized schooners of eleven to thirty men accounting for close to

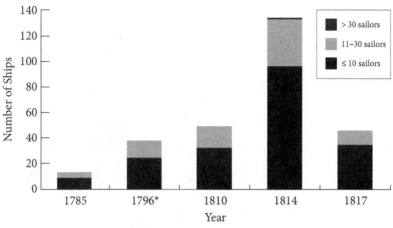

Figure 1.6 Size of Spanish vessels entering Kingston from New Granada, 1785–1817 (by crew size).

30 percent. The only vessel with a crew of more than thirty men was the *Hermosa Americana*, a 200-ton schooner with forty-two men that sailed to Cartagena in August 1814 loaded with dry goods, glassware, and earthenware and returned to Kingston in late September with 120 bags of cotton and 20,000 dollars in bullion.[131]

Since small vessels could only carry very limited cargoes, and thus produced less profit than larger ships, frequent travels constituted an important condition for the trade of small vessels in the Jamaican connection to be profitable. According to Santa Marta's governor, Antonio Narváez y la Torre, a typical schooner traveling to foreign colonies to sell cattle and dyewoods and buy slaves for later sale in Cartagena or Santa Marta, doing eight round-trips to Jamaica and six round-trips to Curaçao, could produce a hefty profit. Assuming average round-trip times of fifteen days to Jamaica and twenty-five days to Curaçao, and after accounting for sailors' salaries and rations, customs duties, and the cost of buying the heads of cattle and the dyewood, Narváez calculated that each schooner engaged in this trade could import about 300 slaves and, after selling them, generate about 30,000 pesos in profit. The transactions, he further explained, would not only be attractively profitable but, most important in his opinion, would greatly contribute to the transformation of the northern provinces into highly productive economies based on the development of commercial plantations.[132]

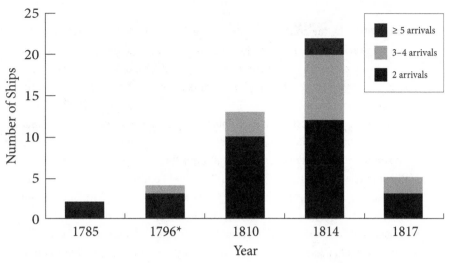

Figure 1.7 Identified peddler vessels trading between New Granada and Kingston, 1785–1817.

Frequency and size were also crucial to diffuse the risk associated with shipwrecks, capture by enemy forces, and seizure of merchandise by Spanish officials in New Granada's ports and coasts. A detailed analysis of the lists of Spanish vessels trading between Kingston and New Granada makes it possible to identify about forty vessels that were actively engaged in this commercial network. New Granada's Jamaican connection, the evidence shows, was largely dependent on a relatively small fleet of frequent visitors. In 1810 and 1814, the heyday of the British free port system and of New Granada's Jamaican connection, about half of the recorded 164 arrivals in Kingston from New Granada's ports (and a similar percentage of the 209 recorded departures) were undertaken by peddler vessels.[133] A conservative estimate of the number of peddler vessels maintaining New Granada's Jamaican connection shows that at least thirteen peddler vessels were in operation in 1810 and no fewer than twenty-two in 1814 (see figure 1.7).[134] This fleet of peddler vessels was not only undertaking trade but also, according to Spanish authorities, undermining Spanish control of New Granada's coasts.

In the context of the revolutionary period, the operations of this fleet of peddler vessels constituted an important matter of concern for Spanish royal officials apprehensive of the diffusion of revolutionary pamphlets, ideas, and news about "the inquietudes France is currently suffering."[135] The existence of this fleet also preoccupied merchants, especially from Cartagena, who faced competition by the contraband these ships surreptitiously introduced in the many hidden coves and uninhabited coasts that surrounded New Granada's Caribbean port cities. In their complaints and proposed solutions, high-ranking imperial authorities and merchants emphasized the interrelation between size and frequency as an important source of the problem created by Caribbean peddler vessels. In two reports on contraband trade in New Granada's ports written in 1800 and 1804, leading Cartagena merchant José Ignacio de Pombo reiteratively referred to small ships' "many trips and entries" and to the practice of "repeated trips" as facilitators of contraband. Combined with the habit of sailing "in ballast" along the coast, frequent trips to Jamaica and other foreign islands were, in Pombo's opinion, the main source of the conspicuousness of contraband in Caribbean New Granada.[136] A decade earlier, Viceroy Ezpeleta had expressed similar concerns, proposing as a possible solution the need to augment the minimum "number of tons of the vessels occupied in the slave trade." This measure, he believed, would reduce the number of trips and limit the ships' efficiency unloading illegal cargoes in the shallow coasts in the vicinities of New Granada's Caribbean ports. Almost counterintuitively, Ezpeleta concluded that in order to curtail the contraband trade that, in his opinion, resulted "from the permits granted to travel to foreign colonies in search of slaves" and the "allowance to ship *frutos del país* to foreign colonies," increasing Caribbean vessels' size and tonnage was the best-suited measure.[137] When it came to helping curtail contraband, bigger was indeed better.

The Limits of a Kingston-Centered Transimperial Greater Caribbean Free Trade Area

In his classic study of the relation between trade and political dominion, J. H. Parry concluded that after the crucial victory at Waterloo, "the British Empire . . . was no longer one of a group of similar competing empires."[138] It was, instead, superior to its traditional European rivals. In Caribbean waters, despite the loss of most of its North American colonies, British maritime, commercial, and political ascendancy had been growing since the Seven Years' War. Through a combination of territorial acquisitions and policy transformations that enabled greater commercial interactions, by the early 1810s Britain had succeeded in creating what can be called a transimperial Greater Caribbean free trade area, which it controlled largely from Jamaica, its most important commercial and naval base. Temporary territorial acquisitions

(Guadeloupe and Martinique in 1794, Curaçao in 1800–1802 and 1807–1815, and Saint Thomas in 1801 and 1807–1815) and permanent new colonies (Trinidad from 1797) contributed to consolidate British commercial hegemony.[139] This hegemony, however, was neither purely commercial nor unquestionably hegemonic. As evidenced by the aforementioned territorial acquisitions and by several failed attempts to acquire further territories (Saint-Domingue in 1793 and Puerto Rico in 1797), the nineteenth-century idea of an exclusively commercial empire was not yet a guiding principle of British relations toward Spanish America.[140]

In the commercial sphere, while British commercial influence over New Granada was strong and clear, the Jamaican connection was by no means the only commercial network in which New Granada's ports participated. While trade with Spain and the French and Dutch Caribbean did not, for most of the 1780s–1810s period, provide a reliable avenue to obtain the coveted manufactures and provisions, nontraditional commercial partners like the Danish Caribbean island of Saint Thomas and the newly independent United States were able to successfully challenge Britain's commercial hegemony. The commercial partnership with the Danish Caribbean, although important during the first two decades of the nineteenth century (despite the British occupation of Saint Thomas between 1807 and 1815), was short-lived and did not leave a significant imprint in the long-term history of the region that became present-day Colombia. Trade with the United States, on the other hand, had both an immediate and a long-term impact in Colombia's history and in giving shape to the transimperial Greater Caribbean. As witnessed by the commercial intercourse between Philadelphia and Cartagena, during the first decade of the nineteenth century the United States was already making important incursions into Spanish America.

In the immediate aftermath of the American Revolutionary War, commercial relations in the Greater Caribbean were dramatically transformed. During the first decade after the end of the American Revolution, Spain's commercial exchanges with its American territories reached unprecedented levels. The Anglo-Spanish War of 1796–1808, however, brought this transatlantic trade to a standstill. As a result New Granada and other Spanish American territories in the circum-Caribbean increased their commercial exchanges with Caribbean foreign colonies and the United States. Between 1780 and 1810, trade with foreigners moved from complementing the Spanish transatlantic commerce to replacing it. The British free port system and Britain's growing maritime power, coupled with an unsatisfied demand for British manufactures in Spanish America, transformed the southwestern Caribbean into a de facto free trade area, where British manufactures, provisions, and, at least in appearance, slaves were exchanged for Spanish American bullion and agricultural produce.

A characteristic of this newly established British-dominated Caribbean commercial system was the participation of a larger set of ports in commercial exchanges with Jamaica. In New Granada, the major port of Cartagena participated in the Jamaican connection in an equal footing with minor ports such as Santa Marta, Riohacha, and Portobelo. Additionally, other ports, which I have called hidden ports, like San Andrés and Sabanilla, maintained an important exchange with Jamaica.

Evidence from Jamaican ports and customs officers demonstrates that, even in times of war, Spanish vessels carried most of the trade with Jamaica. This finding constitutes strong evidence for the success of the British free port system and the important role of New Granada in this success. While Jamaica was the center of New Granada's foreign trade, Britain's dominion of the viceroyalty's commercial relations was far from monopolistic. Other international routes communicating New Granada's ports with foreign Caribbean ports and the United States became important with the advent of the Anglo-Spanish War in 1796. Anglo-American vessels dominated New Granada's trade (mainly Cartagena's) with the United States (largely channeled through Philadelphia). Danish ships, most likely transporting British goods, controlled trade in the Saint Thomas–Cartagena and Saint Thomas–Santa Marta routes. And Dutch vessels, almost completely absent during the periods of British occupation of Curaçao, appear in the records as important commercial partners of Santa Marta in 1807 and of Cartagena in 1817.

The commercial networks presented in this chapter were not only important as producers of revenue for British and Spanish merchants and governments, but also as generators of less tangible, but potentially more enduring, cultural effects. The following chapters explore the ways in which the transimperial commercial networks depicted in this chapter provided the background in which New Granada's Caribbean inhabitants developed geopolitical interpretations about the potential consequences of events in the Kingston-centered transimperial Greater Caribbean.

CHAPTER 2

Sailors

Border Crossers and Region Makers

In the age of sail, the workers of the wooden world were themselves, in their minds and bodies, vectors of global communication.
—MARCUS REDIKER, *Outlaws of the Atlantic*

On September 23, 1791, less than a month after the outbreak of the slave revolt that initiated the Haitian Revolution, news of the slave uprising in French Saint-Domingue reached the port of Santa Marta in the Viceroyalty of New Granada. Like most people and news during the Age of Sail, information about the events in Saint-Domingue traveled by ship. Pedro Pérez Prieto, the twenty-six-year-old captain of the schooner *San Fernando*, told Santa Marta's governor, José de Astigárraga, that a French schooner which Pérez Prieto encountered at sea had informed him that "the blacks and *mulatos* [of the French colony], aided by some white inhabitants had started an uprising and had killed all whites in seventy five plantations." After killing their owners, the rebels proceeded to "burn the plantations." Based on Pérez Prieto's report, Astigárraga began preparations for what he believed, given the proximity of Saint-Domingue and Santa Marta, could be a significant influx of refugees from the French Caribbean colony.[1] News of the Haitian Revolution, mostly transmitted by sailors reaching New Granada from different ports in the Caribbean, continued to capture the attention of Spanish authorities in Caribbean New Granada throughout the 1790s and well into the second decade of the nineteenth century.[2]

While the specific content of Pérez Prieto's account was unexpected and somewhat exceptional—slave rebellions, though not unknown, did not happen every day—the way in which the information was transmitted was typical of an age in which being a ship's captain also included being a transmitter of news. In the late eighteenth and early nineteenth centuries, as the work of Julius Scott and Marcus Rediker has demonstrated, sea captains like Pérez Prieto and the sailors they commanded played a key role in the circulation of news, ideas, rumors, people, and commodities.[3] Through myriad exchanges like the one between Astigárraga and Pérez Prieto and the one that preceded it between Pérez Prieto and the captain of the French schooner, taking place in many ports of the Caribbean Basin as well as on the high seas, Caribbean inhabitants became aware of the events happening on islands, coasts, and continents separated by sea but united by communication networks commanded by sea captains. Focusing on the navigational trajectories of sea captains and sailors who, between the 1780s and the 1810s, connected New Granada's ports with other Caribbean and Atlantic ports, this chapter argues that the circulation of people and information made possible the emergence and consolidation of a transimperial Greater Caribbean geographic space. Sea captains and the crews they commanded were the creators of this transimperial region. Their circulation and the information they spread resulted in the creation of what Michel de Certeau called a "theater of actions," whose configuration challenges preconceived notions about the existence of isolated Spanish, British, and French imperial spheres.[4]

The chapter is organized in two sections. The first one examines the trajectories of seamen who connected New Granada's Caribbean coasts with Spanish and non-Spanish territories in the Caribbean and the Atlantic world. Focusing on two specific types of sailors—captains of Spanish merchant vessels engaged in transimperial trade and ordinary sailors working on board insurgent corsairs—this section stresses the mechanisms of information transmission to show how social interactions resulted in the creation of a region that historians can use as a coherent unit of historical analysis. The second section attempts a characterization of the region sailors created that puts the sea at the center of historical analysis and reflects on the possibility of thinking the transimperial Greater Caribbean as an amorphously demarcated aqueous territory.

Sailors, Information, and the Creation of the Transimperial Greater Caribbean

In their study of the role of sailors, slaves, and commoners in the spread of revolutionary activity in the early modern Atlantic world, Peter Linebaugh and Marcus Rediker present eighteenth-century sailors as "a vector of revolution that traveled from North America out to sea and southward to the Caribbean." Drawing on the work of Julius Scott on Afro-American currents of communications in the Caribbean, Linebaugh and Rediker assert that sailors, through "contact with slaves in the British, French, Spanish, and Dutch port cities of the Caribbean," collected and transmitted "information . . . about slave revolts, abolition, and revolution."[5] Sailors' role as carriers or, in Linebaugh and Rediker's terminology, vectors of information was not limited to spreading revolutionary ideas and plans, nor were their contacts limited to slaves. At sea and on land, sea captains and ordinary sailors also established contact with colonial authorities, merchants, indigenous people, and many other Caribbean dwellers. Through these contacts, they collected and transmitted information—sometimes accurate, sometimes greatly distorted—about European affairs, potential invasions, alliances, and many other details of relevance to colonial authorities and the general public interested in the geopolitical developments of the Atlantic world. The spread of this information made possible the emergence of a way of living and interpreting the world that was common to all those living in the space stretching throughout and beyond the coasts and islands of the Caribbean Sea. Sailors' mobility and the flow of information their mobile lives made possible, in short, produced the loosely bounded transimperial Greater Caribbean region.[6]

Sea captains of Spanish merchant vessels and ordinary sailors on board insurgent corsairs—the two types of seamen I analyze in this chapter—surely experienced the transimperial Greater Caribbean in different ways and with different personal stakes. While captains, especially those whom Spanish authorities trusted, may have interpreted this region from a perspective firmly rooted in their political allegiance to the Spanish Empire, ordinary sailors seemed to inhabit what Julius Scott has called a "masterless Caribbean."[7] Despite the conflicting nature of their geopolitical visions and political allegiances, captains and sailors shared a common experience of circulation across Caribbean and Atlantic waters. This experience allowed them and other less mobile Greater Caribbean dwellers to understand that, despite the existence of many invisible dividing lines crisscrossing the Caribbean (e.g., political boundaries, racial divisions), the lands and waters contained within the Caribbean basin, and sometimes stretching beyond it, constituted a meaningful geographic space of social interaction, a region. Its blurred boundaries, the competing geopolitical projects that emerged within it, and the absence of explicit articulations (in maps, books, and treatises) of its existence as a place did make this geographic unit less visible (to the historian) but not less coherent (to its inhabitant).

Sea Captains

Navigating from one Caribbean port to another, often drawing circular routes that frequently took them to ports they had already visited on several occasions, the sea captains commanding the schooners that I studied in chapter 1 (and the crews manning these schooners) constructed personal geographies that challenged imperial demarcations and were a constant source of concern for colonial authorities. With navigational careers that often surpassed twenty years sailing the Caribbean, sea captains and their experienced crews were aware, like no one else, of the internal coherence—of the *regionness*—of this transimperial geographic space.[8] The professional trajectories of captains Juan Guardiola, Pedro Corrales, Jacinto Ruano, Nicolás Martínez, Pedro Pérez Prieto, and Salvador de los Monteros offer clear examples of the familiarity with the ports, coasts, and islands of the Caribbean that sea captains possessed. An analysis of their travels, including their information exchanges on sea and land, makes it possible to understand the process through which they contributed to the configuration of a transimperial Greater Caribbean.[9]

Guardiola, Corrales, and Ruano were all well acquainted with the geography of the Greater Caribbean, especially its southern coasts and waters. Between 1793 and 1808 (and probably some years before and after) Juan Guardiola captained at least six schooners and frequently navigated from Cartagena to Portobelo, Riohacha, Kingston, and Trinidad in Cuba (see map 2.1). On occasion, as in his 1800 cruises as captain of the schooner *Nuestra Señora de los Dolores* (Our Lady of Sorrows), he also sailed to Curaçao and Santo Domingo. Like Guardiola, Pedro Corrales had many years of experience (at least twenty-five) sailing the Caribbean as captain of the schooners *Carmen*, *Santa Rosa*, and *Carmelita*. Corrales's travels expanded Guardiola's theater of actions further east to incorporate the Danish islands of Saint Croix and Saint Thomas, both of which were important commercial partners of Cartagena and Santa Marta during the 1796–1808 period of Anglo-Spanish warfare and during the 1810s (see map 2.2). Corrales's repeated trips to the Danish Caribbean during 1807 reveal New Granada's need to establish alternative sources to obtain manufactures and victuals when war rendered it impossible to depend on supplies from Spain or the British Caribbean. Jacinto Ruano's Caribbean cruises, in turn, provide a sense of the commercial possibilities that peace had to offer (see map 2.3). In contrast to Corrales and Guardiola, who did most of their traveling after the beginning of the French revolutionary wars, Ruano's recorded travels took place during the peace period between 1785 and 1789. Ruano's Caribbean journeys took him several times to the French Caribbean

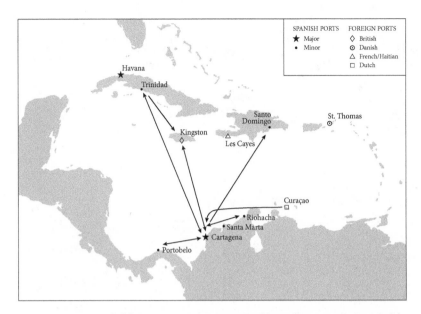

Map 2.1 Juan Guardiola's transimperial Greater Caribbean (1793–1808). Guardiola's circulations took him multiple times to British Jamaica, Dutch Curaçao, and many Spanish Caribbean ports including Cartagena, Riohacha, Portobelo, Trinidad de Cuba, and Santo Domingo.

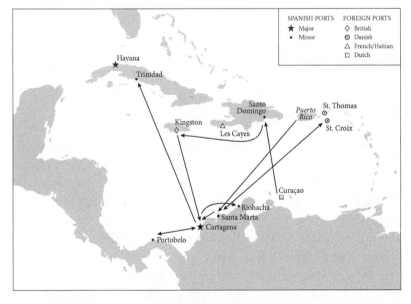

Map 2.2 Pedro Corrales's transimperial Greater Caribbean (1793–1817). A navigational career of over two decades allowed Corrales to become familiar with ports in the Spanish, Dutch, British, and Danish Caribbean.

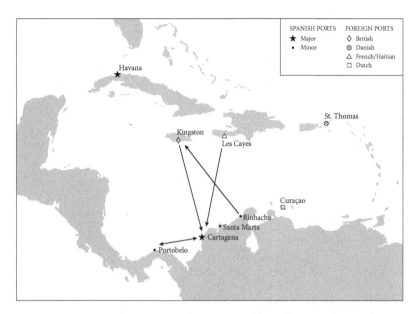

Map 2.3 Jacinto Ruano's transimperial Greater Caribbean (1785–1789). Ruano's frequent trips to Les Cayes show that, before the French and Haitian revolutions, Saint-Domingue rivaled Jamaica as commercial center of the transimperial Greater Caribbean.

port of Les Cayes, where he bought agricultural tools, iron nails, flour, and dried meat, all of which were most likely used to supply the new towns projected for the Darién.[10] Taken together, the navigational trajectories of Guardiola, Corrales, Ruano, and many other sea captains reveal the extent to which geopolitics, commercial legislation, and local needs affected the configuration of a transimperial Greater Caribbean space.

During the 1780s, guided mainly by the need to supply the expeditions to subdue the unconquered indigenous population of the Darién—an important component of which consisted in establishing several towns along the Caribbean coast between Portobelo and Cartagena—Spanish authorities opened Cartagena to trade with foreign neutrals. During the second half of the 1780s, a rare period of peace in a Caribbean world characterized by near-permanent warfare, permission to trade with foreign neutrals resulted in a constant crossing of political borders that made it possible for Caribbean sea captains to circulate almost unrestrictedly between Caribbean port cities controlled by different European powers. While the eruption of the French revolutionary wars, Anglo-Spanish warfare in 1796, and the Napoleonic Wars imposed restrictions on the trade networks of the 1780s, the life trajectories of Guardiola and Corrales reveal that Caribbean sea captains continued to connect New Granada's ports with foreign Caribbean islands. The Caribbean's changing geopolitical landscape, coupled with the successful implementation of the British free port system and Spanish permission to trade with foreign neutrals, resulted in the rise of Kingston as the emporium of the Spanish circum-Caribbean territories.[11] Thus, it should come as no surprise that, like the navigational trajectories of Guardiola and Corrales, those of Abraham Paz (schooner *Marta*), Bonifacio Revilla (schooners *Regencia* and *Samaria*), Josef Aballe (schooners *Malambruno* and *Santo Cristo de la Espiración*), and many other sea captains sailing the Caribbean on Spanish vessels gravitated around Kingston.[12] Kingston's central place in these captains' Caribbean geographies further supports the argument, presented in chapter 1, that toward the end of the eighteenth century the Caribbean was turning into a free trade area largely dominated by the British. In addition, these captains' frequent presence in Kingston allowed this port to emerge as the most important (or one of the most important) site of the transimperial Greater Caribbean.

British commercial hegemony, however, should not be equated with commercial monopoly. Similarly, Kingston's centrality should not be interpreted as exclusivity. As the travels of Ruano and Corrales show, French, Dutch, and Danish Caribbean ports maintained a limited capacity to challenge British commercial dominance. Like Ruano, Manuel Sosa (captain of the Spanish schooner *Carmen*) and Domingo Dixon and Francisco Margeran, both of whom captained French schooners sailing between Les Cayes and Santa Marta, looked to the French Caribbean as source of victuals and clothes to sell in New Granada.[13] The multiple trips of Juan Cruz de Herazo (captain of the sloop *Casildea*) and Pablo Francisco Mora (captain of the Spanish schooner *Nuestra Señora del Carmen*) between Cartagena and Curaçao in 1793, as well as those of José Martínez (schooner *Suceso*), Eudaldo Fiol (schooner *Bella Narcisa*), and Pedro Atencio (schooner *Fancy*), reveal the strategic importance of the Dutch and Danish islands to the construction of the transimperial Greater Caribbean.[14]

From the 1780s, however, the biggest challenge to British commercial hegemony began to come from the newly independent United States. Shipping returns for Cartagena and reports by New Granada's authorities, as chapter 1 shows, shed light on the degree to which the United States became a major player in the Caribbean world of trade. The professional trajectory of Salvador de los Monteros further illustrates the process through which, during the late eighteenth century, the Caribbean networks of trade and information began to expand beyond the Caribbean Sea to reach ports in North America.

During the early 1780s, sailing as captain of the schooner *Amable*, Monteros traveled mainly between Kingston and Cartagena with occasional visits to Portobelo and Trinidad de Cuba. Starting in 1786, by request from New Granada's viceroy Caballero y Góngora, Monteros began to sail beyond the Caribbean, becoming one of the first sea captains to establish direct connections between New Granada and the ports of the newly independent United States. In his capacity as viceregal envoy to the United States, Monteros was charged with obtaining victuals and construction materials (mainly iron tools and ship masts) and recruiting people willing to settle the new towns projected for the Darién. Secretly, Viceroy Caballero y Góngora also trusted Monteros with the confidential mission of finding and capturing a fugitive Jesuit presumably hiding in the United States.[15] The results of Monteros's secret mission are not entirely clear, but his multiple travels between Cartagena and the United States reveal the extent to which ports like Charleston and New York were increasingly participating in New Granada's Caribbean networks of trade and communication. On July 24, 1786, for instance, Monteros entered Cartagena from Charleston as captain of the frigate *San Antonio*, importing "*arboladura* [masts and spats], iron, flour, artillery, bullets," and more.[16] Soon after, navigating with "free and safe passport" granted by the viceroy on September 19, 1786, Monteros sailed from Cartagena to New York. There he spent at least a portion of 1787 obtaining victuals and tools to send to Cartagena. While Monteros remained in New York, the *San Antonio*, this time captained by Olivier Daniel, sailed for Cartagena in March 1787 with a cargo of flour, beer, pepper, clove, hams, cheese, apples, candles, oil, clay plates, iron tools (axes), and boots.[17]

Other captains, including Josef Rodríguez (brig *Fuerte*), Juan Ferrer (polacre *San Agustín*), and Juan Pastor (polacre *Jesús Nazareno*), further pushed the Greater Caribbean boundaries toward the United States through repeated trips to Philadelphia during the late 1780s.[18] Their travels, thus, constituted early predecessors of the stronger commercial connections that, starting in the first decade of the nineteenth century, linked Philadelphia with Cartagena and other ports in the Caribbean coast of the Viceroyalty of New Granada.[19]

Like Guardiola's, Corrales's, and Ruano's, these U.S.-going captains' personal geographies were transimperial. The latters' geography, in contrast to those of Guardiola, Corrales, and Ruano, covered much more terrain. Collectively the trajectories of these sea captains reveal how frequent travel sustained over long periods of time (the archival record reveals that it was common for captains' careers to span more than two decades, characterized by multiple visits to key ports in every single year) made it possible for captains to become main actors in the configuration of transimperial geographies that were, as a scholar of space put it, "always under construction."[20] Just by engaging in frequent travel, Guardiola, Corrales, Ruano, Monteros, and the many other captains and sailors who traversed Caribbean and U.S. Atlantic waters became the main characters of the transimperial Greater Caribbean region they helped create. By transmitting information about life and political events in the many ports they visited, sea captains also made it possible for the many who did not share their mobile lives to live and interpret their lives within the malleable geographical framework of the transimperial Greater Caribbean.

Sea captains not only made possible the flow of information, but they themselves produced some of this information. Isidro Josef Caymani, for instance, as captain of the mail schooner *Postillón*, was responsible for the transportation of official correspondence between Cartagena, Havana, and Puerto Rico. Captain Nicolás Martínez, writing from Jamaica in February 1785, informed Santa Marta's governor, Antonio Narváez y la Torre, that he had learned in Kingston of an alliance between Jamaica's authorities and "three Indian captains from Calidonia" (the Darién), who went to Jamaica to obtain "rifles, gunpowder, bullets and some troops to make war against the Spanish." Attached to this letter, Martínez also sent Jamaican newspapers with information about British actions in Honduras and the Mosquito Coast. Like Monteros in New York, Martínez was in Jamaica under secret orders that included providing military intelligence regarding potential British preparations to attack New Granada's coasts.[21]

Besides these exchanges of printed communications, sea captains also transmitted information orally through the well-established process of ship inspections or *visitas de entrada*. During the visitas conducted in the ports of New Granada, customs officers required captains to provide their name and nationality, the name of the vessel under inspection, the name of the last ports visited, the cargo transported, the number of sailors that made up the ships' crews, and the number of passengers who traveled on the ship. In addition, customs inspectors asked captains to give details about other ships encountered during navigation and about occurrences at sea, in particular if there had been "any ruin because of the disobedience of the members of the crew."[22] The special emphasis port authorities put on events that altered the routine of any given sea journey (mutinies and encounters with foreign ships constituted a special concern for customs officers) reveals the general apprehension that characterized Spanish authorities during a time marked by interimperial warfare and the spread of revolutionary ideas, conspiracies, and uprisings.

Through visitas, Spanish authorities learned about the eruption of the Haitian Revolution and received unofficial information on war declarations and peace settlements (often before the arrival of the official notice). During his visita de entrada in Santa Marta in September 1791, Pedro Pérez Prieto transmitted the news of the outbreak of the slave revolt in Saint-Domingue.[23] In 1802, shortly after entering Puerto Cabello from Puerto Rico, Pedro Corrales relayed to Caracas's authorities information he obtained from a U.S. ship that had just arrived in Puerto Rico from Les Cayes in Haiti. Based on his conversation with the U.S. ship's captain, Corrales prematurely declared the Haitian Revolution over by informing Caracas's captain general that "the black caudillo Toussaint, forced by hunger and thirst . . . , had surrendered," and, as a result, "the whole country" had returned to French possession.[24] In the interrogation that started the visita of the British schooner *Luite Bets*, its captain, Noel Tool, provided information about the presence of British ships and sailors on the Spanish island of San Andrés.[25]

Many times the visitas served as the most efficient mechanism for Spanish authorities to obtain the latest news. Oftentimes captains confirmed previously obtained information about invasion plans prepared by foreign powers. Most of the time, ships' crews, whom port authorities interrogated after captains had given their declarations, corroborated the versions given by their captains. Customs officers, well aware of the limits to the credibility of the information obtained through these official channels, understood the need to take captains' declarations with a grain of salt. Indeed, distrusting captains or, more precisely, knowing who to trust was a fundamental part of the work of customs officers and provincial governors. In 1799 and 1800, just to use two examples, their distrust allowed Cartagena's port authorities—Governor Anastasio Zejudo and customs officer Ignacio Cavero—to discover contraband cargoes that captains Andrés Fernández and Domingo Díaz had naturally not felt inclined to declare.[26] These occurrences made it common for customs officers and provincial governors to complain about the difficulty of obtaining news "straightforwardly from captains" and to declare that captains "do not consider themselves" required "to say what they do not deem convenient" to their ends.[27]

Attempting to solve the problems generated by the general lack of credibility of captains, Spanish officers sought to enlist captains in the service of royal authorities. This procedure allowed them to recruit a set of trusted captains, who were often assigned missions that went beyond navigating the seas transporting goods, people, and information. Monteros and Martínez, discussed previously, were part of a group of trusted captains on whom New Granada's authorities depended to obtain reliable information. The world of Caribbean seafarers and region makers also included Spanish captains allegedly working as spies for British authorities, British adventurers who shifted allegiances and became Spanish subjects, and a host of ordinary sailors employed on merchant vessels, warships, and insurgent corsairs. Like captains, these ordinary sailors were familiar with Caribbean and Atlantic waters and absorbed and transmitted information that made the transimperial Greater Caribbean a lived reality.

Sailors

Ordinary sailors—Jack Tars and Black Jacks, as they are commonly called in maritime history and literature—constituted the majority of the individuals on board Spanish merchant vessels legally crisscrossing Caribbean and Atlantic waters under the protection of imperial legislation facilitating transimperial commercial exchanges.[28] Jack Tars of all colors also manned British, French, Danish, and Dutch sloops and schooners, U.S. brigs, and warships of all imperial and national navies. During the first half of the 1810s they also filled the decks of the vessels sailing under the flag of the newly formed, and ultimately ephemeral, Republic of Cartagena.[29] Like captains, ordinary sailors spent their lives moving from port to port, frequently crossing political borders and connecting imperial spheres historians have traditionally regarded as isolated.[30] Like captains, ordinary sailors encountered multiple opportunities to share information obtained aboard the many ships on which they worked and at the ports, coasts, and islands they visited as part of their Caribbean and Atlantic cruises. While most of the informal conversations sailors had did not enter the archival record and thus remain concealed from historians' eyes, it was common for sailors to be forced to share their personal tales of mobility, border crossing, and region making as part of interrogations following their capture by enemy forces. These interrogatories often revealed—to those conducting the interrogation—the ambiguous nature of sailors' political loyalties and make it possible—for the historian reading through these legal procedures—to identify the extent to which sailors seemed to lack a territorially grounded sense of belonging. Instead of feeling subjects of a particular European crown and firmly attached to a specific town, island, colony, or nation, sailors' experiences point to the existence of an unarticulated but nonetheless strong feeling of being part of a transimperial Greater Caribbean.

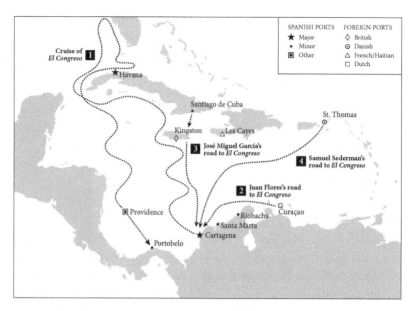

Map 2.4 Cruise of the insurgent schooner *El Congreso de la Nueva Granada*, detailing specific paths different sailors took to embark on it. Constructed based on "Autos . . . *El Congreso*," AGNC, AA-I, Guerra y Marina, 118, 721–933.

The lives of the sailors on the schooners *El Congreso de la Nueva Granada* and the *Altagracia*, all of whom were held in custody and interrogated by Spanish authorities in Portobelo, reveal details about sailors' mobility, professional trajectories, and everyday acts of region making.[31] Both *El Congreso* and the *Altagracia* reached Portobelo's vicinity after several months cruising the Caribbean. *El Congreso*, its twenty-three sailors explained, reached Portobelo after abandoning its captain on Providence Island. Thus, they argued, their arrival in Portobelo was voluntary—a point they needed to emphasize given that *El Congreso* was carrying flags of many different nations and sailing with letters of marque granted by the newly created and, from the perspective of Spanish officials, insurgent Republic of Cartagena.[32] Before reaching Providence Island, *El Congreso*, in typical corsair fashion, had followed a border-crossing path that had taken its sailors from Cartagena "to the coast of Jamaica, . . . then to the coast of Florida, and then to that of Havana" (see map 2.4).[33] At different points throughout this cruise, some sailors abandoned *El Congreso* while others, forcefully or voluntarily, joined its ranks, thus demonstrating the instability of sailing crews and seafaring lives.

The *Altagracia*, its sailors reported, was a Spanish schooner that had been captured by Cartagena's privateers near the western coast of Puerto Rico. Following orders to take the captured vessel to Cartagena, sailors Juan (an Englishman who became captain of the captured schooner but died shortly after reaching the coast of Portobelo), Ilario and Ignacio (both French-speaking sailors from Haiti), and Juan Estevan Rodríguez (a native of Venezuela) jumped from the capturing schooner *La Belona* to the captured *Altagracia*. On board the *Altagracia* they joined Francisco, a young sailor from Venezuela, and slaves María Felipa, Vicenta, Felipa, Dolores, Juana, and Paula and her infant Ramón. While en route to Cartagena, Ignacio declared, "the winds and currents," coupled with the captain's lack of skill, diverted the *Altagracia* from its route and took it to the coast near Portobelo, where it had been stranded.[34]

To Spanish authorities, given the flag under which they sailed, the sailors of both schooners were considered insurgent corsairs loyal to the Republic of Cartagena or, more simply, pirates. Following this logic, prosecutors sought to condemn the sailors "for the crime of sailing with all flags" and for capturing Spanish vessels while "flying [the flag] invented by the insurgents of Cartagena."[35] Sailors of both schooners naturally sought to make the case for their innocence. Of those sailing on the *Altagracia*, Francisco and the slaves were not charged with any crime, while Ignacio, Ilario, and Juan Estevan were tried as corsairs. Francisco avoided charges because all those questioned by Spanish authorities corroborated that he was on board the *Altagracia* before its capture and was forced to remain on board after the corsairs took over. Juan Estevan was acquitted of all charges, and Ignacio and Ilario were sentenced to eight years in jail in Havana. Beyond the ultimate outcome of the judicial procedure, the archival trail left by *El Congreso* and the *Altagracia* reveals the existence of a space of social interaction where sailors of all colors and from many geographic origins sailing under different flags and frequently switching from one ship to another lived lives that were marked by both the risks and opportunities that circulation across the transimperial Greater Caribbean had to offer.

The sailors of *El Congreso* and the *Altagracia*, like the sailors of many other Caribbean- and Atlantic-going corsair vessels, did not just sign up to become corsairs or pirates at the service of the Republic of Cartagena. Their diverse paths to *El Congreso* and the *Altagracia* provide multiple clues to uncover and understand the transimperial Greater Caribbean they created and inhabited. In essence, the stories of the sailors of *El Congreso* and *Altagracia* point to mobile experiences—they moved from port to port and frequently also from

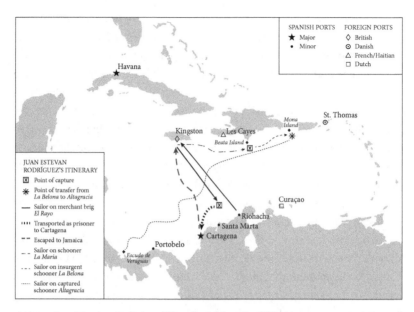

Map 2.5 Juan Estevan Rodríguez's hostile Greater Caribbean experience. Constructed based on "Declaración de Juan Estevan Rodríguez," in "Autos *La Belona*," AGNC, AA-I, Guerra y Marina, 130, 417–419.

ship to ship—that coalesced around a loosely bounded space of social interactions that included Spanish, Dutch, British, French, and independent territories (besides the United States and Haiti, independent territories included the emerging, not fully consolidated, and ephemeral republics of Cartagena, Caracas, and the two Floridas) whose coasts touched the Caribbean and Atlantic waters on which these sailors spent most of their lives.[36]

One such story, that of black sailor Juan Estevan Rodríguez (see map 2.5), points to both the existence of the transimperial Greater Caribbean as a coherent space of social interaction and to the everyday risks experienced by those who gave shape to and lived within this loosely bounded region. Juan Estevan was not just a corsair sailing under the flag of independent Cartagena. In fact, as he was able to demonstrate in court, he had been a prisoner of Cartagena's corsairs, who had forced him to work as a sailor on board both *La Belona* and the *Altagracia*.[37] His route to Portobelo, where he rendered his declaration to Spanish authorities on February 20, 1815, was marked by trouble and reveals the instability and everyday threats characteristic of sailors' lives and of the transimperial Greater Caribbean.

Born in Ocumare, Venezuela, Juan Estevan was a chocolate maker, a trade he had learned while living on the other side of the Atlantic, in Catalonia. Upon returning to the Americas twelve years earlier, he had "worked as a sailor on several merchant vessels." About two years before presenting his declaration to Portobelo's authorities, Juan Estevan was working as a sailor on the Spanish brig *El Rayo*, which "traded mules [from Riohacha] to Jamaica."[38] Returning from Jamaica, *El Rayo* was attacked and captured by a gunboat from Cartagena, where he was taken and held prisoner and forced "for six months to sweep the streets tied to a chain." After those six months, he managed to escape and fled to Jamaica, where he, once again, enlisted as a sailor, this time on the Spanish schooner *La María*. From Jamaica, *La María* sailed east toward Puerto Rico and "by the Beata Island, in front of Santo Domingo," fell prey to Cartagena's insurgent schooner *La Belona*. On board *La Belona*, "because some [of its sailors] knew he had escaped from prison," the captain, infamous French corsair Louis Aury, told Juan Estevan that "the only way for him [Aury] to spare his [Juan Estevan's] life was [if Juan Estevan chose] to enroll as sailor" on the insurgent corsair. Forced into his new status as a corsair for Cartagena, Juan Estevan sailed east on *La Belona* until, south of Mona Island (just west of Puerto Rico), they captured the Spanish schooner *Altagracia*. With three other sailors from *La Belona*, Juan Estevan once again switched vessels, charged with the task of taking the *Altagracia* to Cartagena. Due to the winds and currents, as one of Juan Estevan's fellow sailors explained, the *Altagracia* never reached Cartagena, and Juan Estevan and the schooner's other passengers ended up giving their versions of their Caribbean cruises to Spanish authorities in Portobelo.

Juan Estevan was not alone in living a border-crossing, ship-switching, status-changing life.[39] Like him, Ignacio, one of the black Haitian sailors who accompanied Juan Estevan on the *Altagracia*, had been sailing the Caribbean Sea for years before joining *La Belona*. Born in Port-au-Prince, Ignacio joined the insurgent schooner from Cartagena after working as a sailor on a Dutch vessel, which he joined in Port-au-Prince, and an English vessel, which he joined in Jamaica.[40] Many of the sailors on board *El Congreso*, similarly, came to this insurgent schooner with seafaring experience and information obtained on other ships and islands (see map 2.4). Juan Flores (also known as Juan Fiol, a double naming that also suggests ambiguity about his nationality and the potential for split allegiances—was he Dutch or was he Spanish?), for instance, declared that he had traveled "to Cartagena from Curaçao on an English brig." Once in Cartagena, because "he fell ill and [because] the [English] brig had left," his lack of resources and knowledge of no other occupation left him, so he claimed, no other option but to enlist on *El Congreso*.[41] Sailor José Miguel García also joined *El Congreso* by way of several other ships. First, on board the Spanish schooner *Caridad*, he sailed from El Cobre in Cuba—a town that figured on imperial authorities' radar as a welcoming haven for "all kinds of fugitives from slavery . . . [and] several infamous characters who had been on the run for years"—to Jamaica.[42] In Jamaica, where the *Caridad*'s captain left him stranded, García enlisted on the Cartagena-bound English schooner *Kange Drick*. In Cartagena, after the *Kange Drick*'s captain "disembarked all the crew to avoid the expenses [associated] with their daily maintenance," García and other *Kange Drick* sailors "struggling to make a living," including Brazilian Manuel Pedro, embarked on *El Congreso* as means "to escape misery."[43] English sailor Samuel Sederman, similarly, claimed that hardship (he did not have resources to sustain himself and could not find "another vessel to sail to other port") forced him to become a sailor on board *El Congreso*. His path to *El Congreso*, like that of Juan Estevan to the *Altagracia*, included a violent encounter shortly after he took to sea from Saint Thomas on board the Spanish schooner *Caridad*. *El Congreso*, Sederman claimed, captured the *Caridad* and took it to Cartagena with all its sailors. There, Sederman and others, either voluntarily or forced by economic hardship, joined *El Congreso*'s crew in the cruise that ended with the schooner entering Portobelo in December 1814.[44] Collectively, the biographical snippets of the sailors on board *El Congreso* and the *Altagracia* accurately fit the description of corsairs as "villains of all nations" and of sailors as a "motley crew" made up of veritable "citizens of the world" of different cultural and ethnic backgrounds who joined the ranks of Caribbean- and Atlantic-going vessels from all corners of the Atlantic world.[45] In addition to colored sailors Ilario and Ignacio from Haiti and Manuel Pedro from Brazil, a good number of white sailors from France (Pablo Not, Pedro Robert, Pedro Babal), Malta (Francisco Miguel), Corsica (Antonio Plaza), Majorca (José Rubio), Sicily (Gaspar Core, Mateo de Pauli), England (Samuel Sederman, José Baron), and even Germany (Juan Cort) made up the crews of these insurgent schooners. Caribbean *pardos* and *mulatos* from Cartagena, Cuba, and Venezuela (Manuel Ximénez, José Miguel García, Francisco Díaz, Juan Estevan Rodríguez) further added to *El Congreso*'s and the *Altagracia*'s multinational, multiethnic, polyglot, and cosmopolitan crews.

In their cosmopolitan constitution, *El Congreso* and the *Altagracia* resembled not only the scores of corsair vessels that sailed these seas but also the many imperial warships that sailed the Caribbean and the Atlantic. A contemporary observer described the corsair vessels that roamed the Caribbean as "small schooner[s] with 25 or 30 men on board, [on which] the captain and his officer, as he called him, were the only white men, the rest negroes, and these the very worst drunkards."[46] As Niklas Frykman has shown, during the late eighteenth century, as a result of "the near permanent warfare" that ravaged the Atlantic world, imperial navies required increasing numbers of seamen to man their growing fleets. To recruit the necessary workforce, British, French, Spanish, Dutch, and Danish navies had to force sailors—either through conscription or impressment—to join their crews. Despite a preference for subjects of the empire under whose flag they were going to sail, navies were often forced to recruit foreigners to man their warships. On British and Dutch warships, for instance, it was common for more than half of the sailors to be foreign born.[47] In the British case, despite stipulations of the navigations acts requiring "that three fourths of the crew" of English vessels "be English or Irish . . . , English ships continued to be worked by African, Briton, quashee, Irish, and American (not to mention Dutch, Portuguese, and lascar) sailors."[48] The prevalence of foreigners in these ships and, by extension, in the cities where these navies recruited sailors constituted an important source of concern for imperial officers who, rightly so, distrusted the loyalty of foreign sailors.

An analysis of the crew lists of Spanish warships anchored at Cartagena during the last two decades of the eighteenth century reveals a picture that contrasts Frykman's findings. While sailors from Curaçao were commonly found on board Spanish warships like the *Pentapolin* and the *Santiago*, most of these vessels' common sailors were Spanish subjects hailing from nearby towns and villages including Bocachica, Pasacaballos, Barú, Lorica, and San Bernardo.[49] Proximity, however, did not make the loyalties of most of these sailors less suspect. If imperial officers considered nationality a source of suspicion, they also put great weight on race when determining whose loyalties to consider dubious. In this racialized environment, in which people of color and their political allegiances were not deemed worthy of trust, the seventeen (out of twenty-two) common sailors of the Spanish galliot *Dulcinea* classified as pardos (seven), *zambos* (six), *mulatos* (two), or *aindiados* (two) give a sense of the extent to which Spanish authorities believed they could trust their own seamen.[50] At 45 percent (54 of 119), the proportion of black, zambo, *mulato*, and indigenous sailors and cabin boys on board the *Santiago* also made this crew unworthy of officers' trust.[51]

For Spanish naval commanders, as for the high-ranking officers of other European navies, the threats of mutiny and massive desertion were aspects of their work environment with which they dealt almost on a daily basis. Mutinies, as apparent in the accounts of the sailors of the insurgent schooner *El Congreso*, all of whom agreed that they had captured the schooner and abandoned its captain after learning that he "did not have good intentions and was trying to deceive them," were not confined to the vessels of imperial navies.[52] Desertion, as the story of zambo sailor Simón Hernández shows, also plagued imperial navies and constituted an important element of sailors' mobile lives.

Simón Hernández, a zambo from the town of San Bernardo, lived a ship-switching life. Between 1789 and 1791 he worked as a sailor on the Spanish warships *Liebre, Maristones, Flecha,* and *Micomicona*. On board these vessels he joined crews that, between sea officers, gunners, sailors, cabin boys, and servants, could surpass one hundred men. Hernández's ship-switching life, thus, offered him plenty of opportunities to bond and share information with a relatively large number of fellow sailors. His life also suggests that, as Niklas Frykman pointed out, imperial warships "had a revolving door" that made it necessary for recruiters to be constantly at work in order to keep the decks filled with able men. Not only did sailors move from one ship to another but it was also common for them, as Hernández did in 1791, to simply run away when the discipline of the warship became intolerable.[53]

After his desertion in Cartagena in 1791, nothing else is known about Hernández's life. He could have retired to a life on land or, most likely given that Cartagena was a dynamic port where many sailors found work on board the many merchant vessels that plied the Caribbean frequently crisscrossing imperial boundaries, he could have continued his ship-switching life. Like Juan Estevan, Ignacio, Samuel Sederman, Juan Flores, José Miguel García, and other sailors of *El Congreso* and the *Altagracia*, Hernández could have continued living the border-crossing, region-making life characteristic of transimperial Greater Caribbean sailors.

Hernández's labor mobility (from ship to ship and then, perhaps temporarily, away from ships), coupled with the physical mobility (from port to port) that characterized sailors' lives, suggests the many opportunities sailors had to share information obtained during their frequent Caribbean journeys. While most of the conversations and interactions among these seafaring individuals and between them and coastal inhabitants and islanders are beyond the historian's reach, it is not hard to imagine the type of information and experiences that sailors usually shared. The time they spent in different Caribbean ports and the conditions of their stays reveal that the opportunities to share information were both many and varied. Sailors surely shared stories that created a mild sense of familiarity with distant places from which they had migrated long ago and with which few of their fellow sailors and coastal interlocutors were acquainted. Of most immediate interest to interlocutors must have been stories about the most recent trips and adventures in frequently visited ports, coasts, and islands. The accumulation of stories about recent developments and rumors on nearby Caribbean islands and coasts contributed to the creation of a coherent transimperial Greater Caribbean milieu.

The official accounts sailors like Juan Estevan, Ignacio, Ilario, and those on board *El Congreso* gave port authorities provide a clear sense of the transimperial region that they inhabited, produced, and traversed on a daily basis. Less clear in their accounts are the ways in which their interactions with coastal residents and islanders allowed sailors to spread to others the sense of regionness they experienced on an everyday basis. On occasion, local prisons— to which some sailors were taken after entering specific ports—became sites where sailors could share information with prison guards and other prisoners. Sailors like Bernardo Kennedy of the Danish schooner *Guavaberry* and the seven members that composed the crew of the schooner *San Francisco Xavier*, which entered Santa Marta in July 1803, followed this path. Imprisoned immediately after entering Santa Marta and Riohacha, these sailors' ability to spread news and rumors that they had gathered in other Caribbean ports was initially limited to the few people with which they interacted while in jail. After they were released or escaped from prison, this situation changed. Kennedy, stranded for several months in Riohacha in 1806, became familiar with the Spanish judicial system and, it is not difficult to imagine, also engaged in conversation with multiple members of Riohacha's society. Some, like Luis Polo, the cook of the *San Francisco Xavier*, died in prison unable to transmit to a larger set of coastal inhabitants information about his adventures at sea and in foreign ports. Others, like Juan Rivas (who escaped) and Jaime Sastre and José de Silva (who were released), enjoyed the opportunity to socialize in New Granada's ports, spreading information that made it possible for New Granada's coastal inhabitants to become acquainted with, and feel part of, the Greater Caribbean's transimperial social field.[54]

The picture of sailors' lives that emerges from these tales of mobility is a messy one. Permanently crisscrossing Caribbean waters, legally or otherwise, sailors connected imperial spheres. They were well acquainted with commercial hubs like Kingston, Les Cayes, Saint Thomas, Curaçao, Cartagena, Havana, and other key connecting nodes of the transimperial Greater Caribbean. Their mobile lives not only took them from port to port, frequently returning to a port they had previously visited (perhaps many times) but also, adding to their nomadic existence, from ship to ship, which usually led sailors to shift imperial patrons. It was common for sailors to have experience on board Spanish, British, Dutch, Danish, and, like those on board *El Congreso* and the *Altagracia*, insurgent schooners.

As part of these mobile lives, it was also common for sailors to end up stranded on land after captains unwilling to cover their maintenance expenses forced them off their ships. It was perhaps more common for sailors like zambo Simón Hernández and Bernardo Kennedy to run away and get lost in port cities and their hinterlands. It was not uncommon for sailors, like those on board *El Congreso*, to unite against their captain and take control of the ship.

Through all these experiences, sailors both acted and were acted upon. They voluntarily enrolled on a given vessel and were forced to move from a captured schooner to a capturing one, where they then continued their nomadic lives. The unpleasant encounters Juan Estevan Rodríguez, Francisco Díaz, and others experienced at sea point to the Caribbean as a hostile environment and force us to reconsider notions of "masterless, mobile" lives at sea as closely connected to freedom and autonomy. While the sea, especially for plantation slaves, could have held a "seductive appeal," the distance separating this appealing perception from lived reality could sometimes be substantial.[55] My focus on the circumstances under which sailors moved across Caribbean waters allows me to deromanticize mobility and to identify the coerciveness that belied sailors' mobile existence. Sailors rarely chose where to go or when to return home. For many, in fact, there was no home. Francisco Díaz's answer when asked about his place of residence—he said, "Without fixed residence because I am a sailor"—points to the limits to the opportunities a seafaring life had to offer.[56] In their mobility, voluntary or not, full of opportunities or marked by difficulties and threats, sailors gave coherence to and filled with meaning a transimperial space of social interactions. In short, they created a region. Read in this light, Francisco Díaz's answer becomes much more than a statement about sailors' nomadic existence. When answering, "Without fixed residence because I am sailor," Francisco Díaz was also pointing to the difficulties associated with naming the geographical space sailors inhabited. The absence of a name (a problem also faced by the historian reconstructing this lived geography) did not make the transimperial Greater Caribbean less real.

Filling the Sea, or the Transimperial Greater Caribbean as Aqueous Territory

In his provocative interpretation of the process known in Argentine history as "the conquest of the desert," Claudio Canaparo characterizes this watershed of Argentina's nation-making process as achieved through the use of technologies that made possible the key transformation of terrain (defined as empty space) into territory (characterized as former terrain that has been demarcated and, thus, made legible through "the insertion of signs").[57] Transferred to the Caribbean seascape, Canaparo's distinction resonates with the usual characterization of the sea as empty and typically contrasted with the readable land. This distinction "between the signless sea and the full-of-signs land" takes away an important component of the complexity that characterized the connected processes of creating and experiencing the transimperial Greater Caribbean.[58] A tradition of regarding the sea as signless or empty has hindered historians' ability to give serious consideration to the sea as site where history unfolds, to the reality that, as Nobel laureate Derek Walcott put it, "the sea is history."[59] My focus on sailors' circulation and their social interactions, many of which happened at sea, rescues the sea as historical site and makes it possible to refute what Marcus Rediker has called "the uninspected assumption that only the landed spaces of the earth's surface are real."[60] It, so to speak, fills the sea, turning what most historians have taken as empty space into what following Canaparo's terrain-territory distinction can be called an aqueous territory.[61]

In the mobile lives of captains and sailors it is possible to find the contours of the aqueous territory I call the transimperial Greater Caribbean. Each sailor, by moving frequently from port to port collecting and transmitting news and rumors obtained at sea and in the many ports visited, created a personal geography that cut across political geographies. Collectively, the many captains and sailors crisscrossing Caribbean and Atlantic waters pieced together a transimperial space of social interaction and shared information. Circulation—of people and information—not only created a transimperial Greater Caribbean, of which New Granada's Caribbean coasts and ports were vital components. Circulation also filled with meaning an aqueous territory familiar not only to sailors but also to many others who experienced the transimperial Greater Caribbean from its shores. But what type of region was this transimperial Greater Caribbean?

The transimperial Greater Caribbean, to begin with, was loosely bounded. Because it was formed through mobility and because in their mobile lives the sailors that created this region did not follow fixed, previously determined paths, the edges of the transimperial Greater Caribbean are difficult to determine. Indeed, if we allow for spatial configurations to be permanently under construction, attempting to delimit and fix the shape of the transimperial Greater Caribbean becomes a futile task. This regional configuration was flexible and malleable.

Flexibility and malleability account for rough and unclear edges. But sailors' circulation and interactions make it possible to identify regional nodal points. Analyzing the transimperial Greater Caribbean from the shores of the Viceroyalty of New Granada, my study of the seafaring lives of captains and sailors makes clear that ports like Kingston, Les Cayes, Saint Thomas, Curaçao, Cartagena, Havana, and even Philadelphia were part of a larger, interconnected geographic space. Sailors' circulation brought these ports together, making it possible for people in Cartagena, Curaçao, and Philadelphia to be aware of events taking place in Kingston and other ports of the Greater Caribbean.

Because it spanned empires, the transimperial Greater Caribbean was multicultural. Its inhabitants may not have been able to speak multiple languages, but they surely were aware of the polyglot nature of many of the region's inhabitants, and hearing different languages was certainly an everyday aspect of life on ships and in port cities. In official interrogations (and most likely in informal conversations) sailors were used to telling their tales through translators. Linguistic barriers may have slowed communication but, as the mobile lives of sailors make clear, they did not curtail the flow of information. This information might not have been accurate, but even false rumors contributed to developing a sense of transimperial Greater Caribbean regionness. In fact, it is possible to think of the transimperial Greater Caribbean as an informational space created on the basis of everyday circulation and exchanges, many of which happened at sea, miles away from any of the region's ports. The exchange (of words) between a sailor on a captured schooner and a sailor from the capturing one contributed to the creation of the transimperial Greater Caribbean. Through many recorded exchanges between sailors and port authorities and even more unrecorded ones among sailors and between sailors and port denizens, information flowed across imperial jurisdictions and made possible the emergence and strengthening of a transimperial Greater Caribbean region.

The region, as sailors and coastal residents and islanders experienced it, was both geopolitically unstable and personally threatening. Sailors' mobility, as I have shown, was permanent. It was also contingent on the vagaries of warfare. Geopolitical circumstances, which often resulted in the emergence of new political entities (the United States, Haiti, and the Republic of Cartagena are some examples), made mobility a threatening affair. With every trip captains and sailors risked capture by enemy forces. When taking to sea, sailors usually had a clear idea of where they were headed but could not foresee if and when they were going to reach their destination. At times the winds and currents diverted vessels from their planned itineraries; often hostile encounters with privateers—a frequent occurrence for sailors like Juan Estevan Rodríguez—kept vessels from reaching their planned destination. Despite these adverse circumstances and largely encouraged by commercial policies favoring trade with neutral powers, sailors kept moving and connecting ports and coasts under different imperial jurisdictions.

While increasingly open to interimperial trade, Spanish authorities frequently debated the opportunities and threats that could result from this growing openness. During the 1780s one of these debates, pitting New Granada's viceroy, Antonio Caballero y Góngora, against the head of the Spanish coast guards, Juan Álvarez de Veriñas, left an archival trail that includes what can be seen as cartographical evidence of Spanish awareness and tacit acknowledgment of the existence of the transimperial Greater Caribbean.[62]

As part of his argument against interimperial trade, Veriñas drew a map that depicts a portion of the transimperial Greater Caribbean sailors created and experienced (see figures 2.1–2.3). Drawn as if he was facing the Caribbean Sea and South America from an elevated site on Jamaica, Hispaniola, or Puerto Rico or, perhaps more accurately, from the perspective of a vessel sailing the Caribbean, fore to South America and aft to Jamaica, Hispaniola, and Puerto Rico, Veriñas's 1786 map inverts the usual up-as-north-down-as-south orientation of cartographic representations. Emphasizing the southern portion of the transimperial Greater Caribbean, this upside-down map details the geographic space for whose surveillance Veriñas, in his capacity as head of the coast guards, was responsible. The emphasis on South America's northern coast and the islands of Jamaica, Hispaniola, and Puerto Rico also makes the map an accurate representation of the geographic space that, from the perspective of the ships and sailors that populate the archival sources I use, constituted the core of the transimperial Greater Caribbean. While, as shown by the navigational trajectories of Salvador de los Monteros and the sailors of *El Congreso*, sailors embarking from New Granada's ports often sailed beyond the area depicted in Veriñas's map, their collective experience suggests the centrality of this smaller portion (it may be thought of as a subregion) loosely

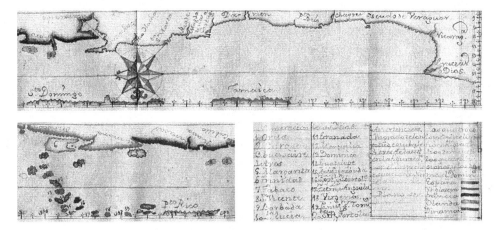

Figures 2.1–2.3 Juan Álvarez de Veriñas's map of the southern portion of the transimperial Greater Caribbean. This "upside-down" map depicts the transimperial space Veriñas was responsible for surveilling. Image courtesy of Archivo General de Indias, Seville, Spain (MP-Panama, 262).

bounded to the north by the southern coasts of the islands of Jamaica, Hispaniola, and Puerto Rico.

For Veriñas, including the islands (twenty-three of them), most of which were under the jurisdiction of Spain's European rivals, allowed him to make his case for the threatening nature of the seascape that constituted his workspace. Including the islands, along with precise measures of the distance separating New Granada's coasts from foreign territories, also allowed him to claim and complain simultaneously that the threat posted by transimperial communication was immediate (the foreign islands are too close), the area too big to patrol, and the resources insufficient to do so effectively (he calls for a raise to the monthly allowance of coast guards and the acquisition of ships and armament).[63] In short, while only depicting a portion of the transimperial Greater Caribbean, Veriñas's 1786 map clearly makes the case for the existence of a transimperial space of social interaction. While Veriñas stopped short of articulating his workspace as a region, it is clear that his map represented a lived geography that he, those sailing under his command, and innumerable other sailors—who, to Veriñas's chagrin, made a living out of crossing political borders—experienced on a daily basis.

Their transimperial Greater Caribbean, thus, was a lived but unarticulated geographical space. It was lived because sailors experienced it in more tangible ways than they experienced the clearly bounded (at least in maps) imperial political geographies. It was unarticulated because sailors did not see themselves and their everyday actions as constructing a region. Sailors did not, nor did they intend to, imagine the transimperial Greater Caribbean as an entity occupying an "objectively identifiable" piece of the earth's surface. Neither did sailors turn the transimperial Greater Caribbean into "a source of pride, loyalty, love, passion, bias, hatred, reason, unreason." The region they created, thus, lacked what Thongchai Winichakul has called a geo-body.[64] Despite all this, the transimperial Greater Caribbean existed as a meaningful space of social interaction.

Finally, and of most relevance to my sea-based regional approach, the transimperial Greater Caribbean of the late eighteenth and early nineteenth centuries was an aqueous territory of mobile markers. Far from being an empty space or an "interval between places," the sea that the region-making sailors navigated was full of signs that captains and ordinary sailors read and cleverly deployed as a strategy to enhance their ability to navigate Caribbean and Atlantic waters safely.[65] Instead of fixed markers ordinarily used to make landed territories legible (e.g., railways, telegraph lines, rivers, roads, and mountains), the transimperial Greater Caribbean was a world of mobile markers.[66] Ships were those markers. Their size and type and the flags they flew conveyed messages that filled with meaning this aqueous region.

The lives of sailors clearly demonstrate the extent to which the sea constituted a site where history happened. Maritime historians have written about labor relations and hierarchies on board vessels, and the term "hydrarchy" has become a well-known designation for the social relations above and below the decks of Atlantic-going vessels.[67] Emphasizing the encounters at sea allows me to make a similar point by interpreting the sea as much more than just an uneventful bridge between ports bursting with human interactions and history.[68]

The life of Juan Estevan Rodríguez, once again, is illustrative of the interactions that filled the sea with history. If Juan Estevan's transimperial Caribbean was hostile, it was not because the ports of the region impeded his mobility or curtailed his opportunities to find work as a sailor. Granted, Juan Estevan was forced to become a sailor because he failed to secure a livelihood as a chocolate maker, the trade he declared as his occupation when interrogated by Spanish officers.[69] The source of the region's hostility, as Juan Estevan experienced it, came from interactions that took place at sea, away from the region's ports and coasts. Capture by enemy forces at sea dramatically changed Juan Estevan's perceived political status, forcing him to demonstrate that, despite being a sailor on an insurgent schooner, he was a loyal subject of the Spanish king. Like Juan Estevan, Domingo Negrón (captain of the schooner *Concepción*), whose schooner, as presented in chapter 1, was captured by the British ship *Veteran*, experienced the sea as workspace, threat, and historical site of human interaction.[70]

As a site of history, the sea that Greater Caribbean sailors navigated on a daily basis was full of signs that sailing experience had taught them to interpret. For Spanish captains, a British brig, depending on the prevailing geopolitical circumstances, could be a potential threat (and therefore needed to be avoided) or an aid to traversing the dangerous Caribbean waters. While Negrón and the crew of the *Concepción* experienced their encounter with the *Veteran* as a hostile capture, for the sailors of the two Spanish schooners the *Veteran* was convoying, this British ship offered protection in their endeavor to extract gold from New Granada and transport it to Jamaica.[71] In both cases, the *Veteran*—through its size, its cannons, and its flag—functioned as a sign that transmitted a message to other vessels cruising the Caribbean. Like the *Veteran*, smaller ships that during the second decade of the nineteenth century sailed the Caribbean flying the flag of the independent Republic of Cartagena (*El Congreso* and the *Altagracia* are two of many) and that of the Republic of Haiti conveyed messages that sailors on board other vessels and coastal inhabitants read.[72] Ships with flags of European powers (British, Spanish, French, Dutch, Danish, etc.) and American republics (United States, Haiti, Cartagena) made the transimperial Greater Caribbean seascape not only a colorful space, but also a readable space full of mobile markers. They filled the sea, transforming it from terrain into territory.

As mobile markers, ships could not provide precise locations but they conveyed messages associated with geopolitical realities. Ships' flags signaled neutrality, hostility, or alliance and, therefore, alerted captains and sailors how to approach or on the advisability of avoiding specific vessels. For Cartagena's corsairs, a Spanish flag indicated a fair prey that could be captured. Ships flying the U.S. flag generally signaled neutrality—a condition that some contemporaries denounced as a "war in disguise," given how neutral status was used by belligerent powers to continue trade through other routes and carriers.[73] The interest of Spanish authorities in learning about the ships that vessels entering Spanish American ports had encountered at sea further points to the centrality of flags as signs that made the transimperial Greater Caribbean readable, eventful, and full of history.[74] Based on this information, Spanish authorities, merchants, and sailors could make calculations and determine not only action plans but specific routes to take or avoid in their border-crossing travels and transactions.

But if ships—through their type, size, and flags—conveyed messages, these messages were neither clear nor straightforward. As demonstrated by the common practice, especially among corsairs and ships conducting contraband trade, of carrying several flags, these signals were often used as bait to lure potential prey, to avoid contraband-searching coast guards like Veriñas, or to trick customs officers. The cases of *El Congreso* and the *Altagracia*, both of which were found to have been "sailing with all flags," demonstrate the skepticism sailors and authorities needed to display when reading the messages flags conveyed.[75] Trustworthy or not, these messages and the interactions they facilitated shed light on the extent to which the sea that Greater Caribbean sailors navigated constituted a site of human interactions that affected the lived experiences and interpretive schemes not only of the many corsairs, coast guards, and sailors navigating on board warships of all nations but also of those who stayed put and experienced these interactions from their less mobile coastal settings. For all these transimperial Greater Caribbean denizens, the sea could not be conceived as merely an interval between ports, as ahistorical space where history was put on hold until ships arrived in ports where history actually happened. To them, the transimperial Greater Caribbean they sailed and inhabited was both a landed and an aqueous space of social interactions, a distinguishable region of loose edges but clear markers. It was an aqueous territory.

Everyday Acts of Region Making

If nations have been defined as "imagined political communities" necessarily associated with a geo-body, regions like the transimperial Greater Caribbean, it can be said, were unimagined.[76] Despite this lack of intentionality— sailors' circulation and information collection and sharing were not part of an explicitly or otherwise formulated region-making project—sailors' lives constituted everyday acts of region formation. In the everydayness of their mobile lives, sailors created a region for whose existence neither they nor any region maker, politician, bureaucrat, or founding father argued.

Historians, with few exceptions, have generally taken space as fixed and geographical units of analysis as given. Cultural geographers, by contrast, have long thought of space and geography as socially constructed and permanently in the process of being made.[77] Historians' tendency to fix geography, coupled with the tendency to project twentieth-century world-regionalization schemes uncritically onto the past, has blinded us to the type of regional configuration that I explored in this chapter.[78]

Historians of Latin America have generally pursued stories that can be told staying within the confines of national histories. Historians of the Atlantic, similarly, have paid excessive respect to imperial political geographies, effectively creating an Atlantic world characterized by what David Hancock self-critically called "imperial self-sufficiency."[79] Histories of border-crossing and mobile subjects whose lives do not fit national or imperial compartments, despite a recent surge, have been generally left untold.[80] Bringing these stories to life allows us to uncover "ways of being in the world" that force us to rethink the usefulness of working within clearly bounded, predetermined, and fixed geographical units of analysis.[81]

Through their multiple Caribbean journeys, sea captains and sailors collected and transmitted information that greatly contributed to making the transimperial Greater Caribbean more coherent, more meaningful. The common pool of information these Caribbean travelers created made it possible for a much larger population—the European subjects and non-European peoples who inhabited the Caribbean islands and basin—to feel part of this regional configuration. Belonging to this transimperial geographic space provided a framework for Caribbean dwellers to make sense of the present and imagine potential future outcomes of present events. Following sailors, letting them show us the geographic space they inhabited and created, and uncovering their everyday acts of region making make it clear that the sailors presented in this chapter made not only their own history but also their own geography. Neither their history nor their geography, as the eventful life of Juan Estevan Rodríguez demonstrates, were theirs to make under circumstances of their own choosing.[82]

II

Geopolitics and Geopolitical
Imagination

CHAPTER 3

Maritime Indians, Cosmopolitan Indians

They have at all times been considered the most ferocious of the maritime Indians.
—FRANÇOIS DEPONS, *Travels in South America*

On July 26, 1787, Cuna chiefs Bernardo, Guillermo (William) Hall, Guaycali, Jorge, and Wrruchurchu (alias Suspani) jumped on board Enrique Hooper's schooner, probably the *Friendship*, to return to their towns in the Darién.[1] For a week, the Cuna chiefs and Hooper and priest Luis Rounellet, whose signatures indicate they were acting as the Cunas' Spanish-to-English translators, had been in Cartagena negotiating the terms of a peace treaty with Spanish authorities. As a result of the treaty the Cunas promised to live as good vassals of the Spanish king in exchange for an amnesty concerning their past crimes (Article 1). In order to demonstrate their good faith, they were required to obey the prohibition to pursue "any trade and communication with foreigners" (Article 7). Spanish authorities, in turn, granted the Cunas permission to sell their produce in any Spanish port at prices at least equal to those offered by the British (Article 5) and pledged to open a road that would allow for swift communication between the Caribbean and Pacific sides of the Darién isthmus (Article 11).[2] The treaty, which temporarily secured peace between Cunas and Spaniards, apparently served both parts equally well: the Spaniards obtained the Cunas' loyalty, and the Cunas secured access to a market and a fair price for their products.

Two years later, in 1789, the Spaniards and the Cunas signed a new Treaty of Friendship in which both parts replicated their 1787 commitments. Soon after, in the first months of 1790, Spanish authorities learned that Bernardo and Guillermo Hall, both signatories of the 1787 treaty, and another Cuna chief, Sebastián, had taken part in a recent trip to Jamaica to obtain "a large number of rifles in exchange for tortoiseshell."[3] The multiple treaties and the Cunas' violation of their commitments (and their ability to get away with it) reveal the extent to which participation in the Caribbean circulation networks made it possible for the Cunas to ascertain their political autonomy and impose their will on what both they and Spanish authorities recognized as independent Cuna territory.

What happened in the years immediately following the signing of the 1787 treaty, moreover, challenges traditional assumptions about indigenous spatial practices and consciousness and the differentiated agencies of Europeans and indigenous peoples. The treaty and its aftermath, in short, allow us to see the Cunas as "full-fledged historical actors who played a formative [and active] role" in shaping indigenous-European relations.[4] The Cunas' mobility (their travels to Jamaica and Cartagena), commercial relations (trade with Jamaica and the Spanish Main), access to and implied ability to use military technology (British rifles were an important component of the Cunas' trade with Jamaica), linguistic talents (the presence of Hooper and Rounellet as translators suggests that Cuna chiefs understood Spanish but felt more comfortable with English), and diplomatic skills (the negotiations show Spanish and Cuna envoys on an equal footing) appear as telling examples that sharply contradict nonindigenous expectations about the indigenous experience.[5]

The Cunas were just one of several indigenous groups of the Greater Caribbean who used this aqueous territory to maintain their independence and successfully advance their political agenda. Together with the Wayuu of the Guajira Peninsula, the Miskitos of Nicaragua's Mosquito Coast, and the Island Caribs of the Lesser Antilles, the Cunas constituted what I will call, following French traveler François Depons, the "maritime Indians."[6] While much has been written about Miskitos and Island Caribs and their relations with Europeans, in the literature on indigenous people in Latin America and the Caribbean the Wayuu and the Cunas shine for their absence.[7]

The Wayuu and the Cunas occupied (and, to a limited extent, continue to occupy) the eastern and western extremes of Colombia's Caribbean coast (see map 3.1). During the late eighteenth century the Wayuu inhabited the Guajira Peninsula, a physical geography most of which fell under the jurisdiction of the newly created province of Riohacha. On the northwestern extreme of what during the eighteenth century was known as the Viceroyalty of New Granada, the Cunas inhabited the Gulf of Darién and its surrounding coast and hinterland, roughly spread throughout what today constitutes the Republic of Panama. Both the Guajira Peninsula and the Darién were nominally part of the Spanish Empire, but, as this chapter shows, everyday interactions between Wayuu and Cunas and Spanish settlers and other Europeans reveal a much more complicated picture of territorial possession.

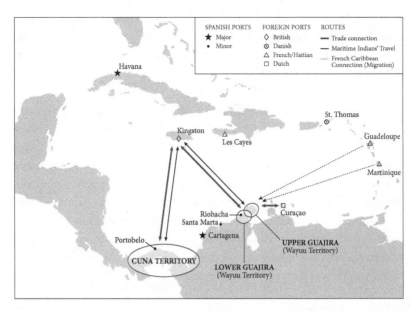

SPANISH PORTS
★ Major
• Minor

FOREIGN PORTS
◇ British
⊙ Danish
△ French/Haitian
□ Dutch

ROUTES
— Trade connection
— Maritime Indians' Travel
····· French Caribbean Connection (Migration)

Havana

St. Thomas

Kingston
Les Cayes

Guadeloupe

Martinique

Riohacha
Santa Marta
Cartagena

Curaçao

UPPER GUAJIRA
(Wayuu Territory)

Portobelo

CUNA TERRITORY

LOWER GUAJIRA
(Wayuu Territory)

Map 3.1 The Maritime Indians' transimperial Greater Caribbean. Maritime Indians' travels and trade made them cosmopolitan and allowed them to maintain their independence.

This chapter studies the connections that allowed Cunas and Wayuu to develop a lifestyle or worldview that, paraphrasing Michel de Certeau, can be called a cosmopolitan, Greater Caribbean "way of being in the world."[8] It also emphasizes how the interactions associated with cosmopolitanism put these indigenous groups on an equal footing with European allies and rivals and allowed them to successfully sustain their challenge to Spanish authorities. In the process, by emphasizing indigenous mobility, multilingualism, technological capacity, and political autonomy, the chapter challenges cartographic fictions of territorial control embedded in European-drawn maps of the Caribbean (and in the language historians and the general public use to speak about Caribbean geography) and sheds light on European perceptions of indigenous peoples (and what these perceptions actually say about the maritime Indians). In short, this chapter argues that the Cunas and the Wayuu, like the people Ira Berlin and Jane Landers called "Atlantic creoles," were "cosmopolitan in the fullest sense." Like Atlantic creoles, maritime Indians were "familiar with the commerce of the Atlantic, fluent in its new languages, and intimate with its trade and cultures."[9] My analysis of maritime Indians' Caribbean connections also democratizes geopolitics because it presents indigenous people engaging questions about "world politics" typically associated with "political elites and educated segments of the general public" (or, in a colonial setting, with white elites), not with the independent indigenous groups whom Spanish authorities called *bárbaros*.[10]

The chapter is organized in three sections. The first one looks at the geographic spaces inhabited by Cunas and Wayuu. Drawing on Spanish maps prepared as part of military campaigns that sought to conquer maritime Indians, this section uses Spanish cartographic narratives to tell the story of maritime Indians' political autonomy and Spanish veiled recognition of that autonomy. The second section analyzes the traits that made maritime Indians cosmopolitan and the ways in which cosmopolitanism allowed them to successfully assert their political independence in the face of constant Spanish attempts to subdue, pacify, reduce, or conquer them. The last section contrasts the ways in which maritime Indians envisioned themselves as actors in the transimperial Greater Caribbean with how Spanish authorities saw them.

Geographic Settings: The Stories Maps Tell

In the late fifteenth and early sixteenth centuries, European powers first began using cartography "to support the assertion of their control over familiar and domestic peoples and territory as well as more distant and alien places" and their native inhabitants.[11] Thus, as historian of cartography J. B. Harley pointed out, "European maps of the period can [perhaps even should] be viewed as statements of territorial appropriation."[12] These cartographic assertions, produced to convey a sense of legitimate territorial possession to an audience of European rivals, presented clear demarcations that produced the appearance of strong empires whose territorial control spread evenly throughout their domains. Historians of the Spanish Empire—in particular those studying geographic locations that based on their distance from imperial centers of power are variously referred to as peripheries, frontiers, borderlands, and claims—have rightly characterized these statements of imperial presence and control as "fiction[s] that existed only in Spanish minds and on European maps."[13] Empires, as Lauren Benton put it, "did not cover space evenly." Instead, especially in peripheral areas (sometimes characterized as "empty" and "lawless" spaces), imperial power was often limited to "narrow bands," "corridors," or "enclaves." These nuances of imperial control, however, are generally silenced by the "monochrome shading [characteristic] of imperial maps."[14]

Imperial maps, however, come in different shapes and scales and were created for different purposes and audiences. Different imperial maps also tell different stories. While global maps (or maps that encompass large portions of an empire's territory) created to show other imperial rivals the vastness of one empire's possessions tell a story of evenly distributed imperial control, more detailed local maps drawn to understand the geopolitics of a particular region within the empire tend to be more self-critical about the exertion of imperial power. In the late eighteenth century, as part of military campaigns that sought to conquer the maritime Indians, Spanish military engineers Antonio de Arévalo and Antonio de la Torre produced detailed maps of the Guajira Peninsula and the Gulf of Darién. Intended for internal consumption (i.e., to be used by Spanish colonial officials), their maps barely attempt to hide the political autonomy of both the Wayuu and the Cunas.

Arévalo's 1773 *General Map of the Province of the Guajiro Indians, also Known as [the province] of Rio del Hacha* (see figure 3.1), drawn after what he considered a successful pacification campaign, implicitly (but clearly) acknowledges Wayuu political autonomy. Naming the province "Province of the Guajiro Indians" constitutes an initial, though tenuous, recognition that the Guajira Peninsula belonged to the Wayuu. Other details further convey the impression of Wayuu autonomy, an autonomy that, Arévalo claims, his pacification campaign was increasingly exterminating. The map's details and the accompanying text, however, make his claim difficult to sustain.

Besides the Spanish provincial capital, located by the coast in the western extreme of the province, and two small Spanish towns located south of the provincial capital (Moreno and Barrancas), the rest of the province is devoid of Spanish presence. According to Arévalo's map, five additional towns—Camarón, Orino, La Cruz, Rincón, and Boronata—were inhabited by now-pacified Wayuu people. Beyond these locations, all in the southern and western half of the Guajira Peninsula—the area called today the Lower Guajira—Arévalo's map constitutes a catalogue of needs and desires.[15] It shows the projected locations of "four new Spanish towns, which need to be founded" and an unspecified number (apparently seven) of "Indian towns that also need to be founded [at least] for now."[16] The locations of the projected Spanish and Indian towns—all in the eastern and northern parts of the peninsula or what is known today as the Upper Guajira—reveal the Spanish perception that it was necessary to extend Spanish influence beyond the Lower Guajira. Furthermore, despite Arévalo's representation of these desires and needs as fait accompli, his vagueness about the number of Indian towns

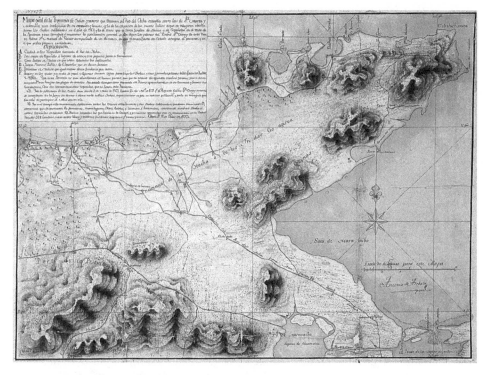

Figure 3.1 "Mapa general de la Provincia de yndios Goagiros que llaman del Río del Hacha" (*General Map of the Province of the Guajiro Indians, also Known as [the province] of Rio del Hacha*) (1773). Image courtesy of Archivo General de Indias, Seville, Spain (MP-Panama, 184Bis)

that needed to be founded (he does not specify a number and he adds the tentative "for now" to the note about the projected Indian towns) suggests that Spanish authorities did not have a realistic sense of the peninsula's eastern and northern territory.[17]

Two other maps (figure 3.2), intended to convey a sense of detailed knowledge of the land, end up reinforcing my suggestion about Spanish authorities' weak presence and inadequate knowledge of the peninsula's physical terrain. In addition to the *General Map*, Arévalo drew detailed maps of the ports of Portete and Bahia Honda on the coast of the Upper Guajira. Despite the detailed information the maps provide about the depth and navigability of the coasts, both maps, like the general map, represent more Arévalo's projects than his achievements. Portete's map, for example, merely signals a location "very appropriate to establish a town." Bahia Honda's map, in contrast, shows an

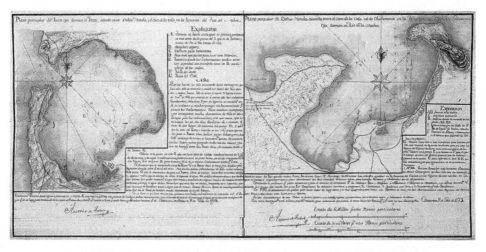

Figure 3.2 "Plano particular del Puerto que llaman el Portete" (1773) and "Plano Particular de Bahia Honda" (1773). Image courtesy of Archivo General de Indias, Seville, Spain (MP-Panama, 182).

already established town—San Joseph de España de Bahia Honda—but an accompanying annotation stating that the bay "has often been frequented by foreigners who have done their commerce there and have extracted mules, cattle, dyewoods, and hides" betrays the limited control Spanish authorities exerted in the area.[18]

Other Spanish sources corroborate the maps' story of a Guajira Peninsula claimed by Spain but independently ruled by the Wayuu. The Spanish claim was theoretically acknowledged by other European powers, but in practical terms Spanish authorities dealt with the Wayuu as an autonomous, belligerent nation that sided with Spain's enemies to undermine the authority of the Spanish monarch. As Riohacha's governor, Josef Medina Galindo, conceded in 1801, "the greater part of the coast [of this province] is inhabited by Guajiro Indians, [who are not] subject to our laws." Because the Wayuu were not subjected to Spanish authorities, Medina concluded, "it is impossible to force them to observe [our laws]."[19] An earlier observer, Francisco Silvestre, writing in 1789, referred to "the famous Guajiro nation, which remains unconquered."[20] Additionally, recurrent calls throughout the 1790s "to conciliate in a friendly manner," through "prudent and soft means" as the only way "to render them docile" and "maintain peace," reinforce the impression that Spanish control over the Guajira Peninsula was very weak.[21] The Wayuu, it seems, were masters of their domains. The Guajira Peninsula, as recognized by Spanish authorities, was only a claim.[22]

Spanish descriptions of the Guajira Peninsula estimated that, by the end of the eighteenth century, the peninsula's population ranged from 16,000 to about 40,000 autonomous indigenous inhabitants plus close to 4,000 people living *a son de campana*.[23] The unconquered Indians did not constitute a single group unified as a political entity. Instead, scholars of the area have argued, three main indigenous groups—the Wayuu, the Cocinas, and the Paraujanos, all of them living independently from the Spanish Crown but willing to reach agreements with its officials—divided the peninsula into clearly identified areas of influence. The Wayuu—themselves subdivided in small groups or *parcialidades* under specific leaders or *caciques*—dominated most of the territory of the peninsula including the immediate surroundings of the provincial capital (the city of Riohacha), the Upper Guajira (including the important ports of Portete, Bahia Honda, and Chimare), and the Lower Guajira (including the surroundings of the Spanish towns of Moreno and Barrancas and important portions of the road connecting the city of Riohacha with the city of Maracaibo in the captaincy-general of Caracas). The Cocinas dominated a small portion of the eastern peninsula, the Sabana del Valle, from where they frequently raided the road to Maracaibo. The Paraujanos lived in the surroundings of the Lake of Maracaibo.[24] While both Cocinas and Paraujanos engaged Europeans and other outsiders in ways similar to those of the Wayuu, this latter group's numerical and territorial superiority made the Wayuu the most pressing concern of Spanish authorities.[25]

Less than a decade after Arévalo drew his maps of the Guajira Peninsula, infantry captain Antonio de la Torre elaborated a map of the Gulf of Darién, its surrounding coasts, and its hinterland, detailing the coast from the mouth of the Sinú River (to the west of the city of Cartagena) to the mouth of the Chagres River (just west of the city of Portobelo; see figure 3.3). Like Arévalo's maps, La Torre's 1784 *Plan Comprising All the Terrain Occupied by the Gentiles of Darién and Calidonia* was drawn as part of a military campaign that sought to conquer the Cunas. Unlike Arévalo, who drew his maps of the Guajira Peninsula after his campaign was officially over, La Torre prepared his map before launching the military operations. Because of this, La Torre's map, even more than Arévalo's, constitutes a catalogue of Spanish plans and desires, and its recognition of Cuna autonomy is less veiled than in Arévalo's maps of the Guajira Peninsula. Because Arévalo's maps reported what was supposed to be a fait accompli, they could not openly acknowledge the Wayuu's continued

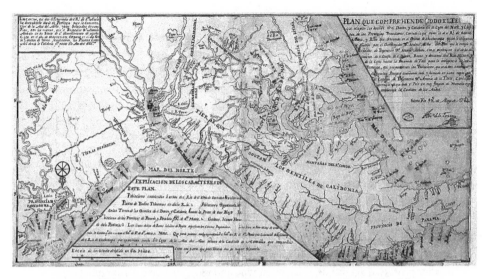

Figure 3.3 "Plan que comprehende todo el terreno que ocupan los jentiles del Darién y Calidonia en la Costa del Norte." Image courtesy of Archivo General de Indias, Seville, Spain (MP-Panama, 202Bis).

independence and, along with it, Arévalo's failure. Since La Torre prepared his map before the actual military campaign, presenting a clear idea of the task ahead was of primary importance.

La Torre's map acknowledges in its title a certain degree of political autonomy for the Cunas, whom Spanish authorities called Darienes or Calidonios. To the right of the map (west of the Gulf of Darién), the map explicitly acknowledges indigenous control by calling the territory from the mouths of the Atrato River (in the center of the Gulf of Darién) to the Punta de San Blas (close to the city of Portobelo) the "lands possessed by the gentiles from Calidonia." East of the Gulf of Darién (to the left of the gulf in this upside-down map), however, La Torre chose the label "deserted lands" for a territory equally populated by Cunas. As in Arévalo's *General Map*, the most telling statement of the lack of imperial presence in the Darién is provided by the number of towns that La Torre proposed to found on both sides of the gulf: eleven.[26] Largely concentrated on the coast to the west of the gulf (the map identifies seven spots where towns needed to be established between the Atrato and the Mandinga rivers), the projected towns reveal Spanish apprehensions over the political autonomy and, as this chapter's opening story concerning the Spanish-Cuna peace treaty illustrated, commercial contacts of the Cunas.

As in the Wayuu case, other sources corroborate the story of Cuna political autonomy that La Torre's map tells. In fact, when read against a background of previous reports—including one Antonio de Arévalo wrote in 1761—La Torre's map appears less as the projected scheme of a mighty imperial power ready and able to conquer the Cunas than as an unrealistic plan that informed observers could have read as the chronicle of a foretold failure. While La Torre's project revealed better knowledge of the terrain, it also made evident that, in the two intervening decades between Arévalo's Darién description and La Torre's map, Spanish officials had been unable to gain any ground in Cuna territory.[27] Despite frequent calls and orders to "punish and subdue" them, by the second half of the 1780s, the Cunas' continued independence was increasingly forcing Spanish officials to argue for the need to "treat them with the humanity proper of our national character and the religion we profess" and to adopt "the method followed by the English, . . . [to] win their will and banish the mortal hatred they professed against us."[28] Between 1799 and 1803, when a hydrographic expedition led by Captain Joaquín Fidalgo surveyed the coast of the Darién, Spanish authorities knew enough about the area to draw very detailed maps—including precise charts of anchorages frequented by foreign smugglers like the Bay of Candelaria, Bay of Calidonia, Cove of Gandí, and Puerto Escondido (Hidden Port), all to the west of the Gulf of Darién—but still acknowledged that the Cunas "do not recognize vassalage to our sovereign, consider themselves independent, and behave according to their whims."[29]

The Cunas and the territory they inhabited and controlled differed from the Wayuu and the Guajira Peninsula in three important respects. First, in demographic terms the number of Cunas inhabiting the Darién was much smaller than that of the Wayuu in the Guajira Peninsula. While estimates for Wayuu population ranged from 16,000 to 40,000, Spanish officials calculated the number of Cunas to fall between 1,500 and 5,000.[30] Despite their small numbers, the Cunas posed a constant threat that required the few Spanish officials and civilian residents of the Darién to be "always alert to defend themselves from these Indians' frequent ambushes."[31] Second, the Darién's physical terrain, in contrast to the mostly arid Guajira Peninsula, was very fertile and, if properly developed, offered profitable commercial possibilities. Growing cacao, sugarcane, tobacco, coffee, indigo, and cotton as well as raising cattle, fishing for turtles, and extracting gold, dyewoods, and woods suited for constructing and repairing ships figured among the list of revenue-making activities identified by contemporary observers.[32] Third, and of most relevance to Spanish authorities, its geographical location and the long history of attempts by Spain's European rivals to establish colonial settlements on its coasts made the Darién a key geopolitical site whose possession, Spain and its rivals understood, opened the doors to the vast Pacific Ocean and its commercial prospects.[33]

These differences notwithstanding, both Cuna and Wayuu territories were contested grounds where the Cunas and the Wayuu met the Spanish colonial state in generally hostile terms. Spanish control in these regions was largely limited to the provincial capitals—Riohacha and Portobelo—whose inhabitants, in typical frontier fashion, lived in perpetual fear of indigenous attacks.[34] Maritime Indians' autonomy increased with distance from the provincial capital. In the ports and coasts of the Upper Guajira, as Eduardo Barrera Monroy put it, the Wayuu "lived [in] a total independence."[35] Similarly, the Cunas of the coast of Calidonia lived in no proximity to any center of Spanish authority. The Lower Guajira and the eastern coast of the Gulf of Darién (between the gulf and the city of Cartagena), because they were closer to Spanish centers of political authority, constituted middle grounds where maritime Indians and Spanish authorities established frequent contacts. In both the Darién and the Guajira Peninsula, the maritime Indians often interacted with non-Spanish Europeans. These connections, generally forbidden by Spanish authorities to no avail, constituted a major source of concern for local, provincial, and viceregal authorities. In these interactions, it is possible to discern the traits of maritime Indians' cosmopolitanism.

Trade, Mobility, Cosmopolitanism, Resistance, and Initiative

Letters and reports exchanged between Spanish officers often emphasized the need to curtail interactions between maritime Indians and non-Spanish Europeans (particularly British merchants). While most of these interactions took place on Spanish territories in the continental Caribbean, Spanish reports also reveal the presence of indigenous people in British colonies (especially Jamaica). The travels of maritime Indians like Cuna chiefs Bernardo, Francisco Cheque, Sebastián, Guillermo Hall, and Pablo del Castillo (alias Golden Hat), as well as those of Wayuu chiefs Caporinche and Martín Rodríguez, attest to the active participation of indigenous people in the Caribbean networks of communication. Many anonymous Cuna and Wayuu Indians, as well as other maritime Indians—the Miskitos of Nicaragua's Mosquito Coast—frequently traveled to Jamaica to buy weapons and gunpowder. Miskitos, including the young Miskito king who attended dinner at the house of Jamaica's governor in 1804 and his grandfather, a former Miskito king who, in 1776, crossed the Atlantic from Britain to the Mosquito Coast with Olaudah Equiano, were a visible presence in the transimperial Greater Caribbean.[36]

Maritime Indians often spent periods of "four to six months" in Jamaica obtaining weapons, gunpowder, and other military materials that they used to maintain their independence from Spanish authorities.[37] On board British ships, maritime Indians like Cuna captain Sebastián traveled to Jamaica to exchange tortoiseshell and other local produce for weapons, gunpowder, and ammunition.[38] European observers commented that it was common for British merchants to "take young Indians to Jamaica" or, allowing for more indigenous agency, that indigenous people, in particular the Wayuu, "send their children to Jamaica in order to learn to speak the English language, to handle their arms and direct the artillery."[39] During these diplomatic visits, Spanish cartographer Joaquín Fidalgo observed, young Cuna Indians "saw" the island, "were entertained" by British authorities and merchants, and acquired basic understanding of the English language.[40]

Maritime Indians' linguistic skills provide another means to reassert the argument about the limited degree of control Spanish authorities exerted on these indigenous groups' territories. The imposition of the colonizer's language on the colonized has long been recognized as a powerful tool of empire.[41] In maritime Indian-Spanish relations, the evidence suggests only limited success in the Spanish pursuit of this imperial strategy. The evidence, in fact, suggests that maritime Indians were more interested in learning English than Spanish. English, after all, was for the maritime Indians a language of trade. Spanish, on the other hand, was a language of war. While there is only limited evidence available to develop a definitive argument on maritime Indians' linguistic skills, the Cuna-Spanish 1787 peace treaty stands out as testimony of maritime Indians' linguistic skills and priorities. The presence of translators Enrique Hooper and Luis Rounellet, because English was the language "spoken by many of the Indians," while making Cuna-Spanish communication possible, also functioned as a painful reminder that in the Cunas' geopolitical landscape Spanish and the Spaniards were far from center stage.[42] Like the English-speaking slaves and free people of color in Bayamo (Cuba) that Matt Childs studied, the Cuna leaders who visited Cartagena in 1787, as well as, more broadly, the maritime Indians of this chapter, "represented a far more cosmopolitan and multilingual population" than the colonial officials who negotiated with them.[43] Both Bayamo's English-speaking slaves and maritime Indians forcefully demonstrate the cultural effects that resulted from sailors' constant circulation between Caribbean ports, islands, and coasts. In the transimperial Greater Caribbean that sailors created, otherwise marginalized populations could position themselves at the cultural and technological avant-garde.

Besides evidencing indigenous cosmopolitanism, maritime Indians' linguistic skills also worked as symbols of political autonomy. Given the geopolitical context of the transimperial Greater Caribbean, maritime Indians' multilingualism (in which Spanish was merely a third language coming after a native indigenous language and English) also functioned as a strong signal for Spanish authorities to worry about the degree to which maritime Indians were gravitating toward other empires' spheres of influence.

The interactions of maritime Indians with non-Spanish European traders and interlopers constituted a constant source of concern for Spanish authorities. In the last three decades of the eighteenth century, Wayuu's commercial relations with foreigners invariably occupied an important place in high-ranking Spanish authorities' official reports on the state of the Viceroyalty of New Granada. According to Francisco Moreno y Escandón, the presence of "several foreigners . . . in many coves of the [Guajira] coast," from where they "supply the Indians with guns . . . and instructions," allowed the Wayuu "to wage continued war on us."[44] Concern with the connections between the Wayuu and foreigners was part of a larger apprehension with how to control indios bárbaros and curtail foreign commercial encroachment on Spanish American territories.

In the case of New Granada, contraband trade with foreigners was perhaps the most important concern of the authorities of the provinces of Panama, Cartagena, Santa Marta, and Riohacha on the Caribbean coast. This apprehension resulted from the fact that, as demonstrated in chapters 1 and 2, the Caribbean provinces of New Granada had stronger commercial ties with Jamaica, Curaçao, Saint-Domingue, Saint Thomas, and the newly independent United States than with Spain. The strength of these connections, and the extent to which Spanish authorities were acquainted and preoccupied with them, led historian Lance Grahn to appropriately label New Granada's Caribbean coast "between Lake Maracaibo (east of the Guajira Peninsula) and the Gulf of Urabá" (today's name for the Gulf of Darién) as "the littoral of contraband."[45] The Guajira Peninsula, "a very long and uninhabited coast with abundant anchorages and few coast guards," and the Darién, with its many rivers and hidden coves, were hubs for contraband trade.[46] Of course, this was only contraband from the perspective of Spanish authorities. From the perspective of the maritime Indians, these connections were just trade.

Through trade the maritime Indians were able to obtain "rifles, gunpowder, bullets . . . blankets, machetes, and even some clothes." In exchange for these products, the Wayuu supplied foreigners with cattle (horses, cows, and mules), dyewoods (*palo brasil*), pearls, salt, "and a bit of cotton."[47] A brief account of the trade in pearls provides a good example of where the trade was carried, who were the Wayuu's main commercial partners, and how trade in general allowed the Wayuu to sustain their independence from Spanish rule. Furthermore, this line of trade offers a window through which it is possible to glimpse what can be called a Wayuu-centric Caribbean.

According to François Depons, an agent of the French government in Caracas who traveled through New Granada between 1801 and 1804, "it is pretended, that the pearls have disappeared from the eastern coast, and the first place of the leeward where that fishery is carried on with some success, is a bay situated between Cape Chichibacoa and Cape de la Vela, occupied by Guihiros [*sic*] Indians, who sell their pearls to the Dutch and English."[48] Depons's geographic area corresponds to the northern coast of the Guajira Peninsula, a territory fully under Wayuu control throughout the eighteenth century. He could have been referring to the Bay of Chimare, where Wayuu chief Antonio Paredes "believe[d] himself to be the only king upon the land."[49] Alternatively, Depons could have been referring to Bahia Honda, a small bay considered "one of the most apparent places for fraud and where it is most often committed."[50] Contraband there, according to Antonio Julián, was one of the greatest sorrows of Riohacha's *vecinos*. They lamented that this "huge and clean [bay], capable of harboring the biggest fleet . . . was only useful to foreign brigs and other ships" that used it "to introduce their goods . . . and take away the *palo del Brasil*, pearls, cottons, and gold from this province."[51] Besides Bahia Honda and Chimare, Spanish authorities also warned of the need to guard the Cabo de la Vela, Portete, Portete Chico, and other important anchorages along the Guajira Peninsula because "experience has taught that [these] have been the ports, coves, and inlets most frequented by smugglers."[52]

Depons's description also mentions the main commercial partners of the Wayuu: Dutch and English merchants. As part of their concern with the rebelliousness characteristic of the Wayuu, Spanish authorities had reported the presence of these foreigners on the Guajira coast for many years. In 1789, for example, Francisco Silvestre reported on the trade the Wayuu carried on with foreigners, "especially with the Dutch from Curaçao."[53] About ten years later, Riohacha's governor, Josef Medina Galindo, informed the viceroy of the mechanisms through which the Wayuu sold cattle to English smugglers in exchange for weapons.[54] In a subsequent letter Medina illustrated a shift in the Caribbean balance of power and how the Wayuu had successfully adapted to the new scenario. Stating that now "it was the English who pursue [most of the] trade with the Guajiro Indians," Medina explained that "in order to better take advantage [of this trade]" the English "seek and have Dutch crews." The reason for this, Medina continued, was that "the Dutch had had the same trade [with the Wayuu] for many years [and] they understand the barbarian language."[55] While Dutch and British traders were certainly the main commercial partners of the Wayuu, ships from the French Caribbean colonies also navigated the Guajira coast.[56]

Commercial exchanges, repeated travels to Jamaica, and frequent verbal exchanges with English-speaking (and Dutch-speaking) merchants and sailors clearly provided maritime Indians with some traits of cosmopolitanism. Through these exchanges, the maritime Indians not only became cosmopolitan Indians, but also, more importantly, given that weapons figured prominently in their commercial transactions, they achieved the technological superiority that made it possible for them to wage successful war against Spaniards. Engagement in Caribbean networks of trade, that is, allowed maritime Indians to develop an enhanced repertoire of resistance, for which Spanish pacification campaigns were not an effective response.

Multilingualism and the ability to master advanced military technologies certainly resulted from maritime Indians' active participation in the networks of communication of the transimperial Greater Caribbean. Mobility, however, should not be equated with freedom to move as one pleases. As Karl Offen showed in his study of intra-Miskito differentiation, Miskito slaving practices and political and ethnic rivalries suggest that the Caribbean not only offered Miskitos the opportunity to sustain their political independence but also the chance to get rid of unwanted or troublesome individuals or, more simply, to make a profit by selling indigenous people to Jamaican buyers. Offen's description of Tawira-Miskito slave raids, which took them south of the Mosquito Coast to Cuna territory in what today constitutes Costa Rica and Panama, also suggests that some Cuna groups could have experienced mobility in very hostile terms.[57] This type of mobility, thus, offers a window to understand indigenous geopolitics and the ways in which maritime Indians could have used the transimperial Greater Caribbean to solve intra-indigenous geopolitical contests.

In the Guajira Peninsula, indigenous people were also familiar with mobility as a coercive force. Wayuu trips to Jamaica were not always temporary, semidiplomatic missions. For many Wayuu, the Caribbean resembled what the Atlantic meant for many Africans during the era of the slave trade: a trip of no return to slavery. As recorded by Antonio de Arévalo in a diary that documented his activities in the Guajira Peninsula between 1772 and 1776, the Wayuu were familiar with the practice of selling Indians—children and adults, men and women—to foreign merchants who then sold them as slaves in Jamaica, Curaçao, Philadelphia, and the French Caribbean.[58] The practice, as far as can be inferred from Arévalo's account, resulted from intra-Wayuu conflict, revealed the limits of the collaboration between Wayuu leaders and British and Dutch merchants, and presented opportunities for Wayuu leaders to deploy their political and military leverage. As historian José Polo Acuña has argued, intra-Wayuu warfare was common and served "an important function of social regulation." Through war, different Wayuu parcialidades shaped political relations, "created clientele networks," and worked out territorial and resource-based grievances.[59]

In October 1772, for instance, intra-Wayuu warfare landed the oldest son of Wayuu chief Antonio Paredes on the vessel of a Dutch merchant known to Paredes as Captain Piche. Paredes's son added to a list of captured Wayuu, which included one of "Paredes's cowboys, three Indian women belonging to his nephew Manare," and "another son of Paredes." While Paredes managed to rescue his two sons—the oldest one by paying a ransom consisting of "three young Indians, ten donkeys, six mules, three hammocks, two blankets, and some seventeen cows" and the other after loyal Wayuu Indians seized the capturing vessel, forcing its captain to release Paredes's son—he continued to exert his negotiating skills in order to secure the release of the remaining captives, who, Paredes had been informed, were being held as domestic slaves in Jamaica. To force the hand of the Dutch hostage takers, Paredes captured and refused to set free "four Dutch men, one woman, and two children" who reached Chimare shortly after fleeing Curaçao.[60] The results of Paredes's negotiations are unknown. The cowboy and the three women, as well as the three young Indians Paredes included as part of the ransom he paid for his oldest son, might have remained enslaved in Jamaica indefinitely. Despite the uncertainty that remains about their ultimate fate, the story clearly illustrates how mobility and participation in transimperial communication networks could pose threats to individuals' freedom.

Similarly, as is evident in the 1787 peace treaty signed between Cuna chiefs and Spanish authorities in Cartagena, treaty making between maritime Indians and Spanish authorities often resulted in the curtailment of freedom for specific individuals. For Cuna chief Bernardo's son, who remained in Cartagena as "hostage of field marshall Antonio de Arévalo," mobility—his travel from Cuna territory to Cartagena—resulted in the loss of freedom.[61] As Equiano's narrative suggests, George—the soon-to-be Miskito king whom he met in London, where George had been brought "by some English merchants for some selfish ends"—also experienced a freedom-curtailing side of mobility.[62] From the perspective of some maritime Indians, thus, it is clear that the communication networks that created the transimperial Greater Caribbean, far from being experienced only as windows to cosmopolitanism, also represented a threat to their individual freedoms.

The most tangible immediate consequence of maritime Indians' active participation in the Caribbean communication networks was their ability to resist Spanish colonization. After reading "the news from Jamaica's . . . newspapers about the aid that some Cuna chiefs from the Darién have asked from [Jamaica's] government," New Granada's viceroy Caballero y Góngora readily acknowledged that the access to British weapons accounted "for the obstinacy with which these *indios bárbaros* [insist] on defending that territory."[63] Possession and mastery of British weapons simply made it impossible for the Spanish to "reduce" the maritime Indians forcibly. Peaceful means, many Spanish generals had to acknowledge during the 1770s, were the only way to deal with the Wayuu (a similar conclusion was reached for the Cunas in the course of the 1780s). Their Caribbean travels thus allowed maritime Indians to deploy a repertoire of resistance that sharply contrasted with that of other indigenous populations confronting European colonizers. Instead of resisting through the use of what James Scott called "weapons of the weak," maritime Indians were well equipped to confront Spaniards militarily and, when negotiating, to do so "from a position of strength."[64] Instead of fruitlessly attempting to resist Spanish conquest with antiquated, primitive weapons, maritime Indians boldly showcased the latest military technology (British rifles) to keep the Spanish at bay.

Just as it was elsewhere in Spanish America, one of the main objectives of Spanish colonization of New Granada's peripheral areas was to pacify independent Indians and other rebellious subjects and incorporate them as tribute payers to the colonial state.[65] Spanish authorities throughout their American domains made constant efforts to subjugate indios bárbaros and turn them into tributaries living in Spanish-controlled pueblos. The imperative nature and difficulties of this mission in the context of New Granada were readily acknowledged in 1772 by Francisco Moreno y Escandón, magistrate protector of Indians, in his general description of the New Kingdom of Granada.

According to Moreno y Escandón, "this kingdom bears the known misfortune that it has barely a province that is not infested in some part by indios bárbaros, who suddenly and disorderly attack Spaniards, causing . . . [many] depredations in lives and haciendas."[66] The Wayuu, numbering 38,150 and generating "continuous uneasiness in the province [of Riohacha]," topped Moreno y Escandón's list of troublesome indios bárbaros; the Cunas were a close second.[67] Turning them and other independent Indians into a subjected population paying taxes and producing agricultural exports, Bourbon officials expected, would generate additional revenue for the mother country.

To cope with the maritime Indians and other indios bárbaros in the Americas, Spanish authorities, especially after the Bourbon ascendance to the Spanish throne, followed a policy that balanced imperial objectives with local realities.[68] In the Guajira Peninsula, this policy was deployed in three clearly identifiable phases that echoed continent-wide efforts by Spanish authorities to deal with indios bárbaros. First, from the 1690s to the late 1760s, Spanish authorities attempted to incorporate the Wayuu through missionary activities (religious conquest); later, during the 1770s, they resorted to incorporation through pacification campaigns (military conquest); and finally, from the 1780s to the end of Spanish rule, they moved to a conciliatory policy that acknowledged the failure of previous efforts of incorporation and awarded the Wayuu a substantial degree of territorial autonomy.[69]

From a continent-wide perspective, as Allan Kuethe has shown, "missionaries, who had traditionally borne the main responsibility for pacification, found themselves relegated to a secondary position at best." Explaining the shift in emphasis from religious to military conquest taking place during the late 1760s, Kuethe asserts that "the distinguishing characteristic of these new frontier actions was the preponderant role played by military force, betraying an increasingly secular approach to the problem of unpacified Indians."[70] Shortly afterward, however, a new shift in emphasis was introduced. According to David Weber, by the late 1780s, "conciliation and negotiation, previously subordinated to force, became the hallmark of Bourbon Indian policy" in territories where subordination efforts had failed.[71]

The first important organized efforts to subdue the Wayuu were assigned to Capuchin friars from Valencia. Starting in 1696, following a royal decree of 1694, Capuchin missionaries attempted to convert the Wayuu to the Catholic faith and to make them loyal subjects of the Spanish Crown.[72] Wayuu reactions to Capuchin advances were immediate and violent, forcing missionaries to flee to Maracaibo. In 1717, a new royal decree ordered the return of

Capuchin missionaries to the province of Riohacha, conferring upon them "the mission of evangelizing and pacifying the Guajiro Indians."[73] Missionary activities suffered several setbacks and during the colonial period missionaries were not able to extend their influence beyond the Capuchin-founded towns of Boronata and Rincón in the Lower Guajira.[74] Their attempts to establish towns in the Upper Guajira (in the Wayuu-controlled ports of Chimare and Bahia Honda) invariably met Indian military resistance and eventual failure. By the end of the 1740s, Spanish authorities had grown increasingly irritated with "Capuchin ineffectiveness in Riohacha."[75] After an apparent surge in missionary activity during the 1750s, Capuchin prefect Antonio de Alcoy informed Santa Marta's governor of the "total distress" of the missionaries and concluded that "it is not in our hands, nor is it feasible to fulfill" the goal of converting the Wayuu to the Catholic faith.[76] This communication provided the final blow to the missionary phase and marked the beginning of the military phase. The first attempt to conquer the Wayuu had proven that Spanish control of the Guajira Peninsula was an imperial fiction that required other means to be turned into a reality.

Political authorities' dismay with "the Guajiros' continued autonomy," Lance Grahn asserts, led New Granada's viceroy to contract "with an ex-convict and former slaverunner, Bernardo Ruiz de Noriego, to conquer the Guajiros."[77] The Wayuu, in turn, responded by launching a massive rebellion in 1769 that, according to Polo Acuña, "burned and razed over thirty Spanish and Indian towns" throughout the Guajira Peninsula.[78] Another account explains the origins of the rebellion as the result of a missionary's order to whip "an Indian of a neighbouring village [who] was in the habit of coming to pass the night with a female Indian in his vicinity."[79] In their attempts to explain the rebellion, secular authorities blamed Capuchin missionaries, claiming that they "not only failed to subdue the Guajiros but provoked them to insolence with their own weakness and ineffectiveness."[80] With the rebellion underway, however, it was time to restore tranquility to the Guajira Peninsula rather than to assign blame.

The task to restore order to the region was assigned to military commander Josef Benito de Enzio. Under his command, close to 1,500 men armed with about 500 guns gathered in the city of Riohacha to launch a massive pacification campaign against the Wayuu. After assessing the situation and finding "that at least six thousand Guajiros, all armed with English weapons awaited him outside the city of Riohacha," Enzio found it advisable to avoid direct confrontation.[81] Claiming that "even if marching from Rio del Hacha with one million men" it would be impossible for the Spanish forces "to achieve anything" except being "finished and extinguished" by the Wayuu, Enzio refused to follow his orders.[82] Accused of depleting royal funds and refusing to follow orders, he was removed from his post.[83] In 1772, Enzio's replacement, Antonio de Arévalo (whose maps I analyzed in the first section of this chapter) advanced a policy based on the foundation of fortified towns designed to mark Spanish territory and prevent Wayuu attacks. By 1775, as evidenced by the establishment of forts in Bahia Honda, Sinamaica, and Pedraza, this strategy appeared to be working. However, after the Wayuu resumed confrontations in 1776, Arévalo reasserted his commitment to a military solution. For him, because the Wayuu were "vengeful," "irreconcilable enemies of the Spaniards" wishing to "rebel and rise up with everything there is in this province," it was necessary to "punish their daring, arrogance, and haughtiness."[84] Given that the Wayuu clearly outnumbered government forces and considering the almost complete lack of Spanish presence in most of the Guajira Peninsula, Arévalo's military solution proved impossible to implement. Moreover, Spanish involvement in the American Revolution in 1779 shifted military priorities away from the Guajira Peninsula.[85] With very limited forces and aware of the dangers of continued animosity with the Wayuu, Spanish authorities adopted a more conciliatory stance toward this independent indigenous group. For the Wayuu, the new Spanish approach marked a victory and the right to continue ruling their domains.

An example of the extent to which Spanish authorities took this new approach seriously is provided by the 1789 events leading to the early dismissal of Riohacha's governor, Juan Álvarez de Veriñas. Shortly after his selection, Spanish authorities were careful to inform Veriñas how he should approach the Wayuu. In his instructions to the newly appointed officer, Santa Marta's governor José de Astigárraga emphasized as the governor's primary task the need "to place the utmost care and diligence in getting along with the Guajiro Indians, trying to deal with them in a friendly manner, entertaining them and presenting them with gifts when necessary."[86] When—several months later—Veriñas, a former head of the Spanish coast guards more used to life at sea than to the perils of a desert frontier, ignored this instruction and "indiscreetly" attacked the Wayuu, exasperating their spirits and raising fears of "a lively and bloody war," Viceroy Ezpeleta hurried to remove him from his post.[87] After previous efforts of military conquest, experience had shown Spanish authorities that peaceful means worked better with these independent maritime Indians.

A former governor of Santa Marta and a connoisseur of the Guajira Peninsula and its people, Antonio Narváez y la Torre, was assigned the task of restoring tranquility. His orders included "to gather the *indios principales* and let them know that governor Veriñas had proceeded to disturb them against expressed orders of the king and the viceroy. . . . Because of this," the order continued, "he had been removed and would be replaced by an officer who will treat them in a different manner without giving them any cause of concern."[88] Toward the end of the year Narváez informed the viceroy of his success in restoring peace to the Guajira Peninsula by declaring that "all captains and indios principales of the recently disturbed parcialidades have entered this city and gone out pacified. . . . Peace has been restored."[89] Soon a new governor, Josef Medina Galindo, was appointed. Medina, unlike Veriñas, made it one of his priorities to establish friendly relations with the Wayuu.

True to the new spirit of conciliation and recognition of Wayuu autonomy, viceroys Ezpeleta and Pedro Mendinueta, in 1796 and 1803, respectively, emphasized in their *relaciones de mando* the need to maintain friendly relations with the Wayuu. While Ezpeleta stressed the need "to conciliate in friendly terms," Mendinueta referred to "maintaining peace" as the only option available after the failures of both attempting "to forcefully subjugate them" and "to reduce them with gentleness."[90] Military might, thus, provided the Wayuu with an enhanced repertoire of resistance that forced Spanish authorities to dramatically change their approach toward the submission of maritime Indians.

That maritime Indians could, and sometimes did, defeat royal troops, does not mean that they did not pursue other strategies to resist Spanish incursions. Diplomatic means were also part of maritime Indians' repertoire of resistance against Spanish conquering attempts. The 1787 peace treaty signed in Cartagena between several Cuna chiefs and New Granada's viceroy Caballero y Góngora that I used to open this chapter not only provides evidence of indigenous cosmopolitanism (language skills, mobility, trade relations) but also demonstrates that maritime Indians were "full-fledged historical actors" capable of taking the initiative in their relations with Europeans.[91]

In their appraisal of the field of borderland studies, Pekka Hämäläinen and Samuel Truett criticize the orthodoxies that assume that "Europeans marked borders, Native Americans resist them; Europeans strive to dominate, Indians try to survive or coexist"; and, most troubling to them and to the perspective advanced in this chapter, that "borderlands are born of European failure rather than indigenous initiative."[92] At the heart of their critique is the persistent tendency to deny indigenous initiative, to limit indigenous agency.

It should come as no surprise that Spanish sources offer a perspective that stresses Spanish agency, initiative, and power to solve critical issues to best serve their own interests. These accounts, however, do not hide the fact that in both military confrontations and diplomatic negotiations, maritime Indians were taking the initiative and obtaining arrangements that served their interests better than they served the Spanish ones. Just the fact that Spanish authorities shifted from an early policy of conquering the maritime Indians to a more peaceful one of dialogue and mutual agreement reveals the extent to which maritime Indians had the upper hand in Spanish-bárbaros relations.[93]

The text of the 1787 peace treaty reflects this tendency to downplay indigenous initiative. When it presents the geopolitical context leading up to the treaty, the text claims that the Cunas, because they were "tired and fatigued of the hostilities they have suffered from the Spaniards, [came] asking for peace."[94] Here the Spanish perspective presents the Cunas almost as begging for peace, implying that Spanish actions in the Darién were leaving the Cunas no other alternative but to follow Spanish orders. Critically contextualizing the text of the treaty, however, makes it possible to subvert this narrative in favor of one that, in light of the stories that maps, mobility, linguistic skills, and trade tell, uncovers a more likely scenario in which the Spaniards are the ones who were tired of their failed attempts to conquer the Cunas.

The language of the treaty also reproduces a fiction of Spanish presence in and control of Cuna territory. When the treaty states that indigenous people "will be allowed to roam freely through the gulf, the coasts, the keys, the rivers, and the interior of the country" or that "the Indians will be free . . . to sell their produce among themselves and to the Spaniards, but any trade and communication with foreigners will be forbidden," it is worth asking who gets to allow whom to do what.[95] Were Spanish authorities in a position to restrict Cuna mobility through the Darién? Could Spanish authorities enforce the prohibition on trade with foreigners? The evidence presented in this section suggests that it was up to the Cunas to decide if they were going to roam freely through the Darién, as well as if they were going to stop trading with foreigners. If the maritime Indians could effectively set the terms of their relations with Spanish authorities, then how did this ability affect the way in which maritime Indians saw themselves as actors in the transimperial Greater Caribbean? How, additionally, did the reality of maritime Indians' independence affect the way in which Spanish authorities saw and thought of these indigenous peoples?

Identities and Geopolitical Imagination:
Maritime Indian versus European

The encounter between maritime Indians and the outside world reveals alternative ways to interpret and legitimate possession of a space that, according to Spanish authorities and other European actors, was Spanish territory.[96] The Wayuu, as implied by the generally hostile nature of their contact with Spanish authorities and their typically friendly encounters with other outsiders, had a different, Wayuu-centric perception. The same, of course, was true of the Cunas and, for that matter, of any group interpreting the world it inhabits from its own cultural perspective. Wayuu interpretations of space were part of a larger process of contesting Spanish-drawn geographical boundaries and participating in the creation and development of a sense of belonging to a community that cut across political borders and connected British, Dutch, and French Caribbean possessions with the Guajira Peninsula and other territories legitimately possessed (from a European perspective) by the Spanish monarchy.

While the previous analysis clearly shows the types of connections that linked maritime Indians with outsiders, it does not provide explicit illustrations of how these interactions led maritime Indians to interpret space in ways that opposed Spanish geographical conceptions and territorial demarcations. In other words, because Wayuu and Cunas did not subscribe to what Neil Smith and Anne Godlewska have called "a European planetary consciousness," it seems reasonable to conclude that, asked to draw a map of his world, an eighteenth-century Wayuu leader would, most likely, have drawn a map showing places such as Portete, Bahia Honda, and Chimare, as well as Curaçao, Jamaica, and Guadeloupe, but excluding Santa Fe, Madrid, and other important centers of Spanish political and economic power. However, because these "rival geographical practices . . . were never recorded other than in group memory," the difficulties of reconstructing a Wayuu-centric Caribbean, as Smith and Godlewska argue, "are extraordinary."[97] Similar difficulties are associated with reconstructing maritime Indians' transimperial identities.

A characterization of identities as "relational and contingent . . . imposed and self-fashioned," when applied to the maritime Indians' case, suggests that these indigenous peoples were part of a transimperial Greater Caribbean community defined, by all the incumbents, largely in terms of their members' antagonism toward Spanish authorities.[98] While primary sources do not include testimonies of maritime Indians asserting their self-fashioned identity, their actions, represented in their conflict with Spanish authorities and their friendly exchanges with other Europeans, provide sufficient evidence to assert that the Wayuu and the Cunas defined themselves in opposition to their Spanish enemies.

Opposition to Spanish authorities, however, does not automatically imply belonging to a transimperial Greater Caribbean community (or even the existence of such a community). Maritime Indians' trade connections with Dutch, British, and French merchants provide a better idea of the community of which these indigenous peoples were active members, of the sense of belonging that they developed. These connections, according to French traveler François Depons's analysis of the Wayuu, transcended the business realm and resulted "in a great deal of friendship . . . We are assured by the Spaniards that this intercourse is maintained upon so intimate a footing that the Goahiros send their children to Jamaica in order to learn to speak the English language, to handle their arms and direct the artillery."[99] As instrumental as this British-Wayuu connection may appear, it seems reasonable to assert that, after several decades of friendly contacts with non-Spanish Europeans and because of their history of confrontation with Spanish authorities, by the end of the eighteenth century maritime Indians had increasingly come to develop a sense of belonging to a larger community, whose configuration informed and was informed by Wayuu conceptualizations of space.

While participation in the communication networks that gave shape to the transimperial Greater Caribbean enabled maritime Indians to resist Spanish conquest and to engage Europeans in favorable terms, travel and familiarity with the Caribbean and its European inhabitants did not automatically result in a shift in Europeans' perceptions regarding maritime Indians' capacity for civilization. Europeans' descriptions of Miskitos, Cunas, and Wayuu, while explicitly condemning these Indians' savage nature, also made evident that maritime Indians did not conform to the preconceived notion of the primitive, technologically incompetent Indian.[100]

Both British and Spanish observers shared a negative perception of maritime Indians as untrustworthy savages. In her recollection of the Miskito king's visit to Jamaica in 1804, Lady Nugent—wife of Jamaica's governor, George Nugent—depicted the young Indian king (he was "about six or eight years old") as "quite savage." The king's behavior—Lady Nugent describes how during dinner he "began to pull off all his clothes" and how she was "obliged to send the little Musquito King *forcibly* to school"—earned him the nickname "his little savage Majesty."[101] The Miskito king's uncle, whom Lady Nugent mocked because of his insistence on being called "Count Stamford, or the

Duke of York," did not fare better than his nephew. Instead of politely eating what was offered during dinner, the "Duke of York" "devoured every thing that came within his reach." Similarly, despite not drinking "much wine," the king's uncle, as expected from a savage Indian, was not able to hold his composure (the little wine "he did take soon got into his head").[102] Spanish cartographer Joaquín Fidalgo shared Lady Nugent's impressions of the maritime Indians. In his opinion, the Cunas were "extremely selfish, suspicious, vindictive, treacherous without faith or word, and very drunk."[103] Drawing on their expectations of how Indians should behave, both Fidalgo and Lady Nugent focused on behaviors that adhered to the image of Indians as untrustworthy savages. Their depictions either willfully ignored (in Lady Nugent's case) or downplayed (in Fidalgo's case) the fact that the same Indians they characterized as savages were interacting with them in European languages.

In a geopolitical context characterized by dramatic political transformations, the maritime Indians' savagery posed more serious threats than those that could arise from Lady Nugent's guests' lack of table manners and inability to hold their composure after drinking wine. The dangers associated with the spread of news and ideas about the Haitian Revolution to the territories inhabited by maritime Indians were at the forefront of Spanish authorities' concerns in the first years of the nineteenth century. The potential outcome of the arrival to the Guajira Peninsula of a group of blacks from the French Caribbean provides an example of Spanish fears and perception regarding the risks associated with maritime Indians' participation in Caribbean networks of communication.

In 1803, the arrival in the port of Chimare, in the Upper Guajira, of a French "sloop from Guadeloupe [carrying] more than two hundred *negros* and *mulatos franceses*" alarmed all New Granada's authorities, from local officials in the provinces of Riohacha and Maracaibo to the viceroy in Santa Fe.[104] As explained by Viceroy Mendinueta, the source of this alarm was an understanding of "how detrimental it could be to the security and calm of the province of Riohacha, and even those of Santa Marta and Maracaibo, the communication between these *negros* and *mulatos* franceses and the Guajiro Indians." Mendinueta's conviction that these *negros* franceses (not much information is given about their legal and socioeconomic status) were "infected with the ideas of liberty, equality and others that have been so pernicious and have caused much harm and many horrors to the unfortunate French islands" led him to believe that their arrival on the Guajira Peninsula could "alter the state of peace in which the Guajiros now are."[105]

Sharing similar impressions and concerns, Caracas's captain general, Manuel de Guevara, ordered Maracaibo's governor, Fernando Miyares, to carry out an investigation of the events. After interrogating several vecinos of Riohacha and sailors from the region, Miyares informed Guevara of an alleged increase in the number of blacks from the French islands after the arrival of "another French sloop . . . with close to five hundred blacks," who were now spread throughout the peninsula.[106] According to Andrés de Luque, one of the vecinos Miyares interrogated, the blacks "were distributed among the Indians to put them to work in field tasks."[107] Other witnesses corroborated Luque's account. Contradictions regarding the relations between the Wayuu and the black expatriates arose when the witnesses were asked about the way in which the Wayuu treated the blacks. While Miguel Francisco Bermúdez declared that "the Indians treated the blacks fairly . . . because they were convinced that the offspring of blacks and Indians are very handsome," Francisco Ramírez stated— based on what he heard from two blacks that the Wayuu took to Riohacha—that this "treatment . . . is somewhat heavy."[108] Despite the contradictions regarding how the Wayuu treated the blacks, the testimonies support the idea that the Wayuu used the blacks as servants. However, the limited number of testimonies (only four witnesses were interrogated) and the distance from which the witnesses perceived the events (Francisco Ramírez, for example, was careful to note that he had "not personally witnessed" what he was declaring) did not provide the Spanish authorities in charge of the investigation sufficient information to understand the outcome of the episode involving the alleged landing in the Guajira Peninsula of several thousand negros and *mulatos* franceses.[109] In spite of the lack of convincing evidence about the deeds, numbers, and whereabouts of the French blacks, Caracas's captain general, reflecting Spanish fears of revolutionary "contamination," rapidly concluded that they were "revolutionary criminals" and that "we should rid ourselves from this pernicious contagion" brought by these "vicious criminals who have already infested their own country and might as well try to infest ours."[110]

There is not sufficient evidence to calculate the number of negros franceses who actually arrived to the Guajira Peninsula in 1803, nor is there information about their previous occupations and deeds or their interactions with the Wayuu and the conversations they held. Yet two points can be raised in terms of what their arrival tells us about the geopolitics of the Guajira Peninsula. First, the fact that these negros franceses arrived to the Upper Guajira and remained there reinforces the idea that this part of the Guajira, more than any other part of the peninsula, was independent Wayuu territory. Spanish control of this territory was so limited that despite colonial officers' conviction of the need to get rid of these French blacks, the decision of what to do about them was ultimately in the hands of the Wayuu. This decision, the scarce evidence shows, included delivering three blacks to the Spanish authorities in Rioha-cha.[111] On what the Wayuu decided to do with the other blacks, the evidence remains silent. In the past, as documented by Lance Grahn, the Wayuu had been known to have owned slaves or to have sold slaves to the interior provinces of New Granada.[112] Similarly, biographical information about Wayuu cacique Cecilio López demonstrates that the Wayuu commonly sold slaves, as well as many other commodities, to the interior provinces of New Granada and, as shown in the previous section, to British and Dutch merchants who frequently visited the peninsula's bays and coves.[113] Whether this was the case of the French blacks of 1803 is not possible to determine based on the information available.

Second, the Spanish authorities' concern with the detrimental effects of the arrival of the French blacks serves as evidence of the existence, even if only in the minds of imperial authorities, of a transimperial community actively spreading revolutionary ideas throughout the Caribbean. The Wayuu, it can be inferred from the investigation and the correspondence, were perceived as active members of this community.

The Wayuu's belonging to a transimperial community appears more clearly from the perspective of Spanish authorities. As shown by the declarations of Viceroy Mendinueta and Governor Medina Galindo with regard to the arrival of negros and *mulatos* franceses on the Guajira Peninsula in 1803, Spanish authorities were unambiguous in their characterization of the Wayuu as members of what can be called a pan-Caribbean revolutionary community of savages. Mendinueta's concerns, as illustrated by Aline Helg, reveal the extent to which "fear of a revolution along Haitian lines in Caribbean Colombia" led Spanish authorities to group together blacks—slaves and free—from all over the Caribbean with the Wayuu and French and frenchified inhabitants of the Caribbean.[114] For Spanish authorities, they were all simply revolutionary criminals.

Identifications of late eighteenth- and early nineteenth-century Wayuu—by themselves, by Spanish authorities, and by myself as a historian—as members of a transimperial community united in their animosity toward Spanish authorities and in their alleged revolutionary fervor do not imply that the Wayuu, and the other maritime Indians, did not also identify themselves in local terms. Identities, as Linda Colley reminds us, "are not like hats. Human beings can and do put on several at a time."[115] Thus, the maritime

Indians belonged simultaneously to a local community (what Spanish authorities, for the Wayuu case, called a parcialidad) and a broader Caribbean-based community of trade and, at least in the minds of Spanish authorities, revolution. The development of these identities influenced and was influenced by maritime Indians' rival geographical practices. Both their identities and spatial commitments resulted from their de facto independence, from the fact that the Guajira Peninsula and the Darién were territories claimed by Spain but autonomously ruled by the maritime Indians.

A Sea of Opportunities

Facing the Caribbean from their coastal territories, the maritime Indians saw a sea of opportunities. Sales of cattle, pearls, dyewoods, and possibly slaves provided them with the financial means to obtain weapons to resist Spanish incursions. Maritime Indians' military might, largely communicated through the possession of British guns, conveyed for Spaniards the message that the best way to gain maritime Indians' favor was through negotiation. The uncertainty about the outcome of the interactions between the Wayuu and the negros and *mulatos* franceses who landed in the Guajira Peninsula in 1803 suggests that Spanish conclusions about the multiethnic Caribbean revolutionary community were exaggerated. Maritime Indians' encounters with the outside world highlight these indigenous peoples' sense of belonging to Wayuu-, Cuna-, and Miskito-envisioned worlds characterized by autonomous rule of their indigenous territories, a determination to defend that autonomy even through violent means, and a willingness to interact with outsiders in ways that contributed to their continued independence.

The study of maritime Indians' interactions with Europeans in the Caribbean also makes it possible to debunk certain ideas associated with the experience of being Indian. Maritime Indians, to use Philip Deloria's term, were in "unexpected places," not only because they were present in a Caribbean world often presented as Indian-less.[116] In a less literal sense, maritime Indians were in unexpected places because they were able to establish effective communication with Europeans (they spoke English and Spanish) and to use British weapons to keep the Spanish at bay. Their adroit use of British weapons challenges preconceived notions of indigenous people as primitive and technologically inferior and reveals how participation in Caribbean communication networks allowed maritime Indians to develop an enhanced repertoire of resistance that they successfully deployed to reassert and maintain their independence. Their spatial practices and consciousness demonstrate that, in the political sphere, maritime Indians were as competent and modern political actors as Europeans were. Despite their language skills and technological and political capacities, maritime Indians were not able to overcome Europeans' perceptions of them as untrustworthy savages. Continued characterization of maritime Indians as savages led Spanish authorities to imagine (perhaps to exaggerate) the threat posed by the potential emergence of a pan-Caribbean revolutionary community of savages. Hiding behind Europeans' negative depictions of maritime Indians lay all the traits of cosmopolitanism that made maritime Indians comparable to Atlantic creoles.

CHAPTER 4

Turning South before Swinging East

I am enthusiastick ab[ou]t India and look up to it as the salvation, as the wealth, the grandeur, the glory of this country.
—JOHN ROBINSON, secretary to the treasury, February 19, 1781

England's confusion upon seeing North America [emerge as] victor is such that all her ideas and secret machinations are directed towards the Spanish American continent.
—LUIS VIDAL Y VILALBA, 1784

Have no doubt Your Majesty that the British will try now with more tenacity than ever before to establish themselves close to the isthmus.
—JOSEPH DE GÁLVEZ, August 4, 1784

On July 21, 1786, a secret meeting took place in the office of the Spanish ambassador in Paris, the count of Aranda. The ambassador, aided by the Irish abbot O'Sullivan (who acted as translator), met John Brooks, a British captain who introduced himself as a loyalist veteran of the American Revolution. Brooks had come to Paris from London, all expenses covered by the Spanish government, to inform Aranda of an expedition projected in Britain to invade the northern coast of South America in the vicinity of the port of Cartagena. According to Brooks, Juan Blommart, a French veteran of the American Revolution, was the leader of the projected expedition. With official British backing—Brooks declared that the marquis of Buckingham was sponsoring the expedition— and the participation of military adventurers John Cruden and Francisco de Miranda, the expedition was scheduled to sail before the end of the year.[1] After receiving Aranda's report, the Spanish Ministry of the Indies relayed the information to New Granada's viceroy, Antonio Caballero y Góngora, for him to make all the necessary preparations to face this potential threat.

Blommart's expedition to Cartagena never actually took place, and it is impossible to establish whether Brooks's information was based on an actual plan or if he invented the plot to obtain an economic reward.[2] It is, nonetheless, a telling example of the geopolitical environment of the times. Rumored and real British plans to invade Spanish American territories were always on the agenda of policy makers and common people of British and Spanish territories on both sides of the Atlantic. Between the 1780s and 1808—when Spain and Britain sealed their alliance against Napoleon—fear of British invasion constituted a pressing concern for Spanish authorities throughout the Americas, in particular on the coasts and islands of the Caribbean Basin where the two empires seemed to be entangled. In the Caribbean coast of the Viceroyalty of New Granada, potential British invasion coexisted with a growing dependence on trade with the British West Indies.[3] The contradictory forces represented by long-standing Anglo-Spanish hostilities and greater commercial exchange between the British West Indies and Spanish America, coupled with the real and perceived economic impact of the American Revolution, nurtured the geopolitical imagination of British, Spanish, and indigenous inhabitants of the Caribbean between the 1780s and the beginning of the nineteenth century.

Northwestern New Granada provides the vantage point from which this chapter analyzes the Greater Caribbean's geopolitics after the American Revolution. The stretch of coast between Central America's Mosquito Coast and the port city of Cartagena in the Viceroyalty of New Granada constituted a highly contested geopolitical site to which New Granada's authorities, Jamaican planters and merchants, and military adventurers still excited by their recent participation in the American Revolution turned their greedy, imperialist eyes in the later decades of the eighteenth century (see map 4.1). This coastal territory, largely populated by independent indigenous groups dexterous in using the Anglo-Spanish rivalry to their own advantage, served as a chalkboard on which merchants and planters, royal officers, and adventurers drew their visions of the future. These visions, in turn, emerged, to a large extent, out of lived experiences marked by the tight connections—by the sense of regionness—that, as explained in chapters 1 and 2, brought together Jamaica and northwestern South America. Acknowledging the existence of a transimperial Greater Caribbean makes it possible to interpret the actions of Jamaican planters, military adventurers, and New Granada's authorities as logical, plausible, and even viable, instead of as outlandish plans born out of desperation, resentment, and lack of political audacity.

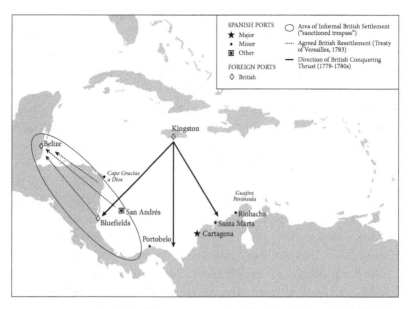

Map 4.1 The American Revolution in the southwestern Caribbean. In what can be characterized as the spirit of the 1780s, disgruntled loyalists and British imperial officers took the American Revolution to the Caribbean.

Jamaican planters and merchants struggling with the scarcities generated by the prohibition on trade with the newly independent United States sought alternative sources from which to obtain foodstuffs, wood, and cattle to feed the island's plantation economy. Northwestern New Granada presented itself as a viable option. Military adventurers—especially British loyalists eager to avenge British defeat in the American Revolution—and merchants with interests in Central and northern South America looked to turn this area into a territory formally or informally dominated by Britain. New Granada's authorities sought to establish effective control of the area—an achievement that, Viceroy Caballero y Góngora believed, required promoting trade and developing the region's productive capacity through the promotion of cotton cultivation.[4] This chapter brings together the geopolitical visions of these three groups to argue that, in the aftermath of the American Revolution, their disparate interests converged around the idea and necessity of keeping the British Empire Atlantic centered. While it is true that in the early 1780s "the future territorial configuration of Britain's empire was . . . becoming clear" (i.e., India's growing importance was shifting imperial interests to the east), interest groups in the Americas were not willing to passively witness the development of what a prominent historian of the British Empire, Vincent Harlow, called the empire's "swing to the east."[5]

A focus on these groups' utilitarian approach to northwestern New Granada inserts northern South America into a growing literature that is reconsidering fundamental aspects of long-standing narratives of British imperial history, in particular the so-called swing to the east and the characterization of British relations with Latin America as constitutive of what has been called an "informal empire."[6] This chapter demonstrates that the swing of British imperial interest to India was neither obvious nor uncontested. In addition, the chapter challenges the notion of the unproblematic adoption of informal empire as a mechanism of international relations that directed Latin America's insertion into the British-led industrial economy of the nineteenth-century Atlantic world. The focus on different groups that, successfully or not, attempted to guide the direction of Britain's imperial future sheds light on the extent to which empire making was a collective enterprise officially sanctioned by London's authorities, but pursued, often in contending fashion, by a heterogeneous group of "imperial" agents scattered throughout the world. In other words, focusing on the efforts to keep the British Empire Atlantic centered, this chapter provides evidence that supports Kathleen Wilson's argument about the existence of "not one but many [British] imperial projects."[7] Ultimately, the analysis of how northwestern New Granada fitted into the designs of the different groups under study advances the larger argument of this study about the richness of the geopolitical imagination of the transimperial Greater Caribbean's denizens. Focusing on how contemporaries interpreted and adapted to the transformations brought about by the American Revolution, this chapter contributes to emerging conversations about the need to connect British imperial history with Latin America and the American Revolution with the Americas.[8] These histories, as Atlantic historians increasingly acknowledge, were entangled.[9]

The analysis is divided in five sections. The first summarizes the literature on the British Empire's swing to the east and the establishment of British informal empire in Latin America. The second presents the proposals of Jamaican planters and merchants to overcome the economic crisis produced by the prohibition on trade between the British West Indies and the newly independent United States. The third turns to the analysis of alleged and real threats of British invasion of Caribbean New Granada. The fourth examines the promotion of cotton cultivation as a way to stimulate economic development in northern New Granada, emphasizing the extent to which this development strategy was linked to the continued British presence in the Americas. The concluding section ties all the interests together to assess the degree of success of all designs and plans to keep the British Empire Atlantic centered.

The British Empire's Swing to the East
and British Informal Empire in Latin America

In *Capitalism and Slavery* (first published in 1944), Eric Williams asserted that the American Revolution "marked the beginning of [the] uninterrupted decline" of the British West Indies.[10] Their decline, a long trail of British imperial historiography has established, took place alongside a shift of imperial interest to India.[11] This shift in geographic emphasis—referred to in British imperial historiography as the swing to the east—was paralleled by the rise of a rhetoric of free-trade imperialism (or informal empire) whose goals have been aptly summarized as "trade with informal control if possible; trade with rule when necessary."[12] The combination of trade, with or without rule, and a growing imperial presence in India led to the emergence in the nineteenth century of a British Empire that was global in scope; a British Empire that has been characterized as "both Atlantic *and* Asian, commercial *and* conquering."[13] While trade without rule became the main imperial strategy in the Americas, conquest developed as the key to British power in many parts of Asia.

Traditional historical accounts of the British Empire take the American Revolution as a dividing line between a first and a second British Empire. The first British Empire was generally characterized as an empire of settlement, located in North America and the West Indies and based on a mercantilist system of commercial regulations that gave overseas communities political autonomy as long as they obeyed the Navigation Acts.[14] The second British Empire, on the contrary, has been presented as an India-centered empire of direct rule over millions of non-British subjects.[15] With historians embracing the idea of the existence of many imperial projects throughout the Georgian period, the old divide between a first and a second British Empire is becoming increasingly untenable.[16]

Agreement persists on the fact that after the American Revolution the British Empire shifted its "center of gravity . . . from the Caribbean Sea to the Indian Ocean, from the West Indies to India."[17] Drawing on contemporary experiences, studies have demonstrated that the prospect of and the final defeat in the American Revolution raised the appeal of India in the minds of imperial bureaucrats, policy makers, and the British public. For war veterans and West Indies bureaucrats like Alured Clarke, Archibald Campbell, Lord Cornwallis, George Nugent, and David Ochterlony, the swing to the east was a lived experience of migration from the Americas to India. After the American Revolution, Clarke, Campbell, and Nugent served time as governors of Jamaica. From there all three moved on to hold higher offices in India. Lord Cornwallis, famous in the Western Hemisphere for his defeat at Yorktown, moved on to become governor general of India between 1786 and 1793.[18] Ochterlony, for his part, migrated to India before the American Revolution. There, he became a "hookah-smoking, turban-wearing, chutney-eating Bostonian" who "had thirteen Indian wives."[19] In Britain, high-ranked policy makers began to openly express their favorable opinion for a potential swing to the east during the critical years of 1781–1782. John Robinson, secretary to the treasury during the North administration, declared, "I am enthusiastick ab[ou]t India and look up to it as the salvation, as the wealth, the grandeur, the glory of this country."[20] Similarly, when defeat in America appeared imminent, Lord Stormont demonstrated his enthusiasm for India, claiming, "We might have found in the East Indies a recompence for all our losses in the west."[21] These statements and personal experiences led British imperial historian P. J. Marshall to argue that the American Revolution signaled the beginning of the unmaking of Britain's empire in the Western Hemisphere.[22] In a similar vein, Maya Jasanoff demonstrates that by 1815 "India was to the British Empire pretty much everything the North American and Caribbean colonies had been forty years earlier."[23]

A common corollary of the swing to the east is that Britain's imperial strategy in the Americas shifted from formal to informal empire. Despite maintaining formal colonies in the British West Indies, British interventions in the Americas increasingly took the form of indirect "control of a territory over which it [did] not exercise sovereignty."[24] The independence of the United States and the growing appeal of Adam Smith's ideas about the financial burden "of maintaining and defending" formal colonies were traditionally used to explain Britain's gradual but steady abandonment of formal colonialism in the Western Hemisphere.[25] More recent studies that emphasize the existence of a "multiplicity of [imperial] visions" and characterize imperial encounters as "complex affairs involving multiple agents ... and unforeseen outcomes" complicate any attempt to establish neat dividing lines between a first British

Atlantic empire and a second British empire centered in India, as well as between a formal and an informal empire in the Western Hemisphere.[26] Because multiple imperial agents advanced different imperial projects, Atlantic and Indian, formal and informal, mercantilism and free-trade empires coexisted. Thus, the unmaking of the British Atlantic empire and its "persistence" were simultaneous processes.[27] Moreover, the contest between mercantilists and supporters of free-trade empire was not a zero-sum game, in which the rise of free-trade imperialism resulted in an immediate decline of mercantilism as imperial economic policy.[28]

During the 1780s, British subjects in the southwestern Caribbean, including thousands of loyalists forced to flee the United States, placed their bets on the side of the persistence of empire. Regaining control of the thirteen colonies, focusing on the remaining colonies, conquering Spanish territories as a way to make up the loss in North America, and establishing greater commercial intercourse with Spanish America were all options up for debate. Spanish authorities in northwestern South America, witnessing with concern the reorganization of the British Empire, understood the threat of British attack was on the rise. The British capture of Saint Eustatius, Curaçao, Demerara, and Trinidad, as well as the attempts to seize Puerto Rico and the multiple rumors of projected invasions, did not look informal in any way. Further south, British assaults on Buenos Aires and Montevideo were equally hard to perceive as informal.[29]

Unlike historians, contemporary observers did not have hindsight to allow them to name processes that were happening around them. They could, however, identify trends and envision a variety of outcomes. In this particular context, Jamaican merchants and planters, imperialist adventurers, and Spanish authorities and South American merchants interested in trading with Jamaica did not coin terms like "swing to the east" or "informal empire." Their actions, however, reveal their interest in avoiding the shift of Britain's imperial emphasis to India and their willingness to explore the possibilities offered by northwestern South America as a strategy to keep the British Empire Atlantic centered. In the aftermath of the American Revolution, turning south, whether to establish formal colonies or to advance an empire of free trade, could provide a sort of replacement for the lost colonies in North America. For some Spanish authorities and local merchants, if carefully handled, this potential turn to the south could contribute to the economic development of the scarcely populated, dangerously autonomous, and largely unproductive provinces of northwestern South America.[30]

Between a Rock and a Hard Place

The prelude to war in North America was followed with great interest in the British West Indies. Fearing for their economic prospects, West Indian planters and merchants—formally associated in the Society of West India Planters and Merchants—attempted to use their economic and political leverage in London to prevent war between Britain and its North American colonies. Their conciliatory efforts, however, were to no avail, and by 1776 West Indian planters and merchants observed with frustration the beginning of a war that was to disrupt the islands' productive system.[31] Given their simultaneous dependence on the U.S. and British markets, the eruption of war trapped West Indian planters and merchants between a rock and a hard place.

The beginning of hostilities resulted in an immediate cessation of the trade between the British West Indies and the rebellious colonies. Failed official efforts to "entice Americans back to the empire" further undermined the prospects for a rapid restoration of this line of American trade.[32] Without it, the British Caribbean islands lost their ability to obtain wood, foodstuffs—especially fish and wheat—and cattle, all necessary inputs to keep sugar production going. In addition, they lost their most important market for rum and molasses.[33] The eruption of war, as Selwyn Carrington summarized it, inaugurated a period of crisis in the British West Indies characterized by "the general scarcity of all articles of food in the islands, approaching famine in some; the shortage of plantation utensils, machinery and packaging cases for sugar and rum; the rising cost of government; the high prices of provisions and lumber; the heavy duties; the advanced cost of transportation; the reduced quantities of tropical products sent to England; [and] the decreasing strength of the labour force."[34] While smuggling and British efforts to supply the Caribbean with foodstuffs imported directly from Ireland and Britain eased the hardships of West Indian inhabitants, these new commercial channels were far from able to make up for the loss of trade with the United States.[35]

With the return of peace and Britain's recognition of the independence of the United States, trade between the British West Indies and the new republic occupied a prominent role in Britain's political agenda. Supporters and opponents of the trade expressed their views on how to fill the "void in the commerce of our Sugar Islands, which the revolt of our former Northern provinces has occasioned."[36] If the independence of the United States made trade between the British West Indies and the new republic illegal, a planter asked, "Can our islands in the West Indies be supplied with provisions and lumber elsewhere?"[37]

While West Indian planters and merchants, interested in restoring the prewar trade, answered that it was not possible, mercantilists in the British Parliament argued that it was not only possible but also necessary. An analysis of the major points of contention in the debate over the trade between the United States and the British West Indies provides insights into the efforts of West Indian planters and merchants to keep the British Empire Atlantic centered.

The contest over trade with the United States became heated months before the signing of the Treaty of Paris officially ended the American Revolution in September 1783. Anticipating the outcome of the war, members of the Society of West India Planters and Merchants had petitioned the king to allow trade between the British West Indies and the United States. In their representation of April 1783, they asked the British monarch to consider

> That the proprietors of estates in the sugar colonies have been put to such enormous expenses for their defence during the late war, and for procuring even the insufficient supplies they have been able to obtain of lumber and other American produce, and have been during the same period visited with so many natural calamities, that their situation is become truly distressful, and loudly calls for attention to every possible means of supporting them, and, with them the manufactures, commerce, navigation, and revenue of the mother country.[38]

And, in defense of the trade with the United States, the planters and merchants reminded the king: "The dominions of the United States of America, and his Majesty's sugar colonies, having been settled in the express view of supplying each other's wants, it cannot be expected that the sugar colonies can subsist, in any degree of prosperity, without those supplies of lumber and provisions from America at cheapest rate, in contemplation of which they were so settled, or without the consumption in North America of their produce in return."[39]

The petition of West Indian planters and merchants inaugurated a dynamic exchange that put some of the most influential planters—including figures like Edward Long and Bryan Edwards, famous among historians of the Caribbean for their histories of Jamaica—at odds with conservative MPs like Lord Sheffield. Between the spring of 1783 and the beginning of 1786, Lord Sheffield presented and expanded his arguments in more than five editions of his *Observations on the Commerce of the American States*. For their part, planters like Edward Long, Bryan Edwards, William Beckford, James Allen, and Stephen Fuller published a series of pamphlets refuting Sheffield's arguments.[40] The controversy revolved around two main questions: Should the British West

Indies be allowed to trade with the newly independent United States? If yes, should this trade be conducted in British ships only, thus excluding American ships—the usual carriers of this trade? On a larger imperial scale, given Britain's recent advance in India and the hopes and fears it generated, the debate was also about the future orientation of the British Empire. For West Indian merchants and planters, avoiding a shift of imperial interest to India was, of course, of paramount importance.

In the British Parliament, Lord Sheffield quickly emerged as the most powerful opponent of trade with the United States. Espousing the mercantilist principles of the Navigation Acts, Lord Sheffield claimed that Canada, Nova Scotia, Newfoundland, and Saint John's Island—the remaining British colonies in North America—could supply the British Caribbean islands.[41] After explaining the agricultural and commercial possibilities of the northernmost British American colonies, Sheffield concluded, "In short, it is unquestionably a fact, that Nova Scotia, Canada, and the island of St. John, will soon become capable, with very little encouragement, of supplying our islands with all the shipping, fish, timber, and lumber of every kind, and with mill or draft horses, with flour and several other articles they may want."[42] In Lord Sheffield's opinion, to open trade with the United States instead of encouraging trade with Canada, Nova Scotia, and Saint John's Island would be unfair to these loyal colonies. More disturbing, allowing trade with the United States would greatly undermine Britain's naval power while favoring the rise of a threatening commercial rival.[43] Like-minded imperial officials in the remaining British North American colonies expectedly echoed Sheffield's claims. Guy Carleton—the future Lord Dorchester—argued for the need "to establish the most close and cordial connection with the provinces which have preserved their allegiance." To this end, he proposed a program to grant land to loyalists migrating to Canada, Nova Scotia, and other British North American colonies as a way of recognizing their sustained effort for the British cause in America.[44] The development of new lands for the production of agricultural exports to supply the British West Indies fitted Sheffield's argument perfectly. In 1784, however, Carleton's scheme was an undeveloped project. Sheffield's argument, as West Indian planters and merchants were quick to notice, offered no immediate solutions, but a mere potential future solution.

West Indian planters and merchants rebutted Sheffield's argument first by pointing to the long history of mutual dependence between the British West Indies and the now-independent United States. This long-standing commercial relation, planter and historian Bryan Edwards claimed, determined "that our subjects in the West India islands have no other alternative for supplying themselves with food (if a free intercourse with America is denied them) than that of raising it themselves." This alternative, of course, could only be pursued at the expense of the islands' sugar production. Therefore, the loss of the trade with the United States would ultimately result in a "loss to the revenues and commerce of Great Britain."[45]

In order to refute Sheffield's argument about the potential of the loyal North American colonies as suppliers of the British West Indies, the planters and merchants produced a statistical account of the imports from North America to the British West Indies in the years immediately preceding the beginning of the American Revolutionary War (see table 4.1). The balance against the remaining British colonies in North America could not have been less favorable. With the sole exception of fish, the participation of the North American colonies loyal to the British Crown rarely exceeded 1 percent for any given commodity. The disparity was so strong that, according to Edward Long, "it requires no comment." That said, Long proceeded to assert "that, to propose making our sugar manufactories in the West Indies dependent upon these two *forlorn hopes* [Canada and Nova Scotia], for their subsistence and supplies, is not less absurd, than if we were to talk of feeding the manufactures, and stocking the looms, of Norwich and Manchester from the deserts of Iceland—we may conceive the one to be just as feasible as the other."[46]

Since Sheffield's argument was largely based on the prospects of Canada and Nova Scotia as suppliers of all the commodities required by the West Indies, the planters did not limit their counterarguments to demonstrating the lack of past commercial intercourse between the British West Indies and the loyal colonies. Instead, Long and Edwards extensively showed the environmental limitations of the new commercial channel proposed by Sheffield. Both planters argued that a combination of Canada's long and very cold winters and the Caribbean hurricane season rendered it impossible to sustain frequent trade. Since "it is only for four, or at most five months in the year, [that] the navigation between Canada and the West Indies is tolerably open," Long claimed, "only one voyage between those two places can be made in the course of one year."[47] Hence, even if Canada and Nova Scotia managed to produce the commodities the West Indies demanded, transporting them would have been basically impossible.

Throughout their tracts in defense of trade with the United States, planters were careful not to dismiss the Navigation Acts. While arguing for a substantial transformation of these laws of trade and navigation, Long did not fail to acknowledge "that *Great Britain* is very much indebted to the *Navigation Act*

TABLE 4.1 Imports from North America to the British West Indies, 1771–1774

| | | PROVENANCE | | | |
| | | EX-COLONIES NOW UNITED STATES | | OTHER BRITISH NORTH AMERICA* | |
Imports	Unit of Measure	No.	%	No.	%
Wood					
Boards and timber	Feet	76,767,695	99.7	234,040	0.3
Shingles	Number	59,586,194	99.7	185,000	0.3
Staves	Number	57,998,661	100.0	27,350	0.0
Masts	Number	157	100.0	0	0.0
Spars	Number	3,074	99.0	30	1.0
Foodstuff					
Corn	Bushels	1,204,389	100.0	24	0.0
Peas and beans	Bushels	64,006	98.4	1,017	1.6
Bread and flour	Barrels	396,329	99.8	991	0.2
	Kegs	13,099	100.0	0	0.0
Rice	Barrels	39,912	100.0	0	0.0
	Tierces	21,777	100.0	0	0.0
Fish	Hogsheads	51,344	94.9	2,756	5.1
	Barrels	47,686	98.3	848	1.7
	Quintals	21,500	59.4	14,722	40.6
	Kegs	3,304	84.4	609	15.6
Beef and pork	Barrels	44,782	99.6	194	0.4
Poultry	Dozens	2,739	99.6	10	0.4
Cattle					
Horses	Number	7,130	99.6	28	0.4
Oxen	Number	3,647	100.0	0	0.0

*Canada, Nova Scotia, and Newfoundland.

Source: James Allen, *Considerations on the Present State of the Intercourse between His Majesty's Sugar Colonies and the Dominions of the United States of America* (London, 1784), 24.

for that grandeur of naval power, to which she has attained within the present century."[48] Similarly, Edwards recognized the importance of the Navigation Acts as guiding principles of Britain's commercial policy, but he argued that reforming these laws was in the best interest of both the West Indies and the whole British Empire.[49] Furthermore, Allen and Long pointed to the most recent modification of the acts—the establishment of free ports in Jamaica and Dominica—to argue that under this new commercial policy it was actually legal for American vessels to conduct trade in the free ports of the British West Indies. Quoting the original Free Port Act and its most recent ratification, Allen declared that it must not be forgotten, that it is still lawful, under the Free Port Act of 6 Geo. III continued by an Act of 21 Geo. III "to import into the ports of Kingston, Savannah La Mar, Montego Bay, and Santa Lucea in Jamaica, from any *foreign* Colony or Plantation in America," (within which description the Dominions of the United States now fall) "in any foreign vessel whatsoever, not having more than one deck, all manner of goods and commodities, the growth or produce of any such Colony or Plantation, manufactures excepted."[50]

Implicit in Allen's quotation of the Free Port Act is a recognition that under current commercial regulations the British West Indies could resort to Spanish America to ease the hardships created by the secession of the United States. Long also recognized that the Free Port Act opened the possibility of trading with Spanish territories that could supply the West Indies with foodstuffs and wood. However, in 1784, the planters' emphasis was on pressuring the government to allow trade with the United States, not on finding alternatives to that trade. Mindful that all efforts to restore trade with the United States could fail, Long did not completely shut the door to other sources. The "Summer Islands" (Bermuda), the Bahamas, and other islands, he believed, offered a more viable option than Canada, Nova Scotia, Newfoundland, and Saint John's Island. "Colonizing these valuable spots," instead of pursuing "the error of colonizing in *northern* latitudes," was, in Long's opinion, an option worth pursuing.[51]

Despite their strong arguments against the viability of supplying the British West Indies with produce from the remaining North American colonies, the planters and merchants of the West Indies lost the debate against Lord Sheffield. The planters' argument for the legality of trading with the United States in American ships under the cover of the Free Port Act did not achieve its expected result either. By the end of 1786, planters' initial hopes of reopening trade with the United States—nurtured by William Pitt's introduction of a bill to allow free trade between the United States and the British West Indies (February 1783)—were definitely crushed.[52] Planters' predictions about the devastating effects of the cessation of trade with the United States, in turn, were traumatically realized.[53]

With all hope for the restoration of trade with the United States gone, Edward Long and his fellow members of the society of planters and merchants turned their eyes south in search of the wood, foodstuffs, and cattle their Jamaican plantations desperately needed. In April 1787, representatives of the

West Indian planters and merchants, including Long, declared in favor of expanding trade between the British West Indies and Spanish American territories. It was their opinion that "the admission of tortoise-shell, bullion and coin, timber being of the growth of the West Indies, asses, horses, livestock, Indian corn, tobacco seed, into the several free ports" of Jamaica and Dominica could supplant, to a certain extent, the lost trade with the United States.[54] The subsequent renewal of the free port act allowed West Indian planters and merchants to import wood, foodstuffs, and cattle from viable alternative sources. The permission to trade with "colonies or plantations in America belonging to . . . a foreign European state," while continuing to forbid trade with the United States, expanded the prospects for trade with the Spanish Main.[55] From the late 1780s, thus, West Indian planters and merchants turned south in an effort to prevent the shift of British imperial interest to the east.

Turning South to Conquer?

While London-based West Indian merchants and planters fell short of proposing to invade Spanish American territories, disgruntled loyalists and other British adventurers were explicit in their promotion of schemes to establish permanent or temporary British settlements in Spanish America's circum-Caribbean territories. Working from London and from the empire's "torrid zones" in the Americas, these adventurers projected expeditions that would avenge British defeat in the American Revolution and restore the greatness of the British Empire.[56] Joining adventurers in these expansionist schemes characteristic of what a historian has called the "spirit of 1783," a number of British subjects who had settled in Central America's Mosquito Coast and in Jamaica constantly roamed the coasts of northwestern South America with purposes that were not always clear to either British or Spanish authorities (see map 4.1).[57] More than the actions of the British government, the activities of these adventurers were responsible for spreading fear among Spanish authorities in the circum-Caribbean. Their actions also shed light on the lack of imperial direction characteristic of British approaches to Spanish America in the aftermath of the American Revolution. In the 1780s, the future of Britain's official stance toward Spanish America was far from settled.[58] Military adventurers, acting independently or with backing from imperial authorities, sought to take the American Revolution to the Caribbean. For them, even after the peace agreement of 1783, the war continued, albeit "in disguise."[59] Just like West Indian merchants and planters, most military adventurers had an interest in the United States, and all strived to keep the British Empire Atlantic centered. Unlike planters and merchants, some of these military adventurers quickly turned their eyes to northern South America with the explicit aim of conquering new territories for the British monarch.

Spain's participation in the American Revolution gained it the enmity of loyalists and imperial officials in Britain's North American and Caribbean colonies. The entrance of France and Spain into the war, in 1778 and 1779, respectively, effectively turned the American Revolution into an international conflict. While actual warfare took place in the thirteen British colonies in North America, British and Spanish authorities in the circum-Caribbean (including the Mosquito Coast) made preparations for the potential opening of a Caribbean theater of operations. While loyalist adventurers like John Cruden and William Augustus Bowles, from their bases of operation in Florida and the Bahamas, envisioned wild plans for conquering the territory stretching from Florida to northern Mexico, Jamaica's governor, John Dalling, supported a series of offensive strategies designed to carve pieces of Central and northern South America from the Spanish monarchy.[60]

Cruden, president of the Assembly of the United Loyalists, led a group of loyalists forced to relocate first to Florida and then, after the cession of East Florida to Spain, to the Bahamas. Firmly "determined neither to become Spanish nor American Subjects," Cruden and "the Loyalists of the Southern Provinces" refused to accept the loss of the thirteen North American colonies.[61] Convinced that it was possible to "bring the Americans back again," Cruden expressed confidence in the final "triumph over the Enemies of our Country."[62] His energy and commitment to the loyalist cause gained Cruden the patronage of fellow loyalist Lord Dunmore, who, from his governor's office in the Bahamas, became one of the most vociferous advocates for British attacks on Spanish Florida and the United States. Lord Cornwallis also entertained Cruden's plans, and Cruden even appeared in the cast of leading characters of the expedition that Juan Blommart was allegedly organizing to invade the vicinity of Cartagena.[63]

Just like Cruden, William Augustus Bowles benefited from Lord Dunmore's patronage. From the Bahamas, Bowles launched several expeditions to Florida with the aim of creating Muskogee, an independent Creek state that he envisioned as being simultaneously "free of Spanish rule, secure against American incursions, and a haven for anyone loyal to British ideals."[64] Bowles's plans went far beyond creating a Creek state. From Florida, he declared, he would "march a strong force across the Mississippi towards Mexico" and once there, "in conjunction with the Natives [would] declare it independent of the Spaniards."[65] Needless to say, Bowles's plan did not work out as he had imagined. Both Cruden's and Bowles's designs, despite their ultimate failure, reveal the interest of British and American loyalists in regaining the United States for the British Crown and robbing Spain of some of its valuable territories in the Americas.[66]

About 750 miles from Florida, in Jamaica, more than 3,000 white loyalists (with about 8,000 slaves) took the sufferings and resentments of the American Revolution to the heart of the Caribbean.[67] The arrival of loyalists in Jamaica and the Mosquito Coast during and immediately after the American Revolution effectively turned the southwestern Caribbean into an alternative theater of operations. Between 1779 and 1781, Jamaica's governor, John Dalling, dispatched two expeditions to Central America. Lured by descriptions of British soldiers who commented on "the great easiness with which opulent cities" in Central America "could be captured," Dalling ordered expeditions that, he hoped, would make him "shine with a brightness equal to that of . . . fortune [seekers] . . . in the east."[68] Far from securing Dalling's glorious aims, the expeditions ended in dramatic failures that weakened Jamaica's defenses, embittered Dalling's relations with the island's assembly, and ultimately led to his dismissal from office in 1781.[69] East of Jamaica, British squadrons roamed around the island of Puerto Rico, leading Spanish observers to believe that an attack was imminent. Luckily for Puerto Ricans, the peace treaty of 1783 put an end, albeit temporary, to British designs on their island.[70]

The peace of 1783 did not bring tranquility to the Caribbean. Less than a year after Spain and Britain signed the Treaty of Paris, minister of the Indies Joseph de Gálvez instructed New Granada's viceroy, Antonio Caballero y Góngora, to remain alert. Despite the peace agreement, Gálvez believed that a desire to avenge the defeat in the American Revolution would cause the British "to try, now with more tenacity than ever, to establish themselves close to the isthmus" of Panama.[71] Another Spanish observer noticed that "England's confusion upon seeing [the republican army in] North America [emerge as a] victor [in the American Revolution] is such that all her ideas and secret machinations are directed towards the Spanish American continent."[72] Partially confirming these hypotheses, Santa Marta's governor, Antonio Narváez y la Torre, informed Viceroy Caballero y Góngora of an expedition prepared in Jamaica to the Mosquito Coast and the Darién.[73] News from Europe about Blommart's expedition to Cartagena and new information about British plans to settle Central America to secure a passage to the Pacific further heightened the apprehensions of New Granada's authorities about a potential British at-tack.[74] For their part, British authorities similarly anticipated the possibility of a Spanish attack on their Caribbean holdings. As a ship captain told Governor Narváez, newspapers in Jamaica suggested that while Spanish authorities were getting ready to attack the Mosquito Coast, British authorities were set to attack the Darién.[75] The peace, thus, was giving British and Spanish authorities in the southwestern Caribbean valuable time to prepare for the imminent resumption of hostilities.

In this climate of impending warfare, the Mosquito Coast and the Spanish territories to its south became key sites of contention. Long settled by British subjects who received Spanish permission to cut wood there in order to export it to Britain via Jamaica, the Mosquito Coast was, as a historian of the area put it, "a sanctioned British trespass on Spanish territory."[76] From a handful of British residents clustered around Bluefields in the late seventeenth century, the British population in Caribbean Central America grew slowly but steadily until the 1780s.[77] From an invasion of Spanish territory, the legal status of the stretch of coast between the Bay of Honduras and northern Panama (see map 4.1) evolved to resemble a British colony or, at the very least, a British protectorate.[78] The increased British presence in the area led Spanish authorities—from the governor of Yucatán to Guatemala's Audiencia president and New Granada's viceroy—to give credence to rumors that the British intended to invade and permanently settle the Spanish possessions "from Yucatán to the Darién," thus extending their reach from the Caribbean to the Pacific coast.[79]

British defeat in the American Revolutionary War gave Spain the leverage necessary to effectively limit British encroachments in Central America. Article 6 of the peace treaty of 1783 carefully demarcated the area where British subjects could reside, limiting British legal presence to Belize and its hinterland (thus, expelling them from Bluefields, the Mosquito Coast, and the vicinity of Portobelo). In addition, Article 6 required that within eighteen months after the treaty's signing (September 3, 1783), "all the English who may be dispersed in any other parts, whether on the Spanish continent, or in any of the islands whatsoever, dependent on the aforesaid Spanish continent, . . . without exception, shall retire within the district which has been above described." The Spanish government agreed "to grant to the dispersed English every convenience possible for their removing to the settlement agreed upon by the present article, or for their retiring wherever they shall think proper."[80]

British residents of the Mosquito Coast, including several hundred recently arrived American loyalists, did not welcome Article 6. While for recently arrived loyalists the article implied yet another involuntary resettlement, for long-term residents of the Mosquito Coast like British colonel Robert Hodgson, Article 6 was to have damaging financial consequences. Like many other long-term residents and recent arrivals to the Mosquito Coast, Hodgson had made valuable investments in the region's woodcutting activities. The cession of the area to Spain thus entailed not only physical displacement but also the likely prospect of financial ruin. While many British residents of the Mosquito Coast were able to postpone their resettlement beyond the initial eighteenth-month deadline, "in 1786 more than 2,000 refugees, three quarters of them slaves, were relocated from the Mosquito Coast to the Bay of Honduras."[81]

Throughout the 1780s, Robert Hodgson was a prominent figure in the southwestern Caribbean. His deeds in the Mosquito Coast, where he had succeeded in gaining the trust of the independent Miskitos, haunted the imagination of British and Spanish colonial authorities alike. At the beginning of the decade, Spanish authorities considered Hodgson one of the most important figures in the British plans to turn south in order to avenge Spanish participation in the American Revolution. By the end of 1791, months before his death, Hodgson's life had taken an unexpected turn.[82]

Hodgson established his residence in Bluefields, at the heart of the Mosquito Coast, in 1749, after he left the military academy to join his father, Robert Hodgson Sr., in his new post as first superintendent of the Mosquito Coast.[83] After nearly two decades of experience in Central America, the younger Hodgson was appointed fourth superintendent to the Mosquito Coast. By that time he was already one of the more experienced individuals in the affairs of the coast, and his rapport with the indigenous population of the area was unmatched. Thus, he became the key piece in British designs for Central and northwestern South America. In fact, there is reason to believe that Dalling's schemes for Central America were partly inspired by Hodgson's project to invade Central America from the British base of Bluefields.[84]

Hodgson's successful career as British officer and spy began to decline in the mid-1770s, when the British government ordered an investigation into his abuse of power and appointed James Lawrie as new superintendent. After a trip to Britain to defend himself, Hodgson returned to the Mosquito Coast in 1782. Shortly thereafter, he was captured by Spanish authorities off the coast of Portobelo.[85] After interrogating him and reviewing a series of maps and documents Hodgson carried with him when he was captured, a Spanish officer assigned the task of translating the documents concluded that Hodgson was a very dangerous individual because "he ha[d] inspected coasts, ports, rivers, and towns from Buenos Aires to Cartagena" and "project[ed] clandestine trade, new navigations, invasions, and the siege of [many] towns."[86] New Granada's viceroy, Caballero y Góngora, was quick to conclude that, since Hodgson had been captured close to Portobelo, he was probably inspecting "our coasts or plotting with the Darién Indians a way to disturb or invade some of our provinces."[87] Given Hodgson's previous trajectory and the current geopolitical climate of the Caribbean, Caballero y Góngora's conclusion hardly seems unjustified.

At this point Hodgson's career took an interesting turn. Probably as part of preliminary peace negotiations, Spanish authorities released Hodgson and sent him to Jamaica. Before being released, Hodgson offered to work for Spain, helping Spanish authorities conquer the indigenous populations of the Caribbean coast between Cape Gracias a Dios and the province of Cartagena. Viceroy Caballero y Góngora recommended Hodgson's proposal to higher authorities and allowed him to settle on the island of San Andrés, 140 miles east of Bluefields.[88] Authorities in Spain, based on information about a trip Hodgson made to England after being released from Cartagena, advised Caballero y Góngora "not to admit this individual in the service of Spain."[89] Using the logic of siding with the enemies of one's enemies, Caballero y Góngora, after acknowledging that Hodgson should be treated with suspicion, argued in favor of granting him Spanish subjecthood. Based on information from London confirming that the British government considered Hodgson "a great picaroon," Caballero y Góngora was inclined "to believe that [Hodgson] will embrace our side with preference."[90] By late 1786, when the ultimatum for British settlers of the Mosquito Coast was about to come into effect, Hodgson was formally asked to swear vassalage to the king of Spain in order to be allowed to remain in Bluefields or, alternatively, "to suffer the fate of the other [British] settlers" of the Mosquito Coast. Less than six months later, in March 1787, Hodgson entered Cartagena to swear loyalty to the Spanish king.[91]

For the next four years, Hodgson performed a balancing act that kept Spanish authorities wondering if his allegiance to the Spanish king was sincere or if he was still loyal to the British Crown. When he died, in June 1791, the question of Hodgson's loyalty remained unresolved.[92] The circumstances of his submission to the Spanish king lead one to think that, as was the case with other British subjects who turned south after the American Revolution, Hodgson was loyal only to himself, to his personal economic interest.

Hodgson's life trajectory illustrates the direction of the British "conquering" thrust between 1779 and the mid-1780s. In this sense, Hodgson is a good example of the attempts by British subjects to turn south in order to keep the British Empire Atlantic centered. But Hodgson's career also sheds light on the dynamic nature of individuals' allegiances in the transimperial Greater Caribbean. Hodgson's late career decision to become a Spanish subject illustrates the importance of personal interest and helps one question preconceived ideas about the meaning and importance of being the subject of a specific crown. In other words, whatever Hodgson's identity as a British subject meant for him, safeguarding his economic investments in the Mosquito Coast ranked higher in his list of priorities. Faced with the tough decision of choosing whether to remain a British subject or pursue his economic interest in the woodcutting business on the Mosquito Coast (given the conditions specified in Article 6 of the Treaty of Paris, these two options were mutually exclusive), Hodgson chose the latter. Unlike Cruden, Hodgson, apparently putting his personal interest before his patriotism, became a Spanish subject in order to be allowed to stay in the Mosquito Coast. In the final analysis, the decisions of military adventurers like Cruden, Bowles, and Hodgson reveal that British subjects interested in keeping the British Empire Atlantic centered were willing to fight to avoid the British departure from the Americas. But when, as in the case of the Mosquito Coast, physical and economic dislocation were an imminent reality, British subjects like Hodgson were willing to explore other ways to secure their economic interests. While Cruden and Bowles remained loyal British subjects, for Hodgson, the exploration of other ways resulted in his pledge of allegiance to the Spanish Crown. Thus, the British subject once perceived by Spanish authorities as among the biggest threats to the Spanish territories in Central and South America died an honored subject of the Spanish king.[93]

The plans of Cruden, Bowles, and Hodgson, along with the officially backed British takeover of Trinidad (1797) and the attempts to capture Buenos Aires (1806, 1807) and Montevideo (1807), demonstrate the lack of a unified British approach to Spanish America. The attacks on Buenos Aires and Montevideo, moreover, show that British sights were not exclusively set on the transimperial Greater Caribbean. While for Jamaican planters and adventurers like Cruden, Bowles, and Hodgson turning south meant to direct their interest to Spanish America's circum-Caribbean, for other British subjects (of whom Home Popham is the best-known example) the turn was to a South Atlantic that, against the hopes of Jamaican planters to keep the empire's interest in the Western Hemisphere, was seen as providing potential stopovers on the way to an expanding British empire in the east.[94]

While the British conquering thrust from 1779 to the late 1780s bore no fruit in Central and northern South America (in fact it resulted in territorial loss in the Mosquito Coast), the multiple plans of invasion—actually undertaken or only projected, realistic or chimeric—convinced Spanish authorities of the importance of establishing a strong presence in these coastal territories. For New Granada's viceroy, being ready to successfully reject potential British invasions required "establishing some towns along all that coast."[95] Populating the area, in turn, required developing an economic base for its prosperity. Caballero y Góngora believed that promoting cotton cultivation to export to Spain, as well as commercial exchanges with foreign territories, especially the British Caribbean, would provide the means to secure effective Spanish possession of the Caribbean coast of northwestern South America. His strategy, thus, called for promoting trade in order to avoid conquest. Given the changing geopolitics of the Atlantic world, Caballero y Góngora's plan and the variations of it that his successors adopted required, among other things, that the British Empire remained Atlantic centered.

Cotton and New Granada's Bid for Insertion into a British-Led Atlantic Economy

Caballero y Góngora's plan to develop cotton cultivation was an essential component of the Bourbon commercial policy aimed at diversifying New Granada's exports to Spain and increasing their value.[96] The promotion of cotton cultivation was devised to serve two additional, though related, purposes. On the one hand, it would increase Spanish control of northwestern New Granada, a territory largely controlled by the independent "Calidonio, Darién or Cunacuna Indians" and frequently threatened by British adventurers like Hodgson.[97] On the other hand, it was expected to supply raw materials for the growing textile industry of Catalonia.

In pursuit of this last aim, the Spanish Crown conceded tax exemptions to stimulate the cultivation and export of cotton. Initially proclaimed in 1776, the exemptions were ratified in the early 1780s, which led to a dramatic increase in raw cotton exports from Cartagena to Spain.[98] Between 1785 and 1794, the boom period of Catalonia's textile industry, Cartagena's cotton exports to Spain grew threefold, from roughly 272,000 pounds to 869,000 pounds.[99] Cartagena's exports contributed significantly to the increase of Catalonia's consumption of raw cotton. Evidence shows that Cartagena's cotton exports amounted to about 30 percent of the 3 billion pounds of raw cotton Catalonia consumed in 1793. Catalonia's consumption, in turn, equaled 15 percent of Britain's, a remarkable fact that tends to go unnoticed in Britain-centered histories of cotton and the Industrial Revolution.[100]

The commercial disruption brought about by the resumption of Anglo-Spanish conflict in 1796, however, brought both Cartagena's exports and Catalonia's cotton-based industrialization to a halt, leaving New Granada's cotton growers with large stocks of cotton waiting for a buyer. Francisco Salceda y Bustamante, for instance, complained in 1798 that he "had more than five thousand quintals [about 500,000 pounds] of cotton and cacao in store." With no prospect of shipping his cargo to Spain in the immediate future, Salceda y Bustamante looked to a potential permission to trade with foreign neutrals as the only avenue to continue his, until then, promising cotton export business.[101] Like him, several other *cartagenero* merchants experienced the 1796–1808 Anglo-Spanish War as a death blow for a business that had raised their hopes for economic development and personal riches. On the other side of the Atlantic, in Catalonia, the lack of supplies put an end to what had been an unprecedented decade of cotton-based growth.

The 1780s expansion of the cotton-based textile industry, of course, was not a process unique to Catalonia. This decade witnessed the beginning of what a historian of the global rise of cotton has called "the late eighteenth-century cotton revolution," a dramatic transformation led by Britain from the cotton-hungry textile industry emerging in Lancashire.[102] Around the world, policy makers, colonial authorities, merchants, and entrepreneurs actively promoted cotton cultivation. Caballero y Góngora's projects were part of a global effort to which his counterparts in the British, French, Dutch, and Portuguese colonial worlds also contributed. While Cartagena increased its cotton exports to Spain, British colonies in the Caribbean and India began to export raw cotton to Britain. Dutch and Portuguese colonies in South America, as well as the French Caribbean (via Jamaica through the free ports trade) and Turkey, were also exporting their cotton to Britain.[103] At a time when cotton had yet to prove that it could be king, promoters of cotton cultivation around the world felt cautiously optimistic. In Jamaica, for instance, a hopeful planter claimed that, if pursued "with the cautions recommended," cotton "will be found highly profitable."[104]

Inventors and societies for the promotion of trade and industry were equally active in the promotion of technologies and schemes to increase cotton cultivation and manufacture. These technological developments were not foreign to the Spanish world. In 1788, five years before Eli Whitney registered his cotton gin, Spanish inventor Antonio de la Carrera asked for permission to travel to New Granada to test his new "cotton ginning machine."[105] Unfortunately, besides the license he obtained to sail to New Granada, Carrera did not leave an archival trail to inform us about the outcome of his travel. What we do know is that processing and exporting cotton was certainly part of a conversation among merchants, *hacendados* (landowners), and imperial officers on how to promote New Granada's economic development, as well as that of the whole Spanish Empire. A lengthy report by the viceroyalty's *director general de rentas* (revenue director) not only listed cotton as one of the most important agricultural products of Cartagena, Santa Marta, Riohacha, and most of the interior provinces, but also recommended the establishment of "a cotton-ginning factory" in Santa Marta.[106] Geopolitical circumstances, as already mentioned, got in the way of New Granada's cotton promotion plans. Carrera's plan and the report of the revenue director, however, reveal not only that many in the Spanish Empire envisioned a future built on cotton, but also that some steps were taken toward that future.

Similar plans and technologies were envisioned, promoted, and actually developed in the North Atlantic. In Philadelphia, the Pennsylvania Society for the Encouragement of Manufactures and the Useful Arts offered a prize to encourage the development of technologies to optimize cotton production.[107] New technologies like James Watt's steam engine, James Hargreaves's spinning jenny, Richard Arkwright's water frame, and Samuel Crompton's spinning mule were rapidly adopted in cotton agriculture, resulting in "a great leap in production" that dramatically transformed the British Midlands into a cotton-manufacturing metropolis and the whole world into Britain's raw cotton supplier.[108]

The great leap in cotton production initiated in the second half of the 1780s continued during the 1790s and on into the nineteenth century. It was characterized by four important trends easily perceived in an analysis of British imports of raw cotton (see figure 4.1).[109] First, Britain's appetite for cotton grew dramatically—nearly tenfold—between 1781 and 1815. (The decline from 1806–1810 to 1811–1815 is largely explained by the lack of information regarding imports from the British West Indies between 1811 and 1813, years that, as explained later, could have witnessed an increase in cotton exports from New Granada to Jamaica and, thus, from there to Britain.) Second, while the amount of raw cotton exported from the British West Indies to Britain showed an upward trend (the same explanation for the decline of total imports

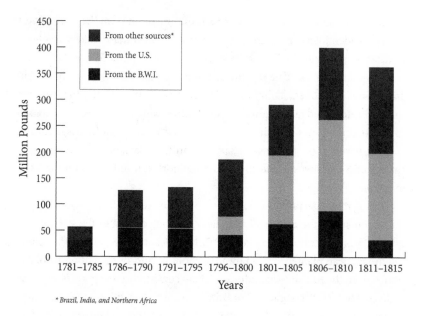

* Brazil, India, and Northern Africa

Figure 4.1 British imports of raw cotton.

from 1806–1810 to 1811–1815 applies for this case), its participation in Britain's total imports declined steadily (from over 50 percent in 1781–1785 to about 20 percent in 1806–1810). Third, initiating what a historian has called "a highly profitable transatlantic partnership centered on cotton," the United States' exports of raw cotton to Britain skyrocketed throughout the period.[110] Measured by both the amount exported and its share of British total imports, the United States emerged as the major player in the cotton world. The decline in U.S. cotton exports to Britain toward the end of the period is largely explained by the commercial breakdown during the War of 1812 between Britain and the United States. Fourth, while the United States grew to become Britain's main cotton supplier, the British thirst for raw cotton continued to require imports from Brazil, India, and northern Africa. Cotton thus connected Britain with the whole world. While the entire world (or its tropical and temperate areas) cultivated and ginned cotton, Britain spun it before returning it to the world in the form of cotton cloth and finished clothing. Britain's imports of raw cotton, its transformation, and subsequent export effectively turned the British Empire into a global empire that combined direct territorial control (formal imperialism) with a range of commercial strategies (informal imperialism) to exert its dominion worldwide.

An important aspect of British imports of raw cotton from the British West Indies not identifiable in the chart is the participation of non-British Caribbean territories in the share of British West Indies cotton exports. While there is no statistical series to calculate the amount of raw cotton that the French, Dutch, and Spanish Caribbean colonies sold to the British West Indies for reexport to Britain, scattered quantitative and qualitative evidence makes it possible to speculate about New Granada's participation in this line of trade. The following analysis, based largely on Kingston's port records, makes it possible to assess the success of Neogranadans' bid to develop the northern provinces on the basis of cotton cultivation.

During the initial phase of the cotton boom, before the United States entered the cotton scene, the British West Indies contributed most of the still-meager quantities of raw cotton demanded by Britain. Between 1784 and 1787, according to Jamaican planter Bryan Edwards, about a third of the cotton wool exported from the British West Indies to Britain consisted of reexports of produce cultivated in foreign colonies.[111] For British policy makers this was a constitutive element of the free ports policy inaugurated in 1766 and expanded in the aftermath of the American Revolution.[112] The British West Indies, either by cultivating cotton or by buying it from foreign colonies, were envisioned as important suppliers of the British market for raw cotton.

While during the 1780s most of the foreign cotton imported into the British West Indies came from French Saint-Domingue, the eruption of the Haitian Revolution (1791) and the subsequent outbreak of Anglo-Spanish War (1796) transformed the Caribbean's cotton supply chain. Since the British Atlantic blockade made it impossible to ship their cotton cargoes to Spain, New Granada's cotton exporters resorted to trade with foreigners (including the British enemy). In 1796, 30 percent (about eleven) of the ships conducting trade between New Granada's ports and Jamaica included cotton in their cargoes.[113] Even before the 1796 war disrupted Spain's transatlantic trade, a good portion of the cotton cultivated in northern New Granada found its way to Britain via Jamaica. According to New Granada's revenue director, while "the greater part" of the cotton produced in northern New Granada was exported to Spain, "some short portions [were shipped] to Jamaica."[114] The 1796–1808 Anglo-Spanish War and the 1808–1814 Napoleonic occupation of the Spanish Peninsula further shifted the balance in favor of Jamaica (and thus Britain). In 1814, at the height of the British free port system, 48 of the 120 Spanish ships that sailed from New Granada to Jamaica transported raw cotton.[115] At this point, more than a third of the raw cotton that entered Jamaica from foreign territories came from New Granada's ports.[116]

New Granada's growing participation in Jamaica's imports of raw cotton could lead one to conclude that Caballero y Góngora's plans succeeded in transforming northern New Granada into a cotton-producing region (although Caballero y Góngora intended this production for export to Spain, not Britain). To take this participation in Jamaica's imports as a measure of success, however, neglects the role geopolitical developments in the transimperial Greater Caribbean played in New Granada's cotton export boom. Closer scrutiny reveals that New Granada's largest contribution to the British cotton trade coincided with the War of 1812, a conflict that temporarily stopped British imports of U.S. cotton. Moreover, New Granada's cotton export boom took place at a time of crisis in Spain. Since Spain was invaded by Napoleon, New Granada's cotton merchants' sole outlet for their raw cotton was British Jamaica.

In the final analysis, while the British Empire's swing to the east did not result in a complete abandonment of its economic interests in the Western Hemisphere, by the late 1810s Britain's Atlantic interests were largely centered on the cotton trade with the United States. Jamaica and the other British West Indies remained part of the British Empire, but they clearly ceased to be what they had been before the American Revolution. New Granada, despite the redirection of its cotton exports to Jamaica, was relegated to the role of secondary supplier of raw cotton.

Only at times when the U.S.-British cotton trade was disrupted could New Granada's merchants hope to tap the British market. In the absence of exceptional circumstances, British thirst for cotton did not need New Granada to be satiated.

Envisioning the Future from the Southwestern Caribbean

Eric Williams was right in identifying the American Revolution as the "beginning of [the British West Indies'] uninterrupted decline."[117] Partially accepting the argument that one of the most important effects of the independence of the United States was the shift of imperial interest to India (to the detriment of the West Indies), this chapter has focused on the southwestern Caribbean to demonstrate that Jamaican planters, British military adventurers—many of them exiled loyalists from the United States—and a sector of New Granada's authorities and merchants actively sought to keep the British Empire Atlantic centered. After analyzing the projects these groups advanced in pursuit of their common aim, this chapter concludes that in the three decades following the American Revolution, Jamaican planters, British military adventurers, and officials and cotton growers in New Granada witnessed the collapse of their expectations for a better future.

While the British Empire did not completely abandon the Americas, its persistence in the Western Hemisphere did not favor the interests of the three groups studied in this chapter. Jamaican planters were not successful in their efforts to reopen trade with the now-independent United States. The two available alternatives—trading with the remaining British colonies in North America and turning south to obtain foodstuffs previously supplied by the thirteen colonies—proved unviable. While trade between Jamaica and northern South America grew, the increase was not large enough to guarantee the prosperity of the British West Indies. By the beginning of the nineteenth century, thus, Jamaica and the rest of the British West Indies had ceased to be the jewels of the crown. The strengthening of the commercial ties with northern South America proved to be only a temporary relief for an impending economic collapse.

Military adventurers, for their part, could not reach their goals of seeing the British Empire retake the thirteen North American colonies. Their alternative scenario—to avenge British defeat by carving out pieces of Spanish America—was plausible enough to put Spanish authorities on the defensive, but not realistic enough to be undertaken successfully. While Cruden, Bowles, and Hodgson all projected schemes to conquer parts of Spanish America, none of them could ultimately convince imperial authorities in London to actively pursue their plans. London's decision to respect the peace treaty with Spain even led Hodgson to abandon his imperial schemes in favor of the pursuit of his private interests. His ultimate decision to become a Spanish subject offers a great example of the complicated meanings of subjecthood and allegiances in an ever-changing revolutionary world.

Finally, New Granada's authorities and cotton growers perceived the new geopolitical environment and Britain's growing appetite for raw cotton as a unique opportunity to promote the economic development of New Granada's Caribbean provinces. Their initial success in tapping into British demand for cotton came to naught when the United States effectively eliminated New Granada from Britain's raw cotton supply system.

In the final analysis, the study of these failed projects to keep the British Empire Atlantic centered reveals that, in the immediate aftermath of the American Revolution, the British Empire did turn south in an attempt to replace the lost North American colonies. Turning south, however, ended up being a temporary strategy quickly superseded by the simultaneous pursuit of formal imperialism in India and informal imperialism geared toward obtaining raw cotton in the United States. Jamaica, Central America, and northern South America were relegated to the periphery of British imperial ventures. The marginalization of these territories from Britain's imperial strategy dramatically affected the future of the transimperial Greater Caribbean and slowly resulted in the silencing of the history of the commercial, geopolitical, and imagined connections linking Jamaica with Spanish and soon-to-be-independent circum-Caribbean territories.[118]

Studying these failed efforts to keep the British Empire Atlantic centered provides a window into the geopolitical imagination of Caribbean dwellers in the aftermath of the American Revolution. Their projects do not tell the story of what ended up happening, but of what contemporaries envisioned as a potential and, from the perspective of the three groups studied in this chapter, desirable future. The study of these different projects to reorganize the post–American Revolution transimperial Greater Caribbean also offers a clear idea of the existence of multiple imperial agents proposing different, often contending imperial projects. To dismiss these projects because they never reached fruition is to underestimate the multiplicity of options available to British and Spanish subjects seeking to gain from the new political environment inaugurated after the independence of the United States. When faced with economic collapse, Jamaican planters, disgruntled British military adventurers, and hopeful officials and cotton growers in New Granada envisioned a viable alternative and, unsuccessfully, sought to pull it off.

CHAPTER 5

Simón Bolívar's Caribbean Adventures

Bolívar: "I am a fugitive who comes to Jamaica and with my exile I will roam through America. . . . My unrest has leaned on the world map and it is to Haiti that I come, to ask, not for the calm upon which one can sleep dreaming of unworthy laurels, but for rifles, canons, and gunpowder. . . . In the name of my bleeding country, President, and to expel the Morillos from the continent . . . I come to request your fraternal aid."

Pétion: "If I were not Haiti's sentinel, by your side without fear I would have chosen to live and die. In all your battles I want you to feel that my heart supports your heart. You will have arms and ammunition, General Bolívar. . . . You come to open new horizons where to place our hopes as well as our cannons. To help you is to consolidate freedom, it is to reject with one stroke all imported yokes, it is to aggrandize the field of human dignity."

—JEAN F. BRIERRE, *Petión y Bolívar*

The arrival of nearly 10,000 Spanish soldiers in Venezuela in early 1815 spelled disaster for the insurgent forces of northern South America. Commanded by Spanish field marshal Pablo Morillo, the Expeditionary Army—aided by numerous royalist forces that had successfully combated the insurgents—rapidly asserted its presence on Venezuela's and New Granada's soil, inaugurating a four-year period known in Colombian historiography as the Reconquista (the Reconquest). In the months immediately following Morillo's arrival in Carúpano (Venezuela) in March 1815, a series of royalist victories made possible the reestablishment of Spanish authority throughout the Viceroyalty of New Granada. The Reconquista, as historian of the wars of independence and leading Colombian statesman José Manuel Restrepo recalled years later, constituted "so unfortunate an epoch" that "will never be forgotten to those of us who survived" it.[1]

During these years of crisis, the insurgency survived in recondite places of New Granada—the Eastern Llanos being the most famous hideout for *independentistas*—and abroad.[2] Exiled insurgent leaders persecuted by Spanish authorities, "diplomatic" envoys representing nonexistent republics and ephemeral states, and freelance, foreign independence entrepreneurs—also known as pirates, corsairs, privateers, or mercenaries—worked in Jamaica, Haiti, Curaçao, Philadelphia, Baltimore, Galveston, and London to keep the independence struggle alive.[3] Simón Bolívar, up to this point renowned for several military and political failures, was among this wandering crew of adventurers, which Spanish authorities characterized as a "wicked mob."[4]

Like Bolívar, many other Spanish American and European military men who sided with the insurgents, as well as many others who became royalists, traveled to Jamaica and Haiti or communicated with their authorities hoping to enlist their support to continue war on the mainland. Focusing on the Caribbean journey of Simón Bolívar during 1815 and 1816, this chapter reveals the Caribbean and Atlantic dimensions of the independence leader's geopolitical calculations at a time when he had yet to achieve fame and glory. Bolívar's Caribbean journey illustrates how the flow of orders, news, and ideas across imperial and national borders influenced how government authorities, pro-independence émigrés, and royalists in the Caribbean developed their military strategies and conceived their action plans. Bolívar's experience in the Caribbean constitutes an invaluable case study to understand the multiple interests that were at stake in the Caribbean and Atlantic worlds during the Age of Revolutions. Jamaican and Haitian authorities used the conflict between Spain and her colonies as an opportunity to advance their geopolitical interests. Jamaican authorities, adapting the orders from London to the Caribbean setting, pursued a policy of neutrality that aimed at preventing Napoleon's influence from reaching the Americas while maintaining Jamaica's strong commercial ties with northern South America. Haiti's government saw in the eventual establishment of republics in South America an opportunity to further legitimize its own independence and spread the ideals of the Haitian Revolution. Insurgent leaders sought whatever support they could get in the Caribbean islands in order to keep their struggle for independence alive. And Spanish authorities in the Caribbean used all their diplomatic leverage to secure the neutrality of Jamaica and Haiti in Spain's struggle against the insurgents. In Bolívar's specific case his expectations of support and the actual support he obtained shed important light about his way of interpreting and positioning himself in an increasingly racialized world.

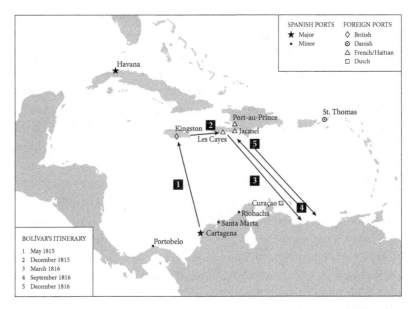

Havana

St. Thomas

Port-au-Prince
Kingston **2** △ △ Jacmel
Les Cayes △
           5

1

3

Curaçao ☐
  • Riohacha **4**
  • Santa Marta
★ Cartagena

Portobelo

BOLÍVAR'S ITINERARY

1 May 1815
2 December 1815
3 March 1816
4 September 1816
5 December 1816

Map 5.1 Simón Bolívar's Caribbean adventures, 1815–1816. In late 1815, after failing to secure support in Jamaica, Bolívar sailed to Haiti, where President Alexandre Pétion offered him guns, vessels, and money to revitalize the struggle and return to Venezuela.

The outline of Simón Bolívar's Caribbean journey is simple (see map 5.1). He arrived in Jamaica in May 1815, after failing to gain support from the independent government of Cartagena to fight royalist forces in Santa Marta. Initially attempting to procure Cartagena's support through peaceful means, Bolívar opted to besiege the city after it became evident that Cartagena's authorities were not willing to contribute the military supplies, men, and provisions his army had requested. The unsuccessful siege forced Bolívar to negotiate his departure from New Granada.[5]

In Jamaica, Bolívar spent the latter half of 1815 attempting to secure diplomatic, financial, military, and logistical support to return to the mainland to fight against the royal troops. Jamaican authorities' strict adherence to the policy of British neutrality, however, made it impossible for him and other Neogranadan and Venezuelan insurgents to obtain anything beyond permission to stay on the island. In December 1815, convinced of the futility of his efforts in Jamaica, Bolívar sailed for Haiti, where President Alexandre Pétion warmly welcomed him.[6] Sponsored by Pétion, Bolívar organized two expeditions to the Venezuelan coast. The first one, in March 1816, failed largely because of Bolívar's inability to secure the allegiance of other military leaders, some of whom regarded him as a traitor to the Venezuelan cause.[7] This debacle forced Bolívar to return to Haiti, where Pétion, once again, supported the Venezuelan's endeavor. In December 1816, three months after his return from Venezuela, Bolívar made his final departure from Haiti. This was the last time Bolívar set foot on any Caribbean island.

Analyzing the confrontation of proindependence insurgents and royalists through the strategies each of these vying parties pursued in their relations with Jamaican and Haitian authorities, this chapter advances the following arguments. First, Pétion's proinsurgent diplomacy and Jamaican authorities' adherence to British neutrality allowed Haiti to emerge as an international revolutionary center actively spreading revolution throughout the Greater Caribbean. Second, the gradual success of British military campaigns against Napoleon and Caribbean-wide fears of the spread of Haitian revolutionary ideals accounted for Jamaican authorities' unwillingness to openly support Spanish American insurgents. Third, guaranteeing British neutrality policy and attempting to hold Pétion to his promise of neutrality required policing and diplomatic pressure from Spanish officials in New Granada, Venezuela, and the Spanish Caribbean islands. Finally, a combination of news about developments in Europe, personal fears of the Haitian Revolution, and Enlightenment ideas about race and civilization informed Bolívar's action plan and expectations for support during his Caribbean journey. Additionally, my analysis of Bolívar's Caribbean adventures, especially the Haitian part of his Caribbean journey, contributes to the recent calls and ongoing efforts to explore the history of postrevolutionary Haiti and the role this self-identified "empire of liberty" played in the political debates of the nineteenth-century Atlantic and in the lives of slaves, revolutionaries, state makers, and other denizens of this fluid and tumultuous world.[8]

The chapter is organized in four sections. The first one presents the Atlantic and Caribbean settings for the international campaigns of Bolívar and many other Venezuelan and Neogranadan émigrés. The second and third sections tackle Bolívar's activities in Jamaica and Haiti, explaining for both cases what Bolívar expected to get and what he actually achieved on both islands. These two sections elaborate on the effectiveness of Bolívar's Caribbean campaign, explaining the reasons of Jamaican authorities to refrain from supporting the insurgents and the rationale behind Haiti's support of numerous insurgent leaders. The final section explains the political and ideological foundations of Bolívar's expectations.

European Warfare and the Western Question

During the first fifteen years of the nineteenth century, Napoleon Bonaparte dominated European battlefields and the political arena of the Atlantic world. Diplomatic relations during the Napoleonic Wars were defined according to a government's stance regarding Napoleon. With all of Europe threatened by Napoleonic invasion, European crowns were either with or against Napoleon. During the first half of the Napoleonic Wars (1799–1808), the system of alliances that confronted the European powers with stronger interests in the Americas resembled that of most eighteenth-century wars: Spain and France were allies against Britain and Portugal. Napoleon's invasion of Spain in 1808 forced Spain into an uncommon alliance with Britain against France, the now-common enemy. Throughout the war, the rivalry over access to Spain's American dominions represented a key point of contention among vying powers. This rivalry over Spanish America, which Rafe Blaufarb has called the "Western Question," greatly influenced the decisions of British, French, and Spanish diplomats.[9] In Spanish America, both royalists and supporters of independence also based their diplomatic and military strategies on their interpretations of the direction of European warfare and the Western Question.

Until 1808 the permanent rivalry between Britain and the Bourbon monarchies of France and Spain made European geopolitics predictable. Framed by a long history of British incursions in Spanish American territories dating back to the sixteenth century, the animosity between the Spanish and British crowns grew exponentially throughout the eighteenth century. After the end of the War of Spanish Succession in 1713, Spanish and British forces faced off in at least four major wars before Napoleon's invasion of the Spanish Peninsula. The balance of the wars generally favored Britain. With the exception of the American Revolutionary War, the course of the wars and the postwar peace treaties resulted in territorial gains for Britain. France and Spain, in contrast, usually paid the price of defeat through the loss of territories and the obligation to grant Britain unwanted commercial concessions.

Defeat in the American Revolutionary War left British authorities sour and generated a new wave of plans to attack Spain's American territories.[10] Adding to the centuries-old strategy of hit, plunder, and run, the Anglo-Spanish War of 1796–1808 included failed and successful British attempts to occupy Spanish territories—Menorca, Trinidad, Puerto Rico, Buenos Aires, and Montevideo—and the drafting of numerous plans to attack Mexico, Venezuela, Buenos Aires, Valdivia, Nicaragua, and other Spanish American posses-sions.[11] The 1796–1808 war also included a humiliating naval blockade that effectively cut communications between Spain and Spanish America and, in 1805, the defeat of the Spanish navy at Trafalgar. In addition, toward the end of the war, a new strategy to tap the riches of Spanish America was gaining strength among top British officials. In February 1808, navy general Arthur Wellesley articulated the new strategy that would have British forces "enter Latin Amer-ica as liberators," thus signaling the abandonment of the idea of taking over as a conquering force.[12] Wellesley declared, "I am convinced, . . . that any attempt to conquer [Spanish American territories] with a view to their future subjec-tion to the British Crown, would certainly fail; and therefore I consider the only mode in which they can be wrested from the Crown of Spain is by a revolution and by the establishment of an independent government within them."[13] Based on the long history of hostilities between Spain and Britain, much of which had taken place in Spanish America, the success of the new British strategy was far from guaranteed. While a history of friendly, though not always legal, Anglo-Spanish commercial exchanges in the Caribbean supported the prospects for British success, a similarly long history of Anglo-Spanish confrontation raised important doubts.[14] In any case, the advance of Napoleon's armies in Europe prevented the new British strategy from being tested.

In fact, in mid-1808, just as Arthur Wellesley was getting ready to sail for the West Indies to test the new strategy, Napoleon's invasion of the Spanish Peninsula forced a dramatic shift in Europe's system of alliances and in Britain's policy toward Spanish America.[15] In less than two months, the British govern-ment abandoned the strategy of promoting independence in Spanish America and embraced its new unlikely ally. A formal proclamation of peace with Spain (July 4, 1808) and a treaty of peace, friendship, and alliance (January 14, 1809) inaugurated a new era in Anglo-Spanish diplomatic relations: alliance against Napoleon in Europe with Britain offering military aid to Spain in ousting the French enemy and British neutrality in Spain's American affairs.[16] Forced to choose between the lesser of two evils, both the British government and the Spanish resistance government favored alliance with their traditional enemy against the invading Napoleon.

In Spain, Napoleon's invasion and the appointment of his brother Joseph Bonaparte as new king of Spain and, by extension, Spanish America resulted in a spontaneous, popular reaction against the invading French forces. While the Spanish authorities, the nobility, and the clergy accepted Joseph Bonaparte as their new king, the Spanish people rejected the authority of the usurper.[17]

Initial resistance against Napoleon has been characterized as "centrifugal." Individual provinces established their own juntas to lead the resistance at a local level. The need to organize a joint resistance led to the creation, in September 1808, of the Junta Suprema Central y Gubernativa de España e Indias (Supreme Central Governing Committee of Spain and the Indies).[18] The advance of Napoleon's troops forced the junta's retreat to Cádiz where the British navy offered it protection from the French. There, the junta appointed a Council of Regency to govern Spain. As its last act before dissolving itself and handling power to the council, the junta ordered the regency to convene a national assembly—the Cortes.[19] The Cortes ruled Spain (and the Spanish American territories that recognized its authority) from September 1810 to May 1814, when Fernando VII returned to power. The joint Anglo-Spanish resistance resulted in the expulsion of the French during the rule of the Cortes and enabled Fernando VII's return. Upon returning to power, Fernando VII abolished the Cortes and the Cádiz Constitution and convicted many liberal constitutionalists. In a word, after reclaiming authority Fernando VII restored absolutism, eliminating most of the accomplishments of what Jaime Rodríguez has called "the political revolution" of the Spanish world.[20] One thing the restored king managed to maintain was the British promise of neutrality in the conflict between Spain and its colonies, which at this point—especially in northern South America—was increasingly turning into a war for independence from Spain.

In the Americas, the Napoleonic invasion of Spain and the consequent Anglo-Spanish alliance decisively influenced the course of events and framed the political options of Spanish Americans. Just as it did in Spain, the initial reaction in Spanish America resulted in the creation of provincial juntas that rushed to express their support for the abducted Fernando VII.[21] In response to these acts of "heroic loyalty and patriotism," the Junta Suprema Central Gubernativa del Reino, considering that "the kingdoms, provinces and islands [of America] should ... constitute part of the Kingdom's Central Government Junta," invited "the viceroyalties of New Spain, Peru, New Kingdom of Granada and Buenos Aires, and the independent captaincy generals of the island of Cuba, Puerto Rico, Guatemala, Chile, ... Venezuela, and the Philippines to appoint one individual each" to represent their respective districts in the Junta Central.[22] Accepting this invitation (and a subsequent one to send representatives to the Cortes in Cádiz), some provinces elected and sent representatives to Spain. While representation was certainly a political revolution, the distribution of seats in both the Junta Suprema and the Cortes was unequal and, in the minds of some Spanish Americans, simply unfair. The problem of unequal representation led some sectors of Spanish America to reject the authority of Spain's temporary government.[23] As Napoleon's troops completed their conquest of the Spanish Peninsula, a growing sense "of the irreversibility of the Napoleonic action in Europe" led some Spanish American provinces to start favoring independence.[24] In northern South America, the emergence of strong parties embracing the cause of independence turned the political revolution into military conflict pitting royalists against insurgent forces. Internal disagreements within the insurgent forces regarding the nature of the government they were to establish also resulted in conflicts among those who favored independence. In the words of historian Anthony McFarlane, "The opposition of royalist and patriot regions was only one manifestation of the divisions that sundered New Granada after 1810; it was paralleled by competition and conflict among the patriot regions themselves."[25]

The proximity of northern South America's provinces to Jamaica and the vital role of the Anglo-Spanish alliance in the peninsular resistance against Napoleon turned Jamaica into a key political arena of the struggle for independence in the circum-Caribbean. As administrators of Britain's most important Caribbean colony, Jamaican authorities received the task of maintaining the Anglo-Spanish alliance in Spanish America. With the emergence in Venezuela and New Granada of groups that favored independence from Spain, the task of Jamaican authorities became increasingly complicated. Since Napoleon had, as early as 1809, expressed his support for the independence of Spanish America, Jamaican authorities faced a difficult dilemma: how to preserve their neutrality—something that South American royalists would appreciate—and simultaneously prevent Spanish American insurgents from swinging toward Napoleon's sphere of influence.[26] In an attempt to minimize the resentment of both royalists and insurgents from South America and in the process continue to harvest the benefits of trade with South America's Caribbean ports, Jamaican authorities adopted the practice of allowing both royalist and insurgent vessels and individuals to conduct private business on the island. At the same time, the island's authorities proposed to offer their services as mediators between the vying parties.[27] In 1812, for instance, Jamaica's vice admiral Charles Stirling offered his mediation in a peace settlement between Cartagena's independent government and New Granada's viceroy. The meeting he facilitated between Viceroy Benito Pérez and Cartagena's representatives, José María del Real and Germán Piñeres, did not result in any agreement.[28] Soon after, Fernando VII's return to the throne in 1814 made Spanish authorities less tolerant of British neutrality in the Caribbean and more capable, now that Napoleon was out of the peninsula, to press for British support. Spanish diplomatic pressure on Jamaica to adhere to the promise of British neutrality constituted one of the major tasks of field marshal Pablo Morillo during the Spanish Reconquista of northern South America.

During the second decade of the nineteenth century, Jamaican politics were not exclusively centered on the British-Spanish alliance and the island's neutrality in the Spanish American conflict. The island's economic decline—felt since the American Revolution first restricted Jamaica's trade with the United States and increasing after Britain abolished the slave trade in 1807—occupied center stage in the preoccupations of colonial authorities and the community of merchants and planters.[29] In this context of economic decline, the opportunity to trade with the vying parties in northern South America constituted a very welcome respite for Jamaica's merchant population.[30] Beyond economic matters, Jamaica's elites also lived in perpetual fear of the spread of the Haitian Revolution to the British island.[31]

Just one hundred miles east of Jamaica, Haiti was as well located as Jamaica to play a vital role in events in northern South America. Haiti's recent successful revolution made it the second republic of the Americas and the first black-led republic in the whole world. By 1815, however, internal confrontations and international pressures made the future of Haiti unpredictable. Internally divided into two political entities—Henry Christophe's northern kingdom and the southern republic ruled by Alexandre Pétion—Haiti was struggling to organize its postindependence economy and secure its sustainability as an independent state.[32] Internationally perceived as a revolutionary threat, Haiti's independent governments—from Dessalines's to Pétion's—took pains to convince western powers that exporting revolution was out of the question. The crisis in northern South America tested Pétion's international commitments and put him at the center of the struggle for independence in northern South America.

With the arrival of Pablo Morillo's Expeditionary Army in Venezuela, Jamaica and Haiti started to receive Venezuelan and Neogranadan émigrés en masse. Thousands of insurgents forced to flee their homelands in northern South America sought in Jamaica and Haiti refuge and support to continue their struggle against royalist forces.[33] Along with many other military men who—like him—eventually became founding fathers of Colombia and Venezuela, Simón Bolívar left South America to secure whatever help he could in the Caribbean. There he was joined by many other European and American adventurers who gathered in the Caribbean expecting to participate in expeditions that targeted Spanish America's circum-Caribbean territories.

"The Strictest Neutrality"

On May 14, 1815, the day he arrived in Jamaica, Bolívar was still years away from achieving fame and glory. His military successes so far had been few, and his recent campaign in New Granada had ended with a dramatic failure that greatly damaged the reputation he had managed to build up. As John Lombardi noted, in 1815 "Simón Bolívar was still little more than a brilliant, ambitious South American general whose short military and political career had been characterized by an erratic record of brilliant successes and dramatic failures."[34] Militarily degraded, unemployed, and financially broke, Bolívar arrived in Jamaica determined to risk the last remains of his meager political capital in the venture of reconstituting the remnants of the independence party.

Convinced after a series of failed attempts that independence could only be obtained with the support of a foreign power, Bolívar set out to secure British support. Britain, Bolívar argued, was called to become "the savior of [Spanish] America."[35] His effort in Jamaica, therefore, centered on convincing British authorities of the benefits that Great Britain could obtain from abandoning its alliance with Spain and openly supporting the independence of Spanish America. His endeavor's success, Bolívar believed, was almost guaranteed. Spain's participation in the American Revolutionary War as an ally of the patriots and the gradual weakening of Napoleon's power increased Bolívar's confidence in his ability to secure British support. To imbue his effort with a sense of urgency, Bolívar concluded one of his first letters in dramatic fashion, claiming that should Great Britain not offer its immediate support to the South American insurgents, "this vast hemisphere" could "succumb or exterminate itself" before "England turn[ed] its view towards America."[36]

Despite this apocalyptic warning, Bolívar's early days in Jamaica were filled with optimism about the future of the revolution and his ability to secure British support, even if this required him to travel to London.[37] Already familiar with a number of British merchants based in Jamaica, Bolívar hoped to use his social network to reach and convince British authorities in Jamaica (Jamaica's governor and the admiral of the British West Indies) and London (Britain's foreign secretary, secretary of state for war and the colonies, and prime minister). Within days of his arrival, Bolívar sent letters to merchant Maxwell Hyslop and former foreign secretary and British ambassador to Spain Richard Wellesley informing them of his intentions. To Manuel Rodríguez Torices, then president of the United Provinces of New Granada, he wrote in late May that the only reason stopping Great Britain from "protecting" the Spanish American colonies was "the elevation of Bonaparte, for the second time, to the French throne."[38] In mid-July, probably before knowing of Napoleon's defeat at Waterloo, a still-hopeful Bolívar expressed confidence in his ability to obtain British support "if not today, tomorrow or [some] other day."[39] By September, as evidenced in a series of letters he submitted to the editor of the *Royal Gazette*, Bolívar's optimism had turned into frustration.[40] His famous Jamaica Letter—written on September 6, 1815, but first published in English in 1818 (and in Spanish only in the 1830s)—contains the best expression of this frustration. In it, Bolívar complains, "We were justified in expecting all civilized nations to rush to our aid, helping us achieve a goal whose advantages are mutual to both hemispheres. Never were reasonable hopes so frustrated! Not only the Europeans but even our brothers to the north stood apart as idle spectators of this struggle, which is in essence the most just and in outcome the most beautiful and important of any ever undertaken in ancient or modern times."[41]

Similarly, in another letter to the editor written and published in late September, Bolívar protested, "We were abandoned by the whole world, no foreign nation has guided us with its wisdom and experience, or defended us with its weapons, or protected us with its resources."[42] Frustration with Britain's unwillingness to support his endeavor, coupled with his lack of financial resources and threats to his life, led him to abandon Jamaica in December 1815 and continue his mission in Haiti.[43]

British authorities' refusal to provide official help to Bolívar was grounded in the British-Spanish alliance sealed shortly after Napoleon's army entered the Spanish Peninsula in 1808. This alliance and the consequent British neutrality in Spanish American affairs were essential features of British policy toward Spanish America during the Napoleonic Wars.[44] Bolívar was not the first South American insurgent leader to experience the negative consequences of British neutrality. Two years before Bolívar's arrival in Kingston, Jamaican authorities had made known to two representatives of the independent government of Cartagena, Ignacio Cavero and John Robertson, the British government's intention not to "interfere in the conflict between the [Spanish] colonies and the mother land."[45] Bolívar, however, was the first *independentista* to be denied British support after Napoleon's final defeat. His Jamaican experience suggests that neutrality continued to be an important feature of British policy, strictly enforced by British authorities in the Caribbean, even after Napoleon's final defeat at Waterloo. British neutrality, it seems, was based on more than just fear of Napoleon's European and overseas expansion. To Bolívar's argument that after Napoleon's defeat there were no reasons for Britain not to support the independence cause, British actions answered that there were no reasons to support it either.

Before Napoleon's defeat, the British-Spanish alliance rested on the need to contain Napoleon's European and overseas expansion. Between 1811 and 1813, when Napoleon seemed uncontainable, British authorities and the Spanish provisional government feared Spanish American insurgents could obtain French support for their fight against Spain. Insurgent leaders had already taken steps in this direction when, in October 1812, they sent a diplomatic mission to the United States and France. The mission's leader, Venezuelan Manuel Palacio Fajardo, was charged with obtaining French support for the insurgent cause in New Granada.[46] The possibility of an alliance between Napoleon's empire and the South American insurgents presented Great Britain with a complicated dilemma: how to maintain its alliance with Spain and simultaneously discourage diplomatic approaches between France and northern South America's insurgents.

The solution, it has been argued, was to "prevent French penetration through a certain support to the independence movement."[47] This line of argument stresses the support that South American insurgents, especially from Cartagena, obtained from Jamaica. The argument, however, does not take into account that New Granada's royalists were as active as insurgents in their attempts to secure "the favors of Jamaica."[48]

Throughout the 1810s, both contending parties sent emissaries to Jamaica to obtain official and private support for their causes. In 1812, Viceroy Benito Pérez sent Pablo Arosemena to urge Jamaican authorities to prohibit insurgents from coming to the island and buying guns and ammunition. In 1813 and again in 1815, the insurgent government of Cartagena sent Ignacio Cavero to obtain weapons and secure aid to force Spain to lift Cartagena's commercial blockade. While both parties were able to obtain aid from merchants—who sold them weapons and provided vital loans—neither party received official endorsements from Jamaican authorities.[49] The private support offered by Kingston's merchant community did not decisively incline the balance in favor of any party.

Jamaican authorities, far from saying that they supported one party or the other, claimed that they were actually encouraging the commercial interests of the island's merchant community. Since some merchants traded with royalists and others negotiated with insurgents, support of trade with both parties allowed Jamaican authorities to maintain their neutrality while furthering Britain's commercial interest and wealth. Vice Admiral Stirling, in a letter to Viceroy Benito Pérez, clearly presented the position of Jamaican authorities during the Napoleonic Wars. According to Stirling, "The trade that is done by [Jamaican] merchants with different ports of Spanish America, whether belonging to the monarchy, or the opposite party, seems to deserve protection, so that Britain can feed its treasury and continue the war against the common enemy."[50] The support of Jamaican authorities to both royalists and insurgents was limited to allowing them to visit the island without interfering in their private transactions with Jamaica's merchants. This laissez-faire attitude allowed Britain to concentrate on European events while not completely alienating the contending parties in the circum-Caribbean.

Napoleon's defeat erased the possibility of an alliance between the South American insurgents and the Napoleonic Empire. The elimination of the Napoleonic threat meant, on the one hand, that Bolívar and the insurgent leaders of South America could no longer bribe Britain by cautiously threatening to side with France. On the other hand, with Napoleon out of the picture, it was apparent that the British and Spanish crowns no longer had reasons to maintain their alliance. The question for British authorities was, Should they sustain the Anglo-Spanish alliance or support Spanish America's independence from Spain? The latter scenario was the one Bolívar was betting on after his arrival in Jamaica. In his opinion, this was the time for Spanish America "to be looked upon with interest by England."[51] Facing the imminent threat of Morillo's reconquering troops, the authorities of the independent government of Cartagena reached a similar conclusion. In an emergency session organized on October 13, 1815, Cartagena's assembly members "unanimously agreed" to place Cartagena "under the protection and direction of the King of Great Britain."[52] After agreeing on their course of action, Cartagena's assembly members instructed their governor, Juan de Dios Amador, to ask Admiral Douglas—the head of the British West Indies fleet—to accept Cartagena's incorporation into the British Empire.[53] Cartagena's petition and Bolívar's plea, as an editorial in the *Royal Gazette and Bahama Advertiser* published in March 1816 indicates, convinced some merchants and a sector of the British public. In addition to including a transcription of Cartagena's petition, the editorial provided the following advice to the British government: "The more you examine the issue in all its aspects, the more this measure should be approved by all friends of humanity and all friends of mercantile advantages and England's prosperity. Do not refuse an offer that no other European power would stop accepting. . . . If this opportunity is lost, there will never be another. Let it be lost and Europe will laugh at your folly."[54]

The British government chose to let Europe laugh at its folly. Expressing the confusion that Britain's negative reply generated among South American insurgents, Bolívar wondered why "Great Britain has not used reprisals against that same Spain that waged war against [the British government] to deprive it of its colonies."[55] Not rushing to help the insurgents, the British government effectively smashed the two pillars of Bolívar's geopolitical calculations: first, that Britain would help the insurgents as payback for Spain's support of the patriots during the American Revolutionary War; and, second, that British support for the insurgency was only being temporarily withheld until Napoleon's defeat. Unfortunately for the South American insurgents, over twenty years of almost continuous warfare had left British authorities and a large sector of the British public exhausted.[56] Spanish diplomatic efforts and the negative connotations that Jamaican authorities attached to a revolution in Spanish America, added to Britain's desire for peace, the potential spread of republicanism to its remaining American colonies, and the commercial benefits Britain hoped to derive from maintaining its alliance with Spain, explain why Bolívar's geopolitical calculations went wrong.[57]

Even before Bolívar's arrival in Jamaica, Spanish military commander Pablo Morillo had launched a diplomatic effort to ensure that British authorities in the Caribbean would either remain neutral or openly collaborate with Spain. Among the first letters Morillo wrote after landing in Venezuela were several missives to the governors of Trinidad, Jamaica, Saint Thomas, and Saint Barthelemy (the last two then under British control) and to Admiral Douglas, the commander in chief of the British Leeward Islands. In these letters, Morillo requested that the British Caribbean authorities "dispatch to him the fugitives of Spanish America," take "timely measures so that no ship brings weapons and ammunition to any coastal point or port" in Spanish America, and, more generally, uphold "the loyalty England has shown to Spain."[58] A central idea in Morillo's correspondence is his interest in convincing British Caribbean authorities that "the independence of the Spanish Main . . . would drag the English [Caribbean] islands to perdition." In his opinion, "the subversive ideas" espoused by South American insurgents seeking refuge in the Caribbean islands could spread beyond Spanish America and contaminate the British Caribbean colonies.[59] These warnings, directed at colonial authorities permanently concerned with the threat of black rebellion, did not fall on deaf ears.

Morillo's correspondence also reveals his appreciation for how the governor of Trinidad, Ralph Woodford, was upholding British neutrality. As for the British authorities of Jamaica, Morillo was less confident that they were doing everything they could to prevent the South American insurgents from using Jamaica as a base for operations. Instead of "policing [the insurgents] and preventing them from perturbing the Spanish possessions," Morillo believed that Jamaican authorities and a sector of the island's population "were aiding them to pursue their detestable plans." Of particular concern to Morillo were the merchants of Kingston, who, he believed, were "supply[ing the insurgents] with weapons, ships, and foodstuffs."[60]

Morillo's repeated complaints of the alleged collaboration between Jamaican authorities and South American insurgents convinced British authorities to order an investigation to establish the extent to which Jamaica's authorities and its inhabitants were participating in the conflict between Spain and its Spanish American territories. The reassurances of Jamaica's governor about how he had "invariably observed the strictest neutrality and avoided all interference between the contending parties in the South American provinces" did not convince Morillo, nor were they completely accepted by Earl Bathurst, the British secretary of war and the colonies.[61] After a formal request by Morillo's second in command, Pascual Enrile, the British government formed a committee to investigate the matter properly.[62]

The committee, "appointed to inquire what protection has been afforded to the commerce of this island," interrogated nearly thirty individuals including a number of merchants, royal officers, and foreigners visiting or residing in Jamaica.[63] Central to the committee's investigation was to establish the degree to which the South American revolutionaries had been and continued to be "assisted or supplied from this island either with money or arms."[64] In particular, the committee members expressed an interest in determining if Simón "Bolívar [had] received any support . . . from any individuals in this country."[65] Additionally, the questionnaires reveal a concern with the existence of a plan—coauthored by Pétion and Bolívar—"to liberate all the slaves in the Spanish dominions of South America" and "establishing a Black Empire in Venezuela."[66]

On the matter of whether Bolívar had been assisted during his stay in Jamaica, the committee established with relative ease that some merchants engaged in the trade with Cartagena—most notably the brothers Maxwell and Wellwood Hyslop—had provided financial and logistical support to the South American revolutionaries. This finding required no major effort from the committee, since Wellwood Hyslop himself admitted during his interrogation that he had "supplied [the insurgents] with money [and] ammunition."[67] Hyslop, who was in Cartagena when Morillo captured the city in December 1815, had personal reasons to support Bolívar. After being "thrown in the prison of the Inquisition" in Cartagena, where he was condemned to death, Hyslop "was miraculously saved" by the intervention of Admiral Douglas and London-based British authorities.[68] Hyslop's support for Bolívar and any other Spanish American insurgents was, therefore, hardly surprising. The impact of this support, the committee concluded based on other testimony, was very limited, merely allowing Bolívar "to go to Aux Cayes" (Haiti) or, more simply, enabling "him to go off."[69] Taking into consideration these other testimonies, the British prime minister closed the file, concluding, "It does not appear clear by this report that Bolívar did receive any considerable assistance from Jamaica," with the exception, perhaps, of that coming "from individuals."[70] As far as the committee was concerned, Jamaican authorities had succeeded in upholding British neutrality.

The alleged collaboration between Pétion and Bolívar to spread revolution and the conviction that such collaboration could "compromise the safety of the [British] colonies in the West Indies" also occupied center stage in the committee's examinations.[71] In particular, the belief that Bolívar, aided by Pétion, was attempting to establish a black empire haunted the minds of committee members. More enlightening about British fears than about Bolívar's plans, this haunting belief, nonetheless, sheds light on the reasons behind British authorities' ultimate decision to remain neutral. The rumors about the plans of Pétion and Bolívar, coupled with information about the presence of "very dangerous characters" from Haiti in Jamaica, unearthed one of the most ingrained fears of colonial authorities all over the Caribbean: the potential spread of the Haitian Revolution.[72] Part paranoia and part well-grounded, lingering fears of a spread of the ideals of the Haitian Revolution throughout the Caribbean ultimately upheld Jamaican authorities in their commitment "to discourage and frustrate any attempts which may be made here to promote the views of the [South American] insurgents."[73]

In the final analysis, as the committee rightfully concluded, Bolívar was only able to obtain aid from individual merchants. While Bolívar's propaganda campaign was good enough to secure him some "assistance from individuals in Jamaica," the Spanish diplomatic effort ultimately succeeded in sustaining Jamaican authorities in their neutrality policy. Morillo's argument about the disastrous consequences that the independence of the Spanish Main could entail for the British Caribbean islands, coupled with the information about Haitian support to the South American insurgents, brought to the surface fears of the possibility of a revolution along Haitian lines. Persistent fears of "another Haiti" or of a "Black Empire in Venezuela" were sufficient reasons for Jamaican authorities to keep Bolívar and other South American insurgents at bay.

As is often the case, the official conclusion, coming two years after Bolívar's initial attempts to obtain British support in Kingston, only reasserted what incumbents in Jamaica, including Bolívar, had experienced on the island. By the time British authorities reached their conclusion, Bolívar, long aware of his failure to obtain British support for his cause, had already departed for Haiti. There, under Pétion's auspices, Bolívar and other Spanish American insurgents and foreign adventurers were able to relaunch the struggle against royalist forces.

"The Receptacle of All the Adventurers"

Upon arriving in Haiti on December 24, 1815, Bolívar's prospects changed dramatically. Even before leaving Jamaica, he had good reasons to believe that in Haiti he was going to get the financial and logistical support Jamaican authorities had denied him. The presence in Haiti of many other South American and European supporters of Spanish America's independence presaged an improvement of Bolívar's prospects.[74] A mere week after arriving in Les Cayes, Bolívar paid a first visit to President Alexandre Pétion. After meeting Pétion, Bolívar declared that he "expected a lot from [Pétion's] love of liberty and justice."[75] Future visits and letters exchanged between Bolívar in Les Cayes and Pétion in Port-au-Prince strengthened the alliance between the two leaders, clarified the type of aid Pétion was going to offer, and ultimately made possible the preparation and departure, on March 31, 1816, of Bolívar's first expedition from Haiti to Venezuela. Characterized by an initial success followed by dramatic defeats in eastern Venezuela, this so-called Expedition from Les Cayes concluded with Bolívar's return to Haiti in September 1816, once again asking for Pétion's support.[76] Pétion's commitment to Spanish America's independence, instead of decreasing with Bolívar's recent failure, seemed to become stronger. Reaffirming his commitment to the insurgents' cause, Pétion consoled a defeated Bolívar by telling him, "If the inconstant fortune has deceived your hopes for a second time, in the third occasion it can be favorable; I, at least, have that presentiment."[77] Three months later, on December 18, 1816, Bolívar set sail from the port of Jacmel to continue his fight for independence. This time, he left Haiti never to come back.

Bolívar was not the only Spanish American insurgent who found support in Haiti; neither were his two expeditions to the Spanish Main the only ones organized in that Caribbean island. Between 1815 and 1817, as two French commissioners dispatched by Louis XVIII to negotiate with Pétion commented, the island of Haiti and especially its capital Port-au-Prince had become "the receptacle of all the adventurers who actively threaten[ed] the possessions of His [Spanish] Catholic Majesty."[78] Around 200 advocates of Spanish American independence from both sides of the Atlantic, including Louis Brion (Bolívar's closest foreign commander), Francisco Xavier Mina, Gregor MacGregor, Pedro Briceño, Carlos Soublette, Mariano Montilla, Francisco Bermúdez, Francisco Antonio Zea, Manuel Piar, Louis Aury, Santiago Mariño, H. L. V. Ducoudray-Holstein, and the brothers Gabriel and Germán Gutiérrez de Piñeres and Miguel and Fernando Carabaño, walked the streets of Les Cayes and Port-au-Prince, giving Haitian cities an unexpected cosmopolitan character.[79]

Benefiting from Pétion's financial, military, and logistical aid, several of these proindependence émigrés used Haiti to organize and launch expeditions to different parts of Spain's crumbling empire (see map 5.2). In late 1815, for instance, the Carabaño brothers sailed from Haiti to the Atrato River, in western New Granada, in a failed attempt to retake New Granada using the Pacific province of Chocó as base of operations.[80] In mid-1816, French corsair Louis Aury, after breaking off relations with Bolívar as a result of a meeting in which émigrés elected Bolívar as their absolute leader, assembled in Haiti an expedition to Galveston.[81] Spanish liberal Francisco Xavier Mina, one of the less-known heroes of Mexican independence, spent about two weeks in Port-au-Prince, in October 1816, repairing his ships and recruiting volunteers to continue his expedition to Mexico. With four ships and an unspecified number of soldiers (of which 270 actually made it to Mexico), Mina sailed from Port-au-Prince to the Mexican island of San Luis (by the Texas coast, southwest of Galveston) on October 24, 1816.[82] And Scotsman Gregor MacGregor used Haiti as a base to organize his expeditions to Amelia Island (in 1817), Portobelo (in 1818), and Riohacha (in 1819).[83]

Orchestrated by Pétion from the presidential office in Port-au-Prince, Haiti's aid was actually delivered through orders executed by Pétion's subalterns. Presidential secretary Inginac and the governor of Les Cayes, General Marion, dealt with the insurgents on a daily basis. In Les Cayes, for example,

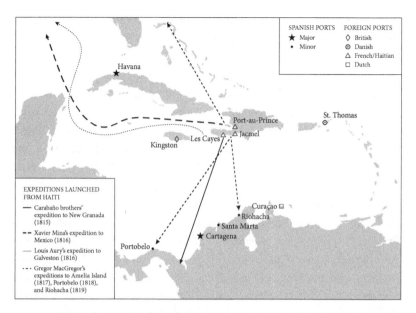

Map within figure:

SPANISH PORTS
★ Major
• Minor

FOREIGN PORTS
◇ British
⊙ Danish
△ French/Haitian
□ Dutch

Havana

Port-au-Prince

St. Thomas

Les Cayes   Jacmel

Kingston

EXPEDITIONS LAUNCHED
FROM HAITI

— Carabaño brothers'
expedition to New Granada
(1815)

-- Xavier Mina's expedition to
Mexico (1816)

···· Louis Aury's expedition to
Galveston (1816)

--- Gregor MacGregor's
expeditions to Amelia Island
(1817), Portobelo (1818),
and Riohacha (1819)

Curaçao □
Riohacha
Santa Marta
★ Cartagena

Portobelo

Map 5.2 Haiti as international revolutionary center. Despite Pétion's commitment not to export revolution, under his auspices Haiti functioned as a meeting ground where adventurers organized expeditions to spread revolution through Spanish America.

Governor Marion's duties included organizing the distribution of humanitarian aid to Spanish American refugees, mediating power disputes among the insurgents, and keeping the population safe from drunken and unoccupied military men.[84] Besides Pétion and his governmental subalterns, the other key figure in the Haitian government's plan to aid the South American insurgents was the English merchant Robert Sutherland. A resident of Port-au-Prince since the first years of the nineteenth century, Sutherland has been called Pétion's "official figurehead" for the Haitian government's supply of arms and ammunition to the insurgents.[85] Bolívar's correspondence during his residence in Haiti, including a series of letters asking Sutherland for money or informing him of a debt recently acquired with his backing, demonstrates the extent to which Sutherland's support made insurgent expeditions possible.[86] Acknowledging Sutherland's decisive role, Bolívar wrote the English merchant a thank-you note, stating, "Without you, dear friend, my expedition would have been something very insignificant. Without you, I'm afraid we would not have been able to sail, because without money nothing can be done, even if you possess everything else."[87]

In Sutherland's house, Bolívar and Mina met to discuss details of Mina's imminent expedition to Mexico. The meeting, on October 13, 1816, shortly after Bolívar's return from his failed expedition to Venezuela and barely a day after Mina's arrival in Haiti, had a significant impact on Bolívar. As he told his friend Louis Brion, after the meeting, Bolívar considered "changing his plans" and joining Mina's expedition.[88] The hospitality and unconditional support of Sutherland, whose house in Port-au-Prince a historian characterized as an "arsenal of freedom," constituted fundamental elements in the resurgence of those fighting for the independence of the Spanish territories in the Caribbean basin.[89]

The characterization of Haiti as a "receptacle" of insurgents should be taken with a grain of salt. Besides conveying the image of an island replete with rebels fighting for independence, this characterization also implies a certain unity among those rebels. In reality, divisions plagued the Haitian exile of South American insurgents, and rivalries inherited from previous disputes in the Spanish Main reemerged alongside new intrainsurgent conflicts created during their Haitian exile. Conflict among insurgent factions, Clément Thibaud asserts, pointing to the teleological tendency to see Bolívar as predestined to be the liberator, might have ended in Bolívar "not being designated as military head."[90] In fact, several personal confrontations involving Bolívar and former and future allies and rivals might well have ended in Bolívar's death.[91] Most importantly, divisions regarding Bolívar's legitimate authority, stemming from the fact that while in Haiti he was no more than a defeated military leader, frequently threatened to destroy Bolívar's liberation project.

The best-documented confrontation among insurgents is that between Bolívar and Louis Aury on the issue of recognizing Bolívar's authority as the principal leader of the rebels in exile. While most émigrés ended up supporting Bolívar, Aury remained firm in his opposition and did not participate in the expeditions from Haiti to northern South America. Ducoudray-Holstein describes a meeting of "all the principal patriots, who had emigrated, and were then [in 1816] at Aux Cayes." At the meeting, attended by "Brion, Piar, Marino [sic] McGregor, Bermudes, myself [Ducoudray-Holstein], the brethern Pineres [sic], the intendant Zea, the commodore Aury[,] . . . it was decided . . . that General Bolivar . . . should unite in himself the civil and military authorities until the convocation of a congress." Aury, Ducoudray-Holstein asserts, was the only one who "opposed to giving Bolivar unlimited power. . . . From that time Bolivar was very angry with Aury; and that resentment lasted until the death of the latter."[92] Contributing to securing the almost unanimous support of the émigrés was Bolívar's ability to win Pétion's favor. Pétion's backing ultimately allowed Bolívar to emerge as the leader among a group of military commanders with similar ambitions to lead the independence struggle.

While Pétion's commitment to Spanish America's independence emerges clearly in his correspondence with Bolívar, an explanation of Haiti's proinsurgent diplomacy requires an analysis of Pétion's actions within a broader geographical framework that takes into account Haiti's recent historical trajectory. Pétion's support for the insurgents resulted from his careful geopolitical calculations based on Haiti's current needs and recent past. In other words, Pétion's willingness to aid those fighting for independence would not have been realized without Jamaican authorities' attachment to the British policy of neutrality explained in the previous section.

One of Pétion's top priorities during the 1810s was to further legitimize the Republic of Haiti in the international arena. Without diplomatic recognition, the future of Haiti as an independent republic was at risk. While commercial agreements allowing Haiti to sell its sugar and coffee to Britain and the United States provided much-needed economic respite and some level of international legitimacy, no republic or monarchy was ready to offer Haiti formal diplomatic recognition.[93] Seeing in the spread of republicanism a potential way of strengthening the future of his country, Pétion found it was in Haiti's interest to support Spanish America's independence. Simply put, the more republics emerged in the Americas, the stronger the case for republicanism as the best political path and the weaker the argument for continued monarchical rule. The fact that Haiti was not merely a republic but a black republic whose president was more than sympathetic to the abolition of slavery, however, took away part of the international appeal of Pétion's bid for republicanism. Aware of the dangers that exporting revolution and abolitionism could entail for Haiti, Pétion observed great discretion regarding his aid to the South American insurgents. His support, he reminded Bolívar shortly before the departure of the Expedition from Les Cayes, rested on two conditions related to the "reserves" he considered necessary "with a nation [Spain] that has not yet pronounced itself in an offensive manner against the [Haitian] Republic." First, he expected Bolívar to abolish slavery in Venezuela and all the other territories to be liberated. Second, Pétion told Bolívar "not to proclaim anything" in the name of Haiti and not "to mention my [Pétion's] name in any of your acts."[94]

Pétion's discretion was partly in line with the promises made and agreements signed by previous Haitian leaders as a way to avoid British maritime blockade—or even invasion—and embark Haiti on a sustained development path.[95] In 1798 and 1799, as part of a preparation for a potential conflict with France, as well as in an attempt to secure markets for Haitian sugar and coffee, Toussaint Louverture signed two secret agreements with British authorities in the Caribbean promising "not to attack or encourage sedition in Jamaica."[96] As part of the same strategy, Louverture signed a trade agreement with the United States that allowed U.S. ships to bring provisions to Haiti in exchange for the island's sugar and coffee.[97] Haiti's commitment not to export revolution was further strengthened with Jean Jacques Dessalines's Imperial Constitution of 1805 and its republican replacement of 1806. Signed by Pétion himself, Haiti's republican constitution of 1806 stated in its second article, "The Republic of Haiti will never form any enterprise with the view to make conquests or to disturb the peace and interior order of foreign islands."[98] At the same time, by declaring Haiti's territory free soil, the constitution made Haiti a beacon, whose light enslaved individuals throughout the Greater Caribbean could see and whose shores they could aspire to reach. As Ada Ferrer has put it, while "fully committed to maintaining emancipation permanently in their territory," the governments of Dessalines and Pétion "publicly renounced all ambition of taking that emancipation to any of the slave societies that surrounded their new country."[99] In helping Bolívar, therefore, Pétion knew he was not only defying a two-decades-old promise of the Haitian Revolution's leaders not to export slave insurrection, but also coming dangerously close to breaking Haitian constitutional law. Discretion, understandably, was of the highest importance.

In a transimperial Greater Caribbean where communication networks had created thick commercial connections between French, British, Spanish, and Dutch territories, however, discretion was not enough to keep a secret. Just as in the late 1790s Louverture found it impossible to keep his secret agreements with Britain and the United States hidden from France, in 1816 Pétion could not prevent Spanish authorities in the Caribbean from finding out about "the plans entertained by the leaders of the insurrection who have taken refuge on that island."[100] Through intelligence activities and diplomatic pressure, Spain acquired information about the insurgents and attempted to force Pétion to uphold Haitian neutrality. Pablo Morillo; Eusebio Escudero, governor of Santiago de Cuba; and Carlos de Urrutia, governor of Spanish Santo Domingo, led the diplomatic effort. Venezuela's captain general Salvador de Moxó, New Granada's viceroy Francisco de Montalvo, Morillo's second in command Pascual Enrile, and Cuba's captain general Juan Ruiz de Apodaca also participated in Spain's diplomatic campaign. Sharing information among themselves and reporting to the Spanish secretary of state, Morillo, Escudero, Urrutia, and the other Spanish officers successfully unmasked Pétion's "pretended adhesion to strict neutrality."[101]

To obtain information about the insurgents' plans and deeds in Haiti, Spanish authorities relied heavily on captains of merchant vessels conducting trade between Spanish American territories and Jamaica, Haiti, and other Caribbean islands. Espionage and correspondence intercepted with captured ships were also important avenues to secure information. As soon as December 1815, after intercepting rebel correspondence sent on board the English schooner *Badger*, Spanish officials were convinced that "Pétion helps the insurgents of Cartagena and will aid all the coast [with] a good quantity of rifles."[102] The most incriminating piece of evidence in Morillo's hands was a note from Sutherland to the president of Cartagena informing him of "200 barrels of flour shipped by me on board the cutter *Badger* on account of my friend President Pétion."[103] Letters by Brion and J. M. Durán, also captured on the *Badger*, further corroborated the role "of our great friend President Pétion" in the shipment of "provisions . . . for Cartagena" and the Haitian president's willingness "to influence in our salvation with whatever is at his reach and circumstances allowed."[104] Choosing to immediately confront Pétion on this matter, Morillo wrote the Haitian president, "I am certain that an expedition [to attack the Spanish Main] is to be formed on that island [Haiti], because I have intercepted the correspondence of those commissioned by the rebels in Jamaica." In very diplomatic language, this first communication culminated by inviting Pétion "to contribute to the tranquility of [Spanish] America by preventing that island's residents from employing themselves in harassing Spanish possessions and commerce."[105]

This initial attempt at pressuring Pétion through diplomatic means proved ineffective. Only a month later, on January 24, 1816, Spanish authorities collected more incriminating evidence of Pétion's support of revolutionary plans. In a joint declaration given in Santiago de Cuba, ship's captain Pedro Bruno and boatswains José Buadas and Francisco Romero gave their account of how, while traveling from Jamaica to Santa Marta on board the Spanish schooner *Rosita* (alias *Pelican*), they were attacked, captured, and brought to a cove near Les Cayes by the insurgent corsair *La Popa*. During their ten-day captivity, the three sailors declared, they overheard conversations related to the presence and deeds of Bolívar, Francisco Bermúdez, and Manuel Piar in Les Cayes. In addition, they declared that they had heard conversations about the arrangements being made in Les Cayes in order "to form, with the protection that general Pétion was expected to provide them, an expedition against Rio de la Hacha, Santa Marta, Portobelo, and . . . Santo Domingo."[106]

Probably unaware of this latest piece of incriminating evidence, Pétion wrote Morillo defending Haiti's "system of neutrality" and restating his argument about the obligation, based on "natural law," to "grant the right of asylum and hospitality to [ships of] all flags that show up in our ports."[107] Seeking to appease Morillo while consciously attempting to deceive him regarding the plans of the insurgents staying in Haiti, Pétion declared, "It is not in the spirit of the [Haitian] Government to allow any type of arming to be done in its ports. . . . Neither do I think that the handful of refugees from Cartagena who are [currently] in this island conceive the idea of an expedition which cannot be assisted by my Government."[108] Pétion's argument, supported as it was on internationally accepted ideas of obligations inspired by humanity, could have worked as a good cover. However, given the firsthand information in their possession, Spanish authorities were no longer speculating when they protested against Pétion's practice of shielding himself behind "the principles of neutrality" while "allowing armed men to congregate" in Haiti.[109]

By mid-1816, Spanish authorities chose not to continue their diplomatic communication with Pétion. Instead, based on information pointing to the preparation of a rebel expedition to Mexico and rumors about a potential plot to "direct the unrest to the pacific island of Cuba," the Spanish secretary of state approved sending a spy to gather information about the rebels' plans.[110] The report of Carlos Préval, the French spy chosen by governor Escudero to visit Port-au-Prince in November 1816, contained little information that Spanish authorities could consider new. Besides details about rebel meetings organized in Sutherland's house and specific information about which rebels were currently in Haiti, Préval only restated what Spanish authorities knew since December 1815: that Pétion was actively supporting Bolívar, Mina, MacGregor, and other insurgents.

By the end of 1816, coinciding with Bolívar's final departure from Haiti, Escudero reiterated the complaint he and his fellow Spanish officers had advanced since December 1815. In an implicit acknowledgment of the failure of Spanish diplomatic pressure, Escudero bemoaned:

> Alejandro Pétion continues in his public papers wanting to persuade us that the strictest neutrality is observed in his ports, publishing as proof of that conduct several pieces about [the] confiscation . . . of interesting preys introduced in his ports, but it is also noted that he does not retain these

preys for the benefit of the legitimate owners of their products, instead destining them to the attentions of the Haitian State, and further proof of his fallacy and hypocrisy is the positive fact of having presented Bolívar with a fully armed sloop.[111]

The failure of the Spanish diplomatic effort in Haiti, especially when compared to its success in Jamaica, points to a fundamental difference between the interests and policies of the authorities of the two Caribbean islands. While Jamaican authorities concluded it was in their best interest to maintain, at least for the time being, Britain's strict neutrality in the Spanish American wars of independence, Pétion saw in this conflict a unique opportunity to "add" re-publics to the map of the Americas. By actively aiding the insurgents, Pétion was ultimately supporting Haiti's political survival. For their part, by choosing to remain neutral, Jamaican authorities concluded they were contributing to curtailing the advance of revolutionary ideas that could threaten the trade and safety of the British island. Spanish authorities, short of soldiers to confront hostilities on the mainland, could only hope that foreign governments in the Caribbean wished to remain neutral or to openly support the Spanish cause. Faced with Haiti's active encouragement of the insurgents, Morillo and Escudero could only protest Pétion's attitude and expect him to fear future Spanish retaliation. Pétion, not perceiving Spanish retaliation as an imminent threat, saw more benefits in the revolutionary promise of a continent of republics free of slavery. The insurgents, unable to secure British support, could only welcome Haiti's aid.

Pétion's help was, without a doubt, decisive, and Bolívar did not fail to thank him and Sutherland, on multiple occasions, for the support he received from Haiti. Despite the many thank-you notes he wrote and the heartfelt message they included, Bolívar's Caribbean trajectory and implicit references in his correspondence reveal a certain caution or wariness toward Haiti. Bolívar, the next section shows, would have been more comfortable had he not been forced to resort to Haiti.[112] No doubt because of this, when Pétion asked him "not to mention my name" in public acts, Bolívar must have been happy to oblige.[113]

Bolívar's Caribbean Labyrinth

Though ultimately successful, Bolívar's Caribbean adventures did not work out exactly as he had imagined they would. Instead of receiving support from Jamaican authorities, from whom, it can be said without exaggeration, he expected everything, Bolívar was aided by the Haitian government, of whose support he felt wary. Both British strict neutrality and Haiti's open support came as surprises that exposed a key flaw in Bolívar's geopolitical calculations. His desires and expectations did not match what he actually encountered. For Bolívar and many other insurgents, given their enlightened education and racial ideas, it was preferable to obtain help from a "civilized" and powerful nation rather than from a black republic.

Bolívar's Caribbean journey and some of his correspondence reveal part of the geopolitical calculations of the Venezuelan leader. As has already been pointed out, during the first weeks of his stay in Jamaica, Bolívar felt optimistic about obtaining British support. At that moment, he believed Britain's support for Spanish America's independence had only been temporarily withheld because of the return of Napoleon to power. Napoleon's final defeat, however, did not translate into the immediate support and protection Bolívar was expecting from the British Crown.[114] In July, still believing that his plan could work, Bolívar politely, but tellingly, rejected Pétion's offer of support. In a letter to his friend, Curaçaoan merchant Louis Brion, who was in contact with Haitian authorities, Bolívar revealed his wariness toward Haiti. In reference to Pétion's invitation to go to Haiti, Bolívar declared, "I myself do not go to that island [Haiti], because I do not want to lose the trust these [British] gentlemen have given me, since, as you know, the aristocratic manias are a terrible thing."[115]

Shielding behind the "aristocratic manias" of Jamaican authorities, Bolívar was hiding his unwillingness to accept Haiti's support. As things turned out, by late 1815, with Jamaican authorities still upholding British strict neutrality, Pétion's invitation was the only offer on Bolívar's table. Forced to choose between renouncing his liberation campaign and accepting help from Haiti, Bolívar opted for the latter. However, as his aide-de-camp Daniel Florencio O'Leary put it, Bolívar "would have willingly avoided [resorting to Haiti], but given his desperate current situation, he had no other way except returning to Jamaica to live a miserable life."[116] Thus, against his own calculations, Haiti, rather than Jamaica, saved the day for Bolívar and the insurgency of northern South America.

Bolívar's rationale was grounded on Enlightenment ideas of race that made everything black suspicious, dangerous, and backward. His expectations were developed within an enlightened context of "panic about Haiti" characterized by what Anthony Maingot called whites' "terrified consciousness of blacks."[117] With "scientific racism ... already a feature of the ideological landscape of the Enlightenment on both sides of the Atlantic," "black," as Michel-Rolph

Trouillot has argued, "was almost universally bad."[118] Therefore, as an enlightened *criollo* Bolívar sought to avoid association with anything that could be perceived as black.[119] His plans, instead, "called for the American nations to become part of the Euro-Atlantic community."[120] Spanish America, according to Bolívar's designs, needed to become "another Europe." The achievement of independence, he believed, should be followed by mass immigration of "continental Europeans," who would secure the establishment of civilized nations in Spanish America.[121] Haiti's support significantly diverted Bolívar from his original plans. Instead of republics belonging to a Euro-Atlantic community, with Haiti's support the nascent South American nations could be perceived as integral components of an awe-inspiring black Atlantic—"Guinea and more Guinea" instead of another Europe.[122] Luckily for Bolívar, Pétion's material aid was conditioned on Bolívar not publicly revealing the source of his support. Given the wariness Bolívar had previously expressed about accepting Pétion's invitation to Haiti, the secrecy Pétion asked him to maintain effectively constituted an additional favor. By keeping his promise to Pétion, Bolívar could use the ships, weapons, and money Pétion gave him while avoiding marking his project with the stain of Haiti.

Some of Bolívar's measures, taken shortly after his first expedition from Haiti reached Venezuela, however, can be interpreted as revealing a degree of ambiguity in his thought. The decree he signed on June 2, 1816, declaring "absolute freedom for the slaves who have groaned under the Spanish yoke during the three previous centuries," for instance, can be interpreted as a public sign of gratitude toward Pétion. The conditions the decree imposed on those it was proclaiming to liberate, however, reveal Bolívar's actual unwillingness to abolish slavery. In order for slaves to obtain their freedom, they had "to enlist under the Venezuelan flag, within twenty-four hours of the publication of this decree. . . . The new citizen," the decree further established, "who refuses to bear arms in fulfillment of the sacred duty to defend his freedom shall be subject to servitude, not only for himself but also for his children under the age of fourteen, his wife, and his aged parents."[123] Around this time, Bolívar's enlightened distrust of everything black started to haunt him. Fear of the rise of *pardos* led Bolívar to order the execution of pardo generals Manuel Piar in 1817 and José Padilla in 1828. Believing that the war with Spain was going to be followed by "a new one with the blacks," Bolívar and some of his close collaborators felt that race war was an imminent threat.[124] Fear of *pardocracia*, coupled with international pressures, also would lead Bolívar to betray Haiti's support, engineering Haiti's exclusion from the 1826 Pan-American Congress of Panama.[125] Regretting his decisions in the cases of Piar and Padilla, Bolívar admitted toward the end of his political career, "This exasperates me so much, that I don't know what to do with myself."[126] The internal contradiction between his supposed gratitude toward the black republic of Haiti and his fear of pardocracia haunted Bolívar until his death in 1830. Britain's failure to respond to Bolívar's plea to become "the savior of [Spanish] America" led Bolívar to a labyrinth from which he could not escape.[127]

Geopolitical Calculations in an Entangled World

A significant historical literature produced during the 1990s, perhaps as an unofficial commemoration of the bicentennial of the slave revolt of Saint-Domingue, brought the Haitian Revolution to the center of historical inquiry.[128] During the first decade of the twenty-first century, Haitian revolutionary studies established itself as one of the most buoyant historical subjects.[129] Many edited volumes and monographs have taught us about the far-reaching geographical impact of the Haitian Revolution.[130] A smaller number of studies attempt to add a temporal component, by depicting the persistence over time of the fears created by the Haitian Revolution.[131] The emphasis of all these studies is on how the events of the 1790s affected the geopolitical imagination of people—elites and subalterns alike—in the Atlantic world from the 1790s to the late nineteenth century. A particular interest of studies of the impact of the Haitian Revolution is to trace the simultaneous fear of slave rebellion and sense of economic opportunity that the revolution generated among colonial elites in the Americas, from the United States to Brazil.[132] Largely excluded from this voluminous historiography is the active role Haiti played in the independence of Spanish America. Bringing Pétion's aid to the South American insurgency to the center stage, this chapter has argued that Haiti's proinsurgent diplomacy was the key piece to bring Bolívar's independence project back on track after the Spanish Reconquista of Venezuela and New Granada.

If, as argued in chapter 1, the British free port system turned Kingston into the Caribbean's commercial center, Pétion's prorevolutionary diplomacy had, by 1816, turned Haiti into an international revolutionary center from which revolution spread toward Spanish America. Turning Haiti into such a center was not a decision to be taken lightly, nor one whose repercussions Pétion could control at will. Quite the contrary, Pétion's decision required careful weighing of the expected political gains and potential damaging consequences of siding with the Spanish American insurgents. Nothing less than

Haiti's political survival was at stake. The potential benefits promised by the expansion of the number of republics in the Americas, however, were strong enough for Pétion to turn a deaf ear to Spanish complaints. Cautiously but decisively calculating the geopolitical implications of his actions, Pétion put Haiti's ports, arsenals, and financial reserves at the service of Spanish America's insurgents.

British authorities in Jamaica and London, on the contrary, chose to listen to and comply with the Spanish diplomatic request to refrain from helping the Spanish American insurgents. Initially wary of the reach of Napoleon's power, Britain considered the possibility of supporting Spanish America's independence as a means to avoid a potential alliance between French forces and the rebels. To contain Napoleon in both Europe and the Americas was, as Simón Bolívar rightly pointed out upon arriving in Jamaica, Britain's most pressing concern until mid-1815. After that, with Napoleon out of the way, Britain's initial thrust to support Spanish American insurgents was replaced by a reassurance of its neutrality in the conflict between Spain and its American territories. Spanish diplomatic efforts, coupled with fear of radicalization of the independence movement, led Britain to favor the status quo. Besides a handful of British merchants in Jamaica motivated by personal interests (e.g., the Hyslop brothers, one of whom spent several months imprisoned by Spanish authorities in Cartagena and was even sentenced to death), South American insurgents failed to secure the support they had expected from Jamaica's British authorities. As the investigation ordered by Britain's secretary of war and the colonies revealed, apprehension about the possibility that Bolívar and other insurgents, aided by Pétion, were willing to liberate all slaves in Spanish America figured prominently in the geopolitical calculations of Jamaican authorities and prevented them from fulfilling Bolívar's expectations. Despite the rise of British abolitionism, the idea of a continent largely populated by ex-slaves was considered a threat that needed to be avoided.

To Bolívar, both the lack of support he found in Jamaica and the decisive and favorably conditioned aid provided by Haiti's president were surprises that drastically changed the path he had traced for himself after departing from Cartagena in 1815. Initially expecting to continue his war effort with British aid, he had to overcome his wariness toward Haiti to accept the aid Pétion was willingly offering. Bolívar's Enlightenment proclivity to distrust everything black coupled with his genuine gratitude toward Pétion created a dilemma that Bolívar was unable to solve. Haiti's support, much to Bolívar's chagrin, put the nations he aspired to create closer to an awe-inspiring black

Atlantic community than to the Euro-Atlantic to which he wanted these nations to belong. Bolívar's desire to create a civilized, Euro-Atlantic nation was a common feature in the vying national projects that comprised enlightened criollos' geopolitical imagination during the Age of Revolutions. His actions and calculations before, during, and after his stay in Haiti, as well as those of the Spanish officers who spied on him and Pétion, reveal the extent to which Haiti, Jamaica, New Granada, and many other locales of the revolutionary Atlantic were connecting nodes of an entangled Atlantic world.

CHAPTER 6

_____

An Andean-Atlantic Nation

How different and decisive features can be noticed between the coastal man and that of the Andean summits!
—FRANCISCO JOSÉ DE CALDAS, "Estado de la geografía"

The country's general boundaries are: to the N. the Atlantic Ocean.
—FELIPE PÉREZ, *Compendio de jeografía*

On November 8, 1819, three months after the crucial patriot victory at the Battle of Boyacá, Simón Bolívar wrote to his second in command, Francisco de Paula Santander, a self-congratulatory letter in which, besides celebrating the recent victories and the promising prospects of the independence struggle, he used the phrase "Esta Patria es Caribe y no Boba" (This fatherland is Caribbean and not foolish) to characterize the emerging nation.[1] While the reasons to characterize the emerging political entity as foolish are well known—the so-called *patria boba* is a staple of Colombia's academic, official, and popular histories—nothing has been made of Bolívar's characterization of the patria as Caribbean.[2] Bolívar's characterization can be read as a tribute to the Caribbean, as private acknowledgment that victory against the Spanish forces would not have been possible had Haitian president Alexandre Pétion, as shown in the previous chapter, not funded two expeditions from Haiti to the coast of Venezuela. The phrase can also be read as a statement of purpose regarding the type of nation he wanted to create. If the new patria was going to be Caribbean, one could expect to find in the years following Bolívar's letter a coherent project to strengthen, or at least maintain, the links between the new Colombian nation and the Caribbean islands. Instead, the opposite took place. From the very beginning of Colombia's independent life, nation makers actively strived to delink the emerging nation from a Caribbean world they perceived as threatening.[3]

Following the key military victories at Boyacá (1819), Carabobo (1821), Cartagena (1821), and Maracaibo (1823), Bolívar, Santander, and many other founding fathers embarked on a nation-building process that had at its heart the goal of establishing a republic that could not only maintain its independence but also secure a place among the civilized nations of the earth. That Colombia's nation makers pursued this goal is hardly surprising. Like all other emerging Latin American nation makers, Colombian founding fathers sought to create a nation that would be welcomed into the Euro-Atlantic community of nations.[4] Doing so, or creating what I call an Andean-Atlantic nation, required erasing the strong links to the Caribbean that I have explored in the previous chapters and replacing them with stronger links to the North Atlantic centers of civilization (Europe and the United States). To create an Andean-Atlantic nation, thus, necessarily entailed the decaribbeanization of the nascent republic. An analysis of these two complementary processes demonstrates that the fact that Colombia ended up becoming an Andean-Atlantic nation does not unequivocally indicate that there were no alternatives. A Caribbean counternarrative, though ultimately defeated, was one of these alternatives.

This chapter shifts geographical vantage point. Instead of embracing the Caribbean Sea and Atlantic Ocean from New Granada's shores, it does so, mostly, from the perspective of the Andean capital of the nascent republic, where a group of enlightened nation makers envisioned a new Colombian nation that could shun the stigma of blackness, barbarism, and obscurantism associated with the Caribbean, and present itself to the world as white, civilized, and enlightened. Focusing on two generations of enlightened nation makers—the *criollos ilustrados* (enlightened creoles) and their successors, the "politician-geographers"—this chapter makes it possible to understand why the transimperial Greater Caribbean did not find its way into Colombia's nation-making narrative.[5]

Drawing on an Enlightenment education that characterized the tropical lowlands (the coast) and their population as backward, enlightened creoles developed an argument that stressed the civilizational possibilities the Andes offered. Politician-geographers, on the other hand, created and used cartographic and geographic representations of the nation to construct an image of Colombia as an Atlantic nation. Together, they made possible the decaribbeanization of the new republic and the creation of an Andean-Atlantic nation. Their efforts did not go unchallenged. From the Caribbean coast, under the leadership first of José Prudencio Padilla and then of Juan José Nieto, a

Caribbean counternarrative evolved as a potential, though ultimately unsuccessful, challenge to the Andean-Atlantic republican project. Both the Andean-Atlantic project and the Caribbean counternarrative illustrate key elements of nation makers' geopolitical imagination, of the way in which they interpreted their present and envisioned the future of the nation they sought to construct. Both projects allow us to understand the dual role of the transimperial Greater Caribbean in Colombia's nation-making process. It was, for some, a threat to be eliminated and, for others, an opportunity to be seized.

Criollos Ilustrados and Their Enlightened Argument for the Andean-Atlantic Nation

During the late eighteenth century and the first years of the nineteenth century, a number of European scientists traveled through the Americas collecting natural specimens, surveying barely explored territories, and performing a variety of scientific experiments.[6] These scientific explorations, a recent literature has demonstrated, ushered in a productive dialogue between European, American, and African knowledge systems that resulted in a mutually constitutive Atlantic scientific tradition.[7] The encounter and collaboration between European scientific travelers and local practitioners occupy a central role in the study of the intellectual genealogy of Colombia's nation makers. During his short visit to New Granada in 1801, Prussian naturalist Alexander von Humboldt marveled at the intellectual dynamism that he encountered in the viceregal capital, Santa Fe. His travels through the viceroyalty allowed him to become acquainted with a group of local savants whose knowledge proved of great use to Humboldt's scientific and cartographic production. In particular, Humboldt benefited from his intellectual exchanges with Francisco José de Caldas and José Celestino Mutis. In Caldas, Humboldt saw not merely a useful local collaborator but a "distinguished physicist, consecrated with unrivaled fervor to the astronomy and many branches of the natural history."[8] From Mutis, a Spanish-born scientist whose experience in New Granada—he had lived in Santa Fe since the early 1760s—made him occupy a liminal space between creole and metropolitan scientific traditions, Humboldt obtained innumerable botanical specimens that he brought with him to Europe and incorporated into his collection and writings. From Caldas and Mutis to the mid-nineteenth-century politician-geographers whose connection with Humboldt has been referred to as an "ideological knot," the figure of the Prussian naturalist loomed large in the enlightened imagination of nineteenth-century Colombian nation makers.[9] Whether through direct (personal or epistolary) contact or indirectly, as in the case of the many other enlightened nation makers who read his work in search for erudition and inspiration, Humboldt was a referent for Neogranadan (later Colombian) criollos ilustrados.

The road to Humboldt or, more generally, to the key European figures associated with the Enlightenment had two distinct branches. While Bolívar reached the Enlightenment in Europe, Santander, Caldas, and many other criollos ilustrados became enlightened in Santa Fe. In educational institutions, like the Colegio Nuestra Señora del Rosario and the Colegio San Bartolomé, and in the less formal settings of political and literary *tertulias*, Caldas, Santander, Francisco Antonio Zea, José Manuel Restrepo, José María Salazar, and José Fernández Madrid, among many others, became enlightened creoles.

In Europe, where he traveled between 1803 and 1806 accompanied by his close friend Fernando del Toro and his long-time tutor Simón Rodríguez and again during 1810 with fellow enlightened creoles Andrés Bello and Luis López Méndez, Bolívar expanded his Enlightenment education.[10] Despite (or maybe as part of) an early Parisian experience that a biographer has characterized as a "crazed life of gambling and sex," Bolívar's time in Europe was a period of intellectual and political awakening.[11] It was also a time of dramatic geopolitical adjustments. While in Europe, Bolívar witnessed Napoleon's proclamation as emperor (1804) and the British victory at Trafalgar (1805). Close observation of these geopolitical arrangements, coupled with readings of "Locke, Candillac, Buffon, D'Alembert, Helvetius, Montesquieu, Mably, Filangieri, Lalande, Rousseau, Voltaire, Rollin, and Verlot" and conversations with Humboldt—whom Bolívar later called the "discoverer of the New World"—about science and politics, attuned Bolívar with the Enlightenment tenets of natural rights, the social contract, popular sovereignty, the separation of powers, and the idea that "the object of government [should be to guarantee] the greatest happiness of the greatest number."[12] In addition, while visiting England, thanks largely to the patronage of Venezuelan patriarch Francisco de Miranda, Bolívar personally met prominent figures of the Enlightenment like Jeremy Bentham and some of the most influential British politicians of the age.[13]

Miranda's Grafton Street house, in the heart of London, effectively became a meeting place for young Spanish Americans enhancing their Enlightenment education through the European experience. During the first decade of the nineteenth century, a number of future leaders of the Spanish American wars of independence found in Miranda's home and his library the perfect setting to further their education and turn the Enlightenment tenets into radical propositions for political independence. Besides Bolívar, Chilean and Argentine founding fathers Bernardo O'Higgins and José de San Martín also benefited from Miranda's hospitality.[14] The list of enlightened creoles who used Miranda's house as temporary residence, educational facility, and conspiracy center also includes Bolívar's friend and tutor Andrés Bello, Ecuadorian patriots José María de Antepara and Vicente Rocafuerte, Mexican propagandist Fray Servando Teresa de Mier, and many others who stayed at Miranda's Grafton Street house even after the patriarch's final departure from London in October 1810.[15]

In New Granada, the leadership of Spanish botanist José Celestino Mutis and Cuban intellectual Manuel del Socorro Rodríguez provided the impetus for the development of a dynamic and politically active scientific community, of which Caldas, Zea, and Antonio Nariño stood out as its most visible members.[16] Under the tutelage of Mutis, who was in New Granada as director of the ambitious Royal Botanical Expedition, Caldas, Zea, Jorge Tadeo Lozano, and other enlightened creoles not only became experienced naturalists and cartographers with great on-the-ground knowledge of the viceroyalty, but also climbed up the colonial bureaucratic ladder.[17] Guided by Manuel del Socorro Rodríguez, the young criollos also became acutely acquainted with the political and philosophical tenets of the Enlightenment. As participants of Rodriguez's Tertulia Eutropélica, many creoles, including future vice president and president of Colombia Francisco de Paula Santander, became familiar with the Enlightenment's arguments for natural rights, popular sovereignty, and the pursuit of happiness. Other tertulias or literary circles (the Arcano Sublime de la Filantropía and the Tertulia del Buen Gusto) and several newspapers (*El Alternativo del Redactor Americano* and the *Semanario del Nuevo Reino de Granada*) also emerged during the late eighteenth and early nineteenth centuries as intellectual platforms for the development and diffusion of the political ideas and scientific arguments of enlightened creoles.[18] Through these meetings and publication venues, enlightened creoles gave shape to a "community of interpretation" built upon new ways of expressing judgments and constructing opinions.[19] Besides sharing books, ideas, and methods of argumentation, criollos ilustrados were also united by a series of obstacles among which a collaborator of the *Semanario* and future nation maker, José María Salazar, counted the "immense sea" separating their unenlightened patrias from "cultured Europe," the inadequate course offerings in educational institutions, and the need for "many important books" and "instruments for physics and the arts."[20] Overcoming these obstacles, especially the real and metaphorical sea separating them from Europe, eventually evolved to become a key element in Colombia's nation-making process.

The *Semanario*, founded by Caldas in 1808, became particularly important as a sounding board for enlightened creoles to develop and spread their sense of appreciation for and appropriation of the territories of the viceroyalty of New Granada. In its pages, enlightened creoles articulated a sense of identity associated with a strong territorial attachment to the viceroyalty, but not necessarily leading to a desire for a radical break with Spain. Instead, according to Colombian historian Mauricio Nieto, criollos ilustrados developed "an eagerness . . . to be recognized as legitimate members of a civilized, dominant, and European community" and a "clear and strong" desire to distinguish and separate themselves from "everything that seems not European," from "the native or the African."[21]

Through the *Semanario*, Caldas, Salazar, and other future nation makers developed an interpretive framework that allowed them to understand society in terms of a dichotomy that opposed civilization and barbarism.[22] Civilized (what both Europeans and criollos ilustrados were) was a term that encompassed positive concepts such as "Enlightenment, light, rationality, wisdom, Christianity, white, good, healthy, clean, prosperity," and other similar ones. Barbarism, on the other hand, was associated with negative terms such as "superstition, obscurity, instinct, ignorance, darkness, paganism, black, bad, sick, dirty, backwardness," and other negative expressions.[23]

In their eagerness to appear civilized, especially to a European community of philosophers and naturalists, enlightened creoles used the *Semanario* as their official platform to participate in scientific debates that brought together scholars on both sides of the Atlantic. The pages of the *Semanario* featured a translation of Humboldt's *Ideas for a Geography of Plants* less than three years after it was first published in Germany. The translation, by enlightened creole Jorge Tadeo Lozano, was followed by critical notes and comments written by Caldas, some of which corrected what Caldas considered Humboldt's mistakes.[24] The friendly tone of Caldas's critiques reveals a great admiration for the Prussian naturalist and contrasts sharply with the tenor of other controversies that populated the *Semanario*.[25]

One particularly controversial issue addressed by Caldas in one of the best-known pieces of the *Semanario* was that of the impact of climate on living beings. Based on his readings of European scientists and philosophers like Georges-Louis Leclerc (comte de Buffon), Corneille de Pauw, and

Montesquieu, Caldas advanced a tropical version of European theories of environmental determinism that assigned degenerative powers to specific climates. While Buffon and de Pauw claimed that the New World's climate rendered living beings (including humans) weak, small, impotent, and inferior to Eurasian ones, Caldas emphasized the stark climatic variations within New World territories in order to maintain that only those creatures living in the tropical lowlands (coasts, valleys, and forests) suffered the degenerative effects of climate.[26] Defiantly asserting that his "knees [did] not bend to any philosopher," Caldas claimed that elevation above sea level was the key variable near the equator. Thus, for him, New Granada was the perfect place to witness the very "different and decisive features . . . [that separated] the coastal man from that of the Andean summits." While the former was generally lacking in virtues and was inclined toward vices, the latter was characterized by "brilliant and decided features."[27] His views, a Colombian historian has argued, decisively contributed to the "demonization of the coastal lands" that came to characterize the nineteenth-century Colombian nation.[28]

In a very similar vein, Caldas's colleague Francisco Antonio de Ulloa asserted that "the dweller of the Andean highlands is so different from that who breathes at its feet, as is the vegetation of these two extremes." In his view, "these regions of fire"—the tropical lowlands—would "never produce a poet, an orator, a musician, a painter, or any other genius capable of honoring his country." By way of conclusion, Ulloa declared that "he who wants to give a step in the sciences, better flee this ill-fated climate [of the equatorial lowlands] and go to breathe under a different sky."[29] With these perceptions of the coasts and other lowland territories of New Granada, it is no wonder that after the wars of independence, criollos ilustrados promoted the creation of an Andean nation. Such a nation, according to their enlightened theories, could resemble civilized Europe; a lowland alternative would only produce backwardness and barbarism.

Enlightened creoles' argument was repeated verbatim by the next generation of elite nation makers, the politician-geographers. One of their leading representatives, cartographer, journalist, and diplomat Manuel Ancízar, like his predecessors Caldas and Ulloa, linked the tropical lowlands with barbarism and, while acknowledging that much needed to be done, never doubted that, with adequate educational and religious institutions, civilization could be achieved in the Colombian highlands.[30] As for enlightened creoles, as demonstrated by a map that Joaquín Acosta dedicated to Humboldt, the Prussian intellectual constituted a fundamental touchstone for politician-geographers.[31]

Decaribbeanizing through Geographical Representations

In his study of Thailand's nation-making process and the invention and meanings of Thainess, Thongchai Winichakul introduced the term "geo-body" to understand the role of geography and mapping in what he considers the arbitrary and artificial process of the creation of Thai nationhood. A nation's geo-body, he explains, depicts that nation's shape (as seen on a map) and the sentiments its inhabitants attach to that shape.[32] The concept is of great use to think about nation-making processes. It is, in the way Thongchai uses it, also greatly terracentric.[33] The geo-body of the Thai nation scrutinized in *Siam Mapped* stresses a shape whose contours are defined by the coast; the sea, in other words, does not figure in Thongchai's Siamese geo-body.[34] Seeing the sea and understanding how nation makers used it to advance particular national visions can greatly enhance our understanding of nation-making processes.

If seeing the sea is important, the words chosen to name it can also be of great relevance to understanding the type of nation that nation makers wish to create. Names are always loaded, never neutral. The act of naming (whether it is to name for the first time or to rename), as Paul Carter reminds us, allows explorers to "invent" places, "to bring them into cultural circulation."[35] In a Latin American context, historians Rebecca Earle and Raymond Craib have paid careful attention to the importance of naming in the nation-building process. Changing names of plazas, streets, mountains, valleys, and roads, these authors have demonstrated, was a key element in the search for order and progress characteristic of national formation in Colombia, Argentina, and Mexico. New names constituted expressions of patriotism and were an effective tool to combat the "cartographic anarchy" that cartographer Agustín Díaz deplored in nineteenth-century Mexico.[36] (Re)naming places, in short, filled with meaning the geo-body of the emerging Latin American nations.

In the particular case of Colombia's nineteenth-century nation formation, the sea and how nation makers (and lay citizens) chose (and were taught) to call it are at the heart of the decaribbeanization process that I explain in this chapter.[37] An analysis of geographical sources (maps, geographical treatises, and geography textbooks) reveals a tendency, among mid-nineteenth-century politician-geographers, to erase the Caribbean, to not use the word "Caribbean" to refer to the sea to the north of Colombia. This decaribbeanizing tendency, I argue, finds its logic in the Enlightenment tenets that associated Europe and North America with civilization and modernity, while characterizing the Caribbean (and the tropical) lowlands as savage and backward.

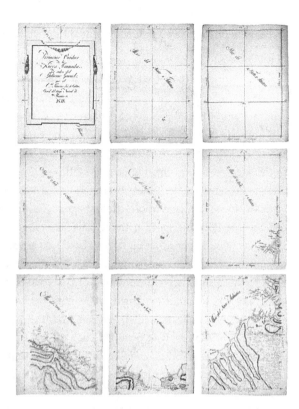

Figures 6.1 and 6.2
Provincias Unidas de la Nueva Granada. Images adapted from Mauricio Nieto Olarte, *La obra cartográfica de Francisco José de Caldas* (Bogotá: Uniandes, 2006), 100–101.

In the middle decades of the nineteenth century, the task of constructing Colombia as a civilized, Europe-like nation fell upon a group of politician-geographers, of which Joaquín Acosta, Agustín Codazzi, Tomás Cipriano de Mosquera, Manuel Ancízar, José María Samper, Manuel María Paz, and the brothers Felipe and Santiago Pérez are the best-known representatives.[38] Their cartographic representations and geographical descriptions of Colombia, as well as those of other cartographers and geographers, present what at first sight seems to be an inconsistent and politically neutral approach to naming the sea to the north of the republic. A quick look at their maps, geographical treatises, and textbooks suggests the use of Mar del Norte (North Sea), Mar Caribe (Caribbean Sea), Mar de las Antillas (Sea of the Antilles), and Mar Atlántico or Oceáno Atlántico (Atlantic Sea or Atlantic Ocean) as synonyms used interchangeably.[39] Reading their maps and texts, as Lina del Castillo puts it, "in terms of what they show and what they hide," however, reveals a tendency and an agenda behind the name they assigned to the sea.[40]

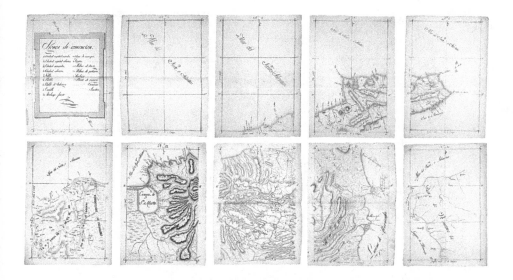

Following independence from Spain in the early 1820s, the new American republics adopted new names as signs of new beginnings. The renaming process, as depicted in cartographic evidence, also reached the sea. Abandoning the centuries-old usage of Mar del Norte, republican cartographers started to use alternative denominations like Mar Atlántico, Mar de las Antillas, and, on occasion, Mar Caribe.[41] Far from simply being used interchangeably, the process of choosing a particular denomination was part and parcel of a nation-making strategy that aimed at establishing Colombia firmly within the community of Euro-Atlantic, civilized nations.

The earliest example of the transition from Mar del Norte to a different toponym is presented (and emphasized through repetition) in a series of nineteen plates drawn by creole naturalist and cartographer Francisco José de Caldas in 1815. The plates, titled *Provincias Unidas de la Nueva Granada*, present the sea and northern coast of the viceroyalty.[42] In them (see figures 6.1 and 6.2), the sea occupies center stage. Of the nineteen plates, only two do not depict the sea. Of the seventeen plates that show and name the sea, five show no land at all, only sea space, which, were it not for the name of the sea crossing the plate, could be interpreted as blank space (see figure 6.3). Drawn in the midst of the wars of independence, these maps constitute the first cartographic representation produced by an independent (although soon reconquered) government.[43] The republican nature of the maps is clearly inscribed in the cartouche that presents Caldas preceded by the title "citizen" and, more tellingly for the

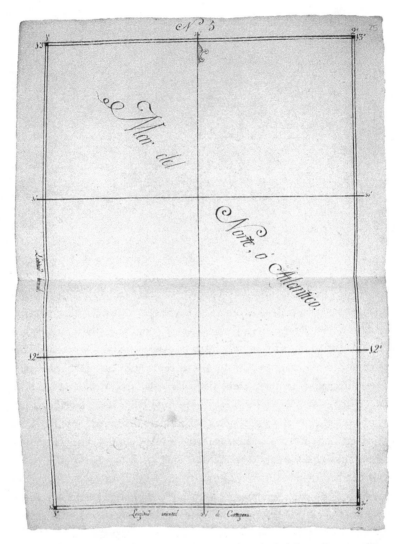

Figure 6.3 Caldas's *Provincias Unidas*. Plate 5. Image adapted from Mauricio Nieto Olarte, *La obra cartográfica de Francisco José de Caldas* (Bogotá: Uniandes, 2006), 105.

careful observer, in the use of Cartagena as the meridian reference to measure longitude, which effectively put an independent Cartagena at the center of the world.[44] Caldas's plates are, in other words, a veritable "cartography of protest" against Spanish imperialism.[45] The anti-Spanish inclination of the maps, as Mauricio Nieto speculates, might have been used against Caldas in the trial that led to his execution in 1816 following the Spanish Reconquest of New Granada.[46]

The sea of Caldas's *Provincias Unidas* is called Mar del Norte o Atlántico. In using both names Caldas is introducing a new denomination (Atlántico) while making sure that viewers of the maps could locate themselves through the traditionally used Mar del Norte. Since some of the plates depict nothing but sea, recognition of the name of the sea is fundamental for viewers to know the location of that sea on the globe. The double naming is significant because it points to a possible transition, a significant break from a colonial Mar del Norte to a republican Mar Atlántico. The new terminology would signal a new republican beginning in which everything, including the name of the sea as well as, perhaps more importantly, the political model, the legislative code, political divisions, commercial legislation, and even racial composition had to be established anew. Whether or not this interpretation fit Caldas's designs, the Spanish Reconquest and the executions of many republican leaders it entailed (including Caldas) ensured that these plates constituted Caldas's last cartographical product. Caldas's logic in naming the sea Mar del Norte o Atlántico, thus, remained undeveloped.

During the 1820s, two other prominent nation makers, Francisco Antonio Zea and José Manuel Restrepo, published, as part of larger geographical and historical accounts of Colombia, two maps of the new republic.[47] The first of these two maps, *Colombia tomado de Humboldt y de otras varias autoridades recientes* (Colombia taken from Humboldt and several other recent authorities), uses the toponym Mar Caribe. Restrepo's *Carta de la República de Colombia* introduces a new variant by referring to the sea to the north of the new republic as Mar Caribe o de las Antillas (Caribbean Sea or Sea of the Antilles). In accompanying maps of the provinces of Magdalena (*Carta del Departamento del Magdalena*) and the Isthmus of Panama (*Carta del Departamento del Ismo*), however, Restrepo eschewed the Caribbean and marked the northern limit of the provinces simply as Mar de las Antillas. How significant were these variations in the naming of the sea? Did the chosen names respond to particular agendas or interests? Were Zea and Restrepo following standard usage in London and Paris, the cities where their maps were published? Were they targeting specific audiences and, therefore, adopting a language under-standable to those audiences? Did they even get to decide what name was going to be printed on the sea space to the north of the landed territory of Colombia?

It was certainly standard usage in the English-speaking Atlantic and Paris to refer to the sea to the north of Colombia as the Caribbean Sea or Mer des Antilles. A sample of twenty-eight maps of Colombia produced in Britain and the United States between 1811 and 1869 reveals a marked tendency to use Caribbean Sea. Prestigious mapmakers on both sides of the Atlantic like J. Arrowsmith, Sidney Hall, and Jeremiah Greenleaf inscribed the Caribbean Sea as the northern limit of Colombia.[48] French maps, on the other hand, as demonstrated by a sample of maps of the new South American republic published between 1825 and 1862, always used Mer des Antilles.[49]

Since Zea's *Colombia* was geared, at least in its English version, toward British and possibly North American audiences, it made sense for Zea (and his collaborators) to choose the name with which British subjects and North American citizens were most familiar: Caribbean Sea. Although Restrepo's maps appeared as part of a work geared toward Spanish-speaking audiences, the choice of Mar de las Antillas could have just been the result of the adoption of French standard usage. In addition, following Lina del Castillo's reflections on the collaborative nature of the production of maps, it is possible to suggest that the name choices of Zea and Restrepo actually reflected the choices of some of their British and French collaborators. This is not to say that, had Zea and Restrepo enjoyed full power to decide how to name the sea, they would have chosen to use a different name. What this reflection intends to convey is that, given the circumstances under which both Zea and Restrepo directed their cartographic projects (Restrepo was not in Paris directly supervising the pro-duction of his *Historia* and the accompanying *Atlas*, while Zea was sick and died shortly before or just after the publication of his map and geographical de-scription), their "editorial voice[s]" might not have been powerful enough to alter European naming traditions.[50]

When compared with the earlier maps of Caldas, those of Zea and Re-strepo point to a complete lack of agreement on how to name the sea. The three maps, produced between 1815 and 1827, include four different names for the sea to the north of the newly established republic. The maps of Zea and Restrepo make my preliminary argument (based on Caldas's plates) regard-ing the possible emergence of a republican sea-naming convention untenable. The only tendency discernable in the three maps points to an unsurprising suppression of colonial naming practices. Instead of using the old, colonial Mar del Norte, the three Colombian mapmakers shifted to Atlantic, Caribbean, or Antilles.

In reference to the evolution of these naming practices, historians Alfonso Múnera and Gustavo Bell Lemus hypothesized that throughout the nineteenth century the term "Atlantic" overrode other uses and "appear[ed] *always*" as the northern "limits of New Granada or the United States of Colombia."[51] Careful examination of the geographical production in the decades following the appearance of Restrepo's map, however, reveals a much more nuanced linguistic turn when it came to naming Colombia's northern sea.

Subsequent maps, produced by Colombia's politician-geographers in a period that a historian of cartography has characterized as "a transformational moment of great dynamism in the process of geographical representation" of the national territory, never called the sea to the north of the republic the Caribbean Sea.[52] Instead, like Restrepo, most of these mapmakers chose Mar de las Antillas, a term that stresses the physical location of the sea (Antilles; ante-isles; preceding the islands or preceded by islands) and is associated neither with colonial naming practices nor with the negative connotations attached to the word "Caribbean."[53] In her analysis of the maps produced by Joaquín Acosta (1847), Mariano Inojosa (1850), Genaro Gaitán and Ramón Posada (1850), Tomás Cipriano de Mosquera (1852), José María Samper (1858), and Manuel Ponce de León and Manuel María Paz (1864), Lucía Duque Muñoz stresses the simultaneous competition and collaboration that characterized the cartographic activities of Colombia's nineteenth-century politician-geographers. Her reading of these maps demonstrates the constant adjustment of the nation's geo-body, especially in its borders with other countries, and generally supports the idea that geographic exploration and the multiplicity of competing cartographic endeavors, including the ambitious, government-funded Chorographic Commission led by Agustín Codazzi, resulted in an increased knowledge of the national territory.[54] In my own reading of these maps—a sea-centered reading—the predominant use of Mar de las Antillas becomes the most remarkable feature. It was, after all, the name chosen by Acosta, Mosquera, Samper, and Ponce de León and Paz.[55]

While the previous analysis based on reading maps—in this case, a specific element of a group of maps of the young republic of Colombia/New Granada—raises some questions about naming practices in early republican maps of Colombia, it does not allow the map reader to reach definitive conclusions regarding the place of maps (and the name of the sea on those maps) in Colombia's nation-building process. That said, my reading of the name of the sea on these national maps allows me to identify a telling feature: Colombian mapmakers, with Zea and, to a certain extent, Restrepo being the only exceptions, avoided the name Caribbean Sea. Like Bolívar's statement about the nascent patria being Caribbean, the use of Caribbean Sea by Zea and Restrepo appears as a slippage in a corpus of cartographic representations that sought to separate the nascent republic from the Caribbean in order to appear as more enlightened, modern, and civilized. The erasure of "Caribbean Sea," in short, reveals a desire to resemble Europe.

This effort to resemble Europe was also evident in the numerous geographical descriptions and compendiums of Colombia published throughout the nineteenth century. The decaribbeanization tendency I identified in the maps becomes more explicit in these geographical treatises, thus making it possible to go beyond the tentative conclusions reached solely on the basis of reading maps. While Zea's 1822 description presented Colombia's northern limits as "the Province of Costa Rica and the Caribbean Sea," Felipe Pérez's 1863 *Compendio* clearly stated that "the general limits of the country are: to the North, the Atlantic Ocean."[56] Like Pérez, Tomás Cipriano de Mosquera and José María Samper identified the Atlantic Ocean as the republic's northern limit.[57] However, the fact that Antonio Cuervo used Mar de las Antillas and Mar Atlántico interchangeably and D. H. Araujo referred to both the Atlantic coast and the Mar de las Antillas reveals that the preference for the name Atlantic (also evident in the writings of Agustín Codazzi and other key figures of the Chorographic Commission) did not completely obliterate the use of Mar de las Antillas.[58]

The works of Mosquera and Samper of the 1850s and 1860s are revealing of the growing tendency to favor the use of Océano Atlántico over other denominations. The names they used for the sea also reveal that both Mosquera and Samper were politician-geographers sensitive to the naming traditions of their audiences. In his *Memoria sobre la geografía física de la Nueva Granada*, "read at the Geographical Society of New York in the sessions of June 8 and October 12, 1852," and dedicated to the members of this learned society, Mosquera generally used Atlantic Ocean when presenting Colombia's boundaries, the location of ports and river mouths, the country's average temperatures and weather regimes, and other features of Colombia's geography.[59] In a telling gesture to the New York audience and their naming practices—a translation effort, one can call it—Mosquera conceded that the islands of San Andrés and Providence were "in the Atlantic, or Caribbean Sea."[60] The word "Caribe" (Spanish for both Caribbean and Carib) for Mosquera, as other passages of the

Memoir demonstrate, was mostly reserved for the indigenous people inhabiting "the *Atlantic* coasts, from Chiriquí on the coast of Veraguas (Panama) to Goajira" (near the Venezuelan border). These people, Mosquera asserted, "were, without doubt, of the Carib race."[61] On specific attributes of the Carib race Mosquera did not comment further in his *Memoir*.

A later publication, *Compendio de geografía general, política, física y especial de los Estados Unidos de Colombia* (1866), more clearly presented Mosquera's views on the Carib race and, in so doing, provides elements to understand the logic behind the decaribbeanization project. In addition, unlike the *Memoir*, the *Compendio* does not include any gesture to appeal to audiences with different naming practices. "Dedicated to the General Congress of the [Colombian] Union," Mosquera's *Compendio* simply presents the republic as limited "to the North" by "the Atlantic Ocean."[62] The term "Caribe" mostly appears in reference to "the indigenous Carib race," which he characterizes as "warlike and indomitable" and, in sharp contrast with the indigenous descendants of the "empires of Mexico and Peru" and "the Muisca nation" of the Colombian highlands, without "political institutions."[63] Given these negative attributes of the Carib race, it should come as no surprise that Mosquera avoided, whenever possible, the association of the Colombian republic with the word "Caribbean." "Atlantic," in contrast, appealed much better to Mosquera's enlightened sensitivities.

Like Mosquera, Samper, whose international projection among Colombian politician-geographers was rivaled only by that of Mosquera himself, demonstrated awareness of European naming conventions as well as a willingness to please his foreign audience.[64] This awareness and willingness explain the apparent contradiction embedded in his shift from using Atlantic in 1857 to Mar de las Antillas in 1860. Samper's 1857 *Ensayo aproximado sobre la jeografía* consistently referred to "the Atlantic" as the limit of the three states—Bolívar, Magdalena, and Panama—with coasts on Colombia's northern sea.[65] Produced with an educational purpose similar to that of geographical catechisms and other geography textbooks of the time, Samper's *Ensayo aproximado* instructed Colombians about the soon-to-be-approved new political division of the country, while continuing to instill among his compatriots the idea of Colombia as an Atlantic nation. Not fortuitously, a depiction of "our coasts" as insalubrious places that "repel . . . the entrepreneurial man with their ardent and inhospitable climates" accompanied his instructional *Ensayo*.[66]

When addressing a French audience, however, Samper found it in his best interest to speak in their language and embrace the French usage Mar de las

Antillas. His essay "La confederación granadina y su población," presented in 1860 to the Society of Ethnography of Paris and "published, in French, in this enlightened corporation's monthly magazine," like Mosquera's work, only uses Caribe in reference to the indigenous people of the country's northern coast.[67] Unlike Mosquera, who did not attach attributes to the Carib race when addressing the international audience of New York's Geographical Society, Samper informed his French peers of the Society of Ethnography about the Carib-like features of "the most barbarous races . . . of the vast territories of the maritime region, from the Guajira Peninsula to the occidental extreme of the Isthmus of Panama." However, not wanting to present his country as an uncivilized one, Samper locates those "barbarous races" mostly in the past (he speaks of them in the past tense—they "inhabited"—and only in his section on the Spanish conquest). In addition, he carefully draws the distinction, in his opinion evident at the time in which he was writing, between the highlands as sites of "civilization" and the lowlands as lands of "violence and the horrors of slavery."[68] Samper's Colombia, thus, was both Andean and Atlantic, not Caribbean.

The argument, thus, insinuates itself. While politician-geographers, conversant as they were with a Euro-Atlantic geographical tradition, recognized the need to facilitate communication through the use of standard naming practices, their own enlightened prejudices and civilizing aspirations led them to privilege the use of Atlantic Ocean over the less glamorous Caribbean Sea. While the term Sea of the Antilles still appeared with certain frequency in the maps and geographical treatises published in the fifty years following Colombia's independence, its use, as became especially clear in Restrepo's and Samper's maps and books, resulted from the need or desire to speak to a French audience long used to the toponym Mer des Antilles. With only one exception—Zea's map and geographical description, both of which, I have argued, used Caribbean in order to speak the language of their primarily British audience—the new republic was never described as limited to the north by the Caribbean Sea. For this decaribbeanization process to have an impact beyond the community of enlightened politician-geographers, however, another set of geographical texts had to be produced: geography textbooks.[69]

Geography textbooks (see figures 6.4–6.7), some of them written as catechisms that students needed to memorize, were the vehicles through which the ideas of politician-geographers about the type of nation that Colombia needed to be were spread. Through these texts, written "for the first instruction of children" or "for the use of primary schools," several generations of Colombians developed a type of "geographical literacy" that allowed them

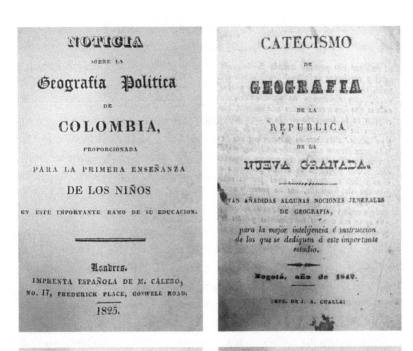

Figures 6.4–6.7 Nineteenth-century geography textbooks that taught Colombians what their nation was (Andean and Atlantic) and what it was not (Caribbean). Images courtesy of Biblioteca Luis Angel Arango, Bogotá, Colombia.

to learn what their country was (and what it was not), how it looked on a map, and where it stood in relation to other countries.[70] Geography textbooks published between the 1820s and the 1860s replicated the decaribbeanizing tendency I identified for maps and geographical treatises.

Like Caldas's maps, Pedro Acevedo Tejada's 1825 *Noticia sobre la geografía política* taught its readers that Colombia "is bounded to the north by the Atlantic or Northern Sea."[71] The equivalence between Mar del Norte and Mar Atlántico, however, is presented only once: at the beginning of the textbook. Throughout the rest of the text, Acevedo Tejada did away with the term "del norte" and simply taught students that the islands of Margarita, San Andrés, and Old Providence were "in the Atlantic Sea," that "the indigenous population of the Atlantic coast was small," that the Magdalena River "finishes its course in the Atlantic," and that "the four maritime states [were] on the Atlantic."[72] In short, while using Atlantic or Northern Sea at the beginning of the textbook facilitated geographical location for both teachers and students, Acevedo Tejada's *Noticia* was ultimately teaching students a new republican denomination for the sea formerly known as "del norte."

Other geography textbooks, like many nineteenth-century maps, also adopted the usage Mar de las Antillas. An anonymous geographical catechism published in 1842, for example, invited students to memorize the following question and answer set:

Q. Where is the Republic of New Granada located?
A. New Granada is that part of South America located between the Sea of the Antilles and Venezuela.[73]

Similarly, Antonio Cuervo's *Resumen de la jeografía* (1852) taught primary school students that the country and the provinces of Riohacha, Sabanilla, and Santa Marta were bounded "to the north by the Sea of the Antilles." Cuervo, however, did not use Mar de las Antillas consistently. Instead his *Resumen* also describes the nation's limits "on the Atlantic Sea." The use of Atlantic—this time consistently—is also a feature of Felipe Pérez's 1865 *Compendio de jeografía*, whose pages describe Colombia's main islands, peninsulas, bays, and ports as located in or by "the Atlantic." "The general boundaries of the country," readers of Pérez's *Compendio* learned, were "to the north, the Atlantic Ocean."[74]

Despite the variety of names adopted to call the sea to the north of the republic, all these geography textbooks, like the vast majority of the maps and geographical treatises, avoided the words "Caribbean Sea." The word "Caribe," in these nation-making manuals, only appeared as a reference to the uncivilized and barbarous nature of the indigenous people known as the Caribs. Thus, to the question of what Columbus did on his second trip, the students learning geography from D. H. Araujo's geographical catechism were taught to answer, "On the second trip, which took place in 1493, Columbus discovered the *Caribbean* islands, . . . inhabited in their vast majority by stupid and anthropophagous Indians."[75] Given this vision of the implications of being Caribbean, it comes as no surprise that the result of the process that a historian of India has called "pedagogical consolidation" of the nation was a Colombian nation that looked for its identity and national character far away from its Caribbean coasts.[76] Through maps, geographical treatises, and geography textbooks, that is, politician-geographers created and spread to a wider audience of Colombian students a mental geography of proximity with the European and American North Atlantic centers of civilization. While central to Colombia's nation-making process, this Andean-Atlantic vision of Colombia was not without its detractors.

A Caribbean Counternarrative?

The desire to mimic (or to be part of the same community as) Europe and the United States that emerges clearly from the analysis of the geographical and cartographical production of Colombia's politician-geographers should not be taken as a sign of the incontestability of the project to create an Andean-Atlantic nation.[77] From the first years of Colombia's independent life, dissenting voices expressed concerns about and pursued alternatives to this dominant nation-making project.

A "letter from a friend," published in the *Gaceta de Cartagena de Colombia* on June 26, 1831, presents us with a critical approach to the notion that imitating North Atlantic centers of civilization constituted the best political and ideological blueprint for nation making. The letter's anonymous author, described by the *Gaceta*'s editors as one of "several friends of the public good, the Constitution, and the legitimate government," asked rhetorically, "When will we abandon the mania of wanting to turn our country into a Great Britain or a North America?" The question allowed the friend to argue that, in his opinion, it was not necessary to mirror the British Parliament and U.S. Congress in terms of number of representatives. "A [constitutional] convention," he continued, does not gain its respect "from the number of its deputies, but from its members' lights [i.e., intellectual abilities] and personal qualities." Given the limited number of Colombians with such desirable qualifications, the friend proposed a Colombian way through which a small legislative body made up of representatives "instructed in the history of the country, will give us a Granadine constitution," not a bad imitation of those of other countries or monarchies.[78]

In pointing to the limits of imitation, the friend was echoing concerns Simón Bolívar had articulated earlier regarding the political system that best suited the emerging republic. In his famous Jamaica Letter (written in 1815), Bolívar praised both Great Britain's parliamentary monarchy and U.S. federalism but felt that neither system was adequate for South America. Believing "that perfectly representative institutions are not appropriate to our character, our customs, and our current level of knowledge and experience," Bolívar argued, "Until our compatriots acquire the political skills and virtues that distinguish our brothers to the north, entirely popular systems . . . will, I greatly fear, lead to our ruin." Based on this lack of "skills and virtues," he rejected both "the federalist system" (he found it to be "*too* perfect") and "the monarchical blend of aristocracy and democracy, which has brought such fortune and splendor to England." In his opinion, it was necessary to "seek a middle way between these two extremes" and "to strive not for the best but for the most likely of attainment." In northern South America this middle way could, he believed, take the form of a "central republic, whose capital might be Maracaibo," on the Caribbean coast of Venezuela, or a new city "built . . . near the magnificent port of Bahia-Honda," in the heart of Wayuu territory in the Guajira Peninsula.[79]

In 1827, according to Britain's first extraordinary envoy and plenipotentiary minister to Colombia, Alexander Cockburn, Bolívar reiterated his vision of a Caribbean-centered republic. "His Excellency" (Bolívar), Cockburn informed British consul Edward Watts, "had resolved to transfer the seat of government from Bogotá to Cartagena, justifying his decision with very convincing arguments."[80] Cockburn did not spell out Bolívar's "very convincing arguments"; neither did Bolívar pursue the decision he had allegedly taken. Given the lack of further references to this project, one must allow for it to have been an invention of Cockburn. Even if this was the case, the mere mention of the idea—at a time of profound transformations and ambitious schemes, including, among others, plans to launch a joint Colombian-Mexican expedition to liberate Cuba from Spain—reveals that the possibility of a Caribbean-centered Colombian nation was far from automatically discarded.[81] The idea, that is, reveals that a Caribbean-centered republic or republican confederation was part of early Colombia's nation makers' geopolitical imagination.

At the very least, Bolívar's calls to establish the new nation's capital by the Caribbean, just like his characterization (with which I opened this chapter) of the new patria as being Caribbean, appear intriguing. His political career after 1815 does not reveal recurrent efforts to create a nation with a Caribbean-based political center. The Jamaica Letter, however, just like Cockburn's missive to Watts and the anonymous "letter from a friend," posed the possibility of an alternative path in which admiration for Europe and North America did not imply unquestioned imitation and blind desire to decaribbeanize the new republic in order to become part of a Euro-Atlantic community of nations. Throughout the nineteenth century, this alternative path became increasingly silenced by the dominant project of creating an Andean-Atlantic nation. Its silencing, in turn, has strengthened the maxim that holds that in the aftermath of the wars of independence, Cartagena, still Caribbean Colombia's most important city, was unable to foster regional development and counter Bogotá's political preeminence.

Among historians of Caribbean Colombia, the proposition that the destruction brought about by the wars of independence made it impossible for the region to challenge the Andean-driven nation-making project has become a truism. Cartagena, the once-powerful counterweight to the Andean viceregal capital, entered the 1820s crippled by war. Morillo's 1815 siege reduced the city's population by more than half and left a trail of devastation throughout the region's countryside. Shortly after entering Cartagena, the Spanish troops executed the most prominent members of the city's political elite. Many of those who managed to flee the city to seek refuge in Haiti, Jamaica, and other Caribbean islands died shortly afterward in their Caribbean exile or a bit later as they returned to the mainland to continue the fighting. While some managed to survive and returned to Cartagena after the wars' end, the city never recovered its colonial prominence.[82] "Cartagena's mendicant weakness," as historian Alfonso Múnera characterized the city's postindependence state, made it and, by extension, the Caribbean provinces subordinated and mostly voiceless participants in Colombia's nation making.[83]

The truism is certainly valid. It is, as studies of the military and political career of pardo hero José Prudencio Padilla have demonstrated, also worthy of further examination.[84] Padilla, Caribbean Colombia's most prominent independence-era military officer, as well as Juan José Nieto, perhaps the most prominent costeño (coastal) politician of the nineteenth century, constitute important, though somewhat lonely, voices of dissent that allow us to understand the attempts to develop an alternative narrative in which Colombia's

Caribbean provinces would appear as a strong counterbalance to the nation's Andean center. Their lives, political and military careers, and intellectual production not only make evident the existence of a Caribbean counternarrative to the Andean-Atlantic nation, but also demonstrate the extent to which free people of color envisioned a role for themselves and the transimperial Greater Caribbean in the emerging republic.

Born in Riohacha to a Saint-Dominguan father and a Wayuu mother, by the early 1820s Padilla (see figure 6.8) was both a seasoned seaman and a high-ranking military officer in Gran Colombia's navy. His illustrious military career began in 1792 when he enlisted as a cabin boy in the Spanish Royal Navy. In 1805, while fighting in the Battle of Trafalgar, he was captured by the British and sent to Britain, where he remained until the end of the British-Spanish war in 1808. Shortly afterward, he crossed the Atlantic to join the army of the then-independent republic of Cartagena. After Morillo besieged and captured Cartagena, Padilla took refuge in Haiti, where he joined Bolívar's expedition from Les Cayes. His participation in the republican siege of Cartagena (1821) and his leadership in the republican victory at Maracaibo (1823) earned him prestige and popularity in both elite political circles and popular sectors.[85] By 1825, his fame had risen to such an extent that Bolívar, in private, referred to him as "the most important man in Colombia." Bolívar also praised "his adherence to me" and, simultaneously acknowledging Padilla's importance and the damage that could result from his potential antagonism, declared, "May God keep him in this feeling."[86]

Bolívar's admiration for Padilla and preoccupation with the pardo general's political and military skills and stature make it possible to understand the extent to which Padilla posed a challenge to the Andean-Atlantic project. Like Bolívar, interior minister José Manuel Restrepo saw in Padilla a threat that presaged the outbreak of a race war across Colombia's Caribbean provinces.[87] Central to their fears were Padilla's proud embrace of his pardo roots and his determination to fight for pardos' equality and political inclusion. In this agenda, Bolívar, Restrepo, and other local and national leaders like Mariano Montilla and Santander saw the imminent threat of pardocracia, as well as the dreaded scenario of the eruption of a revolution along Haitian lines in Caribbean Colombia. Thus, as Marixa Lasso concluded, in the eyes of Colombia's founding fathers, "Padilla's color, political stature, and ascendancy over the *pardos* of the Caribbean coast were too dangerous."[88]

The realization that Padilla's political rise needed to be curtailed led Bolívar and Montilla to engineer Padilla's decline. According to Aline Helg's careful

Figure 6.8 José Prudencio Padilla, the "most important man in Colombia" and one of the key challengers of the Andean-Atlantic republican project. Image courtesy of Museo Nacional de Colombia, Bogotá, Colombia.

reconstruction of the events that led to Padilla's demise, in early March 1828, after Montilla "lured Padilla into assum[ing] military command of the department" of Magdalena, the pardo general failed to mobilize the support he needed to be officially appointed "as the new commander of Magdalena." Realizing "that his supporters had abandoned him," Padilla fled Cartagena and traveled to Ocaña, where he expected to receive support from a majority of the delegates to the constitutional convention gathered in that city. Failing to obtain decisive support from the convention delegates, Padilla headed back to Mompox. From there, he was "forced . . . to proceed to Cartagena," where immediately after his arrival "on 1 April 1828 . . . he was . . . arrested, accused of planning a race war in the city." Shortly afterward, he was imprisoned in Bogotá. While in jail, he was accused of planning and leading an attempt to murder Bolívar on September 25, 1828. Merely a week later, after a swift trial, "a defiant General Padilla was publicly stripped of his rank and shot, his body displayed hanging from the gallows."[89]

In the life story of José Prudencio Padilla, we can identify two elements that point to the emergence, alongside and in opposition to the Andean-Atlantic republican project, of a Caribbean counternarrative. First, as both Lasso and Helg have demonstrated, white political elites saw in Padilla the coming of the dreaded pardocracia. Rule by pardos, early Colombia's nation makers were convinced, would reorient the emerging nation away from their desired goals. Instead of entering the community of Euro-Atlantic nations and being associated with whiteness, civilization, and the Enlightenment, a pardo-run Colombia would be associated with the evils of the Haitian Revolution and with blackness, barbarism, and obscurantism. Second, while Padilla never explicitly articulated a project for pardocracia, his championing of pardos' political rights and equality and actions like turning Cartagena's pardo neighborhood of Getsemaní into the center of the city's political activity constituted a clear critique of an enlightened vision that perceived black as bad, as uncivilized. Despite the threat of his pardo challenge, the events of 1828, as Aline Helg convincingly concluded, demonstrated that Padilla "did not have the qualities of a caudillo" able to decisively counter the Andean-Atlantic republican project. His execution, however, did not put a definitive end to rumors of race war, fears of pardocracia, and attempts to challenge the Andean-Atlantic nation. Throughout the 1830s, rumors of black-led conspiracies connecting Colombia's Caribbean provinces with Haiti and Jamaica continued to alarm the new republic's political elite.[90] While rumors were frequent, visible leaders were few, with Juan José Nieto being the only one able to match and even surpass Padilla's fame.

Like Padilla, Juan José Nieto (see figure 6.9) was of humble origins and of African descent. Nieto was born in Baranoa, a small town in the province of Cartagena, in 1804. The son of *mulato* artisans who wove cotton wicks for candles, Nieto lived his childhood years amid scarcity and the tumultuous politics that characterized the wars of independence of the second decade of the nineteenth century. Despite these inauspicious circumstances, the patronage of Cartagena's independence hero Ignacio Cavero offered Nieto the opportunity to become educated and to enter the political arena. In the late 1820s, Nieto's enthusiasm for democracy made him oppose Bolívar's shift toward authoritarianism. During the 1830s, increasingly established as a local political figure in Cartagena, Nieto criticized the monarchist tendencies of the city's elites.[91] His antimonarchical and federalist stances allowed local elites to voice their concerns about this *mulato* and his growing political stature. For local notable Bartolomé Calvo, Nieto was "an ignorant who wants to make himself noticeable," whose writings were the laughingstock of Cartagena's educated white circles.[92]

Despite the disdain of local elites, Nieto rose to political prominence. Throughout his three-decade political career, Nieto became known, locally and nationally, as one of the staunchest defenders of federalism. In a letter directed to President Santander in 1835, Nieto introduced himself as a "federalist by principle" who acknowledged that the republic was not yet ready to be turned into a federation. However, stressing the need to give more political autonomy to Cartagena's provincial chamber to legislate on local and provincial matters, he argued for an enhanced "provincial system." This letter, in which Nieto also identified a clear "opposition of interests between the coastal provinces and the [Andean] center," constitutes an early articulation of Nieto's Caribbean counternarrative.[93]

Three years later, in a petition to Cartagena's provincial chamber, Nieto asked Cartagena's legislators to "propose to Congress the initiative to deliberate on the question of whether it is convenient to *granadinos* [to adopt] the federal form of government." Nieto's petition revealed a shift in his interpretation of Colombian politics. Whereas in 1835 he only ventured as far as expressing his federalist sympathies, in 1838 Nieto took the additional step of arguing that the republic was ready to adopt federalism. Despite Nieto's conviction about the republic's readiness, Cartagena's provincial chamber—perhaps revealing the antipathy of local elites like Bartolomé Calvo—resolved to reject and archive Nieto's petition.[94]

Frustrated with the political process, Nieto turned to arms and, during the conflict known in Colombian history as the War of the Supremes, fought

Figure 6.9 Juan José Nieto, staunch federalist, president of the short-lived United States of New Granada, and one of the most active proponents of the Caribbean counternarrative. Image adapted from Wikimedia Commons.

alongside military leader Francisco Carmona as one of the chief officers of the United Army of the Federal States of the Coast. Military defeat in 1841 resulted in five years of exile in Jamaica, after which Nieto returned to Cartagena to continue defending his federalist stance. During the 1850s he served twice as governor of the province of Cartagena and before the end of the decade, in 1859, became the elected president of the Sovereign State of Bolívar, an independent political entity with its capital in Cartagena. Shortly afterward, in 1860, he reached the pinnacle of his political career when he became president of a fleeting coastal republic that had Cartagena as its political center. Extending from the Guajira Peninsula to the Gulf of Darién, this political entity comprised what at the time were called the sovereign states of Bolívar and Magdalena. Soon after, on January 1861, Nieto's presidential authority was expanded when he became president of the similarly fleeting but geographically larger United States of New Granada. (In addition to Bolívar and Magdalena on the Caribbean coast, this republican experiment, which a historian has called a "Colombian counterrepublic," incorporated the southwestern province of Cauca.)[95] After only two months in power, Nieto ceded the presidency of the United States of New Granada to politician-geographer Tomás Cipriano de Mosquera and continued, until the end of 1865, presiding over the Sovereign State of Bolívar. On July 16, 1866, less than a year after being deposed from the state's presidency, Nieto died in Cartagena.[96]

This summary of Nieto's political and military careers reveals his consistency in defending the federal model as the one best suited to serve the interests of the republic's coastal provinces. From his 1835 letter to Santander, where he defended federalism as a principle based on the argument that "it cannot be hidden from anyone" that "the bliss" of the province of Cartagena depended on its inhabitants' "liberty to rule their own house," to his death in 1866, shortly after being deposed as president of the Sovereign State of Bolívar, Nieto, as he himself put it, "never lowered my [federalist] flag."[97] His pro-coast federalism clearly constitutes evidence of an alternative nation-making project that privileged the Caribbean coast over the Andean interior.

Nieto's intellectual production—as geographer and novelist—further hints at a worldview and political project antagonistic to the premises of the Andean-Atlantic nation promoted by the enlightened creoles and politician-geographers studied in the previous sections. Unlike the geographic treatises produced by his mid-nineteenth-century peers, Nieto's detailed *Geografía histórica, estadística y local de la Provincia de Cartagena*, written in 1839, did not shy away from the word "Caribbean." When describing the extent of the province, Nieto's *Geografía* states, "To the west its boundaries are, the Caribbean Sea or [Sea] of the Antilles."[98] In light of other politician-geographers' refusal to use the word "Caribbean," Nieto's word choice appears to be a curious deviation that requires explanation. His novel *Yngermina, o la hija de Calamar* offers a partial one.

Published in 1844, *Yngermina* narrates the love story of Spanish conquistador Alonso de Heredia and Yngermina, princess of Calamar.[99] The story takes place during the 1530s in the territory that after the conquest was to become the province of Cartagena. Taking Spanish conquest as inevitable (and therefore making indigenous resistance a predetermined failure), the novel, as a literary critic put it, "does not narrate . . . the antagonism between indigenous people and Spaniards," but focuses on the internal disputes within each group. On the one hand, Nieto distinguishes between the good conquistadors (Pedro de Heredia and his brother, the main character, Alonso, whose approach to conquest stresses mutual understanding, respect, friendship, and even love) and the bad conquistadors (Francisco Badillo and Miguel Peralta, who are presented as greedy, gold-hungry, and violent). On the other hand, he divides *calamareños*—the indigenous inhabitants of Calamar—in two groups: those who identify from an early stage the need to accept conquest and negotiate within oppression (Yngermina and her father, the cacique Ostáron) and those who refuse to accept conquest and pursue armed resistance against Spaniards (Catarpa, Yngermina's brother).[100] Despite their antagonism, all calamareños are portrayed in a positive light that stresses their civilized manners, luxurious and elegant ways, "regularity and orderly behavior," intelligence, nobility, hospitality, and "gentle and loving nature . . . that inspires friendship and trust."[101] It is precisely in this depiction of calamareños and their fate after the conquest that *Yngermina* provides clues to understanding Nieto's nation-making project and its challenge to the Andean-Atlantic nation. Understanding the novel as a "foundational fiction," it is possible to uncover a literary argument that neatly aligns with Nieto's pro-coast federalism.[102]

While the enlightened creoles and politician-geographers of the previous sections created a national narrative that erased the Caribbean and relegated the Caribbean coast (and the other lowland territories of the nation) to the political and ideological periphery, Nieto's *Yngermina* presented an alternative account in which the Caribbean lowlands, because of their glorious indigenous past, could very well be conceived as a source of national pride and patriotism. Effectively making calamareños as civilized as the more celebrated Muiscas of the Andean interior, Nieto was claiming the Caribbean lowlands as a potential "locus of civilization."[103] If calamareños—who were part of the larger group that Tomás Cipriano de Mosquera and José María Samper called the "Carib race"[104]—were (or could have been) civilized, there was no need for Nieto to avoid using the word "Caribbean" when referring to the sea. While Mosquera and Samper took Caribe (as sea and as indigenous group) as a loaded term associated with backwardness and barbarism, Nieto did not see the negative connotations of the term. His province of Cartagena, thus, was bounded on the west by the Mar Caribe.[105]

Nation Making as Atlantic Process

Juan José Nieto's political career and geographical and literary production formed a compelling argument against the narrative of the Andean-Atlantic nation. This dominant nation-making strategy, however, was strong enough to repel compelling arguments coming from the margins of the nation's political center. That the Andean-Atlantic republican project could resist Nieto's challenge, however, did not mean that early nation makers succeeded in creating the nation they envisioned. In fact, it is possible to conclude that, just as Nieto's Caribbean counternarrative failed to pose a significant challenge to the dominant Andean-Atlantic project, the Andean-Atlantic project itself failed to live up to its promoters' expectations.

Enlightened creoles effectively implanted in the emerging nation's psyche the idea of the tropical lowlands as sites of backwardness. Politician-geographers of the mid-nineteenth century, on the other hand, succeeded in erasing the word "Caribbean" from cartographic and geographical representations of the republic. The analysis of the name they assigned to the sea to the north of the republic reveals an almost complete unwillingness to identify the Caribbean Sea as the nation's northern boundary. Instead, it became common to use the name Atlantic Ocean (though the toponym Sea of the Antilles was also used). While enlightened creoles convinced themselves of the civilizational potential of the Andes, for politician-geographers, the name Atlantic Ocean made it possible to create a sense of proximity to the North Atlantic centers of civilization. To feel close to Europe and North America, however, was not the same as to be (or to be perceived as being) close to Europe and North America. The mental proximity that enlightened creoles and politician-geographers felt to Europe and North America was not reciprocated by Europeans and North Americans. While the Caribbean was effectively erased from the national consciousness, Colombia was not incorporated or accepted into the community of Euro-Atlantic nations.

Despite failing in their ultimate aim to incorporate the emerging Republic of Colombia into the Euro-Atlantic community of nations, the logics of enlightened creoles and politician-geographers provide us a great understanding of the geopolitical imagination of these two generations of Colombian nation makers. In their texts and maps we see clearly the enlightened imperative to avoid association with a Caribbean world that was represented in enlightened minds by the disorder, destruction, and barbarism that white elites throughout the transimperial Greater Caribbean associated with the Haitian Revolution. By the same token, the Atlantic, especially the North Atlantic, was perceived as civilized. The black-white, savage-civilized binaries, then, lie at the root of the ways in which enlightened creoles and politician-geographers interpreted their nineteenth-century present and created paths toward a desired future. Their sense of what Doreen Massey called "contemporaneous plurality," or the ability to think of the multiple possibilities of the contemporary moment, was demarcated by the two extremes defined by Bolívar at the early stages of nation making.[106] In order to avoid pardocracia or, as Bolívar explicitly put it, "Guinea and more Guinea," early Colombian nation makers pursued nation-making strategies marked by their desire to create the "other Europe" of Bolívar's dreams.[107]

In addition, the enlightened arguments and geographical representations analyzed in this chapter shed important light on the oft-forgotten Atlantic nature of nation making in Latin America. From its very beginning, when enlightened creoles began to think about independence, nation making connected Spanish America with the North Atlantic in fundamental ways. Independence heroes like Simón Bolívar and Francisco de Miranda conceived plans and recruited sympathizers in Great Britain and the United States. Later in the century, politician-geographers, as their maps and geographical treatises make clear, also imagined their nation in an Atlantic context. National consolidation, for these mid-nineteenth-century nation makers, was not just an internal affair but also a matter of positioning their young republic as part of the Euro-Atlantic community of civilized nations. Many, as James Sanders put it, even imagined themselves and their republics as "the vanguard of the Atlantic world."[108]

Interpreting Colombia's (and Latin America's) nation-making process as fundamentally Atlantic has important historiographical repercussions. In particular, paying attention to the Atlantic nature of Colombia's nation-making process can contribute to "rebalancing Atlantic history" by questioning the field's periodization and the types of connections Atlantic historians privilege.[109] The Atlantic scope of Colombia's nation-making process demonstrates that Atlantic history's temporal horizon does not need to be 1800 or the 1820s. There can be, as Donna Gabaccia put it, "a longer history of the Atlantic."[110] In addition, the Atlantic character of the nation-making process analyzed in this chapter Latinamericanizes the Atlantic by showing that Colombian nation makers actively participated in the political and intellectual currents of the Atlantic world. In so doing, the chapter contributes to the much-needed transformation of a historiographical map that, despite significant progress, still represents the Atlantic world largely as a British North Atlantic world.[111]

Coda: The Atlantic Reaches Land in the Twentieth Century

During the remaining decades of the nineteenth century, geographic texts and lessons continued to inscribe in the minds of Colombians the knowledge that the nation was bounded on the north by the Atlantic Ocean. By the beginning of the twentieth century, the Atlantic nature of the nation was finally inscribed into the national territory (not only its waters). With the creation of a new state called Atlantic, whose capital, Barranquilla, was promoted as the "golden door" through which modernity was to enter the country, Colombia completed (roughly) one hundred years of decaribbeanization.[112] The civilized, modern, Atlantic nature of the nation finally became clearly visible on every national map. Throughout the twentieth century the country's Caribbean past—the history of belonging to a transimperial Greater Caribbean—was successfully erased from Colombia's official history and, to a large extent, historical memory.

Of Alternative Geographies and Plausible Futures

José Manuel Restrepo, a distinguished member of the group of New Granada's enlightened creoles and one of the most prominent political figures of Colombia's early national period, drafted a particular Colombian past and dreamed of a specific Colombian future. His cartographic work, his role as interior minister of Colombia during the 1820s, and his acute fear of race war and of a Haitian-like future for Colombia, as chapter 6 shows, made him one of the masterminds of the Andean-Atlantic republican project and its concomitant process of decaribbeanization of the nascent republic. Restrepo was also Colombia's first national historian. His *Historia de la revolución de la república de Colombia* provided a lasting framework within which many generations of Colombian historians have interpreted the country's transition from colony to nation. The work privileges elite political actors and a narrative of political fragmentation that tragically but inevitably led to the emergence of three republics: Colombia, Venezuela, and Ecuador. Restrepo's *Historia* is a standard bearer of the type of nineteenth-century historical account that sees history, in the words of Lara Putnam, "as the discipline charged with writing each nation-state a usable past" and, by extension, an enduring future of political independence.[1] His account fits neatly into what sociologists have termed "methodological nationalism."[2] Methodological nationalism, the unquestioned use of national borders as geographic units of analysis or "the naturalization of the nation-state" as the analytical unit, effectively creates what in his analysis of Restrepo's *Historia* Colombian historian Germán Colmenares called a "historiographical prison."[3] Actively seeking to rethink and transcend the geographic boundaries and periodization schemes that a nation-state–driven historical account solidifies, historians of the Atlantic world have developed tools to escape this methodological prison. Instead of thinking of the nation-state (and, more generally, of political geographies) as a proper container for historical inquiry, scholars of the Atlantic (and other supranational regions) have increasingly allowed their subjects of study to spill out of their national or imperial containers. Similarly, giving its proper due to contingency as an agent of historical change and opening space for nonstate actors to be at the center of historical analysis, Atlantic historians have begun to interpret the so-called Age of Revolutions as more than just a period of preordained transition from colonies to nation-states.

This book has contributed to the effort to escape the prison of methodological nationalism by advancing an approach that privileges a geographic framework—the transimperial Greater Caribbean—that provides an alternative way to organize and interpret the world. In addition, this book has also questioned the inevitability of the nation-state as a preordained way of organizing global space by showing that from the vantage point of late eighteenth- and early nineteenth-century New Granada's Caribbean shores, it was possible to imagine futures that did not lead to the creation of the Colombian republic that ended up emerging in the aftermath of the Spanish American wars of independence. Using the alternative geography I call the transimperial Greater Caribbean, the subjects of this book envisioned plausible futures developed within this malleable, amorphously demarcated, transimperial aqueous territory.

Lived Geographies as Alternative Ways to Organize and Interpret the World

As in our own contemporary moment, the people who inhabit the preceding pages lived in a world divided—among many other ways—along political lines. Political geographies made their world one in which different empires divided up space and claimed portions of the earth. Unlike our own contemporary moment, the political geographies of the period studied in this book were in constant flux. In the course of the century covered here, some of these empires shattered into pieces and new political geographies—nation-states—came to occupy the surface one or more empires had previously occupied. While political geographies clearly informed the way in which those populating this book's pages lived their lives, there were other ways of experiencing and interpreting the world, other ways of filling space with meaning, of—as articulated in chapter 2—turning space into territory. Focusing on lived geographies—personal and collective geographies developed on the basis of everyday social interactions—this book has made an argument for another way of being in the world. Looking at mobility as a key region-making variable and using the transimperial region that emerged out of sailors' mobility as a geographical framework of analysis, this book has advanced an argument for the existence of what can be called a transimperial Greater Caribbean way of being in the world. Since the transimperial Greater Caribbean, as argued here, was human-made, it has been one of the key arguments of this book that people make both their own history and their own geography.

While lived geographies emerge out of human interactions, these interactions take place within a set of predetermined rules. In the transimperial Greater Caribbean context, this ultimately means that while sailors created the region and both sailors and other less mobile subjects experienced it, none of them created or experienced the transimperial Greater Caribbean under circumstances of their own choosing. Neither did they create nor experience the region in a political and historical vacuum. Instead, as chapter 6 demonstrates, those creating, experiencing, and arguing for the transimperial Greater Caribbean did so alongside others who, like Restrepo, perceived the transimperial Greater Caribbean as a threat that needed to be curtailed. But just what type of region did the sailors and other less mobile transimperial Greater Caribbean dwellers create and experience, and what does uncovering this region entail for our interpretation of the world we study?

Sailors' border-crossing lives not only gave shape to a Kingston-centered transimperial Greater Caribbean, but also—through the information sailors like Pedro Pérez Prieto, Juan Estevan Rodríguez, and thousands more exchanged on the high seas and at many ports—made it possible for other less mobile individuals to be part of this transimperial aqueous territory. In other words, while constant mobility enabled sailors to create and experience the transimperial Greater Caribbean, lack of mobility or less frequent mobility did not automatically exclude others from experiencing this transimperial lived geography. While mobile sailors used their everyday border-crossing experiences to create the malleable, fluid, loosely bounded, aqueous territory of mobile markers that constitutes the transimperial Greater Caribbean, less mobile subjects mostly experiencing this regional configuration from islands and continental shores also lived their lives within this transimperial milieu.

Making the transimperial Greater Caribbean a geographical canvas on which maritime Indians, Jamaican planters, loyalists from the American Revolution, Spanish authorities, South American insurgents, and early Colombian nation makers interpreted their present and envisioned potential futures, this book enables a better understanding of events and processes that are hard to explain by staying within the confines of nation-states, empires, or conventional world-regionalization schemes. Since those whose lives we study did not necessarily live lives bounded by these geographical units of analysis, letting them show us their lived geographies and the potential futures they envisioned within them allows us to better approach the past we are studying. Uncovering alternative geographies like the transimperial Greater Caribbean, thus, makes it possible to approach the lives and times of those we study on their own terms, as opposed to through the limiting gaze afforded by imperial demarcations that clearly informed but did not fully comprehend their experience and interpretation of what they considered their world. By the same token, a transimperial Greater Caribbean framework provides an alternative to the anachronism of interpreting the past through the lens of national borders that were yet to be established.

Maritime Indians' ability to keep Spanish authorities at bay, for instance, can only be properly explained through an approach that allows Cunas and Wayuu to guide us through their lived geographies and the mental maps they produced to make sense of the world they inhabited. The travels and commercial and diplomatic endeavors of Cuna chiefs Bernardo and Guillermo Hall and their Wayuu counterparts Caporinche and Martín Rodríguez reveal the limits of approaching their world through the European perspective Mary Louise Pratt so fittingly termed "imperial eyes."[4] While both Cunas and Wayuu inhabited what Spanish authorities and other European powers considered Spanish territory, all these observers were perfectly aware that these Spanish claims were just that: claims. Both the Darién and the Guajira Peninsula were claimed by Spain but ruled independently by Cunas and Wayuu. Participation in transimperial networks of exchange made it possible for these maritime Indians to remain masters of their domains. From their perspectives, it seems reasonable to conclude, these domains were not peripheral locations within a larger Spanish empire but vital centers of Wayuu and Cuna worlds made possible by sustained interactions across political boundaries.

Similarly, circumscribing the analyses of the American Revolution and Colombia's war of independence within political geographies hinders our ability to understand how the subjects we study experienced these historical events. Neither those fighting in the American Revolution nor the participants in the war that led to Colombia's independence knew the outcomes of these confrontations. They could definitely foresee the ultimate outcome as one of several potential outcomes. But they were far from interpreting these events as just wars for national liberation fought within already-made national territories. As the experiences and projects of Jamaican planters and British loyalists explored in chapter 4 demonstrate, the American Revolution was also fought in the Caribbean and could have had, and indeed had, consequences that went beyond the birth of a new republic. For planters like Edward Long and Bryan Edwards, revenge-thirsty loyalists like John Cruden and William Augustus Bowles, and military adventurers like Robert Hodgson, sitting idly and witnessing their own economic decline as the thirteen British North American colonies turned into the independent United States was simply not an option. And, as Simón Bolívar's Caribbean adventures and his geopolitical calculations made clear, the struggle that ended up leading to the birth of the Republic of Colombia was much more than a civil war pitting patriots against royalists. At stake were also visions of the type of political entity Bolívar and other nation makers, Restrepo included, hoped to create and, in the process, to avoid. The coexistence of conflicting visions and political imaginaries reveals that what ended up happening was not unequivocally bound to happen. It reveals that the geopolitical imagination of the Age of Revolutions allowed for a number of alternative futures to be considered plausible.

Mental Maps and Political Imaginaries as Paths to the Future

The key analytical implication here is that lived geographies foster the development of mental maps, maps in which proximity and belonging are not the direct measure of physical distance and imposed loyalties determined by birthplace. Instead, mental maps distort physical geography in ways that allow us to understand that distance can be relative, that the sense of remoteness or proximity is a matter of perspective. Proximity, in short, is in the eye of the beholder and can be measured in innumerable ways.[5] Mental maps, in addition, transform political geographies to create subjective worlds that reveal key elements of their makers' geopolitical imagination. The case studies of chapters 3 through 6 make it possible to trace a number of mental maps through which the subjects of this book interpreted the world they inhabited.

My analysis of the maritime Indians' transimperial interactions provides us with two examples of mental maps that resulted from these indigenous groups' participation in the communication networks that created the transimperial Greater Caribbean. On the one hand, based on the ways in which Wayuu and Cunas encountered Spanish authorities and other Europeans, it seems reasonable to imagine a Wayuu leader (or his Cuna counterpart) picturing a world in which the Guajira Peninsula and some of its most important ports (e.g., Portete, Bahia Honda, and Chimare) occupy center stage, with islands like Curaçao and Jamaica figuring as the main international points of reference. By contrast, Spanish centers of political and economic power like Madrid, Santa Fe, and Cartagena, one can further imagine, would barely appear in this Wayuu leader's mental map of the Wayuu-centric transimperial Greater Caribbean. In this case, thus, imagining the world from a Wayuu perspective forces us to reconceptualize political geographies in favor of geographical frameworks that more closely represent the world that the subjects we study experienced and envisioned. For maritime Indians, in sharp contrast with dominant renditions of indigenous people as primitive and technologically incompetent beings inhabiting an exotic and somewhat pristine world, cosmopolitanism and its associated political, military, and diplomatic skills were at the core of their transimperial Greater Caribbean world.

On the other hand, Spanish concerns about the spread among the Wayuu of revolutionary ideas imported from the French Caribbean gave shape to a mental map of the geographic area Spanish authorities considered at risk of revolutionary contagion. Like many of their contemporary and future colonial and early national administrators, Spanish bureaucrats used their apprehension over Haiti's revolutionary process as a tool to organize their experience and understanding of the world they inhabited. In short, they built a mental map in which the communication networks that gave shape to the transimperial Greater Caribbean carried the seeds of a fear-inducing, black-dominated, Haitian-like future that needed to be avoided. If political geographies tend to be the main organizing principle of world-regionalization schemes, these two examples show us the potential for organizing geographic regions through other means. Revolutionary fears and commercial interactions can (and did) work as ways of organizing global space that rival(ed) conventional ways of dividing and making sense of the world.

Another clear example of a mental map that, like the hypothetical map a Wayuu leader would have drawn, distorts physical geography in order to come up with a vision of the future emerges clearly from the analysis of nineteenth-century Colombian nation makers. In their eagerness to construct a Colombian nation that could qualify as a member of the Euro-Atlantic community of nations, they pursued a nation-making project geared toward both establishing a sense of proximity to the civilized nations of the North Atlantic and marking a clear distance from the Caribbean. The mental map resulting from this pursuit was one that erased the Caribbean and brought the North Atlantic nations—especially Great Britain and the United States—closer to South America's shores. It is possible to imagine this mental map by thinking of the Atlantic world as a tablecloth. Pulling the tablecloth down from the Caribbean would send Jamaica, Haiti, Cuba, and the rest of the Caribbean islands into the abyss while bringing the North Atlantic closer to Colombia's shores. This way of envisioning the world and the community of nations to which they wanted the emerging Colombian nation to belong allowed Colombian nation makers to create a national fiction that, in spite of geographical proximity, stressed real and imagined linkages to the North Atlantic centers of civilization while erasing real and derided connections to a Caribbean world perceived as black, savage, uncivilized, and, therefore, threatening. While the Caribbean counternarratives of José Prudencio Padilla and Juan José Nieto sought to challenge this Euro-Atlantic vision of the future, the geographical distortion at the heart of the Andean-Atlantic republican project ended up prevailing as Colombia's official way of presenting itself to the world.

The plans of Jamaican planters and loyalists forced to flee the United States in the immediate aftermath of the American Revolution give us another type of mental map, one that instead of distorting physical geographies simply transforms political ones. In this case, the new world Long, Edwards, Cruden, Bowles, and Hodgson, among others, envisioned in their attempts to keep the British Empire Atlantic centered was one in which the obvious solution to the economic crisis that the American Revolution generated in the British Caribbean was to turn south and change the political map of the Americas by painting the Caribbean coasts of Central and South America imperial pink. For planters and adventurers like Hodgson, this way of redrawing the future political map of the Americas offered a potential solution to the threat of economic ruin. For disgruntled loyalists, it functioned as a gratifying way to avenge the wrongs Spain had caused by contributing to the independence of the United States.

Most of the futures envisioned in these mental maps failed to become influential at the time they were envisioned. The alternative geographical and political scenarios they projected also failed to become dominant ways for future analysts to organize and interpret the world. The British Empire, despite the collective effort of planters and loyalists, did not choose to conquer northern South America. British authorities, to the great chagrin of Bolívar, did not abandon their neutrality policy and refused to aid Bolívar during his stay in Jamaica. Colombian politician-geographers, while successfully erasing the Caribbean from the geographical representations of the nascent republic, failed to convince their North Atlantic counterparts that the Colombian republic did, indeed, belong to the civilized, Euro-Atlantic community of nations. Because they did not come to fruition, these visions were, to paraphrase E. P. Thompson, condemned to "the enormous condescension of posterity."[6]

Like many other political imaginaries and strategies that flourished through the Atlantic world during the Age of Revolutions, the visions of maritime Indians, Jamaican planters, creole military adventurers, and Colombian nation makers allow us to reinterpret the period as much more than one characterized by a straightforward transition from colony to nation. As more recent works on the revolutionary Atlantic have demonstrated, the period between the 1760s and the 1860s offered a wide variety of options and opportunities for Caribbean and Atlantic dwellers of all socioeconomic and racial backgrounds. While many embraced independence and republicanism as paths to the future, countless others favored monarchy. In the transimperial Greater Caribbean (and the Atlantic) theater of actions, many worlds were plausible. The maritime Indians, Jamaican planters, and Colombian nation makers who populate this book's pages, thus, like the Indian and slave royalists of southwestern New Granada; the "black and mulatto Cubans who explicitly supported the continuation of Spanish rule"; the many public intellectuals in nineteenth-century Mexico, Argentina, and Colombia who tended "to see monarchy as the answer"; the Atlantic creoles for whom "monarchy was . . . the best option"; and the Dominicans and Haitians who "dream[ed] together" of a unified Hispaniola, among many others, force us to step out of our geographical and historiographical comfort zones to make sense of the worlds and projects they created and envisioned.[7] Their unfulfilled visions and failed projects were as integral to the Age of Revolutions as the ones that ended up coming into being.

Despite the ultimate failure of their projects, the fact that their promoters spent time, energy, ink, paper, money, and other resources trying to turn them into reality speaks to their importance. A history that is attentive to how the subjects we study developed mental maps to envision potential futures allows us to better capture the "sense of the perils and possibilities of the contemporary" moment.[8] It allows us to understand what ended up happening within a larger interpretational framework that also contemplates options that those we are studying considered plausible. Considering plausibility, in turn, can help us reconsider the notion of the unthinkable by allowing historical subjects inhabiting the rapidly changing world of the Age of Revolutions to envision possible futures that only a historical approach dismissive of its subjects' agency and geopolitical imagination would disregard as improbable or unthinkable delusions. While historian and anthropologist Michel-Rolph Trouillot made a convincing argument for the different ways in which the Haitian Revolution constituted "an unthinkable history," my approach to the dynamic transimperial Greater Caribbean world during the Age of Revolutions, I hope, makes a strong case for the analytical potential of unfulfilled visions.[9]

These visions—some of them realistic projects, some chimerical delusions—were fundamental components of the "open-ended constellation of political futures" that allowed those whose lives we study to interpret, organize, and make sense of the tumultuous world they inhabited.[10] The multiple visions of transimperial Greater Caribbean dwellers like Juan Estevan Rodríguez, Pedro Pérez Prieto, Guillermo Hall, Bernardo, Caporinche, Martín Rodríguez, Edward Long, Bryan Edwards, John Cruden, William Augustus Bowles, Robert Hodgson, Simón Bolívar, José Prudencio Padilla, Juan José Nieto, and innumerable others restore complexity to the past by presenting the world of the Age of Revolutions as one in which multiple futures were plausible. If the century between the 1760s and the 1860s ended up being characterized by the emergence of an Atlantic world in which nation-states gradually became the norm, the multiple visions studied in this book demonstrate that, despite what ended up happening, other worlds were possible; other outcomes were considered plausible.

Note on Method and Sources to
Establish the Routes of Vessels Crisscrossing
the Transimperial Greater Caribbean

As any historian who has attempted to trace the route of a schooner navigating Caribbean waters during the late eighteenth and early nineteenth centuries knows, following ships in the archives is a difficult task.[1] The problem—mostly— has to do with the fragmentary nature of the information available in archival repositories. In theory, retrieving the itinerary of any given ship requires consulting the records of the port of departure and of the port to which the ship declared it was sailing. For the purposes of this study, given the centrality of Jamaica, I consulted New Granada's books of departures and arrivals and Jamaica's shipping returns. In practice, the meticulous process of cross-checking these port records seldom yields a clear-cut navigational trajectory.

Neither the Spanish colonial archives nor the British imperial archive allows for a complete reconstruction of the dynamic world of transimperial exchanges in which New Granada's Caribbean ports were actively involved. Port records for important ports in the transimperial Greater Caribbean, such as Riohacha, Portobelo, San Andrés, and Sabanilla, are not available. For Kingston, Cartagena, and Santa Marta information is available only for selected years. While this is enough to provide a general idea of the movement of these ports and the itineraries of many of the vessels that continuously traversed Caribbean waters, an exploration of the port records of other important Caribbean entrepôts like Curaçao, Saint Thomas, and Les Cayes could add further nuances to our understanding of the workings of the transimperial Greater Caribbean.

To the problem of fragmentary information (shipping returns are available only for selected ports and selected years), one must add others that can be summarized as follows: (1) An important part of the trade was consciously hidden from authorities attempting to keep track of ships and creating historical records; (2) ships did not usually sail from one port to another and then back to the initial port, itineraries instead including multiple stopovers; (3) often different ships had the same name; and (4) ships changed captains frequently.

Consciously Hidden Trade

Many ships engaged in transimperial trade simply do not appear in the historical records. Ships illegally sailing the Caribbean only made it to the historical record when authorities seized them or when other captains mentioned encounters with them at sea. Thus, especially at times when exchanges with foreigners were completely forbidden, it is difficult to acquire a good sense of the volume of ships engaged in illicit transimperial trade. Frequent seizures and multiple complaints about contraband give the idea of the existence of a conspicuous illegal intercourse with foreigners, but can lead to either exaggerating or underestimating the reality of illegal trade.

Itineraries with Multiple Stopovers

Caribbean vessels worked as peddlers, visiting many ports before returning to their initial port of departure. Therefore, ships tend to "get lost" in the middle of the Caribbean before reappearing in the shipping returns of Kingston, Cartagena, or Santa Marta. A Spanish ship entering Jamaica from a Neogranadan port could then sail to Cuba or Puerto Rico or any other foreign port before it reappears entering Cartagena from Riohacha. Ultimately this means that the available information to reconstruct ships' itineraries can simplify the actual routes traversed by Caribbean vessels. The limited information available can also hide certain ships or reduce their importance on Caribbean commercial routes.

Common Names for Ships

There were many Spanish ships sailing Caribbean waters, many of which had the same name. *San Josef* (or *San Joseph* or *San Josef y las Ánimas* and many other variations) and *Carmen* (or *Nuestra Señora del Carmen* or *El Carmen* and many variations thereof) were very common names. With multiple ships bearing the same name it is impossible, in many cases, to avoid confusion. Some times ship aliases, captains' names, and tonnage are helpful in distinguishing between two ships of the same name. But aliases and tonnage are not always available. Captains' names, for their part, introduce a new difficulty.

Frequent Captain Changes

Associating a ship with a captain is often a good way to avoid confusion among ships with the same or similar names. However, since captains changed ships frequently and these changes were not always accounted for in the shipping returns, this method leads to many dead ends. It was common for ships to change captains several times in the course of a single year. In 1793, for example, the *Santiago*, a Spanish vessel sailing between Cartagena and Jamaica with frequent visits to Sabanilla and Riohacha, sailed under five different captains.[2] The port records, in this particular case, include annotations registering the captain changes, which eliminates ambiguity. For ships with common names like *Carmen* or *San Josef*, even with annotations about captain changes, confusion is inevitable.

The description just provided includes just some of the most common problems. Many other difficulties, including flag changes, sales that led to renaming, and shipwrecks, could make a ship disappear from the historical record. Despite these difficulties, as chapters 1 and 2 demonstrate, a careful juxtaposition of Spanish and British port records makes it possible to reconstruct a transimperial Greater Caribbean from New Granada's shores. In other words, while distinguishing between two ships called *Carmen* or *San Josef* can be a difficult task, it is not always an impossible one.

Detailed Itineraries and Basic Information
on Selected Spanish Schooners

1. *Soledad* (1785)

Captain   Manuel Bliz

Known itinerary
1. Jan. 4: Entered Cartagena from Cuba with tobacco.
2. Mar. 3: Entered Kingston from Santa Marta with Nicaraguan wood.
3. Jun. 1: Entered Kingston from Riohacha with Nicaraguan wood.
4. Jun. 27: Sailed for Cartagena with sixty-five slaves.
5. Jul. 2: Entered Cartagena with slaves.
6. Oct. 21: Sailed from Kingston to Cartagena with forty-three slaves and dry goods.

2. *Santiago* (1793)

Captains   Josef Soler, Joaquín Vidarres, Domingo Herrera, Manuel de Estrada, Josef Añino

Known itinerary
1. Jan. 10: Sailed for Riohacha (from Cartagena) with *frutos*.
2. Apr. 3: Entered Cartagena from Jamaica with three *bozales* and 784 *pesos* and four *reales*.
3. May 29: Sailed for Riohacha with *frutos* and bullion.
4. Jun. 25: Entered Cartagena from Jamaica with twenty-four *negros bozales*.

5. Jul. 12: Sailed for Sabanilla in ballast to get *palo mora* for sale in Jamaica.

6. Sep. 21: Entered Cartagena from Jamaica in ballast.

7. Oct. 19: Sailed for foreign colonies with *frutos*.

8. Nov. 23: Entered Cartagena from Jamaica in ballast.

9. Dec. 7: Sailed for Sabanilla to get *palo mora*.

10. Dec. 23: Entered Cartagena from Sabanilla with *palo mora*.

11. Dec. 24: Sailed for Jamaica with *frutos*.

3. *Esperanza* (1793)

Captain	Ramón Echandía
Known itinerary	1. Jan. 22: Sailed for Sabanilla (from Cartagena) in ballast to get cotton.

2. Feb. 14: Entered Cartagena from Sabanilla with hides, sugar, and other *efectos*.

3. Mar. 6: Sailed for Sabanilla in ballast to get cotton for sale in Jamaica.

4. Aug. 7: Entered Cartagena from Jamaica in ballast.

5. Dec. 24: Sailed for Riohacha and Coro with corn.

4. *Santo Cristo de la Espiración* (1793)

Captains	Josef Aballe, Juan Guardiola
Known itinerary	1. Apr. 4: Sailed for Portobelo (from Cartagena) with *frutos* and *efectos*.

2. May. 2: Entered Cartagena from Portobelo in ballast.

3. Jul. 19: Sailed for foreign colonies to buy slaves and tools.

4. Aug. 19: Entered Cartagena from Jamaica in ballast.

5. Sep. 5: Sailed for Sabanilla to get cotton.

6. Sep. 16: Entered Cartagena from Sabanilla with cotton.

7. Oct. 9: Sailed for foreign colonies with *frutos*.

8. Nov. 16: Entered Cartagena from Jamaica with four *bozales*.

5. *Ana María* (1793)

Captain	Josef García
Known itinerary	1. Jan. 3: Entered Cartagena from Portobelo with wax and 500 silver pesos.
	2. Jan. 12: Sailed for Zapote and Portobelo in ballast.
	3. Jun. 26: Entered Cartagena from Portobelo with 500 pesos.
	4. Jul. 11: Sailed for Jamaica with *frutos* to buy slaves.
	5. Sep. 3: Entered Cartagena from Jamaica in ballast.
	6. Sep. 14: Sailed for Zapote in ballast.

6. *Bella Narcisa* (1807)

Captains	Francisco Martínez, Eudaldo Fiol
Known itinerary	1. Apr. 19: Entered Santa Marta from Cartagena with *registro*.
	2. May 4: Sailed for Cuba with *registro*.
	3. Jun. 10: Entered Santa Marta from Cuba with *registro*.
	4. Jun. 24: Sailed for Riohacha in ballast.
	5. Jul. 2: Entered Santa Marta from Riohacha with *registro*.
	6. Jul. 24: Sailed for neutral foreign colonies with *frutos* to exchange for slaves.
	7. Aug. 27: Entered Santa Marta from Saint Thomas with unspecified cargo.
	8. Sep. 24: Sailed for Saint Thomas with *frutos* and bullion to buy slaves.
	9. Nov. 14: Entered Santa Marta from Danish Saint Croix in ballast.

7. *Samaria* (1814)

Captains	Jaime Gilbert, Francisco Manes, Bonifacio Revilla, Juan Santos
Known itinerary	1. Mar. 26: Sailed for Santa Marta from Kingston with rum, candles, and dry goods.

2. Apr. 6: Entered Santa Marta from Jamaica with unspecified cargo.

3. Apr. 20: Sailed from Santa Marta to Riohacha in ballast.

4. May 12: Entered Kingston from Riohacha with Nicaraguan wood and hides.

5. May 21: Sailed from Kingston to Santa Marta with rum and dry goods.

6. May 30: Entered Santa Marta from Jamaica with unspecified cargo.

7. Jun. 20: Sailed from Santa Marta to Riohacha and Maracaibo in ballast.

8. Jul. 30: Entered Santa Marta from Riohacha with *registro* from Maracaibo.

9. Aug. 8: Sailed from Santa Marta to Riohacha in ballast.

10. Oct. 11: Entered Santa Marta from Riohacha with *registro* from La Guaira and Puerto Cabello.

11. Nov. 3: Sailed from Santa Marta to Riohacha in ballast.

12. Nov. 16: Entered Kingston from Riohacha with Nicaraguan wood.

13. Nov. 24: Sailed from Kingston to Santa Marta in ballast.

14. Dec. 1: Entered Santa Marta from Jamaica in ballast.

15. Dec. 20: Sailed from Santa Marta to Riohacha in ballast.

16. Dec. 22: Returned to Santa Marta in ballast because of the strong winds.

17. Dec. 30: Sailed from Santa Marta to Riohacha in ballast.

8. _Esperanza_ (1814)

Captains   Domingo Pisco, Josef Borregio

Known itinerary   1. Unspecified date (Jan.): Entered Kingston from Riohacha with Nicaraguan wood and hides.

2. Jan. 31: Sailed for Riohacha from Kingston with rum, beer, dry goods, and earthenware.

3. Mar. 4: Entered Kingston from Riohacha with Nicaraguan wood, turtles, and hides.

4. Mar. 12: Sailed for Riohacha from Kingston with rum and dry goods.

5. May 2: Entered Kingston from Riohacha with Nicaraguan wood and hides.

6. Unspecified date (May): Sailed for Riohacha from Kingston with rum, dry goods, and earthenware.

7. May 28: Entered Kingston from Riohacha with Nicaraguan wood and hides.

8. Jun. 2: Sailed for Riohacha from Kingston with rum, candles, and chairs.

9. Jun. 24: Entered Kingston from Riohacha with Nicaraguan wood and hides.

10. Jul. 5: Sailed for Riohacha from Kingston with rum and dry goods.

11. Oct. 15: Sailed for Riohacha from Kingston with dry goods.

12. Nov. 7: Entered Kingston from Riohacha with Nicaraguan wood and hides.

13. Nov. 12: Sailed for Riohacha from Kingston with rum and dry goods.

14. Dec. 8: Entered Kingston from Riohacha with Nicaraguan wood and hides.

9. *Providencia* (1814)

Captain	Antonio Garriga
Known itinerary	1. Apr. 21: Entered Kingston from Santa Marta with cotton, Nicaraguan wood, and hides.
	2. Oct. 22: Sailed for Riohacha from Kingston with rum and dry goods.
	3. Nov. 9: Entered Kingston from Santa Marta with Nicaraguan wood.
	4. Nov. 15: Sailed for Riohacha from Kingston with rum and dry goods.
	5. Dec. 10: Sailed for Riohacha from Kingston with rum and dry goods.

10. *Alexandre* (1817)

Captains	Megin Beltbirg, Antonio Tolesa, Thomas Pérez, Josef Mayamo
Known itinerary	1. Feb. 1: Entered Kingston from Cartagena with bullion.
	2. Mar. 15: Sailed for Portobelo from Kingston with dry goods.
	3. Apr. 19: Entered Kingston from Cartagena with bullion.
	4. May 17: Sailed for Portobelo from Kingston with dry goods and earthenware.
	5. Jul. 3: Entered Kingston from Portobelo with bark.
	6. Aug. 18: Sailed for Portobelo from Kingston with dry goods.
	7. Nov. 6: Entered Kingston from Portobelo with bullion.
	8. Dec. 13: Sailed for Portobelo from Kingston with dry goods and rum.

APPENDIX 3

Tables of Ships' Arrivals and Departures

TABLE A3.1 Port of Origin of Ships Entering Cartagena, 1785–1817 (Number of Arrivals)

			PORT OF ORIGIN		
Year	Santa Marta	Portobelo	Riohacha	San Andrés	Sabanilla
1785	11	19	15	0	0
1789	26	27	12	2	0
1793	10	28	7	0	6
1800	1	26	0	0	0
1808	4	19	6	6	0
1817	22	23	2	0	0
Total	74	142	42	8	6

			PORT OF ORIGIN		
Year	Venezuela	Cuba	Jamaica	Haiti	Danish Caribbean
1785	4	17	8	2	0
1789	10	17	5	1	0
1793	10	17	21	0	0
1800	5	28	4	1	3
1808	8	21	5	0	1
1817	1	13	17	0	6
Total	38	113	60	4	10

			PORT OF ORIGIN		
Year	U.S.	Spain	Other Spanish	Other Foreign	Unknown
1785	0	24	18	0	0
1789	6	32	19	0	3
1793	0	15	11	6	2
1800	6	0	5	3	5
1808	0	2	8	0	0
1817	4	2	2	4	1
Total	16	75	63	13	11

Note: The number of arrivals excludes those returning *de arribada* (in distress).

Source: 1785, AGNC, AA-I, Aduanas, 8, 195–219; 1789, AGNC, AA-I, Aduanas, 16, 1009–1042; 1793, AGNC, AA-I, Aduanas, 22, 539–569; 1800, AGNC, AA-I, Aduanas, 33, 307–343; 1808, AGNC, AA-I, Aduanas, 44, 1–21; 1817, AGNC, AA-I, Aduanas, 51, 1–17.

TABLE A3.2 Destination of Ships Departing from Cartagena, 1785–1817 (Number of Departures)

DESTINATION

Year	Santa Marta	Portobelo	Riohacha	San Andrés	Sabanilla
1785	2	13	0	0	0
1789	7	21	7	0	0
1793	2	19	7	0	10
1800	1	22	4	0	0
1808	7	14	12	4	0
1817	16	17	2	0	0
Total	35	106	32	4	10

DESTINATION

Year	Venezuela	Cuba	Jamaica	Haiti	Danish Caribbean
1785	0	20	0	0	0
1789	9	26	0	0	0
1793	9	27	12	0	1
1800	4	22	2	0	3
1808	5	19	3	0	0
1817	1	11	25	0	5
Total	28	125	42	0	9

DESTINATION

Year	U.S.	Spain	Other Spanish	Other Foreign	Unknown
1785	0	18	0	0	0
1789	0	29	0	0	1
1793	0	13	0	13	1
1800	0	6	4	3	0
1808	1	1	17	0	0
1817	3	1	0	6	0
Total	4	68	21	22	2

Note: Other Foreign: 1793 (4 sailed for Curaçao, 1 for St. Eustatius, and 8 for neutral foreign colonies); 1800 (1 sailed for Curaçao and 2 for neutral foreign colonies); 1817 (5 sailed for Curaçao and 1 for Martinique). Other Spanish: mostly Puerto Rico; Santo Domingo was also common; rare departures toward Mexico (Campeche and Veracruz) and Nicaragua (San Juan and Granada).

Source: 1785, AGNC, AA-I, Aduanas, 8, 195–219; 1789, AGNC, AA-I, Aduanas, 16, 1009–1042; 1793, AGNC, AA-I, Aduanas, 22, 539–569; 1800, AGNC, AA-I, Aduanas, 33, 307–343; 1808, AGNC, AA-I, Aduanas, 44, 1–21; 1817, AGNC, AA-I, Aduanas, 51, 1–17.

TABLE A3.3 Port of Origin of Ships Entering Santa Marta, 1801–1814 (Number of Arrivals)

Year	PORT OF ORIGIN Cartagena	Portobelo	Riohacha	San Andrés	Venezuela
1801	8	1	12	1	8
1807	5	1	23	1	6
1814	1	8	17	0	2
Total	14	10	52	2	16

Year	PORT OF ORIGIN Cuba	Jamaica	Haiti	Danish Caribbean	U.S.
1801	8	0	9	1	0
1807	4	1	0	7	0
1814	6	21	0	0	0
Total	18	22	9	8	0

Year	PORT OF ORIGIN Spain	Other Spanish	Other Foreign	Unknown
1801	0	12	0	1
1807	1	10	1	2
1814	0	1	0	1
Total	1	23	1	4

Note: The number of arrivals excludes those returning de arribada (in distress).

Source: 1801, AGNC, AA-I, Aduanas, 34, 1–10; 1807, AGNC, AA-I, Aduanas, 41, 768–787; 1814, AGNC, AA-I, Aduanas, 47, 286–300.

TABLE A3.4 Destination of Ships Departing from Santa Marta, 1801–1814 (Number of Departures)

			DESTINATION		
Year	Cartagena	Portobelo	Riohacha	San Andrés	Venezuela
1801	8	2	16	0	8
1807	5	1	31	0	10
1814	0	7	30	0	8
Total	13	10	77	0	26

			DESTINATION		
Year	Cuba	Jamaica	Haiti	Danish Caribbean	U.S.
1801	5	0	4	3	1
1807	1	0	0	5	0
1814	5	10	0	0	0
Total	11	10	4	8	1

		DESTINATION		
Year	Spain	Other Spanish	Other Foreign	Unknown
1801	1	7	1	0
1807	1	6	5	2
1814	0	0	1	4
Total	2	13	7	6

Note: Other Foreign: 1807 (*colonias amigas*, most likely in the Danish Caribbean).

Source: 1801, AGNC, AA-I, Aduanas, 34, 1–10; 1807, AGNC, AA-I, Aduanas, 41, 768–787; 1814, AGNC, AA-I, Aduanas, 47, 286–300.

TABLE A3.5 Spanish Vessels Entering Kingston from Spanish Territories, 1784–1817

PORT OF ORIGIN

| | | NEW GRANADA | | | | | | | | |
| | | | MINOR PORTS | | | | | | | |
Year	Total	Cart.	Port.	S.M.	Rio.	H.P.	Uns.	Cuba	Ven.	Other
1784	26	0	2	2	3	0	1	8	1	9
1785	63	2	1	4	5	0	0	21	4	26
1796*	112	15	2	5	12	2	0	44	9	23
1810	166	2	7	7	14	11	4	48	12	61
1814	402	32	18	8	25	35	1	160	19	104
1817	161	10	7	9	5	8	2	70	8	42
Total	930	61	37	35	64	56	8	351	53	265

PORT OF ORIGIN (%)

| | | NEW GRANADA | | | | | | | | |
| | | | MINOR PORTS | | | | | | | |
Year	Total	Cart.	Port.	S.M.	Rio.	H.P.	Uns.	Cuba	Ven.	Other
1784	26	0.0	7.7	7.7	11.5	0.0	3.8	30.8	3.8	34.6
1785	63	3.2	1.6	6.3	7.9	0.0	0.0	33.3	6.3	41.3
1796*	112	13.4	1.8	4.5	10.7	1.8	0.0	39.3	8.0	20.5
1810	166	1.2	4.2	4.2	8.4	6.6	2.4	28.9	7.2	36.7
1814	402	8.0	4.5	2.0	6.2	8.7	0.2	39.8	4.7	25.9
1817	161	6.2	4.3	5.6	3.1	5.0	1.2	43.5	5.0	26.1
Total	930	6.6	4.0	3.8	6.9	6.0	0.9	37.7	5.7	28.5

*Does not include data for the April–June trimester.

Cart., Cartagena; Port., Portobelo; S.M., Santa Marta; Rio., Riohacha; H.P., Hidden Ports: San Andrés, Old Providence, San Blas, Sabanilla; Uns., Unspecified: Spanish Main; Ven., Venezuela.

Source: 1784, TNA, CO, 142/22; 1785, TNA, CO, 142/22; 1796, TNA, CO, 142/23; 1810, TNA, CO, 142/26; 1814, TNA, CO, 142/28; 1817, TNA, CO, 142/29.

TABLE A3.6 Spanish Vessels Departing from Kingston to Spanish Territories, 1784–1817

PORT OF ORIGIN

		NEW GRANADA								
			MINOR PORTS							
Year	Total	Cart.	Port.	S.M.	Rio.	H.P.	Uns.	Cuba	Ven.	Other
1784	34	1	3	1	3	0	1	2	0	23
1785	87	4	3	11	4	0	0	32	3	30
1796*	75	4	0	5	8	0	0	43	14	1
1810	290	14	16	11	28	11	13	57	23	117
1814	461	28	19	8	21	35	5	151	22	172
1817	165	3	8	9	5	7	1	68	11	53
Total	1,112	54	49	45	69	53	20	353	73	396

PORT OF ORIGIN (%)

		NEW GRANADA								
			MINOR PORTS							
Year	Total	Cart.	Port.	S.M.	Rio.	H.P.	Uns.	Cuba	Ven.	Other
1784	34	2.9	8.8	2.9	8.8	0.0	2.9	5.9	0.0	67.6
1785	87	4.6	3.4	12.6	4.6	0.0	0.0	36.8	3.4	34.5
1796*	75	5.3	0.0	6.7	10.7	0.0	0.0	57.3	18.7	1.3
1810	290	4.8	5.5	3.8	9.7	3.8	4.5	19.7	7.9	40.3
1814	461	6.1	4.1	1.7	4.6	7.6	1.1	32.8	4.8	37.3
1817	165	1.8	4.8	5.5	3.0	4.2	0.6	41.2	6.7	32.1
Total	1,112	4.9	4.4	4.0	6.2	4.8	1.8	31.7	6.6	35.6

*Does not include data for the April–June trimester.

Cart., Cartagena; Port., Portobelo; S.M., Santa Marta; Rio., Riohacha; H.P., Hidden Ports: San Andrés, Old Providence, San Blas, Sabanilla; Uns., Unspecified: Spanish Main; Ven., Venezuela.

Source: 1784, TNA, CO, 142/22; 1785, TNA, CO, 142/22; 1796, TNA, CO, 142/23; 1810, TNA, CO, 142/26; 1814, TNA, CO, 142/28; 1817, TNA, CO, 142/29.

TABLE A4.1 Professional Trajectories of Caribbean Sea Captains, 1784–1817

Name	Ships	Recorded Years of Activity	Estimated Years Traveling	Ports Visited
Andrés Capiruchique	*Dentapolin* (S), *NS Carmen* (S)	1789, 1800	12	Cartagena, Portobelo, Maracaibo
Andrés Fernández	*NS Carmen* (S), *Esperanza* (S)	1793, 1810	18	Cartagena, Portobelo, Riohacha, Kingston
Antonio Vidal	*Ranger* (F, S), *Fortuna* (S)	1784, 1817	34	Riohacha, San Blas, Kingston
Antonio Morales	*Isabella* (S), *Flor de la Mar* (S)	1810, 1814	5	Riohacha, Kingston
Antonio Royé	*Soledad* (S)	1785, 1793	9	Cartagena, Portobelo, Havana
Cristóbal Vidal	*San Antonio* (S), *Betsey* (S), *NS Carmen* (S)	1785, 1786, 1793	9	Cartagena, Santa Marta, Portobelo, Kingston
Emanuel Batties	*George* (B), *Fidelity* (B)	1782, 1786	5	Kingston, Mosquito Coast
Esteban Balpardos	*San Carlos* (S), *NS Rosario* (S)	1789, 1793	5	Cartagena, Cádiz, Santander
Francisco Javier de Ainzuriza	*NS Carmen* (S), *Chula* (S), *Bella Narcisa* (S), *Lugan* (S)	1789, 1793, 1808, 1810	22	Cartagena, Santa Marta, Riohacha, Kingston, Veracruz
Francisco Llopis	*San Antonio* (S), *Candelaria* (S)	1793, 1808	16	Cartagena, Portobelo, Cuba (Havana, Trinidad), Jamaica (Kingston?), Barcelona
Francisco Martínez	*San Jose y el Carmen* (S), *Bella Narcisa* (S), *NS Carmen* (S)	1789, 1807	19	Cartagena, Santa Marta, Riohacha, Chagres, Guaranao, Santo Domingo, Cuba
Francisco Sánchez	*Casildea* (S), *San Josef* (S)	1789, 1810	22	Cartagena, Kingston, Coro

(*continued*)

Name	Ships	Recorded Years of Activity	Estimated Years Traveling	Ports Visited
Francisco Santoyo	San Joaquín (S), NS Carmen (S), San Miguel (S)	1785, 1789	5	Cartagena, Riohacha, Bahia Honda
Francisco Vichera	San Josef (S), NS Mercedes (S)	1785, 1793	9	Cartagena, Portobelo, Chagres, Mandinga
Gabriel Simó	Bella Rosa (S), La Dolores (S)	1807, 1810	4	Cartagena, Santa Marta, Portobelo, Kingston, Puerto Cabello
Henry Hooper	Fortune (B), Friendship (B)	1782, 1784, 1785, 1786	5	Riohacha, Kingston, Mosquito Coast, San Andrés
Isidoro Hernández	San Juan Nepomuceno (S), Alvarado (S), Diligente (S), Postillón (S)	1785, 1789	5	Cartagena, Havana, Puerto Rico
Isidro Antonio Pombo	Princesa (S), Florida Blanca (S), San Carlos (S)	1789, 1793, 1800	12	Cartagena, Cuba (Havana, Trinidad), Puerto Rico
Isidro Josef Caymani	Postillón (S), Pinzón (S)	1785, 1793	9	Cartagena, Havana, Puerto Rico
Jacinto Ruano	San Carlos (S, F), Buena Esperanza (S)	1785, 1786, 1789	5	Cartagena, Portobelo, Riohacha, Kingston, Chagres, Les Cayes
Jaime Estella	Santa Rosalía (S), Fortuna (S)	1800, 1807, 1808	9	Cartagena, Santa Marta, Portobelo, Santo Domingo, Puerto Rico
Jaime Vidal	Santa Rosa (S)	1801, 1808	8	Cartagena, Santa Marta, Puerto Cabello, Puerto Rico
John Glenn	Pitt (B), Sally (B)	1782, 1784, 1785, 1786	5	Kingston, Mosquito Coast
José Gallardo	NS Carmen (S), Caridad (S), Mariana (S)	1808, 1814, 1817	10	Cartagena, Portobelo, Riohacha, Kingston, San Andrés, San Blas, Nicaragua
José M. López	Cristo (S), Santa Ana (S), Luisa (S)	1810, 1814	5	Riohacha, Kingston
José Martínez	San Fernando (S), Suceso (Da.)	1796, 1800	5	Cartagena, Saint Thomas
Josef Aballe	Malambruno (S), San Josef y las Ánimas (S), Santo Cristo de la Espiración (S)	1789, 1793, 1796, 1800	12	Cartagena, Portobelo, Kingston
Josef de Osma	Sandoval (S), Príncipe de Asturias (S), Rey (S)	1785, 1789	5	Cartagena, Havana, Puerto Rico

Name	Ships	Recorded Years of Activity	Estimated Years Traveling	Ports Visited
Josef Frahin	NS Soledad (S), NS Carmen (S)	1783, 1785, 1786, 1789	7	Cartagena, Portobelo, Riohacha, Kingston, Chagres
Josef González	Rainbow (S), San Josef y las Ánimas (S)	1786, 1789, 1796	11	Cartagena, Portobelo, Riohacha, Kingston
Josef Leal	Amable (S), NS Carmen (S), NS Dolores (S)	1785, 1789, 1793	9	Cartagena, Portobelo, Bahia Honda, Zapote
Josef Rodríguez	San Josef (S), La Popa (S), Fuerte (S)	1785, 1786, 1789	5	Cartagena, Portobelo, Riohacha, Kingston, Philadelphia
Josef Torres	San Josef y las Ánimas (S)	1789, 1793	5	Cartagena, Kingston, Coro, Barcelona
Juan Allende	Despacho (S)	1789, 1793	5	Cartagena, Havana, Puerto Rico
Juan Bautista Codima	Señor San Josef (S), Dolores (S)	1789, 1800	12	Cartagena, Havana, Cádiz, Barcelona
Juan de la Vega	NS Carmen (S)	1785, 1810	26	Santa Marta, Riohacha, Kingston, Chagres
Juan Díaz	San Josef (S)	1784, 1789	6	Cartagena, Santa Marta, Riohacha, Kingston
Juan Ferrer	San Agustín (S), María (S), Veloz (S), Felix (S), Mariana (S), Betsy (B)	1789, 1810, 1814, 1817	29	Cartagena, Santa Marta, Riohacha, Kingston, Chagres, Cuba, Philadelphia
Juan Guardiola	San Antonio (S), Santo Cristo (S), San Josef y las Ánimas (S), NS Dolores (S), NS Candelaria (S), NS Carmen (S)	1793, 1796, 1800, 1808	16	Cartagena, Portobelo, Riohacha, Kingston, Sabanilla, Cuba, Curaçao, Santo Domingo
Juan Guillermo	Santa Bárbara (S), Santa Clara (S), Notus (S)	1808, 1814, 1817	10	Cartagena, Portobelo, Riohacha, Kingston, San Andrés
Juan Josef de Arriola	Neptuno (S), Concepción (S), Lugan (S)	1800, 1814, 1817	18	Cartagena, Santa Marta, Riohacha, Kingston, Cuba (Trinidad, Batabano)
Juan Miró	Concepción (S)	1789, 1814	26	Cartagena, Portobelo, Riohacha, Kingston
Juan Pastor	Jesús Nazareno (S)	1785, 1789	5	Cartagena, Puerto Rico, Philadelphia, Málaga, Barcelona

(continued)

Name	Ships	Recorded Years of Activity	Estimated Years Traveling	Ports Visited
Juan Quintana	*Concepción* (S), *NS Carmen* (S)	1796, 1800, 1801	6	Cartagena, Santa Marta, Riohacha, Kingston, Havana
Juan Santos	*NS Carmen* (S), *Samaria* (S)	1800, 1814	15	Cartagena, Santa Marta, Riohacha, Maracaibo
Juan Suárez	*Burla* (S)	1810, 1814	5	Portobelo, Kingston
Juan Vicente Llue	*San Josef y las Ánimas* (S), *NS Carmen* (S), *Candelaria* (S)	1793, 1796, 1800	8	Cartagena, Portobelo, Kingston
Manuel Benítez	*Rosario* (S), *Santa Ana* (S), *Concepción* (S)	1800, 1807, 1810	11	Cartagena, Santa Marta, Riohacha, Kingston
Manuel Bliz	*Soledad* (S), *NS Carmen* (S)	1785, 1786, 1789	5	Cartagena, Santa Marta, Riohacha, Kingston, Cuba
Manuel Cuello	*Santa Ana* (S), *Criolla* (S)	1800, 1810	11	Cartagena, Kingston, Cuba (Batabano, Havana)
Manuel del Río	*Carmen* (S), *Unión* (S)	1801, 1817	17	Cartagena, Santa Marta, Havana, Puerto Rico
Marcos Marcantoni	*Beauty* (S, Da.), *Veterano* (S)	1808, 1814	7	Cartagena, Kingston, Puerto Rico
Miguel Bruguera	*Santa Bárbara* (S), *Félix* (S), *Tres Hermanos* (S), *Regencia* (S)	1808, 1810, 1814	7	Cartagena, Santa Marta, Portobelo, Riohacha, Kingston
Miguel Cope	*Clarissa* (S), *Manuel* (S), *Triste* (S)	1810, 1817	8	Riohacha, Kingston
Miguel Iglesia	*María* (S), *Merced* (S), *Dos Amigos* (S), *Flecha* (S), *Dicha* (S), *San Miguel* (S)	1810, 1814	5	Santa Marta, Portobelo, Kingston, Chagres, Cuba
Miguel Millán	*San Antonio* (S), *La Venganza* (S)	1800, 1808	9	Cartagena, Portobelo, Cuba
Nicolás Franco	*Santa Bárbara* (S), *NS Carmen* (S)	1800, 1808	9	Cartagena, Portobelo, Riohacha, Kingston, Islas Mulatas
Pablo Juri	*Alejandro* (S), *Soledad* (S), *Rosalía* (S)	1785, 1796, 1807	23	Cartagena, Santa Marta, Riohacha, Kingston, Puerto Cabello, Havana
Pedro Atencio	*Fancy* (Da.), *NS Carmen* (S)	1800, 1814	15	Cartagena, Santa Marta, Portobelo, Riohacha, Saint Thomas, Maracaibo

Name	Ships	Recorded Years of Activity	Estimated Years Traveling	Ports Visited
Pedro Corrales	*NS Carmen* (S), *Santa Rosa* (S), *Carmelita* (S)	1793, 1800, 1807, 1817	25	Cartagena, Santa Marta, Portobelo, Kingston, Curaçao, Saint Croix, Santo Domingo, Puerto Rico
Pedro Pérez Prieto	*San Fernando* (S), *Santo Cristo* (S)	1789, 1801	13	Cartagena, Santa Marta, Riohacha, Zapote, Coro
Rosendo Baamonde	*Princesa* (S), *Príncipe de Asturias* (S)	1785, 1789	5	Cartagena, Havana, Puerto Rico
Salvador Carbonell	*Feliciana* (S), *San Francisco Xavier* (S)	1785, 1789	5	Cartagena, Santa Marta, Havana, Cádiz, Málaga, Barcelona
Salvador de los Monteros	*Amable* (S)	1784, 1785, 1786, 1787	4	Cartagena, Portobelo, Kingston, Cuba (Trinidad), Charleston, New York
Salvador Rocha	*San Josef* (S)	1785, 1789	5	Cartagena, Havana, Cádiz
Sebastián Cantero	*San Josef y la Popa* (S), *NS Concepción* (S)	1789, 1793, 1796	8	Cartagena, Portobelo, Kingston
Sebastián Mori	*Esperanza* (S), *Carmen* (S)	1796, 1801	6	Cartagena, Santa Marta, Riohacha, Kingston
Silvestre Moiño	*Fortuna* (S), *NS Carmen* (S), *San Josef y las Ánimas* (S)	1789, 1793, 1796, 1800	12	Cartagena, Santa Marta, Portobelo, Riohacha, Kingston, Chagres, Coro, Guaranao

Note: S, Spanish; F, French; B, British; Da., Danish.

Source: Trajectories constructed based on TNA, CO, 142/22; TNA, CO, 142/22; TNA, CO, 142/23; TNA, CO, 142/26; TNA, CO, 142/28; TNA, CO, 142/29; AGNC, AA-I, Aduanas, 8, 195–219; AGNC, AA-I, Aduanas, 16, 1009–1042; AGNC, AA-I, Aduanas, 22, 539–569; AGNC, AA-I, Aduanas, 33, 307–343; AGNC, AA-I, Aduanas, 34, 1–10; AGNC, AA-I, Aduanas, 41, 768–787; AGNC, AA-I, Aduanas, 44, 1–21; AGNC, AA-I, Aduanas, 47, 286–300; AGNC, AA-I, Aduanas, 51, 1–17.

Detailed Itineraries of Specific Caribbean Sea Captains

TABLE A5.1 Juan Guardiola

Ship Name	Year	Anchored At	Entering From	Date	Sailing For	Date
San Antonio	1793	Cartagena	Jamaica	Jun. 10	Cuba and Jamaica	Jul. 6
Santo Cristo de la Espiración	1793	Cartagena	Jamaica	Aug. 19	Sabanilla	Sep. 5
Santo Cristo de la Espiración	1793	Cartagena	Sabanilla	Sep. 16	Foreign neutral colonies	Oct. 9
Santo Cristo de la Espiración	1793	Cartagena	Jamaica	Nov. 16		
Santo Cristo	1796	Kingston	Cartagena	Feb. 5		
Santo Cristo	1796	Kingston	Cartagena	Mar. 15	Cartagena	Mar. 17
Santo Cristo	1796	Kingston	Cartagena	Jul. 1		
San Josef y las Ánimas	1800	Cartagena	Portobelo	Apr. 25		
NS de los Dolores	1800	Cartagena	Jamaica	Jul. 2	Foreign neutral colonies	Jul. 29
NS de los Dolores	1800	Cartagena	Curaçao	Sep. 24	Santo Domingo	Dec. 19
NS de la Candelaria	1800	Cartagena	Portobelo	Nov. 28	Portobelo	Dec. 19
NS de los Dolores	1800	Cartagena		Dec. 23	Jamaica	May 14
NS del Carmen	1808	Cartagena	Trinidad	Jan. 28	Trinidad	Mar. 9
NS del Carmen	1808	Cartagena	Trinidad	Apr. 17		
San José y las Ánimas	1808	Cartagena			Ríohacha	Aug. 1
San José y las Ánimas	1808	Cartagena	Ríohacha	Aug. 16	Trinidad	Aug. 26

Source: AGNC, AA-I, Aduanas, 22, 539–569; TNA, CO, 142/23; AGNC, AA-I, Aduanas, 33, 307–343; AGNC, AA-I, Aduanas, 44, 1–21.

TABLE A5.2 Pedro Corrales

Ship Name	Year	Anchored At	Entering From	Date	Sailing For	Date
NS del Carmen	1793	Cartagena	Panama	Apr. 3	Cuba	Apr. 6
NS del Carmen	1800	Cartagena	Santo Domingo, Curaçao, Jamaica	Apr. 30	Riohacha	Jul. 28
NS del Carmen	1800	Cartagena		Aug. 1		
Santa Rosa (alias *Minerva*)	1807	Santa Marta	Puerto Rico	Mar. 29	Neutral colonies	Jun. 9
Santa Rosa (alias *Minerva*)	1807	Santa Marta	Saint Croix	Jul. 10	Neutral colonies	Aug. 24
Carmelita (alias *Golondrina*)	1817	Cartagena	Santa Marta	Apr. 4	Portobelo	May 2
Carmelita (alias *Golondrina*)	1817	Cartagena	Portobelo	May 22	Portobelo	May 29
Carmelita (alias *Golondrina*)	1817	Cartagena	Portobelo	Aug. 28	Portobelo	Dec. 28

Source: AGNC, AA-I, Aduanas, 22, 539–569; AGNC, AA-I, Aduanas, 33, 307–343; AGNC, AA-I, Aduanas, 41, 768–787; AGNC, AA-I, Aduanas, 51, 1–17.

TABLE A5.3 Jacinto Ruano

Ship Name	Year	Anchored At	Entering From	Date	Sailing For	Date
Saint Charles	1785	Kingston			Cartagena	Apr. 19
San Carlos	1785	Cartagena	Les Cayes	Apr. 27		
San Carlos	1785	Cartagena	Saint-Domingue	Jul. 15		
San Carlos	1786	Kingston	Riohacha	May 25		
Buena Esperanza	1789	Cartagena	Chagres	Oct. 29	Portobelo and Chagres	Dec. 18

Source: AGNC, AA-I, Aduanas, 8, 195–219; TNA, CO, 142/22; AGNC, AA-I, Aduanas, 16, 1009–1042.

TABLE A5.4 Salvador de los Monteros

Ship Name	Year	Anchored At	Entering From	Date	Sailing For	Date
La Amable Elena	1784	Kingston			Portobelo	Dec. 11
Amable Eliza	1785	Kingston			Cartagena	Dec. 4
Amable Elena	1785	Cartagena	Trinidad and Jamaica	Dec. 15		
La Amable	1786	Kingston	Cartagena	Jan. 15	Cartagena	Feb. 8

Source: TNA, CO, 142/19; TNA, CO, 142/22; AGNC, AA-I, Aduanas, 8, 195–219.

TABLE A5.5 Pedro Pérez Prieto

Ship Name	Year	Anchored At	Entering From	Date	Sailing For	Date
San Fernando	1789	Cartagena			Zapote, Santa Marta, Riohacha	Jul. 13
Santo Cristo	1801	Santa Marta	Coro	Dec. 20		

Source: AGNC, AA-I, Aduanas, 16, 1009–1042; AGNC, AA-I, Aduanas, 34, 1–10.

TABLE A6.1 The Name of the Sea in Maps of New Granada and Colombia

	Year	Author	Nationality of Author	Title	Place	Name of the Sea
1	1657			*Tierra Firme: Nuevo Reino de Granada y Popayan*		Mar del Norte
2	1663			*Tierra Firme y Nuevo Reino de Granada y Popayan*		Mar del Norte
3	1748	R. Vaugondy	Foreigner	*Pertie Occidentale de la Terre Ferme*		Mer du Nord
4	1772	Josep Aparico Morata	Foreigner	*Plan Geografico del Vireynato de Santafe de Bogota Nuevo Reyno de Granada*		Mar Septentrional o Mar del Norte
5	1808	Vicente Talledo y Rivera	Foreigner	*Mapa Corografico del Nuevo Reyno de Granada*		Mar del Norte
6	1811	Francisco José de Caldas	Colombian	*Muestra de una plancha del Atlas de Caldas*	Bogotá	Mar del Norte o Atlántico
7	1811	John Pinkerton	Foreigner	*New Granada*	London	Caribbean Sea
8	1821			*Colombia tomado de Humboldt y de varias otras autoridades recientes*	London	Mar Caribe
9	1822			*Mapa general de Colombia formado según las observaciones e indagaciones astronómicas de Mr. A. de Humboldt*	Paris	Mar de las Antillas
10	1822	H. C. Carey and I. Lea	Foreigner	*Geographical, Historical, and Statistical Map of Colombia*	Philadelphia	Caribbean Sea

(continued)

	Year	Author	Nationality of Author	Title	Place	Name of the Sea
11	1823	B. R. Baker	Foreigner	*Colombia*	London	Caribbean Sea
12	1824	F. Lucas Jr.	Foreigner	*Colombia*	Baltimore	Caribbean Sea
13	1824	C. Smith	Foreigner	*Colombia*	London	Caribbean Sea
14	1825	Sidney Hall	Foreigner	*Map of Colombia Engraved for the Modern Traveller*	London	Caribbean Sea
15	1825	J. A. Buchon	Foreigner	*Carte geographique, statistique et historique de la Republique Colombienne*	Paris	Mer des Antilles
16	1826	A. Brue	Foreigner	*Carte Générale de Colombie, de la Guyane Française, Hollandaise et Anglaise*	Paris	Mer des Antilles
17	1827	José Manuel Restrepo	Colombian	*Carta de la República de Colombia*	Paris	Mar Caribe o de las Antillas
18	1827	José Manuel Restrepo	Colombian	*Carta del Departamento del Magdalena*	Paris	Mar de las Antillas
19	1828	Sidney Hall	Foreigner	*Colombia*	London	Caribbean Sea
20	1828	Lapie	Foreigner	*Carte de Colombie et des Guyanes*	Paris	Mer des Antilles
21	1828	H. S. Tanner	Foreigner	*A New Map of Colombia with Its Departments and Provinces*	Philadelphia	Sea of Antilles
22	1830	Langlois	Foreigner	*Colombie et Guyanes*	Paris	Mer des Antilles
23	1830	John Grigg	Foreigner	*Colombia and Guiana*	Philadelphia	Caribbean Sea
24	1831	T. Cadell	Foreigner	*Colombia and Peru*	London	Caribbean Sea
25	1832	John Dower	Foreigner	*Colombia*	London	Caribbean Sea
26	1833	T. Starling	Foreigner	*Colombia*	London	Caribbean Sea
27	1834	J. Arrowsmith	Foreigner	*Colombia*	London	Caribbean Sea
28	1834	Henry Teesdale	Foreigner	*Columbia*	London	Atlantic Ocean
29	1835	Thierry	Foreigner	*Carte de la Colombie et des Guyanes*		Mer des Antilles
30	1835			*Colombia and Guiana*		Caribbean Sea
31	1835	Joseph Thomas	Foreigner	*Colombia*	London	Caribbean Sea
32	1835	David H. Burr	Foreigner	*Colombia*	New York	Caribbean Sea

	Year	Author	Nationality of Author	Title	Place	Name of the Sea
33	1836	H. S. Tanner	Foreigner	*Venezuela, New Granada and Equador*	Philadelphia	Sea of Antilles
34	1837	A. R. Fremin	Foreigner	*Colombie et Guyanes*	Paris	Mer des Antilles
35	1838	Andres de Castillejo		*Plano del puerto de Sabanilla*		Mar del Norte
36	1840	Jeremiah Greenleaf	Foreigner	*Colombia*	Brattleboro	Caribbean Sea
37	1840			*Colombie et Guyanes*	Paris	Mer des Antilles
38	1840	D. Lizars	Foreigner	*Colombia and Guyana*	Edinburgh	Caribbean Sea
39	1840	Agustín Codazzi	Colombian	*Mapa de los tres departamentos Venezuela, Cundina-marca y Ecuador que formaron la República de Colombia para servir a la historia de las campañas de la guerra de independencia en los años de 1821, 1822 y 1823*	Caracas	Mar de las Antillas
40	1842	J. Arrowsmith	Foreigner	*Colombia*	London	Caribbean Sea
41	1847	Mitchell	Foreigner	*Venezuela, New Granada and Equador*	Philadelphia	Sea of Antilles
42	1847	Joaquín Acosta	Colombian	*Mapa de la Republica de la Nueva Granada dedicado al baron de Humboldt*		Mar de las Antillas
43	1848	Jeremiah Greenleaf	Foreigner	*New Grenada, Venezuela and Ecuador*		Caribbean Sea
44	1850	C. Smith	Foreigner	*Colombia*	London	Caribbean Sea
45	1850	Mariano Inojosa	Colombian	*Plan corográfico de la Nueva Granada*		Mar del Norte
46	1852	T. C. Mosquera	Colombian	*Carta de la Repub-lica de N. Granada conforme a su ultima division politica*		Mar de las Antillas
47	1852	J. G. Barbie du Bocage	Foreigner	*Colombie et Guyanes*	Paris	Mer des Antilles
48	1853	S. A. Mitchell	Foreigner	*Venezuela, New Granada and Equador*	Philadelphia	Sea of Antilles
49	1855	J. H. Colton	Foreigner	*Venezuela, New Granada and Ecuador*	New York	Caribbean Sea

(*continued*)

	Year	Author	Nationality of Author	Title	Place	Name of the Sea
50	1862	F. A. Garnier	Foreigner	*Ancienne Colombie*	Paris	Mer des Antilles
51	1864	Manuel Ponce de Leon and Manuel Maria Paz	Colombian	*Carta jeografica de los Estados Unidos de Colombia antigua Nueva Granada*	Bogotá	Mar de las Antillas
52	1864	Manuel Ponce de Leon and Manuel Maria Paz	Colombian	*Carta corográfica del estado del Magdalena*		Mar de las Antillas
53	1864	James Wyld	Foreigner	*Map of Colombia and British Guyana*	London	Caribbean Sea
54	1865	Mitchell	Foreigner	*Venezuela, United States of Colombia and Ecuador*	Philadelphia	Caribbean Sea
55	1869	G. W. Colton	Foreigner	*Colton's Venezuela, United States of Colombia or New Granada and Ecuador*	New York	Caribbean Sea
56	1920	Oficina de Longitudes del Ministerio de Relaciones Exteriores	Colombian	*Mapa de la Republica de Colombia destinado a la instruccion publica*	Bogotá	Oceano Atlantico

Source: 11–14, 19, 20, 22, 24, 26, 28–30, 33, 35–38, 40, 41, 44, 49, 54: Archivo General de la Nación, Colombia (AGNC), Mapoteca 4; 21, 42, 56: AGNC, Mapoteca 6; 51: AGNC, Mapoteca 3; 1–5, 42, 46: *Atlas histórico geográfico de Colombia*; 45, 52: *Atlas de cartografía histórica de Colombia*; 6, 8, 9: *Atlas de mapas antiguos de Colombia*; 7, 10, 15–18, 23, 25, 27, 31, 32, 34, 39, 43, 47, 48, 50, 53, 55: David Rumsey Map Collection, www.davidrumsey.com.

Introduction: Uncovering Other Possible Worlds

Epigraph: McKittrick, *Demonic Grounds*, xi, emphasis added.

1. "Acta de la legislatura de la provincia de Cartagena," 68, 70–71. For a brief account of "the day *cartageneros* declared themselves subjects of His Britannic Majesty," see Bell Lemus, "Cartagena de Indias británica." For Cartagena's short-lived independence, see Sourdís, *Cartagena de Indias*. For different responses to the French invasion, see Rodríguez O., *The Independence of Spanish America*, 51–74; Dym, *From Sovereign Villages*, 65–97; Gutiérrez Ardila, *Un nuevo reino*, 187–233.

2. Bell Lemus, "Cartagena de Indias británica," 64.

3. For contemporary accounts of the siege, see Rodríguez Villa, *El Teniente General*, 2:575–578, 2:585–586, 3:9–11; Ducoudray-Holstein, *Memoirs of Simón Bolívar*, 111–122; Pombo, "Reminiscencias del sitio de Cartagena"; and García del Río, "Página de oro." For more recent analyses, see Earle, *Spain and the Independence*, 61–64, 101–104, 147–154; Cuño Bonito, *El retorno del rey*; and Sourdís, *Cartagena de Indias*, 113–152.

4. Throughout the colonial period and most of the nineteenth century the political entity we now call Colombia was called New Granada. Until 1819 it was known as the Viceroyalty of New Granada. Between 1819 and 1830, following the nation's Fundamental Law of December 17, 1819, "the republics of Venezuela and New Granada are . . . united as one, under the glorious title of Colombia" (Article 1). Since Ecuador was part of the former Viceroyalty of New Granada, the new nation's territory covered the area that now constitutes the republics of Venezuela, Colombia, and Ecuador, as well as Panama. Starting in 1826, Colombia—or Gran Colombia, as it has come to be known in the historiography—began to disintegrate until, by the end of 1830, it broke down into three republics: Ecuador, New Granada, and Venezuela. From then, the territory that now constitutes the Republic of Colombia adopted several names, including New Granada (1830), Granadan Confederation (1858), United States of Colombia (1863), and Republic of Colombia (1886). For

the Fundamental Law of 1819 and the many other constitutions that renamed the republic and redrew its map, see Pombo and Guerra, *Constituciones de Colombia*.

5. Linebaugh and Rediker, *The Many-Headed Hydra*, 7.

6. For the editors of a special issue of the *Radical History Review*, "another world *was* possible" in the sense that "historically, the relentless effort to deny the possibility of alternative political and social forms has been matched by determined struggles to recognize and realize such possibilities." Corpis and Fletcher, "Editors' Introduction," 1. My project aligns with this conceptualization in its aim to account for what geographer Edward Soja called, following Marshall Berman, "a collective sense of the 'perils and possibilities' of the contemporary." Soja, *Postmodern Geographies*, 28; Berman, *All That Is Solid*, 15.

7. The "horizon of expectation," according to historian Reinhart Koselleck, comprises "what is expected of the future" or, formulated otherwise, the potential future outcomes that the historical actors we study believed could result from their present. Koselleck, *Futures Pasts*, 261.

8. Goswami, "Imaginary Futures," 1462. For counterfactuals, possibility, and plausibility in history, see Bunzl, "Counterfactual History"; and Hawthorn, *Plausible Worlds*.

9. The term Greater Caribbean has gained traction as a way to think beyond conventional definitions that limit the Caribbean region to the island range stretching from the Bahamas to Trinidad. For works that embrace the term and the wider geographical perspective, see McNeill, *Mosquito Empires*; Mulcahy, *Hurricanes and Society*; Schwartz, *Sea of Storms*; and Gaspar and Geggus, *A Turbulent Time*. The use of the Spanish term "Gran Caribe" is also becoming more common in the Spanish-language literature. See for example García de León Griego, *El mar de los deseos*; and Pérez Morales, *El gran diablo*.

10. The quotation marks are intended to show that the British Caribbean, the French Caribbean, the Dutch Caribbean, and Danish Saint Thomas were formally British, French, Dutch, and Danish, but their residents could experience them as much more than British, French, and Danish.

11. See Scott, *Degrees of Freedom*; Guterl, *American Mediterranean*; Scott and Hébrard, *Freedom Papers*; Johnson, *The Fear of French Negroes*, 91–121; Landers, *Atlantic Creoles*; Grafenstein, *Nueva España en el Circuncaribe*, 169–195; Souto Mantecón, *Mar abierto*.

12. Ferrer, *Freedom's Mirror*; Sartorius, *Ever Faithful*; Childs, *The 1812 Aponte Rebellion*.

13. Ferrer, *Freedom's Mirror*, 17. See also Knight, *Slave Society in Cuba*; Goveia, *Slave Society in the British Leeward Islands*; and McGraw, *The Work of Recognition*, 4.

14. Hoffnung-Garskof, *A Tale of Two Cities*, xvi; Seigel, *Uneven Encounters*, 3. For a similar analysis based on the role of the "extensive circulation of people" and media in the creation of a sort of "intellectual and cultural" cohesiveness that brought together "far-flung locales" throughout the Americas, see Putnam, *Radical Moves*, 5.

15. As chapter 1 shows, empires, including the Spanish one, gradually moved toward free trade, but imperial officials, especially Spanish ones, vociferously complained about contraband trade.

16. Denmark abolished the slave trade in 1803, Britain and the United States in 1807, and Haiti—the first republic to do so—abolished slavery immediately after its independence in 1804. According to the Trans-Atlantic Slave Trade Database, 47 percent of the total slaves that reached the Americas did so after the outbreak of the American Revolution. The corresponding percentages for Spanish America and Cuba are 60 percent and 98 percent. More surprisingly, despite the fear of slave revolt triggered by the Haitian Revolution, 58 percent of the slaves that reached Spanish America did so after the outbreak of the Haitian Revolution in 1791. For Cuba, the percentage is 97 percent. In the struggle between fear and greed inaugurated by the Haitian Revolution, the statistics of the Trans-Atlantic Slave Trade Database make a compelling case for the victory of greed. See http://www.slavevoyages.org /assessment/estimates, accessed March 11, 2016. Percentages calculated by the author.

17. Grandin, *The Empire of Necessity*, 6, 7, 22–30. See also Ferrer, *Freedom's Mirror*, 17–43; Schmidt-Nowara and Fradera, *Slavery and Antislavery*; Tomich, "The Wealth of Empire."

18. For Massey, "contemporaneous plurality" refers to the "possibility of the existence of multiplicity" or the "simultaneous coexistence of others with their own trajectories and their own stories to tell." Massey, *For Space*, 9–11. For a study that takes seriously the set of chimeric and unrealistic projects developed by Spanish, British, and French early modern explorers on the best way to reach "the alluring Pacific Ocean," see Mapp, *The Elusive West*, 101–121.

19. "Structures of feelings" and "ways of being in the world" are related terms that refer to the way in which people make sense of their world and experience it. Raymond Williams stresses a distinction between "structures of feeling" and the "more formal concepts of 'world-view' and 'ideology,'" because his term allows him to "go beyond formally held and systematic beliefs." Williams, *Marxism and Literature*, 132. For "ways of being in the world," see de Certeau, *The Practice of Everyday Life*, 97.

20. Soja, *Postmodern Geographies*, 14. See also Lefebvre, *The Production of Space*; Massey, *For Space*. For a historical study that takes space seriously and carefully challenges the fixity of "stage spaces" in a Latin American context, see Craib, *Cartographic Mexico*.

21. Massey, *For Space*, 11, 9. The notion of space as a human construction is also a key feature of the way in which Australian historian Greg Dening approached the South Pacific. Dening described his work as "a metaphor for the different ways in which human beings construct their worlds and for the boundaries that they construct between them." Dening, *Islands and Beaches*, 3.

22. For subnational definitions, see Applegate, "A Europe of Regions"; Van Young, "Doing Regional History"; and Appelbaum, *Muddied Waters*. For supranational

definitions, see Goebel, *Overlapping Geographies of Belonging*; Conrad and Duara, *Viewing Regionalisms*; Reid, *Southeast Asia in the Age of Commerce*; and Wigen and Lewis, *The Myth of Continents*. For a short introduction to regional definitions, see Young, "Regions."

23. Goebel, *Overlapping Geographies of Belonging*, 45.

24. Studying the subnational regional configuration known as the South East in the United Kingdom, John Allen, Doreen Massey, and Allan Cochrane make the case for the need to understand regions in terms of time-space. For them the question "Where is the south east?" is as relevant as that of "When is the south east?" Allen, Massey, and Cochrane, *Re-Thinking the Region*, 50.

25. Van Young, "Doing Regional History," 172; Goebel, *Overlapping Geographies of Belonging*, 45.

26. Allen, Massey, and Cochrane, *Re-Thinking the Region*; Massey, *For Space*; and de Certeau, *The Practice of Everyday Life*. See also Horton and Kraftl, *Cultural Geographies*, 181–199.

27. Van Young, "Doing Regional History," 167.

28. Smith and Godlewska, "Introduction," 7–8.

29. Coronil, "Beyond Occidentalism," 54.

30. Zahra, "Imagined Noncommunities," 96–97; Smith and Godlewska, "Introduction," 8. For archival visibility and, most importantly, invisibility, see Trouillot, *Silencing the Past*.

31. For "imagined communities," see Anderson, *Imagined Communities*.

32. Cresswell and Merriman, "Introduction," 5. See also Cresswell, *On the Move*; and Merriman, *Mobility, Space and Culture*.

33. Tuan, "Space and Place," 410–411; Gupta, "The Song of the Nonaligned World," 73. Scholarship on relations between different Native American groups and between Native Americans and Europeans in the territory that eventually became the United States has emphasized the role of mobility in the configuration of geographic spaces that did not match European empires' political geographies. See for example Parmenter, *The Edge of the Woods*, xii; Hämäläinen, *The Comanche Empire*; and Dubcovsky, "One Hundred Sixty-One Knots."

34. Steinberg, "Of Other Seas," 156.

35. Gillis, *Islands of the Mind*, 83. In his argument against "terracentric" ways of interpreting the world, historian Marcus Rediker critiques "the unspoken proposition that the seas of the world are unreal spaces, voids between the real places, which are landed and national." Rediker, *Outlaws of the Atlantic*, 2.

36. Manning, *Navigating World History*, 155, 170.

37. Instead of framing his account within a "nationalist . . . spatial framing" that foregrounds "conflict over slavery within the boundaries of today's United States" (i.e., perpetuating a narrative that "projects a definition of spaces which *resulted* from the Civil War . . . backward onto its narrative of the description of the conflict over slavery before the war"), Johnson develops "an alternative vision of what 'the South' might [have] looke[d] like," one that "instead of looking at what 'the South'

was leaving" asks "where Southerners . . . thought they were going and how they thought they could pull it off in the first place." Johnson, *River of Dark Dreams*, 15–16. For another analysis that thinks of the U.S. Civil War and U.S. nation building beyond the conventional national framework, see Scott and Hébrard, *Freedom Papers*, 121–138.

38. Rupert, *Creolization and Contraband*, 9.

39. Gould, "Entangled Histories, Entangled Worlds"; Cañizares-Esguerra, "Entangled Histories."

40. Lewis and Wigen, "A Maritime Response." For their larger critique of world regionalization schemes, see Wigen and Lewis, *The Myth of Continents*.

41. Stoler calls for the need "to account for the *temporary* fixity of terms such as 'white prestige,' 'poor whites,' 'métissage,' and 'bourgeois respectability,' " arguing, following anthropologist Bernard Cohn, that these "summary statements" tend to "preclude rather than promote further historical analysis." Stoler, *Carnal Knowledge*, 202.

42. José Moya described Latin America as both inaccurate and convenient. Moya, "Introduction," 1. For history becoming teleology, see Craib, *Cartographic Mexico*, 5.

43. For useful summaries of the definitions and debates on the question, see Bassi, "La importancia de ser Caribe"; Grafenstein, *Nueva España en el Circuncaribe*, 21–29; Giovannetti, "Caribbean Studies as Practice."

44. Mintz, "The Caribbean as Socio-Cultural Area," 20; Benítez-Rojo, *The Repeating Island*, 33–81; Knight, *The Caribbean*.

45. Giusti-Cordero, "Beyond Sugar Revolutions"; Abello and Bassi, "Un Caribe."

46. Mulcahy, *Hurricanes and Society*; Johnson, *Climate and Catastrophe*; Schwartz, *Sea of Storms*.

47. McNeill, *Mosquito Empires*, 2.

48. Wigen and Lewis, *The Myth of Continents*, ix.

49. Marx, *The Eighteenth Brumaire*, paragraph 2.

50. Agnew, *Geopolitics*, 11–31 ("visualizing global space"); Ó Tuathail, "General Introduction," 1 ("future direction" and "coming shape"). For a larger discussion of geopolitics, including a history of the term and the notion of a critical geopolitics, see Ó Tuathail, *Critical Geopolitics*.

51. Agnew is particularly interested in "the modern geopolitical imagination," which he defines as "the predominant ways world politics have been represented and acted on geographically by both major actors and commentators over the past two centuries." Defining geopolitical imagination in such terms appears to deny powerless actors the ability to have a geopolitical imagination. Agnew, *Geopolitics*, 11.

52. Anderson, *Imagined Communities*.

53. Gupta, "Song of the Nonaligned World," 73, 64.

54. Chaterjee, *The Nation and Its Fragments*, 11. Inviting us "to think ourselves beyond the nation," Appadurai laments the lack of an "idiom . . . to capture the

collective interest of many groups in translocal solidarities, cross-border mobilizations, and postnational identities." Appadurai, "Patriotism and Its Futures," 411, 418. See also Appadurai, *The Future as Cultural Fact*. In fairness to Anderson, his latest book explores precisely these forms of border-crossing solidarities. Anderson, *Under Three Flags*.

55. Anderson, *Imagined Communities*, 6.

56. Gould and White, *Mental Maps*, 3. For Yi-Fu Tuan, "mental maps are [among other things] imaginary worlds." Tuan, "Images and Mental Maps," 211.

57. White, "What Is Spatial History?"

58. Sellers-García's study of how documents traveled from and to colonial Guatemala is based on the premise that for people living in remote towns in the *audiencia* of Guatemala, as for all people, "conceptions of distance were contextual." These conceptions (and the mental maps directly associated with them) were "created not only by geographical circumstances but also by political, social, economic, and cultural conditions." Sellers-García, *Distance and Documents*, 1–3.

59. For ephemeral states, a term I borrow from Jane Landers, see Landers, *Atlantic Creoles*, 95–137; Racine, *Francisco de Miranda*, 211–241; Sourdís, *Cartagena de Indias*; and Pérez Morales, *El gran diablo*, 77–112, 145–173. For the hemispheric confederation that Simón Bolívar envisioned in the mid-1820s when he called for a Pan-American meeting of heads of state in Panama, see Lynch, *Simón Bolívar*, 212–217; and Collier, "Nationality, Nationalism, and Supranationalism."

60. Juan García del Río's argument for the need to "adopt the constitutional monarchy, or approach ourselves to this form whenever it becomes possible" is well known among historians of Colombia. See García del Río, "Meditaciones colombianas," 331. For other imaginaries of monarchism, see Sanders, *The Vanguard of the Atlantic*, 34–37, 46–49; and Brown, *The Struggle for Power*, 44–49. For standard accounts of the heated debates between federalists and centralists that ran through Colombia's independent history, see Bushnell, *The Making of Modern Colombia*; and Safford and Palacios, *Colombia*. For projects to turn northern New Granada into a British colony, see chapter 4.

61. The geo-body of a nation can be understood as the "portion of the earth's surface" that nation occupies. But the geo-body "is not merely space or territory. It is a component of the life of a nation. It is a source of pride, loyalty, love, passion, bias, hatred, reason, unreason." Thongchai, *Siam Mapped*, 16–17. An imagined geo-body, thus, would refer to the earth's surface a political entity is envisioned to occupy, to the surface a particular geopolitical project would cover on a map.

62. Rediker, *Outlaws of the Atlantic*, 178. See also Scott, "The Common Wind"; and Bolster, *Black Jacks*.

63. Lasso, *Myths of Harmony*; Helg, *Liberty and Equality*. See also Ferrer, "Haiti, Free Soil, and Antislavery."

64. For sailors, see Linebaugh and Rediker, *The Many-Headed Hydra*; Rediker, *Between the Devil and the Deep Blue Sea*; Bolster, *Black Jacks*; Vickers, *Young Men and the Sea*; and Scott, "The Common Wind." For interimperial trade, see Armytage, *The Free Port System*; Adelman, *Sovereignty and Revolution*; Pearce, *Brit-*

ish Trade with Spanish America; Rupert, *Creolization and Contraband*; Jarvis, *In the Eye of All Trade*; and Prado, *Edge of Empire*.

65. See chapters 3 to 6 for historiographical references on these topics.

66. Hancock, *Oceans of Wine*, xvi.

67. Cañizares-Esguerra and Breen, "Hybrid Atlantics," 597. See also Bassi, "Beyond Compartmentalized Atlantics."

68. Greer, "National, Transnational, and Hypernational," 717–718.

69. Ferreira, *Cross-Cultural Exchange*, 242–248.

70. Cañizares-Esguerra, *Puritan Conquistadors*, 218 ("global awareness"); Greer, "National, Transnational, and Hypernational," 700 ("brave new borderless world"). For the rise of U.S. historians' global awareness, see Taylor, *American Colonies* and *The Civil War of 1812*; Bender, *A Nation among Nations*; and Gould, *Among the Powers*.

71. For these characterizations of the Atlantic and overviews of the most recent works in Atlantic history, see Gould, "Entangled Histories, Entangled Worlds"; Cañizares-Esguerra, "Entangled Histories"; Cañizares-Esguerra and Breen, "Hybrid Atlantics"; Sweet, *Domingos Álvares*, 229; Taylor, *The Civil War of 1812*, 10; Gould, *Among the Powers*, 8; Hancock, *Oceans of Wine*, xv; Benton, *A Search for Sovereignty*, 2; Bassi, "Beyond Compartmentalized Atlantics."

72. Epstein, *Scandal of Colonial Rule*.

73. Ferrer, *Freedom's Mirror*; Childs, *The 1812 Aponte Rebellion*.

74. Landers, *Atlantic Creoles*; Millett, *The Maroons of Prospect Bluff*.

75. De Certeau, *The Practice of Everyday Life*, 123.

76. Berlin, "From Creole to African," 254. Landers adopts Berlin's term to study "a diverse group" of individuals of African descent united by their "determined quest for freedom," whose lives were characterized by extraordinary social and geographical mobility and marked by the political instability of the Age of Revolutions and the multiple dangers and opportunities it entailed. Landers, *Atlantic Creoles*, 14.

77. For thought-provoking, enlightening, innovative approaches that use food as a key variable to develop cultural geographies that make it possible to see the world otherwise, see Carney and Rosomoff, *In the Shadow of Slavery*; and Goucher, *Congotay! Congotay!*

78. Craib, *Cartographic Mexico*, 259.

79. De Certeau, *The Practice of Everyday Life*, 97.

Chapter 1: Vessels

Epigraph: "From Havana to Portobelo / from Jamaica to Trinidad / roams and roams the ship ship / without captain." Guillén, "Un son para niños antillanos," 145. All translations are mine unless otherwise stated.

1. Antonio Amar to Miguel Cayetano Soler, December 7, 1806, AGI, Santa Fe, 653, no. 10.

2. While 1814 was a year of war, the war was against internal insurgents and France, not against Britain. In this case, commercial legislation allowing Riohacha

to trade with foreign neutrals, coupled with current geopolitical circumstances, made the *Esperanza*'s trade legal as long as its cargo consisted of authorized products.

3. See appendix 1 and Bassi, "The Space Between" for the methodological difficulties associated with following ships, and appendix 2 for a detailed itinerary of the *Esperanza*'s 1814 journey.

4. Guillén, "Un son," 145. Guillén's poem tells the story of a paper ship that sails the Sea of the Antilles, passing many islands and describing a circulatory pattern that resembles that of many of the schooners whose trajectories I analyze in this chapter.

5. "Informe de Manuel Hernández . . . sobre el estado del comercio en el virreinato de Santa Fe," AGI, Santa Fe, 959, no. 67. San Andrés is also 250 miles north of Portobelo, 450 miles northwest of Cartagena, and 480 miles southwest of Jamaica. See also Pombo, *Comercio y contrabando*.

6. For works that emphasize the central role of Cartagena, see McFarlane, *Colombia before Independence* and "El comercio exterior del virreinato"; Múnera, *El fracaso de la nación*; and Bell Lemus, "La conexión Jamaiquina."

7. Scott, "The Common Wind," 68. Like Scott, in their pioneering works Olga Pantaleão and Frances Armytage analyzed the shift in imperial policies toward less restrictive commercial legislation in the aftermath of the Seven Years' War. Their insights, however, continue to this day to be minimized by the weight of historiographical traditions operating within compartmentalized Atlantics that tend to present each Atlantic (i.e., British, Spanish, French, Portuguese) as autonomous and isolated. Pantaleão, *A penetracão comercial*; Armytage, *The Free Port System*.

8. In a different historical and geographical setting, Eric Tagliacozzo has referred to this dynamic definition of contraband as "undertrading" or "the passage of goods underneath, or at the legal and geographic interstices of, the majority of items traded in this arena." For Tagliacozzo, undertrading in Southeast Asia's Anglo-Dutch frontier was a function of "particular historical moments" that created the conditions for "certain products and even some ports [to] pass . . . in and out of an undertrade category." Tagliacozzo, *Secret Trades, Porous Borders*, 5. I tend to think of the distinction in terms of a transition from a definition of contraband based on mercantilist principles to one that can be called a modern definition, based on the adaptation of commercial policies to the new ideas associated with free trade.

9. Shipping returns for Cartagena are available only for 1785, 1789, 1793, 1800, 1808, and 1817. Santa Marta's returns are available only for 1801, 1807, and 1814. For Cartagena's shipping returns, by year, see: 1785, AGNC, AA-I, Aduanas, 8, 195–219; 1789, AGNC, AA-I, Aduanas, 16, 1009–1042; 1793, AGNC, AA-I, Aduanas, 22, 539–569; 1800, AGNC, AA-I, Aduanas, 33, 307–343; 1808, AGNC, AA-I, Aduanas, 44, 1–21; 1817, AGNC, AA-I, Aduanas, 51, 1–17. For Santa Marta, see (by year): 1801, AGNC, AA-I, Aduanas, 34, 1–10; 1807, AGNC, AA-I, Aduanas, 41, 768–787; 1814, AGNC, AA-I, Aduanas, 47, 286–300.

10. Comercio libre y protegido was decreed in 1778 but, due to the commercial disruptions created by Spain's participation in the American Revolution, was only

effectively introduced in 1784 or 1785. See Torres Ramírez and Ortiz de la Tabla, *Reglamento y aranceles reales para el comercio libre*; and, for the effective introduction of the policy, Fisher, *The Economic Aspects of Spanish Imperialism*, 134–196; and McFarlane, *Colombia before Independence*, 126–184.

11. For early incursions of British, French, and Dutch smugglers, pirates, and privateers as well as colonists, see Lane, *Pillaging the Empire*; Kupperman, *Providence Island*; Pearce, *British Trade with Spanish America*, 1–40; and Rediker, *Villains of All Nations*.

12. Jamaica shipping returns for the period 1766–1818 are found in the Colonial Office documents of London's National Archives, TNA, CO, 142/22–29. The only previous studies using these documents are Armytage, *The Free Port System*; and Pearce, *British Trade with Spanish America*.

13. Rodríguez O., "We Are Now the True Spaniards," 34. The Bourbon Family Compact refers to the alliance sealed between France and Spain at the end of the War of Spanish Succession, when Louis XIV's grandson was recognized as the Spanish King Felipe V. The Family Compact lasted until the French revolutionary wars, securing the French-Spanish alliance against Great Britain for most of the eighteenth century.

14. For a succinct analysis of the role of Spain in these wars, see Rodríguez O., "We Are Now the True Spaniards," 34–38. For an innovative analysis that puts the Pacific Ocean at the center of the eighteenth-century interimperial disputes, see Mapp, *The Elusive West*.

15. See Pares, *War and Trade in the West Indies*; and Grafenstein, *Nueva España en el Circuncaribe*.

16. The argument for free trade is usually traced back to the publication of Adam Smith's *An Inquiry into the Nature and Causes of the Wealth of Nations* in 1776. It is worth stressing that Smith's ideas were developed within an intellectual and policy-making milieu in which many political economists throughout the Atlantic world were increasingly arguing against mercantilist principles. Spanish political economists like Joseph Campillo y Cosío, Bernardo Ward, and Pedro Rodríguez Campomanes, as modern scholarship has demonstrated, were critical of Spanish commercial policies and looked favorably toward free trade. See Stein and Stein, *Silver, Trade, and War* and *Apogee of Empire*; Ferrer, *Freedom's Mirror*, 20–23; and Tomich, "The Wealth of Empire."

17. Parry, *Trade and Dominion*, 96–97.

18. Pearce, *British Trade with Spanish America*, 18. See also Parry, *Trade and Dominion*, 102–103; and Pantaleão, *A penetracão commercial*, 46–56, 95–102.

19. The concessions and mild openness to trade with foreigners were subject to controversy. An early nineteenth-century critic of the increased openness to trade with foreign neutrals, based on the possibilities this trade created for fraud, described the "universal system" of trade prevailing "in time of peace" as follows: "The colonizing powers of Europe, it is well known, have always monopolized the trade of their respective colonies; allowing no supplies to be carried to them under any

foreign flag, or on account of any foreign importers; and prohibiting the exportation of their produce in foreign ships, or to any foreign country, till it has been previously brought into the ports of the parent state." [Stephen], *War in Disguise*, 11–12.

20. In 1764 Halifax referred to the British practice of giving "Spanish vessels coming to . . . Jamaica, thro' distress, or for refreshments, . . . the assistance they have been always allowed." Halifax to Lords of Trade, May 12, 1764, quoted in Pearce, *British Trade with Spanish America*, 46. In Spanish documents there are frequent references to *auxilios de humanidad* (humanitarian aid) and the "hospitality" provided to foreign ships in distress. See for example "Expediente sobre la arribada legítima del bergantín holandés Cornelia Luisa, su capitán Thimoteo Seud a Portobelo, de donde fue llevado a Cartagena," AGI, Santa Fe, 955. See also Pantaleão, *A penetracão commercial*, 120–121.

21. [Stephen], *War in Disguise*, 12. Reappraisals of the global outreach of the Seven Years' War include Baugh, *The Global Seven Years War*; Anderson, *Crucible of War*; McLynn, *1759*; Dull, *The French Navy and the Seven Years' War*; and Mapp, *The Elusive West*, 261–428.

22. Stein and Stein, *Apogee of Empire*, 56. See also Childs, *The 1812 Aponte Rebellion*, 23–33.

23. For a more detailed analysis of the effects of the British siege and occupation of Havana, see Schneider, *The Occupation of Havana*.

24. Antonio Benítez-Rojo's succinct description of the sistema de flotas is worth quoting. Designed by Pedro Menéndez de Avilés, the sistema de flotas required that "all navigation between the West Indies and Seville (the only port that allowed transatlantic trade) would be undertaken in convoys consisting of cargo ships, warships, and light craft for reconnaissance and dispatch; the cargoes of gold and silver were to be boarded only on given dates and in only a few Caribbean ports (Cartagena, Nombre de Dios, San Juan de Ulúa, and some other secondary ones); forts would be built and garrisons stationed not only at these ports but also at those defending the entrances to the Caribbean (San Juan de Puerto Rico, Santo Domingo, Santiago de Cuba, the eastern coast of Florida, and, especially, Havana); all these ports would be bases for squadrons of coast guard and patrol ships, whose mission would be to sweep the waters and coastal keys clean of pirates, privateers, and smugglers, while at the same time providing rescue service to convoys in trouble." Benítez-Rojo, *The Repeating Island*, 7. More recently and even more succinctly, Greg Grandin described the Spanish mercantilist commercial system as follows: "Spain prohibited its colonies from trading with one another, banned foreign ships from entering American ports, prohibited individual merchants from owning their own fleets of cargo ships, and limited manufacturing. . . . The idea was to prevent the development of a too-powerful merchant class in America, making sure its colonies remained a source of gold and silver and an exclusive [market] for goods made in or shipped through Spain." Grandin, *The Empire of Necessity*, 24–25. For more substantive and detailed descriptions of the convoy system also known as the Carrera de Indias, see the classic works of Pierre and Huguette Chaunu and

Clarence Haring. Chaunu and Chaunu, *Sevilla y América*; and Haring, *Trade and Navigation*.

25. Stein and Stein, *Apogee of Empire*, 69, 73–75. See also Adelman, *Sovereignty and Revolution*, 13–100.

26. Stein and Stein, *Apogee of Empire*, 57.

27. Pearce, *British Trade with Spanish America*, 51. The Jamaican ports opened at this time were Kingston, Savannah la Mar, Montego Bay, and Santa Lucea; the ports opened in Dominica were Prince Rupert's Bay and Roseau. Armytage, *The Free Port System*, 42.

28. Armytage, *The Free Port System*, 46.

29. Stein and Stein, *Apogee of Empire*, 143–185; Rodríguez O., *The Independence of Spanish America*, 30–32; Fisher, *The Economic Aspects of Spanish Imperialism*; Torres Ramírez and Ortiz de la Tabla, *Reglamento y aranceles reales para el comercio libre*; and García-Baquero, *Comercio colonial y guerras revolucionarias*.

30. According to Armytage in 1781, only thirty-five foreign vessels (Dutch and Danish) entered the British free ports. Armytage, *The Free Port System*, 51.

31. McFarlane, *Colombia before Independence*, 152–153; Ripoll, "El comercio ilícito," 157–160. For contemporary arguments on trade with foreign neutrals, see the reports by Viceroy Josef Ezpeleta opposing trade with foreign neutrals and Cartagena's *consulado de comercio* (merchant guild) and field general Antonio Narváez y la Torre favoring it. "Reservada del virrey de Santa Fe," May 19, 1795, AGI, Santa Fe, 645, no. 21; "El Consulado," July 24, 1804, AGI, Santa Fe, 960, no. 83; and Narváez, "Discurso del Mariscal de Campo."

32. See chapter 4 for British debates regarding the future of empire in the aftermath of the American Revolution, in particular the schemes to avoid the shift of imperial interest to India.

33. Fisher, *The Economic Aspects of Spanish Imperialism*, 144, 163.

34. In his study of foreign influences on Spanish Bourbon reformism, Gabriel Paquette refers to the similarities of British and Spanish development models as "policy convergence." "Incessant war, mercantile rivalry, and the drive for geopolitical power," he writes, "resulted in policy convergence and a move towards institutional isomorphism across Europe's Atlantic empires." Paquette, *Enlightenment, Governance, and Reform*, 6.

35. Armytage, *The Free Port System*, 52–71; Caballero y Góngora, "Relación del estado del Nuevo Reino de Granada," 1:443–459.

36. For Cartagena's trade during the sixteenth and seventeenth centuries see del Castillo Mathieu, *La llave de las Indias*; Vidal, *Cartagena de Indias*; Landers, "The African Landscape of Seventeenth-Century Cartagena"; and Wheat, "The First Great Waves."

37. This tendency is evident in studies of Colombia's colonial trade (e.g., McFarlane, *Colombia before Independence*; and Múnera, *El fracaso de la nación*), as well as in edited volumes on Caribbean and Atlantic port cities, which only include Cartagena in their chapters about Colombia's ports (i.e., Knight and Liss, *Atlantic*

Port Cities; Grafenstein, *El Golfo Caribe*). One of the most recent publications on Caribbean ports (Vidal and Caro, *Ciudades portuarias*) includes a long-needed correction. It includes chapters on Santa Marta and Riohacha that stress, especially for the case of Riohacha, their commercial connections with the Dutch Caribbean.

38. The *Nazareno* entered Cartagena from Cádiz on January 17, 1785, and departed for Cádiz on June 22, 1785. AGNC, AA-I, Aduanas, 8, 195–219. In 1789, the ship *Purísima Concepción* entered Cartagena from Cádiz on July 20 and, after three months in Cartagena, departed for Cádiz on October 24. AGNC, AA-I, Aduanas, 16, 1009–1042v.

39. For detailed itineraries of selected ships, including the *Santiago*, see appendix 2.

40. AGNC, AA-I, Aduanas, 8, 195–219; AGNC, AA-I, Aduanas, 16, 1009–1042; AGNC, AA-I, Aduanas, 22, 539–569; AGNC, AA-I, Aduanas, 33, 307–343; AGNC, AA-I, Aduanas, 34, 1–10; AGNC, AA-I, Aduanas, 41, 768–787; AGNC, AA-I, Aduanas, 44, 1–21; AGNC, AA-I, Aduanas, 47, 286–300; AGNC, AA-I, Aduanas, 51, 1–17.

41. AGI, Santa Fe, 1091.

42. Appendix 3, tables A3.1 and A3.3. See also McFarlane, *Colombia before Independence*, 130–131, 370.

43. "Resumen de un cuatrienio de las embarcaciones . . . que han salido de . . . Cartagena para . . . la Península desde . . . 1785 hasta . . . 1788," AGI, Santa Fe, 957.

44. Appendix 3, tables A3.1 and A3.2.

45. Appendix 3, tables A3.3 and A3.4; AGNC, AA-I, Aduanas, 47, 780v. The *Lightning* or *El Rayo* entered Santa Marta from the Spanish port of Vigo on February 22, 1807, and sailed back to Spain on April 1 of that same year. Given the dates of its trip, it seems that the *Lightning* was one of the few ships that successfully crossed the Atlantic (at least in its trip westward) during the Anglo-Spanish War of 1803–1808.

46. Appendix 3, table A3.4.

47. Quoted in Stein and Stein, *Apogee of Empire*, 268.

48. Fisher, *Commercial Relations*, 88–89; and McFarlane, *Colombia before Independence*, 160.

49. Rodríguez O., *The Independence of Spanish America*, 8; Humboldt, *Personal Narrative*, 3:129. Humboldt's population figures are given for 1823. If the population impact of the wars of independence is considered, it is highly probable that New Granada's participation in Spanish America's population was higher during the late eighteenth century.

50. Narváez to Minister of Finance, Panama, March 9, 1799, AGI, Santa Fe, 959.

51. Royal orders allowing the ports of Cartagena, Santa Marta, and Riohacha to trade with foreigners are mentioned, described, or alluded to in the correspondence of Viceroy Ezpeleta with authorities in Madrid. See for example Ezpeleta to Lerena, Santa Fe, July 19, 1791, AGI, Santa Fe, 640, no. 12; and Ezpeleta to Lerena, Santa Fe, June 19, 1791, AGI, Santa Fe, 640, no. 129.

52. Trade with foreigners was subject to restrictions in the commodities to be exchanged, the ports where transactions could be made, and the nationality of ships allowed to conduct the commerce.

53. "El Consulado," July 24, 1804, AGI, Santa Fe, 960, no. 83; "Reservada del virrey de Santa Fe," May 19, 1795, AGI, Santa Fe, 645, no. 21.

54. Pombo, *Comercio y contrabando*, 20.

55. AGI, Santa Fe, 640; "Don Juan Alvarez de Verina, comandante de los guarda costas de la Indias Occidentales y sus islas, se queja reverentemente a SM . . . de los desaires que se hacen a su empleo por el arzobispo virrey de Santa Fe," Cartagena, December 31, 1787, AGI, Santa Fe, 655; Álvarez de Veriñas to Antonio de Valdés, Cartagena, February 28, 1789, AGI, Santa Fe, 655; Gil y Lemos, "Relación de D. Francisco Gil y Lemos," 2:5–33.

56. AGI, Santa Fe, 1015, no. 6; AGI, Santa Fe, 641, no. 129.

57. For a typical cargo, see the report of the inspection of the U.S. ship *Amable* in AGNC, SC, Aduanas, 21, 836–851.

58. Caballero y Góngora, "Relación del estado del Nuevo Reino de Granada," 1:448.

59. It was possible to identify the nationality of thirty-four ships: twenty-three were Spanish, four French, four English, two Dutch, and one Danish. "Nota de las embarcaciones de colonias que han entrado en este puerto de Cartagena de Indias desde primero de enero de 1786 hasta 16 de abril del presente con sus nombres, el de sus capitanes y carga," AGI, Santa Fe, 955.

60. Cabildo de Santa Fe to Antonio Bazan, Santa Fe, October, 26, 1789, AGI, Santa Fe, 955; and Gutiérrez de Piñeres to Antonio Valdés, August 29, 1787, AGI, Santa Fe, 955.

61. Josef García de Pizarro to Antonio Valdés, Madrid, August 20, 1787, AGI, Santa Fe, 955. See also Múnera, *El fracaso de la nación*, 111–139.

62. Veriñas to H. M., Cartagena, December 31, 1787, AGI, Santa Fe, 655.

63. Cartagena-born Antonio Narváez y la Torre, renowned military officer and governor of Santa Marta in 1778, and José de Astigárraga, governor of Santa Marta in the early 1790s, were among the most high-profile proponents of importing slaves in order to develop an export agriculture like that of Saint-Domingue. Narváez y la Torre, "Provincia de Santa Marta y Río Hacha"; Astigárraga to Antonio Porlier, Santa Marta, March 22, 1789, AGI, Santa Fe, 1181, no. 14. See also Helg, *Liberty and Equality*, 54–56.

64. The royal orders granting permission to Cartagena and Riohacha are mentioned in Ezpeleta to Lerena, Santa Fe, July 19, 1791, AGI, Santa Fe, 640, no. 12; and Ezpeleta to Lerena, Santa Fe, June 19, 1791, AGI, Santa Fe, 640, no. 129.

65. "Informe de Juan de León Pérez al virrey," Cartagena, October 30, 1794, AGI, Santa Fe, 645.

66. Appendix 3, table A3.1. A report of the trade of Santa Marta with foreign colonies put the number of vessels sailing from Santa Marta to foreign colonies in 1794 to buy slaves at eighteen. "Relación de las embarcaciones que han navegado desde el puerto de Santa Marta para colonias extranjeras con frutos del país para el comercio de negros," AGI, Santa Fe, 645.

67. AGNC, AA-I, Aduanas, 22, 539–569.

68. AGNC, AA-I, Aduanas, 22, 539–569.

69. Ezpeleta to Lerena, Santa Fe, December 19, 1791, AGI, Santa Fe, 640, no. 201.

70. Ezpeleta to Gardoqui, Santa Fe, May 19, 1795, AGI, Santa Fe, 645.

71. The extraction of gold by British smugglers was a central point of Domingo Negrón's narrative. In his account of the capture of his brig *Concepción*, he recounted how the *Veteran* was loaded with "eight hundred thousand gold pesos." Amar to Soler, December 7, 1806, AGI, Santa Fe, 653, no. 10.

72. Ezpeleta to Lerena, Santa Fe, December 19, 1791, AGI, Santa Fe, 641, no. 201.

73. Lorenzo Corbacho to Ezpeleta, Portobelo, November 6, 1794, AGI, Santa Fe, 645, no. 4; Corbacho to Ezpeleta, Portobelo, February 22, 1795, AGI, Santa Fe, 645, no. 5; Juan de León y Páez to Ezpeleta, Cartagena, October 30, 1794, AGI, Santa Fe, 645, no. 1.

74. Depons, *Travels in South America*, 2:59.

75. Appendix 3, table A3.1.

76. AGNC, AA-I, Aduanas, 33, 307–343; and AGNC, AA-I, Aduanas, 44, 1–21.

77. Appendix 3, table A3.3; and AGNC, AA-I, Aduanas, 41, 768–787.

78. Appendix 3, table A3.1.

79. "Estado general que manifiesta el comercio de esta plaza de Cartagena de Indias, correspondiente al año de 1805, formado en cumplimiento de reales ordenes," AGI, Santa Fe, 960.

80. Appendix 3, table A3.3; and AGNC, AA-I, Aduanas, 41, 768–787.

81. [Stephen], *War in Disguise*, 20.

82. Nissen, *Reminiscences of a 46 Years' Residence*, 34, 37, 50, 60, 105, 110, 113.

83. Armytage, *The Free Port System*, 95–112; and Pearce, *British Trade with Spanish America*, 119–229.

84. Walton, *Present State of the Spanish Colonies*, 2:168–169.

85. Depons, *Travels in South America*, 2:56.

86. Pearce, *British Trade with Spanish America*, 170–176.

87. Rodríguez O., *The Independence of Spanish America*, 49–59, 155.

88. Bassi, "Raza, clase y lealtades políticas."

89. For the most recent analyses of the wars of independence in Caribbean New Granada, see Múnera, *El fracaso de la nación*; Helg, *Liberty and Equality*; Lasso, *Myths of Harmony*; Saether, *Identidades e independencia*; and Pérez Morales, *El gran diablo*.

90. Armytage, *The Free Port System*, 113.

91. For British neutrality, see Esdaile, "Latin America and the Anglo-Spanish Alliance"; and Wadell, *Gran Bretaña y la independencia*. Chapter 5 presents a detailed explanation of the Anglo-Spanish alliance and of British neutrality in Spanish America.

92. Appendix 3, table A3.3; and AGNC, AA-I, Aduanas, 47, 286–300.

93. In 1817, Cartagena was again under Spanish control. After declaring its independence in November 1811, Cartagena remained an independent state until December 1815, when Spanish troops under Pablo Morillo entered the city. Cartagena remained under Spanish control until October 1821. Contemporary accounts of Cartagena's declaration of independence, its siege and conquest by Spanish

troops, and its definitive recapture by republican troops in 1821 are provided in Restrepo, *Historia de la revolución*, 1:189–194, 2:51–59, 76–90; 4:147–156, 208–209, 235–236, 287–293; Sevilla, *Memorias de un oficial*. For analyses of Cartagena's early independence and the Spanish reconquest of the city, see Earle, *Spain and the Independence*, 61–64, 101–104, 147–154; and Cuño Bonito, *El retorno del rey*.

94. Armytage, *The Free Port System*, 113–137.

95. See appendix 2 for detailed itineraries of these vessels.

96. Appendix 2; AGNC, AA-I, Aduanas, 41, 768–787.

97. Bell Lemus, "La conexión jamaiquina."

98. McFarlane, "El comercio exterior."

99. Information for foreign vessels entering and clearing out of Kingston is available for 1783–1787, 1796, and 1810–1818 in TNA, CO, 142/22–29.

100. The number of free ports in Jamaica was initially established at four (Kingston, Montego Bay, Savannah la Mar, and Santa Lucea). In the same year, 1766, two free ports were opened in Dominica (Prince Rupert's Bay and Roseau). Two other ports, one in Grenada and other in the Bahamas (New Providence), were added in 1787. By the end of 1805, there were free ports in Jamaica, Dominica, Grenada, Antigua, Trinidad, Tobago, the Bahamas, Tortola, Saint Vincent, and Bermuda. Armytage, *The Free Port System*, 42, 59, 141.

101. Armytage, *The Free Port System*, 148–149.

102. At the time, according to Trevor Burnard, Kingston was also "one of the most important centers of Black Atlantic life in the New World" and "one of the five major towns in British America, the other four being Boston, New York, Philadelphia and Charleston." Comparing Kingston with these North American ports, Burnard asserts, "From the perspective of Kingston, the North American port cities were not especially impressive. Kingston was wealthier and, to some commentators at least, more beautiful than towns in British North America." Burnard, "Kingston, Jamaica," 126, 129, 125.

103. TNA, CO, 142/22; Armytage, *The Free Port System*, 113–137.

104. TNA, CO, 142/22.

105. Armytage found, based on customs accounts for 1792, "that 265 Spanish vessels entered, against 224 French vessels, and only 30 Dutch." Armytage, *The Free Port System*, 64. The percentages for 1810 and 1814 come from TNA, CO, 142/26 and TNA, CO, 142/28.

106. Clarke, *Kingston, Jamaica*, 27; Depons, *Travels in South America*, 2:56.

107. Scott, *Tom Cringle's Log*, 127.

108. Quoted in Pearce, *British Trade with Spanish America*, 82.

109. Scott, *Tom Cringle's Log*, 129.

110. Appendix 3, table A3.5.

111. Appendix 3, table A3.5.

112. For a chronology of the British free port system, see Armytage, who refers to the 1808–1822 period as the height and decline of the free port system. Armytage, *The Free Port System*, 113–137.

113. The total number of vessels entering Kingston from Neogranadan ports in 1810 and 1814 was 45 and 119. See appendix 3, table A3.5.

114. See for example Pombo, *Comercio y contrabando*; "Representación de los comerciantes de Cartagena al virrey Ezpeleta," Cartagena, April 30, 1795, AGI, Santa Fe, 1019.

115. "Representación de los comerciantes de Cartagena al virrey Ezpeleta."

116. The *Annette*, for example, sailed from Kingston to Cartagena in April and returned to Kingston on May 24. After about three weeks in Kingston, it sailed again for Cartagena on June 11, proceeding afterward to Sabanilla, from where it entered Kingston on July 12. On July 29, after seventeen days in port, it sailed again for Cartagena. After its return on September 15, it stayed in Kingston for less than two weeks before it sailed again for Cartagena. Through all these trips the *Annette* was captained by Francisco Díaz. Except for the trip of June 11, in which it transported dry goods, the *Annette* cleared out of Kingston in ballast, returning with cotton and on one occasion bullion (36,000 dollars). TNA, CO, 142/28.

117. Appendix 2. In addition to the *Esperanza* at least three more schooners made several Kingston-Riohacha round-trips during 1814. José Diaz's *Cosmopolita* made five and Luis Zúñiga and Antonio Morales's *Flor de la Mar* made three. TNA, CO, 142/28.

118. Appendix 2.

119. Appendix 2.

120. AGI, Santa Fe, 641, no. 11; "El virrey de Santafé da cuenta . . . del expediente promovido sobre exacción del derecho de avería a una partida de dinero que se extrajo de Portobelo para . . . San Andrés," Santa Fe, December 19, 1805, AGI, Santa Fe, 653.

121. "Informe de Manuel Hernández," AGI, Santa Fe, 959, no. 67.

122. "Consulta de Amar sobre derechos a pagar," Santa Fe, December 19, 1805, AGI, Santa Fe, 960.

123. Appendix 3, table A3.5; and TNA, CO, 142/28.

124. Appendix 2.

125. Braudel, *Civilization and Capitalism*, vol. 2, *The Wheels of Commerce*, 120.

126. Alfonso Mola, "The Spanish Colonial Fleet," 373. For a useful comparison, it is worth noting that, according to Herbert Klein, the average Liverpool slaver in the 1790s weighed 201 tons. Klein, *The Atlantic Slave Trade*, 133.

127. "Resumen en un cuatrienio de las embarcaciones y su carga," AGI, Santa Fe, 957.

128. I use the term "peddler vessel" for small vessels with frequent entries into and clearances from the port of Kingston. Size (small) and frequency (two or more visits) are the defining characteristics of peddler vessels.

129. Jarvis, *In the Eye of All Trade*, 122–125.

130. TNA, CO, 142/28.

131. TNA, CO, 142/28.

132. Narváez y la Torre, "Provincia de Santa Marta y Río Hacha," 69–73.

133. Appendix 3, tables A3.5 and A3.6; and TNA, CO, 146/26, 146/28.

134. The estimate is conservative because I only included those vessels for which, based on name, captain, destination and origin, and size, it was possible to confidently eliminate the risk of counting as one ship what were actually two or more ships. In the process, I chose not to include in the list of peddler vessels some ships with common names like *Carmen* and *San Josef*. See appendix 1 for the difficulties associated with ships' names.

135. Ezpeleta to Lerena, "Sobre la suspensión del comercio de negros por el contrabando que incentiva," Santa Fe, December 19, 1791, AGI, Santa Fe, 641, no. 201.

136. Pombo, *Comercio y contrabando*, 68, 87, 97.

137. Ezpeleta to Lerena, Santa Fe, March 19, 1792, AGI, Santa Fe, 641, no. 228.

138. Parry, *Trade and Dominion*, 330.

139. Moya Pons, *History of the Caribbean*, 186–188.

140. The possibility of British invasion of sectors of Caribbean New Granada and the fears it triggered are the subject of chapter 4.

Chapter 2: Sailors

Epigraph: Rediker, *Outlaws of the Atlantic*, 9–10.

1. AGNC, AA-I, Gobierno, 13, 463–469.

2. For the spread of information about events in Haiti, see Geggus, *Haitian Revolutionary Studies*; Geggus, *The Impact of the Haitian Revolution*; Scott, "The Common Wind"; Lasso, *Myths of Harmony*; Childs, *The 1812 Aponte Rebellion*; Ferrer, *Freedom's Mirror*.

3. Scott, "The Common Wind"; Linebaugh and Rediker, *The Many-Headed Hydra*; Rediker, *Outlaws of the Atlantic*.

4. De Certeau, *The Practice of Everyday Life*, 123.

5. Linebaugh and Rediker, *The Many-Headed Hydra*, 241; Scott, "The Common Wind." See also Rediker, *Outlaws of the Atlantic*, 116–119.

6. For the notion of space as "produced," see Lefebvre, *The Production of Space*; Smith, *Uneven Development*.

7. Scott, "The Common Wind," 6–58. See also Pérez Morales, *El gran diablo*.

8. Based on shipping returns for the ports of Cartagena and Santa Marta in New Granada and Kingston, Jamaica, I have put together a list of sea captains with navigational careers of more than three years. Many of these captains spent over twenty years navigating the Caribbean and the Atlantic. See appendixes 4 and 5.

9. See appendix 5 for details of the professional trajectories of these sea captains.

10. The so-called *establecimientos del Darién* were a central element of the Spanish strategy to establish effective control of the Darién territory. The strategy, directed by Viceroy Caballero y Góngora during the 1780s, called for the promotion of immigration (white settlers from Philadelphia and Germany settled in the area with permission from Spanish authorities), the importation of construction materials and victuals to support the population, the pacification of the area's indigenous population, and the promotion of cotton cultivation to secure the prosperity of the

towns and their inhabitants. For a brief description of the pacification campaigns, see Helg, *Liberty and Equality*, 25–31. For complaints about the benefits Caballero y Góngora's strategy promised, see "Don Juan Alvarez de Veriña . . . se queja reverentemente a SM desde Cartagena de Indias," Cartagena, December 31, 1787, AGI, Santa Fe, 655. For the ultimate fate of the settlers from Philadelphia (which included British, German, and Irish subjects), see Joaquín Cañaveral to Antonio Valdez y Bazán, Cartagena, April 27, 1790, AGI, Santa Fe, 1015.

11. Depons, *Travels in South America*, 2:56; Scott, *Tom Cringle's Log*, 127.

12. See appendix 4.

13. AGNC, AA-I, Aduanas, 34, 1–10.

14. AGNC, AA-I, Aduanas, 22, 539–569; AGNC, AA-I, Aduanas, 33, 307–343; AGNC, AA-I, Aduanas, 41, 768–787.

15. Caballero y Góngora to Salvador de los Monteros, Cartagena, December 7, 1787, AGI, Santa Fe, 645.

16. "Nota de las embarcaciones de colonias que han entrado en este puerto de Cartagena de Indias desde primero de enero de 1786 hasta 16 de abril del presente con sus nombres, el de sus capitanes y carga," AGI, Santa Fe, 955.

17. "Relación de la carga que conduce al puerto de Cartagena de Indias la fragata San Antonio alias la Cordobesa, capitán don Olivier Daniel," AGI, Santa Fe, 955.

18. AGNC, AA-I, Aduanas, 16, 1009–1042.

19. Evidence of the growing importance of Philadelphia in New Granada's foreign trade is available in the customs records of the Colombian archives. See for example AGNC, SC, Aduanas, 12, 17, 464–468 (brig *María de Filadelfia*); AGNC, SC, Aduanas, 5, 18, 973–997 (ship *Aya Pigot*); AGNC, SC, Aduanas, 4, 22, 37–48 (schooner *Nancy*).

20. Massey, *For Space*, 9.

21. Martínez to Narváez y la Torre, Kingston, February 15, 1785, AGNC, SC, Milicias y Marina, 115, 544–553.

22. "Diligencia de entrada de la balandra española *La Leonor*," Santa Marta, April 16, 1784, AGNC, AA-I, Aduanas, 8, 1–26. See also AGNC, AA-I, Aduanas, 8, 27–53; AGNC, SC, Aduanas, 21, 32; and AGNC, SC, Milicias y Marina, 80, 754–762.

23. AGNC, AA-I, Gobierno, 13, 463–469.

24. Corrales to Captain General of Caracas, Puerto Cabello, May 27, 1802, AGI, Estado, 60, no. 21.

25. "Declaración dada por Noel Tool," May 5, 1775, AGNC, SC, Milicias y Marina, 80, 754–762.

26. AGNC, SC, Aduanas, 2, 20, 832r–835v; AGNC, SC, Aduanas, 2, 13, 382r–384.

27. Anastasio Zejudo to Viceroy Mendinueta, Cartagena, September 19, 1801, AGNC, SC, Milicias y Marina, 81, 165–172; "Información sobre goleta inglesa varada en Galerazamba," AGNC, SC, Milicias y Marina, 82, 311–315.

28. For prosopographical studies of Jack Tars, see Rediker, *Between the Devil and the Deep Blue Sea*; Bolster, *Black Jacks*; and Vickers, *Young Men and the Sea*.

29. For a study of the corsairs sailing under the flag of the Republic of Cartagena, an independent state that, in lieu of a formal navy, made its naval presence in

Caribbean waters through the grant of letters of marque, see Pérez Morales, *El gran diablo*. For ephemeral states see Landers, *Atlantic Creoles*, 95–137.

30. For a critique of the tendency to think of imperial spheres as disconnected, see Hancock, *Oceans of Wine*.

31. The analysis that follows is mostly based on the interrogations of the sailors of the schooners *El Congreso de la Nueva Granada* (1814) and *Altagracia* (1815). For *El Congreso*, see "Autos obrados sobre la entrada del corsario insurgente titulado *El Congreso*" (hereafter "Autos *El Congreso*"), AGNC, AA-I, Guerra y Marina, 118, 721–933. For the *Altagracia*, see "Autos seguidos en el gobierno de esta capital de Santiago de Veraguas contra los individuos que sirvieron de corsarios con nación leal, en la goleta nombrada *La Belona* y la suerte les condujo a varar en el Escudo de Veraguas en la goleta apresada por aquella nombrada *Altagracia*" (hereafter "Autos *La Belona*"), AGNC, AA-I, Guerra y Marina, 130, 395–481.

32. "Patente de corso," in "Autos *El Congreso*," 741–743. The schooner's letter of marque said its crew was composed of thirty-three sailors, including eleven officers, twenty-one ordinary sailors, and one cabin boy; only twenty-three were interrogated in Portobelo.

33. "Declaración de Juan Flores," in "Autos *El Congreso*," 757–758. Insurgent corsairs did not follow predetermined routes. Instead, they cruised the sea in search of prey. Their cruises resembled those of tramp steamers, whose improvised itineraries Colombian novelist Álvaro Mutis described as taking them "from port to port in search of occasional cargo to transport to no-matter-where." Mutis, *La última escala del tramp steamer*, 16.

34. "Declaración de Ignacio, marinero," in "Autos *La Belona*," 402–407.

35. "Autos *La Belona*," 470.

36. For these ephemeral states, see Landers, *Atlantic Creoles*, 95–137; Racine, *Francisco de Miranda*, 211–241; Sourdís, *Cartagena de Indias*; and Pérez Morales, *El gran diablo*, 77–112, 145–173.

37. "Declaración de Juan Estevan Rodríguez, negro marinero de la goleta corsaria *Belona*," February 20, 1815, in "Autos *La Belona*," 417–419.

38. Juan Estevan did not specify the dates of any of the incidents he narrates in his declaration. Besides stating that he returned to the Americas from Spain "twelve years ago," he remained ambiguous about when any of the events he was recollecting happened. Based on the time he spent as a prisoner in Cartagena (six months) and the time he spent on board the *Altagracia* (five months), it is clear that it had been more than a year—perhaps two, given that before sailing on the *Altagracia* he had sailed on *La Belona* and other Spanish vessels and had also escaped from Cartagena to Jamaica—since he had been employed on *El Rayo*.

39. The work of Greg Grandin includes eloquent examples of the status-changing effects sailors experienced as a direct consequence of the geopolitical instability characteristic of the Age of Revolutions. In an example from the eastern Atlantic, in the vicinities of Cape Coast castle, Grandin writes, "Early in Britain's fight against France, a British merchant ship calling at Cape Coast castle,

purchased a cargo of captured Africans. They were considered slaves, locked in the ship's hold, and destined for the West Indies to work on sugar plantations. That ship was captured by the French navy, which took the Africans not as slaves but as conscripts, distributing them among its frigates and men-of-war. The Africans were now sailors. By 1803, however, the British had recaptured sixty-five of them. After some debate within the councils of the Admiralty, the British deemed the Africans to be not slaves but prisoners of war, subjects—or, as the French preferred, citizens—of a legitimate, if rogue, nation. But since the British couldn't get France to live up to its customary obligations and provide for these (or any other, for that matter, white or black) captured sailors, the British had them distributed on ships throughout the Royal Navy. They were sailors once again, as well as, presumably, new British subjects." Grandin, *The Empire of Necessity*, 300.

40. "Declaración de Ignacio, marinero," in "Autos *La Belona*," 402–407.

41. "Declaración de Juan Flores," in "Autos *El Congreso*," 757–758.

42. Scott, "The Common Wind," 22.

43. "Declaración de José Miguel García," in "Autos *El Congreso*," 761–762; "Declaración de Manuel Pedro del Brasil," in "Autos *El Congreso*," 762–763.

44. "Declaración de Samuel Sederman," in "Autos *El Congreso*," 781–783.

45. Rediker, *Villains of All Nations*; Linebaugh and Rediker, *The Many-Headed Hydra*, 154, 212, 246–247; Rediker, *Outlaws of the Atlantic*, 119; Pérez Morales, *El gran diablo*, 71; Grandin, *The Empire of Necessity*, 19–21.

46. Nissen, *Reminiscences of a 46 Years' Residence*, 38. For corsairs and privateers navigating primarily in the Gulf of Mexico and the U.S. Atlantic coast during this period, see Head, *Privateers of the Americas*.

47. Frykman, "Seamen," 68–76.

48. Linebaugh and Rediker, *The Many-Headed Hydra*, 151. See also Costello, *Black Salt*.

49. "Lista de la tripulación, guarnición y brigada del balahú del rey nombrado *Pentapolin*," AGNC, AA-I, Guerra y Marina, 44, 15–84; "Lista que comprende los oficiales mayores de mar, artilleros, marineros, grumetes, pajes, infantería, brigada y criados que sirven al rey sobre su balandra nombrada *Santiago*," AGNC, AA-I, Guerra y Marina, 61, 431–541.

50. "Lista que comprende los oficiales mayores de mar, artilleros, marineros y grumetes que sirven al rey sobre su galeota nombrada *Dulcinea*," AGNC, AA-I, Guerra y Marina, 48, 542–557.

51. "Lista que comprende los oficiales mayores de mar, artilleros, marineros, grumetes, pajes, infantería, brigada y criados que sirven al rey sobre su balandra nombrada *Santiago*," AGNC, AA-I, Guerra y Marina, 61, 431–541.

52. "Declaración de Juan Flores," in "Autos *El Congreso*," 757–758.

53. Frykman, "Seamen," 83.

54. "Querella de Bernardo Kennedy, tripulante de la goleta danesa *Guavaberry*, porque lo dejaron preso en Riohacha," 1806, AGNC, SC, Milicias y Marina, 82, 311–315; "Diligencias que se actúan por este gobierno sobre la aprehensión hecha

por el comandante del bergantín Cartagenero guarda costa de sm a una goleta que de arribada entró en este puerto nombrada *San Francisco Xavier*," Santa Marta, July 15, 1803, AGI, Sante Fe, 952. See also "Informe sobre comiso en Cartagena de la balandra *La Victoria*," September 25, 1806, AGI, Santa Fe, 1149.

55. Scott, "The Common Wind," 8. For similar approaches emphasizing the opportunities that life at sea offered, see Bolster, *Black Jacks*; Pérez Morales, *El gran diablo*.

56. "Declaración de Francisco Díaz," April 17, 1815, in "Autos *La Belona*," 449.

57. Canaparo, "Marconi and Other Artifices," 242. For longer treatments of the transformation of terrain into territory in an Argentine setting, see Canaparo, *Muerte y transfiguración* and *Geo-Epistemology*.

58. In his argument for the need to "historiciz[e]" and "civiliz[e]" the sea, Greg Dening questions "[Roland] Barthes's polarity between the signless sea and the full-of-signs land." See Dening, "Deep Times, Deep Spaces," 13–14.

59. Walcott, "The Sea Is History."

60. Accompanying this "uninspected assumption," Rediker rightly points out, is "the unspoken proposition that the seas of the world are unreal spaces, voids between the real places, which are landed and national." Rediker, *Outlaws of the Atlantic*, 2–3.

61. In addition to Dening and Walcott, my approach to thinking the sea as historical site is also informed by the works of Epeli Hauʻofa and John Gillis. In developing his "vision of Oceania," Hauʻofa explains the process of "world enlargement . . . carried out by tens of thousands of ordinary Pacific Islanders . . . crisscrossing an ocean that had been boundless for ages before Captain Cook's apotheosis." This perspective allows him to shift from thinking about "islands on the far sea"—an analytical framework that emphasizes "dry surfaces in a vast ocean" and "the smallness and remoteness of the islands"—to envisioning "a sea of islands"—a framework that stresses Oceania as "a large sea full of places to explore" and the notion that, to Pacific Islanders, "the sea is home." Gillis (drawing on Hauʻofa) questions historians' tendency to see the sea as empty and claims, "We have difficulty grasping such a world because we think of the sea as a void rather than a place and we treat islands as if they are always small, remote, and isolated whatever their size and proximity." Hauʻofa, "Our Sea of Islands," 28, 30, 31, 32; Gillis, *Islands of the Mind*, 83–84. For a more recent analysis of the sea—specifically the South Atlantic and the South Pacific—as site where history happens, see Grandin, *The Empire of Necessity*.

62. See chapter 1 for a short summary of the debate between Caballero y Góngora and Álvarez de Veriñas.

63. For the text accompanying the map, see AGI, MP-Panamá, 262.

64. Thongchai, *Siam Mapped*, 17.

65. Gillis, *Islands of the Mind*, 83. See also Steinberg, "Of Other Seas"; Carter, *The Road to Botany Bay*, xxii–xxv.

66. For markers on land and the act of naming them as means to transform space into place or terrain into territory, see Canaparo, "Marconi and Other Artifices" and *Muerte y transfiguración*, 53–69, 85–105; and Carter, *The Road to Botany*

Bay, 1–68. For a view that emphasizes the sea's lack of markers, see Studnicki-Gizbert, *A Nation upon the Ocean Sea*. For Studnicki-Gizbert, in the ocean, which he rightly characterizes as "a *via* that linked disparate lands and peoples," there were "no markers despite the best efforts of early modern cartographers to divide seas and oceans" (6–7). He is right in pointing to the lack of markers useful for cartographers, but my claim here is that oceans were marked otherwise. Mobile markers might not have been of use to cartographers, but they provided good-enough signals that conveyed messages to sailors.

67. Linebaugh and Rediker, *The Many-Headed Hydra*, 143–173.

68. For a take on the experience on board an Atlantic crossing vessel that emphasizes tedium, storms, and social life aboard, see Berry, *A Path in the Mighty Waters*.

69. "Declaración de Juan Estevan Rodríguez," in "Autos *La Belona*," 417–419.

70. Amar to Soler, December 7, 1806, AGI, Santa Fe, 653, no. 10.

71. Amar to Soler, December 7, 1806, AGI, Santa Fe, 653, no. 10.

72. In 1817, the appearance of a sloop flying the red-and-blue flag of the Republic of Haiti caused great consternation among local authorities in the Guajira Peninsula. Viceroy Francisco de Montalvo, no doubt reflecting concerns based on the recent history of Haiti's collaboration with Colombian and Venezuelan insurgents and a longer history of anti-Spanish collaboration between European foreigners and the Guajira's indigenous people, quickly informed authorities in Spain. Montalvo to Secretario del Despacho Universal de Estado, Cartagena, November 13, 1817, AGI, Estado, 53, no. 42. See chapters 3 and 5 for the connections between the Guajira's indigenous people and non-Spanish Europeans and for Haitian-insurgent collaboration.

73. [Stephen], *War in Disguise*, 20.

74. See "Diligencia de entrada de la balandra española *La Leonor*," AGNC, AA-I, Aduanas, 8, 1–26.

75. "Autos *La Belona*," 470. In southern South America, U.S. captains used similar tactics to trick customs officers. According to Greg Grandin, "New England captains, upon approaching Montevideo or Buenos Aires in ships laden with Manchester broadcloth, New Haven pistols, or Gold Coast slaves would lower the stars and stripes, raise the royal Spanish standard, ready their counterfeit papers, and prepare to tell port authorities that the ship they were sailing was owned by a local Spaniard." Grandin, *The Empire of Necessity*, 27.

76. Anderson, *Imagined Communities*, 6.

77. See for example Massey, *For Space*; Soja, *Postmodern Geographies*; Smith, *Uneven Development*; Lefebvre, *The Production of Space*.

78. Historian John Gillis warned "against the temptation to project contemporary understandings of geography onto a past in which a very different set of relationships was operative." Gillis, *Islands of the Mind*, 3.

79. Hancock, *Oceans of Wine*, xvi.

80. For two recent examples of this growing literature focusing on Chinese migration to the Americas and on Afro-Caribbean mobility, see Young, *Alien Nation*; Putnam, *Radical Moves*.

81. De Certeau, *The Practice of Everyday Life*, 97.

82. Marx, *The Eighteenth Brumaire*, paragraph 2.

Chapter 3: Maritime Indians, Cosmopolitan Indians

Epigraph: Depons, *Travels in South America*, 1:217.

1. Between 1782 and 1786, Enrique (or Henry) Hooper appears in Kingston's shipping returns as captain of two British schooners—the *Fortune* and the *Friendship*—traveling mainly between Kingston and the Mosquito Coast, but also visiting San Andrés and Riohacha. In December 1786 he sailed from Kingston to Riohacha as captain of the *Friendship*. Maybe this was the schooner he used to transport the Cuna Indians in July 1787 (see appendix 4). The Cunas were also referred to, by Spanish authorities, as Cunacunas, Calidonios, or Darienes. Ignacio Gallup-Díaz prefers to use the term Tule, because this is how the members of this indigenous group refer to themselves today. I keep the term Cuna or Cunas because the geographical scope of actions of the indigenous people that I cover under this term makes it difficult to assert that all these maritime Indians thought of themselves as Tule. See Gallup-Díaz, *The Door of the Seas*. For the other group of maritime Indians that appear in this chapter—the Wayuu, whom Spanish authorities called Guajiros—I chose the former name because this is how they self-identified and continue to self-identify.

2. "Convención de paz y vasallaje."

3. AGS, SGU, 7242, 40.

4. Hämäläinen, *The Comanche Empire*, 6. See also Wunder and Hämäläinen, "Of Lethal Places"; and Hämäläinen and Truett, "On Borderlands." For indigenous spatial practices (i.e., "any political feat, economic activity, forceful claim, or social performance that asserts and demonstrates authority over people, resources, and space"), see Offen, "Creating Mosquitia," 259. For spatial consciousness, understood as the way in which "people perceived their changing spatial environment and functioned within it," see Parmenter, *The Edge of the Woods*, xxvii.

5. Mobility, commercial relations, technological appropriation, linguistic talents, and diplomatic skills have recently been put at the center of Iroquois people's encounter with Europeans. See Parmenter, *The Edge of the Woods*. For telling examples that challenge paradigms and, in particular, "strong presumption[s] of *absence*," see Putnam, "To Study the Fragments/Whole," 618. For nonindigenous expectations about and perceptions of indigenous people, see Deloria, *Indians in Unexpected Places*; Earle, *The Return of the Native*; and Barr, *Peace Came in the Form of a Woman*.

6. Depons, *Travels in South America*, 1:217. Depons used the term ambiguously. By saying that the Wayuu—whom he and other European observers, following Spanish authorities' usage, called Guajiros—were "the most ferocious of the maritime Indians," he implied that the term was also used in reference to other groups. While I focus on the Wayuu and the Cunas, based on the similar ways in which Saint Vincent's Island Caribs and the Miskitos of Nicaragua's Mosquito Coast used Caribbean networks of trade and migration, I believe that Depons's term can be applied to the four indigenous groups.

7. Both groups make fleeting appearances in David Weber's comprehensive study of indigenous groups who successfully resisted Spanish conquest. Weber, *Bárbaros*. Rare studies of the Cunas include Gallup-Díaz's *The Door of the Seas*; and Castillero Calvo, *Conquista, evangelización y resistencia*. For the Wayuu, see Barrera Monroy, *Mestizaje, comercio y resistencia*; Polo Acuña, *Etnicidad, conflicto social y cultura fronteriza*; and Polo Acuña, *Indígenas, poderes y mediaciones*. The literature on Caribs and Miskitos informs my approach to Cunas and Wayuu. For studies of the Caribs, stressing their encounter with Europeans and the attempts to "write them out" of the Caribbean, see Whitehead, "Introduction"; Sued Badillo, "The Island Caribs"; Hulme, "The Rhetoric of Description"; Boucher, *Cannibal Encounters*; Fabel, *Colonial Challenges*, 134–205; Garraway, *The Libertine Colony*, 39–92; Newton, "Geographies of the Indigenous." For Miskito politics, diplomacy, ethnicity, and spatial practices, see Offen, "Creating Mosquitia"; Offen, "The Sambo and Tawira Miskitu"; Offen, "Race and Place in Colonial Mosquitia"; García, "Interacción étnica y diplomacia de fronteras"; and García, "Ambivalencia de las representaciones coloniales."

8. De Certeau, *The Practice of Everyday Life*, 97.

9. Berlin, "From Creole to African," 254; Landers, *Atlantic Creoles*.

10. Ó Tuathail, "General Introduction," 1, 2. For the best available study of *indios bárbaros*, the label Spaniards attached to "Indians who lived independently within territories claimed by Spain," see Weber, *Bárbaros*, 12. The term implies a dichotomy distinguishing indios bárbaros from those who had been incorporated—those whom Spaniards called *indios domésticos* (domestic or domesticated Indians).

11. Akerman, "Introduction," 2.

12. Harley, "Rereading the Maps of the Columbian Encounter," 522. Unpacking this statement, Harley further explains, "Early European maps of America usually are stridently *geopolitical documents*. Above all they bear the traces of the territorial moves by which the colonial powers of early modern Europe *sought to* delimit, divide, and assert control over *their* overseas territories" (528–529, emphasis added).

13. Hämäläinen, *The Comanche Empire*, 5. According to David Weber, by the end of the eighteenth century "independent Indians still held effective dominion over at least half of the actual land mass of what is today continental Latin America, from Tierra del Fuego to present-day Mexico." Moving north of present-day Mexico, Juliana Barr similarly argued that for geographical settings "far from metropolitan cores . . . maps served to assert possession" and to "solidify national [or imperial] borders" by "silencing an Indian presence." Weber, *Bárbaros*, 12; Barr, "Geographies of Power," 7. For sharp analyses of European maps as dialogues among European powers that reflected the "machinations of geopolitics," see Barr and Countryman, "Introduction," 4; and Craib, "Cartography and Power."

14. Benton, *A Search for Sovereignty*, 2–3, 161. "Peripheral" is a loaded term that generally reproduces geographic space as perceived from the centers of imperial power. From the perspective of maritime Indians, the land they inhabited did not constitute a periphery; instead, they lived at the center. For recent interpretations of centers, peripheries, frontiers, borderlands, and claims and the historiographical

debate about these terms, see Weber, *Bárbaros*; Adelman and Aron, "From Border-lands to Borders"; Hämäläinen, *The Comanche Empire*; Wunder and Hämäläinen, "Of Lethal Places"; Hämäläinen and Truett, "On Borderlands"; and the essays in Daniels and Kennedy, *Negotiated Empires*.

15. For maps as "expressions of desire," see Barr and Countryman, "Introduction," 4.

16. AGI, MP-Panama, 184Bis.

17. For a detailed physical description of the Guajira Peninsula's territory, including the division into Lower and Upper Guajira, see Polo Acuña, *Indígenas, poderes y mediaciones*, 25–40.

18. AGI, MP-Panama, 182.

19. "Informe reservado del governador de Rio Hacha," Riohacha, October 14, 1801, 289.

20. Silvestre, "Apuntes reservados," 2:80.

21. Ezpeleta, "Relación del gobierno," 2:256; AGS, SGU, 7072, no. 10; AGS, SGU, 7072, no. 10; and Mendinueta, "Relación del estado," 3:161.

22. Amy Turner Bushnell defined a claim as "a vast cartographic expanse to which an early modern monarch held title under European international law." Bushnell, "Gates, Patterns, and Peripheries," 18. For similar scenarios in which "Europeans claimed sovereignty against other Europeans . . . but were not able to enforce those claims on Indians" and for occasions when "colonization" was a claim at which "the colonized" would have scoffed," see DuVal, *The Native Ground*, 7–8, 10.

23. Antonio Julián calculated the number of Wayuu between 16,000 and 20,000; Antonio de Arévalo declared that "some have claimed that there were up to 26,000 Indians," and Francisco Silvestre estimated their numbers reached 40,000. According to Silvestre, the number of people living *a son de campana* (under Spanish law and religion) amounted to 3,966 souls; 1,920 men and 2,046 women; 351 whites (including 18 ecclesiastics), 633 tributary Indians, 2,513 freedmen, and 469 slaves. Julián, *La perla de América*, 189; Arévalo, "Plan de operaciones," 182; and Silvestre, "Apuntes reservados," 2:80–82.

24. Barrera Monroy, *Mestizaje, comercio y resistencia*, 28–30. See also Polo Acuña, *Indígenas, poderes y mediaciones*, 65–117. Polo Acuña identifies the main Wayuu parcialidades, identifying for each its main leader (also referred to as cacique, *capitán*, or *mayoral de parcialidad*) and the sites they inhabited (sometimes formally established towns, most times merely regarded as *sitios* or sites).

25. References to the Cocinas stealing cattle and molesting travelers along the road from Riohacha to Maracaibo are common, but it is clear that they were a minor concern. See for example Guirior, "Instrucción," 1:341. The Paraujanos are barely mentioned in Spanish documents.

26. AGI, MP-Panama, 202Bis.

27. In 1761 Arévalo argued for the need to establish towns throughout the province, emphasizing the coasts to the east (by the mouth of the Cayman River) and the

west of the Gulf of Darién (at the Bay of Calidonia). Arévalo's 1761 project, in turn, coincided in both its diagnosis and its prescription with the proposal Dionisio de Alsedo y Herrera prepared in the 1740s. Arévalo, "Descripción o relación del Golfo de el Darién." For Alsedo's plan, see Gallup-Díaz, *The Door of the Seas*, chapter 7.

28. Caballero y Góngora, "Relación del estado," 1:461; Arguedas, "Diario de una expedición," 1:391. See also Monty, "Reconocimiento y exploración"; Morante and Abances, "Exploración de la costa atlántica."

29. Fidalgo, *Derrotero y cartografía*, 284–315 (quote from 285).

30. Arévalo, "Descripción o relación del Golfo de el Darién," 259; Silvestre, "Apuntes reservados," 2:104; and Helg, *Liberty and Equality*, 30.

31. Silvestre, "Apuntes reservados," 2:70.

32. Arévalo, "Descripción o relación del Golfo de el Darién," 252–254; Silvestre, "Apuntes reservados," 2:68–69.

33. The most famous attempt to create a non-Spanish colony in the Darién was pursued by Scottish colonists who settled the isthmus from 1698 to 1700. During the early eighteenth century, French pirates-turned-settlers raised cacao in Cuna territory, but their presence was never formalized as a colonial claim. See Hart, *The Disaster of Darien*; Gallup-Díaz, *The Door of the Seas*, chapter 4; Howe, *A People Who Would Not Kneel*, 10–20; and Caballero y Góngora, "Relación del estado," 460–461.

34. For other frontier settings in which similar European-indigenous relationships developed, see Hämäläinen, *The Comanche Empire*; Barr, *Peace Came in the Form of a Woman*; DeLay, *War of a Thousand Deserts*; Resendez, *Changing National Identities*; Rushforth, *Bonds of Alliance*.

35. Barrera Monroy, *Mestizaje, comercio y resistencia*, 51.

36. AGS, SGU, 7242, 40; AGI, Santa Fe, 956; AGI, Santa Fe, 1095; Polo Acuña, *Indígenas, poderes y mediaciones*, 127, 129; Depons, *Travels in South America*, 1:218–219; Nugent, *Lady Nugent's Journal*, 269–273; Equiano, *The Life of Olaudah Equiano*, 250–251.

37. "Declaración que Antonio de Arévalo le tomó al capitán Sombrero de Oro," Cartagena, June 15, 1782, AGI, Santa Fe, 956.

38. AGS, SGU, 7242, 40.

39. Fidalgo, *Derrotero y cartografía*, 309; Depons, *Travels in South America*, 1:219.

40. Fidalgo, *Derrotero y cartografía*, 309.

41. See for example Mignolo, *The Darker Side of the Renaissance*, 29–67.

42. "Convención de paz y vasallaje," 163–176.

43. Childs, *The 1812 Aponte Rebellion*, 131.

44. Moreno y Escandón, "Estado del Virreinato," 1:247.

45. Grahn, *The Political Economy*, 1.

46. Mendinueta, "Relación del estado," 3:104.

47. Astigárraga to Antonio Valdez, Santa Marta, February 3, 1789, AGS, SGU, 7072, no. 10. See also Moreno y Escandón, "Estado del Virreinato," 1:187; Silvestre, "Apuntes reservados," 2:82, 103; and Grahn, *The Political Economy*, 31–64.

48. Depons, *Travels in South America*, 1:59.

49. Arébalo, *La pacificación de la Provincia del Río del Hacha*, 56.

50. Guirior, "Instrucción," 1:337.

51. Julián, *La perla de América*, 241. According to Julián, palo de Brasil, pearls, and cotton were produced by Indians in the Guajira Peninsula. Gold was extracted from the interior provinces of New Granada, transported through internal contraband routes, and sold to the Wayuu by smugglers from the viceroyalty's interior.

52. Caballero y Góngora, "Relación del estado," 1:480.

53. Silvestre, "Apuntes reservados," 2:82.

54. "Informe reservado del governador de Rio Hacha," 289.

55. Medina to viceroy, Riohacha, November 30, 1801, in Moreno and Tarazona, *Materiales para el estudio*, 293.

56. Throughout the eighteenth century, British traders increasingly "stole" the Caribbean trade out of Dutch hands. The ultimate step in this process was the British occupation of Curaçao in 1801. For British Curaçao, see Fortman, "The Colony of Curaçao under British Rule."

57. Offen, "The Sambo and Tawira Miskitu," 343–345.

58. Arébalo, *La pacificación de la Provincia del Río del Hacha*, 123, 197, 216.

59. Polo Acuña, *Indígenas, poderes y mediaciones*, 98–115.

60. Arébalo, *La pacificación de la Provincia del Río del Hacha*, 216.

61. "Convención de paz y vasallaje," 171–172.

62. Equiano, *The Life of Olaudah Equiano*, 250.

63. Caballero y Góngora to Joseph de Gálvez, Cartagena, May 28, 1785, AGI, Santa Fe, 1095.

64. Scott describes "the weapons of the weak" as a set of strategies designed to obtain respite within domination. "Foot dragging, dissimulation, desertion, false compliance, pilfering, feigned ignorance, slander, arson, [and] sabotage" were all part of these "*everyday* forms" of resistance. Scott, *The Weapons of the Weak*, xvi–xvii, 241–303. For negotiating "from a position of strength," see Parmenter, *The Edge of the Woods*, 200.

65. For campaigns of pacification and incorporation undertaken by Spanish authorities during the last three decades of the eighteenth century, see Helg, *Liberty and Equality*, 27–40; Herrera, *Ordenar para controlar*.

66. Moreno y Escandón, "Estado del Virreinato," 1:184.

67. Moreno y Escandón, "Estado del Virreinato," 1:197.

68. Weber, "Bourbons and Bárbaros," 84.

69. For the best analysis of the continent-wide approach, see Weber, *Bárbaros*.

70. Kuethe, "The Pacification Campaign," 467. Panamanian historian Alfredo Castillero Calvo echoes Kuethe's analysis, writing that "in traditionally conflictive zones, like the Guajira [Peninsula], . . . the Darién, Mosquitia, the territorial vastness dominated by the elusive Apache Indians, or the Rio de la Plata, the role of the missionary is increasingly less important and, in many of the new frontier

projects, . . . [he] remains virtually excluded or reduced to an insignificant role."
Castillero Calvo, *Conquista, evangelización y resistencia*, 326.

71. Weber, "Bourbons and Bárbaros," 84.

72. Grahn, "Guajiro Culture," 130–156; Barrera Monroy, *Mestizaje, comercio y resistencia*, 52–76; and Polo Acuña, *Etnicidad, conflicto social y cultura fronteriza*, 42–50.

73. Polo Acuña, *Etnicidad, conflicto social y cultura fronteriza*, 43. See also Polo Acuña, *Indígenas, poderes y mediaciones*, 132–142.

74. Barrera Monroy, *Mestizaje, comercio y resistencia*, 57.

75. Grahn, "Guajiro Culture," 144.

76. Alcoy to Andrés Pérez, Riohacha, April 10, 1764, in Moreno and Tarazona, *Materiales para el estudio*, 119.

77. Grahn, "Guajiro Culture," 146. See also Polo Acuña, *Indígenas, poderes y mediaciones*, 149–155.

78. Polo Acuña, *Etnicidad, conflicto social y cultura fronteriza*, 81. "Indian towns" here refers to Spanish-controlled *pueblos de indios*, not to Wayuu-controlled towns. See also Polo Acuña, *Indígenas, poderes y mediaciones*, 183–229.

79. Depons, *Travels in South America*, 1:217.

80. Grahn, "Guajiro Culture," 148.

81. De la Pedraja, "La Guajira en el siglo XIX," 9.

82. Arébalo, *La pacificación de la Provincia del Río del Hacha*, 43.

83. Polo Acuña, *Indígenas, poderes y mediaciones*, 156.

84. Arévalo, "Plan de operaciones," 174, 179, 180, 187.

85. Kuethe, "The Pacification Campaign," 479.

86. Astigárraga to Álvarez de Veriñas, "Instrucciones que el gobernador de Santa Marta . . . entrega al del Río Hacha," Santa Marta, April 10, 1789, AGS, SGU, 7072, no. 10.

87. Ezpeleta to Antonio Váldez, 1789, AGS, SGU, 7072, no. 10.

88. Ezpeleta to Antonio Váldez, 1789, AGS, SGU, 7072, no. 10.

89. Narváez to Ezpeleta, December 26, 1789, in Moreno and Tarazona, *Materiales para el estudio*, 283.

90. Ezpeleta, "Relación del gobierno," 2:256; Mendinueta, "Relación del estado," 3:161.

91. Hämäläinen, *The Comanche Empire*, 6.

92. Hämäläinen and Truett, "On Borderlands," 352. See also Barr, "Geographies of Power," 43.

93. For a similar approach that emphasizes Iroquois initiative and the need to read beyond the text of treaties written in European languages by European scribes, see Parmenter, *The Edge of the Woods*, 231–273.

94. "Convención de paz y vasallaje," 163.

95. "Convención de paz y vasallaje," 165, 167.

96. Alternative interpretations of space have been studied by Edward Said, who uses the term "rival geographies"; Linda Rupert, who speaks of "parallel human geographies"; and Akhil Gupta, who refers to "other forms of spatial commitment."

See Said, *Culture and Imperialism*, xx; Rupert, "Contraband Trade," 48; and Gupta, "The Song of the Nonaligned World," 63. European ways of legitimizing territorial possession and how they differed from indigenous ways are schematically presented in Seed, *Ceremonies of Possession*. For indigenous conceptualizations of space expressed through cartographic representations, see Mundy, *The Mapping of New Spain*; and Barr and Countryman, "Introduction."

97. Smith and Godlewska, "Introduction," 7–8.

98. Mitchell, *Belongings*, chapter 4, paragraphs 6–7. See also Vaughan, "Slavery and Colonial Identity"; Cooper and Brubaker, "Identity"; and Colley, *Britons*.

99. Depons, *Travels in South America*, 1:218–219.

100. In a North American setting, Philip Deloria has studied how "primitivism, technological incompetence, physical distance, and cultural difference" have determined how "many Americans have imagined Indians." Juliana Barr refers to the "assumptions we bring to the reading and writing of European-Indian relations" as "often still freighted with unspoken or unconscious presumptions of European technological superiority, Indian 'primitivism,' Indian resistance, and implicit, corresponding European dominance." Deloria, *Indians in Unexpected Places*, 4; Barr, *Peace Came in the Form of a Woman*, 289.

101. *Forcibly* appears in italics in the original; this can be read as pointing out Lady Nugent's surprise at having to force a child to go to school. Emphasizing the fact that she had to force their king to go to school signals the savagery of the Miskitos.

102. Nugent, *Lady Nugent's Journal*, 269–273.

103. Fidalgo, *Derrotero y cartografía*, 285.

104. Mendinueta to Pedro Ceballos, Santa Fe, April 19, 1803, AGI, Estado, 52, no. 137.

105. Mendinueta to Pedro Ceballos, Santa Fe, April 19, 1803, AGI, Estado, 52, no. 137. For the apprehension of imperial authorities with negros franceses see Johnson, *The Fear of French Negroes*; Scott, "The Common Wind"; Mongey, "A Tale of Two Brothers"; Ferrer, "Speaking of Haiti"; Childs, *The 1812 Aponte Rebellion*; Helg, *Liberty and Equality*; and Lasso, *Myths of Harmony*.

106. Miyares to Capitán General de Caracas, Maracaibo, November 28, 1803, AGI, Estado, 61, no. 47.

107. Declaration of Andrés de Luque to Miyares, 1803, AGI, Estado, 61, no. 47.

108. Declaration of Miguel Francisco Bermúdez to Miyares, 1803, AGI, Estado, 61, no. 47; and Declaration of Francisco Ramírez to Miyares, 1803, AGI, Estado, 61, no. 47.

109. Declaration of Francisco Ramírez to Miyares, 1803, AGI, Estado, 61, no. 47.

110. Guevara to Ministro de Estado, Caracas, December 20, 1803, AGI, Estado, 61, no. 47.

111. Mendinueta to Ceballos, Santa Fe, April 19, 1803, AGI, Estado, 52, no. 137.

112. See Grahn, *The Political Economy*, 62–63, 197–199.

113. Weber, *Bárbaros*, 247–248.

114. Helg, "A Fragmented Majority," 160.

115. Colley, *Britons*, 6.

116. Deloria, *Indians in Unexpected Places*.

Chapter 4: Turning South before Swinging East

Epigraphs: Robinson, quoted in Marshall, *The Making and Unmaking*, 368.
Vidal y Villalba to Joseph de Gálvez, 1784, AGNC, SC, Negocios Exteriores, 2, D. 51, 734v.
"La Inglaterra se halla con tal confusión de ver el Norte de América vencedor, que todas sus ideas y máquinas secretas las endereza al continente de la América española." Gálvez to Archbishop-Viceroy Caballero y Góngora (in reference to British plans to invade the Isthmus of Darién), San Ildefonso, August 4, 1784, AGNC, SC, Milicias y Marina, 112, 529. "No dude S.M. que los ingleses intentarán ahora con más tezón que antes establecerse cerca del istmo."

1. "Traducción hecha por el Abate Osullivan," AGNC, AA-I, Historia, 3, 285–290.

2. In his meeting with the Spanish ambassador, Brooks requested a "small pension" in exchange for the information he had just provided and for the promise of obtaining more information regarding the expedition. The count of Aranda, while acknowledging that Brooks's information could be a scam, recommended that the Ministry of the Indies grant him the pension. Conde de Aranda to Conde de Floridablanca, Paris, July 22, 1786, AGNC, AA-I, Historia, 3, 291–301.

3. See chapter 1.

4. Caballero y Góngora, "Relación del estado," 3:443–459.

5. Marshall, *The Making and Unmaking*, 2; Harlow, *The Founding of the Second British Empire*, 1:62–102.

6. See for instance Wilson, "Introduction"; Brown, "Introduction"; Stern and Wennerlind, "Introduction."

7. Wilson, "Introduction," 11.

8. See Brown, "Introduction"; O'Shaughnessy, *An Empire Divided*; Gould, *The Persistence of Empire*; and Jasanoff, *Liberty's Exiles*.

9. The acknowledgment of entanglement is not followed by agreement on how the entanglement happened, nor why and where the entanglement mattered. For a well-publicized debate on the issue, see Gould, "Entangled Histories, Entangled Worlds"; Cañizares-Esguerra, "Entangled Histories"; and Gould, "Entangled Atlantic Histories."

10. Williams, *Capitalism and Slavery*, 120.

11. Harlow, *The Founding of the Second British Empire*, 1:62–102; Marshall, *The Making and Unmaking*; Bayly, *Imperial Meridian*; Armitage, *The Ideological Origins*; Wilson, *The Island Race*; Wilson, "Introduction"; Jasanoff, *Edge of Empire*; and Jasanoff, *Liberty's Exiles*.

12. Gallagher and Robinson, "The Imperialism of Free Trade," 13. See also Semmel, *The Rise of Free Trade Imperialism*; Bayly, *Imperial Meridian*, 9–10; Harlow, *The Founding of the Second British Empire*, 1:62–102.

13. Jasanoff, *Edge of Empire*, 21.

14. Marshall, "The First British Empire," 43–44.

15. Bayly, "The Second British Empire"; Jasanoff, *Liberty's Exiles*, 12.

16. According to Kathleen Wilson, "There was not one but many imperial projects in the Georgian period, engaged with by planters, reformers, merchants,

explorers, missionaries, settlers, adventurers, indigenes, and the enslaved." Wilson, "Introduction," 11. See also Wilson, *The Island Race*, 15; and Marshall, *The Making and Unmaking*, 379.

17. Williams, *Capitalism and Slavery*, 123.

18. Jasanoff, *Liberty's Exiles*, 338; Nugent, *Lady Nugent's Diary*.

19. Jasanoff, *Liberty's Exiles*, 339.

20. Robinson to Warren Hastings, February 19, 1781, quoted in Marshall, *The Making and Unmaking*, 368.

21. Lord Stormont, February 17, 1783, quoted in Marshall, *The Making and Unmaking*, 369.

22. Marshall, *The Making and Unmaking*, especially 368–379.

23. Jasanoff, *Liberty's Exiles*, 335.

24. Brown, "Introduction," 3. Hesitantly embracing the usefulness of the notion of informal empire to understand Britain-Latin American relations during the nineteenth century, Alan Knight concedes that "the adjective 'imperialist' seems appropriate" to describe these relations because the "coercive, interventionist, and political nature" of British policy toward Latin America, while not geared toward "territorial possession," clearly "constitute[d] some sort of imperialism." Knight, "Britain and Latin America," 123, 129. For a review of the historiography, see Miller, "Informal Empire in Latin America."

25. Smith, *An Inquiry into the Nature and Causes*, 3:29.

26. Wilson, *The Island Race*, 15; Coronil, "Foreword," iv.

27. Gould, *The Persistence of Empire*, especially 208–214.

28. For innovative approaches to mercantilism, see the essays in Stern and Wennerlind, *Mercantilism Reimagined*.

29. Fortman, "The Colony of Curaçao under British Rule"; Epstein, *Scandal of Colonial Rule*; Johnson, *Workshop of Revolution*, 250–262.

30. In his most recent book, P. J. Marshall devotes a chapter to what he calls "the swing to the south," which he defines as "a shift in focus of British preoccupations from the northern colonies with their large white populations not only to the plantation colonies of the West Indies, but also to the lands round the Gulf of Mexico and further south into Spanish America" (176). In his analysis Marshall focuses on the military expeditions projected (though not always launched) in British colonies (in particular Jamaica and the Bahamas) against Spanish American territories (especially in Central America). Marshall, *Remaking the British Atlantic*, 176–192. While I pay attention to these expeditions, the drive to conquer constitutes just one of several elements of my analysis.

31. O'Shaughnessy, *An Empire Divided*, 137–159.

32. Taylor, *The Civil War of 1812*, 30–42; McFarlane, *The British in the Americas*, 294.

33. Edwards, *The History*, 2: 483–489. Edward Long gave a succinct description of the trade between Jamaica and the United States before the American Revolution: "Jamaica takes lumber, flour, and certain other articles from North America,

and to a certain annual value; North America takes molasses, sugar, and rum, from Jamaica, but in an inferior value." Long, *The History of Jamaica*, 1:539.

34. Carrington, *The British West Indies*, 126.

35. Carrington, *The British West Indies*, 162; O'Shaughnessy, *An Empire Divided*, 160–184.

36. Long, *A Free and Candid Review*, 9.

37. Edwards, *Thoughts on the Late Proceedings*, 64.

38. "Representation of the West India Planters and Merchants to His Majesty's Ministers," London, April 11, 1783, in Edwards, *Thoughts on the Late Proceedings*, 45–46.

39. "Representation of the West India Planters and Merchants to His Majesty's Ministers," 47–48.

40. O'Shaughnessy, *An Empire Divided*, 239–243. In this section I draw heavily on the following pamphlets: Long, *A Free and Candid Review*; Edwards, *Thoughts on the Late Proceedings*; and Allen, *Considerations on the Present State*.

41. The Navigation Acts were a series of laws regulating trade in the British dominions. Originally passed in 1651, the Navigation Act was mercantilist in nature. A basic principle of the Navigation Act was the exclusion of foreign ships from British trade. British policy makers regarded this principle as the foundation of British maritime power. As seen in chapter 1, from the 1760s the British government introduced a series of modifications to the Navigation Acts. From 1766 it became legal for foreign ships to conduct trade in a number of free ports established throughout the British Caribbean. Attachment to the mercantilist nature of the Navigation Acts, despite exceptional allowances, was strong. Hence, the debate regarding trade between the newly independent United States and the British West Indies often took the form of a debate concerning the modification of the Navigation Acts.

42. Sheffield, *Observations on the Commerce*, 145–146.

43. Milobar, "Conservative Ideology," 58; Taylor, *The Civil War of 1812*, 31.

44. Jasanoff, *Liberty's Exiles*, 85–88.

45. Edwards, *Thoughts on the Late Proceedings*, 83.

46. Long, *A Free and Candid Review*, 44–45.

47. Long, *A Free and Candid Review*, 14. See also Edwards, *Thoughts on the Late Proceedings*, 21–22, 38.

48. Long, *A Free and Candid Review*, 1.

49. Edwards, *Thoughts on the Late Proceedings*, 72–73.

50. Allen, *Considerations on the Present State*, 49. The parenthetical comment is part of Allen's text. The acts mentioned in the quote were approved in 1766 and 1781. See chapter 1 for a discussion of the effects of the British free port regulations. Upholding the principles of the free ports legislation, Long rhetorically asked, "Could the king's officer (*no* prohibition *then* appearing) hesitate to admit American vessels upon the *same* footing as any *other foreigners*, subject to the regulations of that act? Nay, could he suppose himself warrantable, in *refusing* them admittance; with such an unrepealed act of parliament in his hands, to authorize

that admittance?" Long's answer to both questions, of course, was negative. Long, *A Free and Candid Review*, 106.

51. Long, *A Free and Candid Review*, 79–81.

52. Carrington, *The British West Indies*, 163, 166. Pitt's bill was rejected.

53. According to Bryan Edwards, famine and diseases associated with poor diets resulted in the death of over 15,000 slaves between 1780 and the end of 1786. Edwards, *The History*, 2:511–515. See also Jasanoff, *Liberty's Exiles*, 251–257; and Williams, *Capitalism and Slavery*, 121.

54. Minutes of May 27, 1787, TNA, BT, 5–4, 128v.

55. Armytage, *The Free Port System*, 59.

56. Prokopow, "'To the Torrid Zones'"; "Traducción hecha por el Abate Osullivan," AGNC, AA-I, Historia, 3, 285–290; Jasanoff, *Liberty's Exiles*, 215–277.

57. The best example of this type of merchant-adventurer is Robert Hodgson, a British officer living in the Mosquito Coast who swore loyalty to the Spanish king. This chapter's presentation of Hodgson's story is largely based on a long file about his life available in AGS, SGU, 6945. John Reeder, a British ship owner, also figured frequently in Jamaica's ship records and the reports of Spanish authorities. Antonio Narváez y la Torre to Viceroy Caballero y Góngora, Riohacha, October 12, 1784, AGNC, SC, Milicias y Marina, 115, 663–667. For the "spirit of 1783" and its three key components—drive toward imperial expansion, "clarified commitment to liberty and humanitarian ideals," and confrontation between rulers and subjects over issues of representation—see Jasanoff, *Liberty's Exiles*, 5–17, especially 11–14.

58. See chapter 5 for a discussion of British policy toward Spanish America during the Napoleonic Wars. For "lack of direction" or improvisation in British policy toward Latin America in the 1780s, see Lynch, "British Policy and Spanish America"; Kaufmann, *British Policy*.

59. The metaphor of a "war in disguise" was used at the time in reference to the use of neutral flags by enemy ships in order to conduct trade with enemy territories. See [Stephen], *War in Disguise*. Stephen's metaphor works perfectly to explain the Anglo-Spanish peace that followed 1783.

60. Jasanoff, *Liberty's Exiles*, 215–243; O'Shaughnessy, *An Empire Divided*, 185–191; Marshall, *Remaking the British Atlantic*, 186–192.

61. Cruden, *An Address*, 3–5.

62. Jasanoff, *Liberty's Exiles*, 216; Cruden, *An Address*, 20.

63. Jasanoff, *Liberty's Exiles*, 215–218, 227–234; "Traducción hecha por el Abate Osullivan," AGNC, AA-I, Historia, 3, 285–290.

64. Jasanoff, *Liberty's Exiles*, 237. See also Landers, *Atlantic Creoles*, 100–110.

65. William Augustus Bowles to Lord Grenville, Adelphi, January 13, 1791, reprinted in Turner, "English Policy toward America," 729.

66. Cruden's plans came to an early end in 1787, when he died in the Bahamas, insane but still optimistic about reconquering the United States. Bowles's designs were thwarted on several occasions by Spanish troops who captured him in 1792

and again in 1803. He died, in 1805, in a Spanish prison in Havana. For brief biographical sketches, see Jasanoff, *Liberty's Exiles*, xiv–xv.

67. Jasanoff, *Liberty's Exiles*, 356–357; Prokopow, "'To the Torrid Zones,'" 38–47.

68. Excerpts from Jamaican news about Dalling's expeditions to Nicaragua, July 1781, AGS, SGU, 6945, no. 1.

69. O'Shaughnessy, *An Empire Divided*, 188–191. See also Marshall, *Remaking the British Atlantic*, 186–192.

70. Luis Vidal y Villalba to Gálvez, 1784, AGNC, SC, Negocios Exteriores, 2, D. 51, 733–734. A decade later, in 1797, the British made yet another unsuccessful attempt to conquer Puerto Rico. AGNC, AA-I, Historia, 3, 566.

71. Gálvez to Caballero y Góngora, San Ildefonso, August 4, 1784, AGNC, SC, Milicias y Marina, 112, 529.

72. Luis Vidal y Villalba to Gálvez, 1784, AGNC, SC, Negocios Exteriores, 2, D. 51, 735v.

73. Narváez y la Torre to viceroy, Riohacha, February 26, 1785, AGNC, SC, Milicias y Marina, 115, 544–553.

74. Gálvez to Caballero y Góngora, San Ildefonso, August 26, 1786, AGNC, AA-I, Historia, 3, 282; "Extracto . . . de lo ocurrido con el coronel inglés Don Roberto Hodgson," December 31, 1784, AGS, SGU, 6945, no. 1; Marshall, *Remaking the British Atlantic*, 187; Anderson, *Mahogany*, 112–114.

75. AGNC, SC, Milicias y Marina, 115, 544–553.

76. Prokopow, "'To the Torrid Zones,'" 299. See also Offen, "British Logwood Extraction."

77. See Helms, "Miskito Slaving and Culture Contact."

78. Naylor, *Penny Ante Imperialism*, 39–63.

79. Josef de Estachería (President of Guatemala's Audiencia) to Viceroy Caballero y Góngora, Guatemala, June 11, 1784, AGNC, SC, Virreyes, 16, D. 95, 593–594.

80. "The Definitive Treaty of Peace and Friendship," 3:392–399. For article 6, see 397–398.

81. Anderson, *Mahogany*, 119.

82. This discussion of Robert Hodgson is largely based on a long file about his life available in AGS, SGU, 6945, no. 1.

83. Naylor, *Penny Ante Imperialism*, 46–50.

84. Naylor, *Penny Ante Imperialism*, 61.

85. "Expediente sobre el coronel Robert Hodgson," AGS, SGU, 6945, no. 1. See also Basilio Gascón to Gálvez, Cartagena, July 25, 1784, in Torre Revollo, "Escritos hallados," 78–79.

86. Gascón to Gálvez, in Torre Revollo, "Escritos hallados," 79.

87. Caballero y Góngora to Gálvez, Santa Fe, March 27, 1783, AGS, SGU, 6945, no. 1.

88. "Extracto . . . de lo ocurrido con el coronel inglés don Roberto Hodgson," December 31, 1784, AGS, SGU, 6945, no. 1.

89. Gálvez to Caballero y Góngora, San Ildefonso, August 4, 1784, AGS, SGU, 6945, no. 1.

90. "Extracto . . . de lo ocurrido con el coronel inglés don Roberto Hodgson," December 31, 1784, AGS, SGU, 6945, no. 1; Viceroy Caballero y Góngora, June 9, 1786, AGS, SGU, 6945, no. 1.

91. Report of Caballero y Góngora, undated, AGS, SGU, 6945, no. 1.

92. President of Guatemala, Bernardo Troncoso, to Conde del Campo de Alange, Guatemala, June 19, 1791, AGS, SGU, 6949, 16.

93. According to Naylor, the Spanish king "conferred on [Hodgson] the Knight of the Order of Carlos III, he being the first foreigner so honored." Naylor, *Penny Ante Imperialism*, 242n27.

94. See Johnson, *Workshop of Revolution*, 250–262; di Meglio, ¡*Viva el bajo pueblo!*, 78–90; Blanchard, "An Institution Defended."

95. Caballero y Góngora to Gálvez, Santa Fe, April 15, 1784, AGS, SGU, 6945, no. 1.

96. See chapter 1 for a discussion of Bourbon commercial policy.

97. For the perspective of the indigenous inhabitants of northwestern New Granada, see chapter 3. Spanish authorities used the terms Calidonios, Darienes, and Cunacunas to refer to the indigenous people inhabiting the territory stretching from Cartagena to Panama. "Parecer del regente general sobre permitir o no la navegación del Río Atrato," November 27, 1783, AGI, Santa Fe, 956.

98. Viceroy Mendinueta to Soler, Santa Fe, June 19, 1803, AGI, Santa Fe, 651, no. 892; "Representación del consulado de comercio de Cartagena al virrey," Cartagena, February 20, 1801, AGI, Santa Fe, 651.

99. McFarlane, "El comercio exterior," 114; Ellison, *The Cotton Trade*, 84.

100. McFarlane, "El comercio exterior," 114; Thomson, *A Distinctive Industrialization*, 275; Ellison, *The Cotton Trade*, 84.

101. Salceda y Bustamante to Minister of State, Cartagena, September 1, 1798, AGI, Santa Fe, 1019.

102. Beckert, *Empire of Cotton*, 84. For examples of the vast literature on the expansion of the cotton industry, see Edwards, *The Growth of the British Cotton Trade*; Farnie, *The English Cotton Industry*; Dodge, *Cotton*; Lemire, *Cotton*; Riello, *Cotton*; Farnie and Jeremy, *The Fibre That Changed the World*; Riello and Parthasarathi, *The Spinning World*. For a brief overview of the emergence of Lancashire's cotton industry, see Singleton, "The Lancashire Cotton Industry."

103. Edwards, *The Growth of the British Cotton Trade*, 79–83; Jasanoff, *Liberty's Exiles*, 230; Donnell, *Chronological and Statistical History*, 41, 43; Armytage, *The Free Port System*, 74–75; Edwards, *The History*, 2:322–323; Drescher, *Econocide*, 56–58; Riello, *Cotton*, 200–203; Schoen, *The Fragile Fabric*, 47; Beckert, *Empire of Cotton*, 121.

104. Edwards, *The History*, 2:321.

105. "Licencia de embarque para que Antonio de la Carrera viaje de España a Cartagena para poner a prueba su máquina de despepitar algodones," AGI, Santa Fe, 954.

106. "Informe del director general de rentas del virreinato de Santa Fe," Madrid, May 1795, AGI, Santa Fe, 957.

107. Donnell, *Chronological and Statistical History*, 52.

108. Lemire, *Cotton*, 81–82; Schoen, *The Fragile Fabric*, 23–60; Beckert, *Empire of Cotton*, 56–82. For an analysis of the impact the development of these technologies had on slaves in the U.S. South, see Baptist, *The Half Has Never Been Told*.

109. This analysis is based on the statistical information from Edwards, *The Growth of the British Cotton Trade*, 250–251. Drescher's statistical evidence for the period 1786–1805 and Beckert's analysis corroborate the trends observable in Edwards's data. Drescher, *Econocide*, 83–87; Beckert, *Empire of Cotton*, 83–135.

110. Schoen, *The Fragile Fabric*, 39.

111. Edwards, *The History*, 2:321–324.

112. See chapter 1.

113. TNA, CO 142/23.

114. "Informe del director general de rentas del virreinato de Santa Fe," Madrid, May 1795, AGI, Santa Fe, 957.

115. TNA, CO 142/28.

116. Armytage, *The Free Port System*, 79.

117. Williams, *Capitalism and Slavery*, 120. Emphasizing the word "beginning" is important to understand the continued validity of Williams's claim. Like Williams, P. J. Marshall emphasizes the word "beginning" to stress that the "unmaking" of the British American Empire was a gradual process. Seymour Drescher's analysis demonstrates that the 1790s witnessed an expansion of the British West Indies' trade. Drescher's argument is not incompatible with Williams's and Marshall's. Together the three studies demonstrate Eliga Gould's claim for the "persistence of [the British American] empire" in the aftermath of the American Revolution. Marshall, *The Making and Unmaking*; Drescher, *Econocide*, 113–121; Gould, *The Persistence of Empire*.

118. For the idea of silencing history, see Trouillot, *Silencing the Past*.

Chapter 5: Simón Bolívar's Caribbean Adventures

Epigraph: "Bolívar: 'Yo soy un fugitivo que viene de Jamaica y con mi exilio recorreré América. . . . Mi inquietud se ha inclinado sobre el mapa del mundo y es hacia Haití que vengo, no a pedir la calma donde puede uno adormecerse soñando los indignos laureles, sino fusiles, cañones y pólvora. . . . En nombre de mi país que sangra, Presidente, y para arrojar a los Morillo del continente . . . vengo a pediros vuestra fraternal ayuda.'

"Pétion: 'Si no fuera yo el centinela de Haití, a vuestro lado sin miedo, hubiera escogido vivir y morir. En todas vuestras batallas quiero que sintáis que mi corazón apoya al vuestro. Tendréis armas y municiones, general Bolívar. . . . Venís a abrirme nuevos horizontes donde colocar nuestras esperanzas tanto como nuestros cañones. Ayudaros es consolidar la libertad, es rechazar de un golpe todos lo yugos importados, es agrandar el campo de la dignidad del hombre.'"

This fictionalized version of the conversation that Simón Bolívar and Alexandre Pétion had shortly after Bolívar arrived in Haiti in December 1815 summarizes the relationship between the two political leaders. Brierre, *Petión y Bolívar*, 47–48.

1. Restrepo, *Autobiografía*, 17.

2. For the resistance in the Llanos, see Thibaud, *Repúblicas en armas*, 261–309.

3. The participation of foreign mercenaries in the wars of independence in Colombia and Venezuela has been widely studied, including Brown, *Adventuring through Spanish Colonies*; and Rodríguez, *Freedom's Mercenaries*. Interesting studies of the foreign adventurers Louis Aury, Luis Brión, Renato Beluche, and other corsairs of the era include Duarte French, *Los tres Luises del Caribe*; Grummond, *Renato Beluche*; Hartog, *Biografía del Almirante Luis Brión*; Head, *Privateers of the Americas*. For "ephemeral states," see Landers, *Atlantic Creoles*, 95–137. For corsairs in the period immediately preceding the Reconquista, see Pérez Morales, *El gran diablo*.

4. [Apodaca] to Ministry of State, Cuba, June 7, 1816, in Franco, *Documentos para la historia*, 180.

5. The main account of the events leading to Bolívar's departure from Cartagena is Restrepo, *Historia de la revolución*, 2:5–49.

6. At the time, Haiti did not exist as a unified political entity. While Pétion presided over a polity called the Republic of Haiti, his power was circumscribed to what during the colonial period had been called the southern and western provinces. The northern province, known at that time as the Kingdom of Haiti, was ruled by Henry Christophe, who deemed himself emperor of Haiti. For brief summaries of Haiti's political history and the civil war pitting Pétion against Christophe, see Dubois, *Haiti*, 54–65; and Ferrer, "Haiti, Free Soil, and Antislavery," 44.

7. Rodríguez O., *The Independence of Spanish America*, 186.

8. Ferrer, "Haiti, Free Soil, and Antislavery" (41 and 42 for Haiti as "empire of freedom"); Dubois, "Thinking Haiti's Nineteenth Century"; Fischer, "Bolívar in Haiti"; Gaffield, *Haitian Connections*.

9. Blaufarb, "The Western Question."

10. Lynch, "British Policy," 1. See chapter 4 for a detailed analysis of the complex geopolitical environment of the 1780s.

11. Kaufmann, *British Policy*, 31; Esdaile, "Latin America and the Anglo-Spanish Alliance," 56. Lynch, "British Policy," 5–6, 16–20. Britain had occupied Spanish territories in previous wars. Some occupations were temporary (e.g., Menorca, Havana, the coast of Nicaragua, and Florida); others were permanent (e.g., Gibraltar). The nature of the British occupations of Trinidad and Buenos Aires was not known to contemporaries. By 1815, British hold on Trinidad was strong, but there was no guarantee of perpetuity. In contrast, the British occupation of Buenos Aires was quickly repelled. See Epstein, *Scandal of Colonial Rule*; Johnson, *Workshop of Revolution*, 250–262; and Di Meglio, *¡Viva el bajo pueblo!*, 78–90.

12. Kaufmann, *British Policy*, 31; Robson, *Britain, Portugal and South America*, 197.

13. Quoted in Kaufmann, *British Policy*, 39.

14. See chapter 1 for the commercial exchanges between Jamaica and New Granada.

15. Kaufmann, *British Policy*, 42; Rydjord, "British Mediation," 29.

16. Lynch, "British Policy," 23; Kaufmann, *British Policy*, 43–44.

17. Rodríguez O., *The Independence of Spanish America*, 51–53.

18. Rodríguez O., *The Independence of Spanish America*, 59.

19. Rodríguez O., *The Independence of Spanish America*, 64–65, 76–77.

20. Rodríguez O., *The Independence of Spanish America*, 82–92, 103–106, 169–174. The political revolution included the birth of representative government (Spanish and Spanish American provinces elected and sent representatives to the Cortes) and the drafting of a liberal constitution—the Constitution of Cádiz—that served as a model for many of the constitutions later drafted and adopted by the new Latin American republics. For the impact of the Constitution of Cádiz in the Atlantic world, see Chust, *Doceañismos, constituciones e independencias*.

21. Rodríguez O., *The Independence of Spanish America*, 52–59; Martínez Garnica, "La independencia," 201.

22. "Real Orden de la Junta Suprema Central Gubernativa del Reino," 51–52.

23. Thibaud, *Repúblicas en armas*, 11. Initially, Seville's Junta Suprema granted nine representatives to Spanish America. The number of American representatives was increased for the Cortes, but the problem of unequal representation was not solved. The exclusion of the population of African descent from the formula to determine the number of representatives of each province left many Spanish American provinces feeling underrepresented and with vast sectors of the population painfully aware of their exclusion. Alfonso Múnera and Marixa Lasso have explained the exclusion of free people of color from the benefits of citizenship as one important factor in the radicalization of Cartagena. Múnera, *El fracaso de la nación*; Lasso, *Myths of Harmony*, 36–57.

24. Martínez Garnica, "La independencia," 218.

25. McFarlane, "Building Political Order," 16.

26. Esdaile, "Latin America and the Anglo-Spanish Alliance," 62; Kaufmann, *British Policy*, 53.

27. Rydjord, "British Mediation," 29–50.

28. Restrepo, *Historia de la revolución*, 1:243–244; Gutiérrez Ardila, *Un nuevo reino*, 438–451.

29. Ward, "The British West Indies," 415–439. See also chapter 4 for the reaction of merchants and planters to the potential economic repercussions of the American Revolution.

30. Armytage, *The Free Port System*, 113–137. See also chapter 1 for the importance of trade between Jamaica and northern South America during the second decade of the nineteenth century.

31. Maingot, "Haiti and the Terrified Consciousness."

32. Girard, *Haiti*, 55–66; Dubois, *Haiti*, 89–134; Ferrer, "Haiti, Free Soil, and Antislavery," 44.

33. Verna, *Bolívar y los emigrados patriotas*.

34. Quoted in Rodríguez O., *The Independence of Spanish America*, 185.

35. Bolívar to Richard Wellesley, Kingston, May 27, 1815, in Bolívar, *Cartas del Libertador: Tomo I*, 188.

36. Bolívar to Maxwell Hyslop, Kingston, May 19, 1815, in Bolívar, *Cartas del Libertador: Tomo I*, 183.

37. Bolívar to Richard Wellesley, Kingston, May 27, 1815, in Bolívar, *Cartas del Libertador: Tomo I*, 188.

38. Bolívar to Rodríguez Torices, Kingston, May 27, 1815, in Bolívar, *Cartas del Libertador: Tomo I*, 185.

39. Bolívar to Louis Brión, Kingston, July 16, 1815, in Bolívar, *Cartas del Libertador: Tomo I*, 205.

40. Bolívar to the Editor of "The Royal Gazette," Kingston, August 18, 1815 (published in the *Royal Gazette* 37, no. 32, August 1815), in Bolívar, *Cartas del Libertador: Tomo I*, 206–211; Bolívar to the Editor of "The Royal Gazette," Kingston, September 6, 1815, in Bolívar, *Cartas del Libertador: Tomo I*, 215–236; Bolívar to the Editor of "The Royal Gazette," Kingston, September 28, 1815 (published in the *Royal Gazette* 37, no. 39, September 1815), in Bolívar, *Cartas del Libertador: Tomo I*, 236–239.

41. Bolívar, "The Jamaica Letter," 16.

42. Bolívar to the Editor of "The Royal Gazette," Kingston, September 28, 1815 (published in the *Royal Gazette* 37, no. 39, September 1815), in Bolívar, *Cartas del Libertador: Tomo I*, 236–239.

43. During his last two months in Jamaica, Bolívar survived a murder attempt and complained frequently about living in poverty. For the murder attempt, see Scott, *Tom Cringle's Log*, 56–58; and Madariaga, *Bolívar*, 518. For Bolívar's financial complaints, see Bolívar to Hyslop, Kingston, October 4, 1815, in Bolívar, *Cartas del Libertador: Tomo I*, 245; and Bolívar to Hyslop, Kingston, December 4, 1815, in Bolívar, *Cartas del Libertador: Tomo I*, 249–250.

44. Wadell, *Gran Bretaña y la independencia*, 29.

45. Wadell, *Gran Bretaña y la independencia*, 165. Gutiérrez Ardila, *Un nuevo reino*, 572–574.

46. Gutiérrez Ardila, *Un nuevo reino*, 522–533.

47. Bell Lemus, "Cartagena de Indias británica," 47.

48. Gutiérrez Ardila, *Un nuevo reino*, 563–577.

49. Gutiérrez Ardila, *Un nuevo reino*, 570–574.

50. Vice Admiral Stirling to Benito Pérez, Port Royal, January 19, 1813, quoted in Gutiérrez Ardila, *Un nuevo reino*, 570.

51. Bolívar to Rodríguez Torices, Kingston, May 27, 1815, in Bolívar, *Cartas del Libertador: Tomo I*, 185.

52. "El Gobernador Don Juan Ruiz de Apodaca instruye de las ideas que tenía el gobierno de Cartagena," Havana, April 8, 1816, AGI, Estado, 57, no. 32.

53. For a summary of the events leading to Cartagena's petition, see Restrepo, *Historia de la revolución*, 2:77–79; and Bell Lemus, "Cartagena de Indias británica," 39–67.

54. "El Gobernador Don Juan Ruiz de Apodaca instruye de las ideas que tenía el gobierno de Cartagena," Havana, April 8, 1816, AGI, Estado, 57, no. 32.

55. Bolívar to the Editor of "The Royal Gazette," Kingston, September 28, 1815 (published in the *Royal Gazette* 37, no. 39, September 1815), in Bolívar, *Cartas del Libertador: Tomo I*, 237.

56. Kaufmann, *British Policy*, 78.

57. For the political, ideological, and commercial elements informing Britain's decision, see Blaufarb, "The Western Question"; and Kaufmann, *British Policy*, 103–135.

58. Morillo to Governor of St. Barthelemy, Pampatar, April 13, 1815; Morillo to Governor of St. Thomas, Pampatar, April 13, 1815; and Morillo to Governor of Trinidad, Pampatar, April 13, 1815, all in Rodríguez Villa, *El Teniente General*, 2:458, 2:451, and 2:450.

59. Morillo to Governor of Trinidad, Pampatar, April 13, 1815, in Rodríguez Villa, *El Teniente General*, 2:450.

60. Morillo to Admiral Douglas, Cartagena, January 7, 1816; Morillo to Admiral Douglas, Santa Marta, July 30, 1815; and Morillo to Admiral Douglas, Cartagena, December 12, 1815, all in Rodríguez Villa, *El Teniente General*, 3:1, 2:573–574, and 2:589–590.

61. Duke of Manchester to Earl Bathurst, Kingston, November 4, 1815, TNA, CO 137/142, no. 73, 95.

62. Enrile to Duke of Manchester, Cartagena, November 23, 1815, TNA, CO 137/142.

63. TNA, CO 137/142, 143.

64. "The Examination of Wellwood Hyslop," November 27, 1816, TNA, CO 137/142, 154. The question asked of Wellwood Hyslop was, "Have the independants from your knowledge or belief been assisted or supplied from this island either with money or with arms and to what extent?" Hector Mitchell, Henry Josselyn, and Louis Perrotin were asked variations of this question. "The Examination of Hector Mitchell," November 27, 1816, TNA, CO 137/142, 152–153; "The Examination of Henry Josselyn," December 2, 1815, TNA, CO 137/142, 163–164v; and "The Examination of Louis Perrotin," December 3, 1816, TNA, CO 137/142, 167–168.

65. "The Examination of Edward Cowell," December 2, 1816, TNA, CO 137/142, 164v. The question Cowell was asked to answer was, "Do you know or have you heard that Bolivar received any support in funds from any individuals in this country?" John Morce and Achille Onfroy were asked to answer the same question. "The Examination of John Morce," December 2, 1816, TNA, CO 137/142, 165v–167; and "The Examination of Achille Onfroy," December 3, 1816, TNA, CO 137/142, 172v.

66. "The Examination of Wellwood Hyslop," 154v; unsigned report headed "Downing Street, 17 July 1817," TNA, CO 137/142, 141.

67. "The Examination of Wellwood Hyslop," 154.

68. *Nile's Weekly Register* 10 (March–August 1816), 384–385; W. Maxwell to Earl Bathurst, Liverpool, March 9, 1816, TNA, CO 137/143, 104; and W. Maxwell to Earl Bathurst, Liverpool, April 10, 1816, TNA, CO 137/143, 115v.

69. "The Examination of Louis Perrotin," 167; "The Examination of John Morce," 166.

70. "Downing Street, 17 July 1817," TNA, CO 137/142, 141.

71. Manchester to Bathurst, Jamaica, October, 18, 1816, TNA, CO 137/142, no. 109, 101v.

72. "The Examination of Robert Ouchterlony," December 2, 1816, TNA, CO 137/142, 162.

73. Manchester to Bathurst, Jamaica, October 18, 1816, TNA, CO 137/142, no. 109, 101v.

74. For information on proindependence émigrés who were in Haiti in 1816, see Ducoudray-Holstein, *Memoirs of Simón Bolívar*, 123; and Restrepo, *Historia de la revolución*, 3:261–264.

75. Bolívar to Brion, Port-au-Prince, January 2, 1816, in Bolívar, *Cartas del Libertador: Tomo I*, 255. There is no surviving documentation of the words Pétion and Bolívar exchanged during the meeting, but, given the support Bolívar obtained immediately afterward, Brierre's imaginative reconstruction of the conversation between the two leaders (see epigraph) certainly appears to be a close approximation of what could have transpired during the meeting.

76. For detailed, though conflicting, accounts of the confusing events that led to Bolívar's return to Haiti, see Restrepo, *Historia de la revolución*, 3:261–275; Ducoudray-Holstein, *Memoirs of Simón Bolívar*, 122–139; Madariaga, *Bolívar*, 285–287; Rodríguez O., *The Independence of Spanish America*, 186; and Masur, *Simon Bolivar*, 201.

77. Pétion to Bolívar, Port-au-Prince, September 7, 1816, in Verna, *Petión y Bolívar*, 538.

78. Esmangart and Fontanges to Eusebio Escudero, Cuba, November 25, 1816, in Franco, *Documentos para la historia*, 192.

79. Thibaud, *Repúblicas en armas*, 293; Ducoudray-Holstein, *Memoirs of Simón Bolívar*, 123–125. Sybille Fischer compellingly argues for the cosmopolitan character of Haiti's southern cities, while tracing the history that explains the unexpectedness of this Haitian cosmopolitanism as a result of the process that she calls "the disappearance of Haiti." Fischer, "Bolívar in Haiti," 28–29.

80. Escudero to Morillo, Cuba, March 2, 1816, and Morillo to Escudero, Ocaña, March 31, 1816, in Franco, *Documentos para la historia*, 174, 175–176.

81. Duarte French, *Los tres Luises*, 112–128.

82. The time Mina spent in Haiti as well as his date of departure and the number of men who landed in Mexico are based on William Robinson's account. Harris Gaylord Warren puts Mina's departure date at October 27. Robinson, *Memorias de la revolución*, 78–83; Warren, "The Origin of General Mina's Invasion," 13.

83. See Rafter, *Memoirs of Gregor M'Gregor*, 64–73, 142–155, 165–177, 247–283, 294–303; Brown, *Adventuring through Spanish Colonies*, 40–41, 65–66, 116–118; and Rodríguez, *Freedom's Mercenaries*, 87–133.

84. Verna, *Petión y Bolívar*, 181–197.

85. Verna, *Robert Sutherland*, 30.

86. Bolívar to Sutherland, Les Cayes, February 11, 1816; Bolívar to Sutherland, Les Cayes, February 13, 1816; Bolívar to Sutherland, Les Cayes, February 11,

1816; and Bolívar to Sutherland, Les Cayes, February 11, 1816, all in Verna, *Robert Sutherland*, 107, 108–109, and 111.

87. Bolívar to Sutherland, Jacmel, December 11, 1816, in Verna, *Robert Sutherland*, 112.

88. Bolívar to Brion, Port-au-Prince, October 14, 1816, quoted in Verna, *Robert Sutherland*, 49.

89. Verna, *Robert Sutherland*, 37.

90. Thibaud, *Repúblicas en armas*, 303.

91. While in Haiti, Bolívar clashed with Ducoudray-Holstein, Montilla, Bermúdez, and Aury. Ducoudray-Holstein, *Memoirs of Simón Bolívar*, 122–139, 169–173; Verna, *Petión y Bolívar*, 181–197.

92. Ducoudray-Holstein, *Memoirs of Simón Bolívar*, 123–125. Duarte French, *Los tres Luises*, 94–107.

93. Girard, *Haiti*, 46–57. On Haiti's long path to recognition by France, Great Britain, and the United States, see Gaffield, *Haitian Connections*, 190–94.

94. Pétion to Bolívar, Port-au-Prince, February 18, 1816, in Verna, *Petión y Bolívar*, 537.

95. Geggus, "Preface," xiii.

96. Dubois, *Avengers of the New World*, 223. See also Girard, *Haiti*, 57.

97. Dubois, *Avengers of the New World*, 223–226; and Girard, *Haiti*, 46, 55–58.

98. Janvier, *Les constitutions d'Haïti*, 49.

99. Ferrer, "Haiti, Free Soil, and Antislavery," 41.

100. Morillo to Pétion, Ocaña, March 31, 1816, in Franco, *Documentos para la historia*, 175. For Louverture's failure to hide his agreements from France, see Dubois, *Avengers of the New World*, 225–226.

101. Escudero to Minister of State, Cuba, December 15, 1816, in Franco, *Documentos para la historia*, 194.

102. Morillo to Minister of War, Cartagena, December 31, 1815, AGI, Estado, 57, no. 33, 1.

103. Sutherland to President of Cartagena, Port-au-Prince, December 22, 1815, AGI, Estado, 57, no. 33.

104. Brion to Bermúdez, undated, AGI, Estado, 57, no. 33; and J. M. Durán to Dunglada, Port-au-Prince, December 20, 1815, AGI, Estado, 57, no. 33.

105. Morillo to Pétion, Cartagena, December 12, 1815, in Rodríguez Villa, *El Teniente General*, 3:115.

106. "Declaración dada por Don Pedro Bruno y otros socios en 24 de Enero de 1816 sobre las circunstancias ocurridas en su apresamiento por el Corsario Insurgente la Popa de Cartagena y observaciones que hicieron sobre el asilo que recibieron del Gobierno del General Alexandro Petion," Santiago de Cuba, January 24, 1816, in Franco, *Documentos para la historia*, 169–172.

107. Pétion to Carlos de Urrutia, Port-au-Prince, January 16, 1816, in Franco, *Documentos para la historia*, 167–168; and Pétion to Morillo, Port-au-Prince, February 25, 1816, in Franco, *Documentos para la historia*, 173.

108. Pétion to Morillo, Port-au-Prince, February 25, 1816, in Franco, *Documentos para la historia*, 173.

109. Morillo to Pétion, Ocaña, March 31, 1816, in Franco, *Documentos para la historia*, 174–175.

110. Escudero to Morillo, Cuba, September 25, 1816, in Franco, *Documentos para la historia*, 184–185; Escudero to Minister of State, Cuba, November 5, 1816, in Franco, *Documentos para la historia*, 185–186.

111. Escudero to Secretary of War, Cuba, December 16, 1816, AGI, Estado, 12, no. 19.

112. On this point my interpretation differs from that of Sibylle Fischer, who argues that Bolívar embraced Haiti's republicanism as "a kind of blueprint for the establishment of American republics." While I agree that, at least during the 1810s, Bolívar wanted to establish republics (and the portion of Haiti ruled by Pétion was, indeed, a republic), Haiti, I believe, shone in Bolívar's mind more as an example of what not to look for than of what to look for. I agree with Fischer's claim that "we have good reasons . . . for thinking that the Haitian experience might have had a significant impact on the political refugees from Venezuela and Nueva Granada, and thus ultimately on political thought during the struggle for independence." Exploring the ideological impact of Haiti on the hundreds of foreigners who used Haiti as a political refuge is clearly necessary. Fischer, "Bolívar in Haiti," 27, 33.

113. Pétion to Bolívar, Port-au-Prince, February 18, 1816, in Verna, *Petión y Bolívar*, 537.

114. Bolívar to Rodríguez Torices, Kingston, May 27, 1815, in Bolívar, *Cartas del libertador: Tomo I*, 185–186.

115. Bolívar to Brion, Kingston, July 16, 1815, in Bolívar, *Cartas del libertador: Tomo I*, 205.

116. Quoted in Verna, *Petión y Bolívar*, 158.

117. Maingot, "Haiti and the Terrified Consciousness," 53, 55–56.

118. Trouillot, *Silencing the Past*, 76–78.

119. Studies of enlightened criollos in Colombia's nation-building process include Silva, *Los ilustrados*; and Nieto Olarte, *Orden natural*.

120. Ewell, "Bolívar's Atlantic World Diplomacy," 35.

121. Bolívar to Hyslop, Kingston, May 19, 1815, in Bolívar, *Cartas del libertador: Tomo I*, 183.

122. The phrase "Guinea and more Guinea" is from a letter Bolívar wrote to Francisco de Paula Santander in 1826. The letter is quoted in Helg, "Simón Bolívar and the Spectre," 455.

123. Bolívar, "Decree for the Emancipation," 65–66. For an analysis of this decree and, more broadly, the participation of slaves in the wars of independence in Spanish South America, see Blanchard, *Under the Flags of Freedom*, especially 64–85.

124. Lasso, *Myths of Harmony*, 129.

125. "Pardo" was the Spanish term for people of African descent; "pardocracia" was Bolívar's term for rule by pardos. Aline Helg analyzed Bolívar's fear of pardocracia, coining the term "the spectre of pardocracia." Helg, "Simón Bolívar and the Spectre,"

447–471. For the diplomatic "dis-encounter" between Haiti and Colombia immediately after Colombia's independence, see Gutiérrez Ardila, "Colombia y Haití," 67–93. For the international pressures, see Stinchcombe, "Class Conflict and Diplomacy."

126. Bolívar to Páez, Bogotá, November 16, 1828, in Bolívar, *Cartas del libertador: Tomo VI*, 515.

127. Bolívar to Wellesley, Kingston, May 27, 1815, in Bolívar, *Cartas del Libertador: Tomo I*, 188.

128. Fick, *The Making of Haiti*; Trouillot, *Silencing the Past*. Examples of pre-1990s studies of the Haitian Revolution are Geggus, *Slavery, War, and Revolution*; Scott, "The Common Wind."

129. Geggus, *Haitian Revolutionary Studies*; and Dubois, *Avengers of the New World*.

130. See for example Geggus, *The Impact of the Haitian Revolution*; Gaspar and Geggus, *A Turbulent Time*; Geggus and Fiering, *The World of the Haitian Revolution*; White, *Encountering Revolution*; Brown, *Toussaint's Clause*; Popkin, *You Are All Free*.

131. Clavin, *Toussaint Louverture*.

132. See Ferrer, *Freedom's Mirror*; and Reis and Gomes, "Repercussions of the Haitian Revolution."

Chapter 6: An Andean-Atlantic Nation

Epigraphs: "¡qué rasgos tan diferentes y decisivos no se advierten entre el hombre de la costa y el de la cima de los Andes!" Caldas, "Estado de la geografía," 1:21.

"Los limites generales del país son: al N. el océano Atlántico." Pérez, *Compendio de jeografía*, 23.

1. Bolívar to Santander, Pamplona, November 8, 1819, in Cortázar, *Correspondencia*, 2:64.

2. The general explanation of "patria boba," a label widely used in Bolívar's time that until very recently remained the standard term to refer to the 1810–1815 period, states that the lack of agreement about how to organize the territory of the Viceroyalty of New Granada after Napoleon's invasion of Spain thwarted the possibility of an early (and peaceful) independence and made it possible for Spanish forces to reconquer the viceroyalty in 1816. Patriots' foolishness in being unable to agree on the most convenient political system, so the story goes, doomed the early independence movement. The richness of the debates about what political model best suited the nation that could emerge in the absence of Spanish power has been emphasized in order to argue that there was nothing foolish about the rich political culture of the first half of the 1810s. For a critique of the term, see Garrido, *Reclamos y representaciones*. For studies that rely on the label "patria boba" as analytical guide and periodization tool, see Liévano Aguirre, *Los grandes conflictos sociales y económicos*, 1:189–210; Ocampo López, *La patria boba*.

3. Throughout this chapter I use the term "Colombia" as a way of distinguishing between the colonial and the republican entity. As explained in the introduction, the colonial name New Granada continued to be used until the 1860s.

4. For studies of nation formation in Latin America, see Earle, *The Return of the Native*; Sanders, *The Vanguard of the Atlantic*; and Beckman, *Capital Fictions*. For the specific cases of Colombia and Venezuela, see Brown, *The Struggle for Power*.

5. I borrow the term "politician-geographers" from Margarita Serje, who uses it to refer to a group of mid-nineteenth-century Colombian politicians who received formal education in geography as part of their professional formation. Serje, *El revés de la nación*, 88–103.

6. The cast of scientific travelers included Charles-Marie de La Condamine, who traveled through Quito, navigated the Amazon River, and spent time in French Guiana between 1735 and 1745; Alexander von Humboldt and Aimé Bonpland, who traveled through Venezuela, New Granada, Quito, Cuba, Mexico, and the United States between 1799 and 1804; and Alessandro Malaspina, whose Pacific expedition took him from Cádiz (in 1789) to the Río de la Plata, Chile, Peru, New Spain, Alaska, the California coast, and then across the Pacific to Manila, Australia, and New Zealand before returning to Cádiz in 1794.

7. For examples of the literature on science and empire, see Safier, *Measuring the New World*; Cañizares-Esguerra, *Nature, Empire, and Nation*; Schiebinger, *Plants and Empire*; and Bleichmar, *Visible Empire*. For other examples of the Atlantic dialogue and the borrowings and transformations that characterized it, see Norton, *Sacred Gifts*; Carney, *Black Rice*; Carney and Rosomoff, *In the Shadow of Slavery*; Barrera-Osorio, *Experiencing Nature*; Sweet, *Domingos Álvarez*; Dubois, "An Enslaved Enlightenment"; and Gómez, "Bodies of Encouter."

8. Nieto Olarte, *Orden natural y orden social*, 239.

9. Serje, *El revés de la nación*, 88.

10. Lynch, *Simón Bolívar*, 22–40, 48–54.

11. Lynch, *Simón Bolívar*, 23. On the potential connection between sex, vices, political engagement, and exile, Winston James, in his study of Caribbean migrants in the United States, wrote, "Exile made it easier for many of these young migrants to embrace radical ideas precisely because the social pressures abroad were not as great as they were at home. Just as exile enabled them to dance more and smoke more, it also gave them a greater opportunity than hitherto to engage with new political ideas and behavior, including some that would have been definitely frowned upon back home." James, *Holding Aloft the Banner*, 77.

12. Bolívar's European reading list also included Hobbes, Spinoza, Holbach, Hume, Paine, Raynal, de Pradt, and a wide selection of ancient history. Lynch, *Simón Bolívar*, 22–40. For Bolívar and Humboldt, see Wulf, *The Invention of Nature*, 139–147, 171–190; and Rippy and Brann, "Alexander von Humboldt and Simón Bolívar" (701 for Humboldt as "discoverer of the New World").

13. Miranda arranged meetings with Britain's foreign minister, the marquis of Wellesley, Nicholas Vansittart, and William Wilberforce. Lynch, *Simón Bolívar*, 50–53; Racine, *Francisco de Miranda*, 200–205.

14. Bolívar, O'Higgins, and San Martín did not visit Miranda's house at the same time, but the fact that they all spent time there speaks volumes to the role of

Miranda as intellectual and political mentor of a younger generation of enlightened creoles. Racine, *Francisco de Miranda*, 150; Jaksic, *Andrés Bello*, 33.

15. Jaksic, *Andrés Bello*; Berruezo León, *La lucha de Hispanoamérica*, 61–66, 85–92, 99–121; Racine, *Francisco de Miranda*, 207.

16. For the role of Mutis and Rodríguez, see Silva, *Los ilustrados*; Soto Arango, *Mutis*; Padilla Chasing, "Despotismo ilustrado y contrarrevolución"; Serrato Gómez, "Un ilustrado ante la Revolución francesa"; Moreno Chuquén, "Manuel del Socorro Rodríguez"; and Díaz Consuegra, "La búsqueda de lo *Americano*."

17. Caldas became a lecturer in mathematics at the prestigious Colegio de Nuestra Señora del Rosario. He also served as director of the Royal Astronomical Observatory of Santa Fe and was a member of the Royal Botanical Expedition. Zea was a lecturer in philosophy at the Colegio San Bartolomé and became the subdirector of the Royal Botanical Expedition. Lozano directed the zoological component of the Royal Botanical Expedition. For details about their scientific careers, see Nieto Olarte, *Orden natural y orden social*, 59–95; and Soto Arango, *Francisco Antonio Zea*.

18. Enlightened creole José Fernández Madrid, for example, was an active participant in the Tertulia del Buen Gusto and published literary and scientific works in *El Alternativo* and the *Semanario*. See Solano Alonso, *El Caribe colombiano*, 49–65. See also del Castillo, "La Gran Colombia de la Gran Bretaña," 129.

19. Silva, *Los ilustrados*, 245–247, 315–319, 575.

20. Salazar, "Memoria descriptiva," 2:226–227.

21. Nieto Olarte, *Orden natural y orden social*, 107–108.

22. This framework, one that was shared by enlightened creoles throughout Spanish America, is usually associated with Argentine intellectual and nation maker Domingo Faustino Sarmiento and his book *Facundo: Civilización y Barbarie*. In *Facundo* Sarmiento presents one of the most fundamental elements of Latin America's nation-building processes, namely that in order to reach civilization it was necessary to whiten the population of the new republics. For an English translation, see Sarmiento, *Facundo*.

23. Nieto Olarte, *Orden natural y orden social*, 305.

24. Humboldt, "Geografía de las plantas," 2:21–162 (for Caldas's notes, see 2:141–162).

25. In his "Memoria descriptiva," for example, José María Salazar impugned "several mistakes of the [memoir] of Mr. [Jean Baptiste] Leblond on the same subject." Salazar, "Memoria descriptiva," 2:198.

26. Nieto Olarte, *Orden natural y orden social*, 159–174. For European theories of the inferiority of animals and humans in the Americas, see Gerbi, *The Dispute for the New World*.

27. Caldas, "Del influjo del clima," 1:137, 160–161, 167, 195; Caldas, "Estado de la geografía," 1:21.

28. Múnera, "José Ignacio de Pombo y Francisco José de Caldas," 82.

29. Ulloa, "Ensayo sobre el influjo del clima en la educación física y moral del hombre," quoted in Nieto Olarte, *Orden natural y orden social*, 195–196.

30. Appelbaum, *Mapping the Country of Regions*.

31. The title of Acosta's map is *Mapa de la República de la Nueva Granada dedicado al Barón de Humboldt* (Map of the Republic of New Granada Dedicated to Baron von Humboldt). The map is available in Blanco, *Atlas histórico-geográfico*, 119.

32. Thongchai, *Siam Mapped*, 16–17. Emphasizing "the territorial factor," a Colombian geographer makes a similar claim when he states that "in the national states of the modern world," territory "becomes the basic structure that locates and makes a country tangible"; it "constitutes the particular identity that distinguishes [that country] from other national states in the planet." Under the term "territorial patriotism," Dominguez, like Thongchai, incorporates the feelings citizens attach to the national territory. Dominguez Ossa, "Territorio e identidad nacional," 337, 339.

33. Maritime historian Marcus Rediker uses "terracentric" in reference to historical narratives that understand—explicitly or not—that "the seas of the world are unreal spaces," allowing only "landed and national" spaces to be "real places." Rediker, *Outlaws of the Atlantic*, 2.

34. This exclusion or taking for granted of the sea is by no means exclusive to Thongchai's work. In their studies of boundaries, mapping, and surveying in southwestern Europe, British Guiana, and India, D. Graham Burnett, Matthew Edney, and Peter Sahlins similarly favor land over water territories. While focusing on land-based territories and territorialities does work for these authors, incorporating the sea into a nation's geo-body can add interpretational layers to nation-building processes. See Sahlins, *Boundaries*; Edney, *Mapping an Empire*; Burnett, *Masters of All They Surveyed*.

35. Carter, *The Road to Botany Bay*, 27–28. For a similarly rich take on the act of naming, see Harley, "New England Cartography."

36. Craib, *Cartographic Mexico*, 128–132; Earle, *The Return of the Native*, 47–78; and Earle, "*Sobre Héroes y Tumbas*." See also del Castillo, "La Gran Colombia de la Gran Bretaña." For thought-provoking examples about the naming of Brazil and renaming sacred places as a way to desacralize them, see Cañizares-Esguerra, *Puritan Conquistadors*, 112–113, 118.

37. For attempts to put the name of the sea at the center of the nation-making process, see Bell Lemus, "¿Costa atlántica?"; and Múnera, "El Caribe colombiano." Both Bell Lemus and Múnera point to a substitution of Atlantic for Caribbean. My position, based on a revision of a broad array of maps (see appendix 6), geographical treatises, and geography texts, is more nuanced. For a global take on the lack of consensus about how to name different oceans and the political and ideological ramifications of choosing certain toponyms over others, see Lewis, "Dividing the Ocean Sea."

38. Margarita Serje, Efraín Sánchez, and Fernando Cubides have pointed to geography as a common professional background of many politicians and other influential Colombian elites. See Serje, *El revés de la nación*; Sánchez, *Gobierno y geografía*, 620–652; and Cubides, "Representaciones del territorio," 319–343. Joaquín Acosta was president of the House of Representatives and secretary of foreign

relations during the 1840s; Agustín Codazzi directed the ambitious corographic expedition that mapped the nineteenth-century republic; Tomás Cipriano de Mosquera was president of the republic on three occasions (1845–1849, 1861–1864, and 1866–1867); Manuel Ancízar was secretary of foreign relations; José María Samper worked for several administrations; Felipe Pérez was secretary of war and the navy and president of the republic during the late 1870s; and Santiago Pérez was president of the republic from 1874 to 1876. For short biographical sketches of these and other politician-geographers and nation makers, see Banco de la República, Actividad Cultural, Biografías, http://www.banrepcultural.org /blaavirtual/biografias/a; and Appelbaum, *Mapping the Country of Regions*. For interpretations that emphasize other professional backgrounds for Colombian politicians, namely linguistics and law, see Deas, *Del poder y la gramática*; and Palacios, "La Regeneración."

39. The following analysis on the politics of naming the sea is based on cartographic evidence summarized in appendix 6.

40. Del Castillo, "Cartography in the Production."

41. Late colonial maps of New Granada invariably used Mar del Norte to refer to the sea to the north of the viceroyalty. Two examples are Josep Aparicio Morata's *Plan geográfico del vireynato de Santafe de Bogota Nuevo Reyno de Granada* (1772) and Vicente Talledo y Rivera's *Mapa Corográfico del Nuevo Reyno de Granada* (1808). Both maps are reproduced in Blanco, *Atlas histórico-geográfico de Colombia*, 59, 71. Maps of specific provinces, like Antonio de la Torre's map of the Darién (1782; figure 3.3), Juan López's *Carta Plana de la Provincia de la Hacha* (1786), and Vicente Talledo y Rivera's *Mapa corográfico de la Provincia de Cartagena de Indias* (1815) also used Mar del Norte. For reproductions of these last two maps, see Díaz Angel, Muñoz Arbeláez, and Nieto Olarte, *Ensamblando la nación*, 45, 64.

42. While the title suggests a map of all the provinces that used to constitute the viceroyalty of New Granada, the plates only show the northern provinces of Cartagena, Santa Marta, and Riohacha. This inconsistency, coupled with the tumultuous geopolitical environment of the 1810s, has led historian Mauricio Nieto to characterize the nineteen available plates as part of an unfinished project. Nieto Olarte, "Caldas," 34.

43. See chapter 5.

44. In a clear rejection of the Spanish tradition of using Cádiz as reference, the prime meridian used to measure longitude in the nineteen plates is situated at Cartagena. Other maps produced by Caldas locate the prime meridian in Quito. Nieto Olarte, "Caldas," 33. For the nineteen plates, see Nieto Olarte, *La obra cartográfica*, 99–119.

45. Harley, "Power and Legitimation," 117.

46. Nieto Olarte, "Caldas," 29.

47. Zea's map accompanied the work *Colombia* and its English translation. Restrepo's map of Colombia and accompanying maps of the nation's provinces appeared in an atlas that was part of his *Historia de la Revolución de la República de*

Colombia. The maps of Restrepo's atlas are available at David Rumsey Map Collection, http://www.davidrumsey.com.

48. Of the twenty-eight maps, printed mostly in London (14) and Philadelphia (7) but also in New York (3), Edinburgh (1), Baltimore (1), and Brattleboro (1), only four adopted the term Sea of Antilles and one—Henry Teesdale's 1834 "Columbia" [*sic*]—used Atlantic Ocean. See appendix 6.

49. In the sources consulted, nine out of nine French maps (i.e., maps published in French, in France, and by authors with French last names) of Colombia used Mer des Antilles. See appendix 6.

50. In reference to Zea's map, Lina del Castillo discusses the collaborative nature of its production as well as the limited but still important "editorial voice" that Zea maintained throughout the production process. Her analysis favors January 1823 as the publication date for the map, while also pointing out that the map appeared as part of the two-volume publication *Colombia* that appeared in 1822. Zea died in November 1822. Del Castillo, "La Gran Colombia de la Gran Bretaña," especially 125–128.

51. Bell Lemus, "¿Costa atlántica?," 139–140; and Múnera, "El Caribe colombiano," 49. Both Múnera and Bell, in Bell's words, merely "pose hypotheses." My argument is greatly indebted to their hypotheses but also seeks to add nuances to their thought-provoking generalizations. Múnera anticipates key elements of my argument by stating, "In school maps of the twentieth century, Cartagena, and more generally the whole northern littoral of Colombia, appears located by . . . the Atlantic Ocean" (49). Bell claims, slightly exaggerating, that "in all the [geographical] texts published in the second half of the nineteenth century, the Atlantic Ocean *always* appears as the [northern] limits of New Granada or the United States of Colombia" (139).

52. Duque Muñoz, "Geografía y cartografía," 12. Using the map collection of Colombia's National Archives as her main source, Duque Muñoz counted 114 maps produced between 1840 and 1865. Of these, six were maps of the whole national territory. The six national maps were drawn by Joaquín Acosta (1847), Mariano Inojosa (1850), Genaro Gaitán and Ramón Posada (1850), Tomás Cipriano de Mosquera (1852), José María Samper (1858), and Manuel Ponce de León and Manuel María Paz (1865). Digital images of these maps are available on several websites. For a comprehensive list of cartographic resources available online, see Razón Cartográfica, http://razoncartografica.com/mapoteca/. For specific collections, see Biblioteca Nacional de Colombia, Ministerio de Cultura, Mapoteca Digital, http://www.bibliotecanacional.gov.co/content/mapas-de-colombia; and Banco de la República, Cartografía Histórica, http://www.banrepcultural.org/blaavirtual/cartografia.

53. The use of Antilles as physical location was not newly introduced in the nineteenth century. The cartographer Herman Moll, for instance, used it in 1701. Describing the "Antilles Islands," he said, "They are all in general call'd by divers Geographers *Antillae*, q.d. *Ante-Insulae*, i.e. *The Fore-Islands*, by reason of their situation before the Gulph of *Mexico*, and in regard that they first come in sight

to those that sail from *Europe*, or *Africa*, before the Coasts of *New Spain*." Moll, *A System of Geography*, 2:183.

54. Duque Muñoz, "Geografía y cartografía"; and Duque Muñoz, "Territorio nacional, cartografía y poder." For studies of the Chorographic Commission, see Sánchez, *Gobierno y geografía*; and Appelbaum, *Mapping the Country of Regions*.

55. The intriguing exception to the tendency to use Mar de las Antillas was Mariano Inojosa, whose 1850 map, produced under the "inspection of Joaquín de Acosta and Benedicto Domínguez," uses Mar del Norte. Lina del Castillo suggested to me, in a personal communication, the possibility that some of these maps were drawn as part of classes taught by Acosta at the Colegio Militar (military school). At the risk of anachronistically assigning twenty-first-century grading criteria to nineteenth-century assessment practices, one can wonder if Acosta gave Inojosa a bad grade for referring to the sea in colonial terms.

56. While Zea uses Caribbean throughout his account (and in its accompanying map), he hinted that this usage aimed at facilitating British subjects' geographical location. In an early passage of his geographical description, Zea states that the sea "that bathes [Colombia's] northern [coasts] is that which the English call Caribbean Sea." Throughout the text he adopts this usage without explaining if Colombians generally preferred another term. [Walker and Zea], *Colombia*, 1, 31, 272, 274, 280, 293, 296, 305; Pérez, *Compendio de jeografía*, 23.

57. Mosquera, *Compendio de geografía*, 104, 106, 286, 289; Samper, *Ensayo aproximado*, 10, 12, 13, 19.

58. Cuervo, *Resumen de la jeografía*; Araujo, *Tratado de geografía*. For examples that show the preference for the name Atlantic by key members of the Chorographic Commission, see Codazzi, *Geografía física y política*; Pérez, *Geografía general*; and Pérez, *Jeografía física i política*.

59. Mosquera, *Memoria* (1852) and its English translation *Memoir* (1853), 5, 21, 76, 11, 15, 17, 20, 83, 27.

60. Mosquera, *Memoir*, 8. In this memoir, Mosquera used Caribbean Sea on four more occasions. Atlantic, on the other hand, appears more than twenty times.

61. Mosquera, *Memoir*, 41 (emphasis added).

62. Mosquera, *Compendio de geografía*, 106. In a section devoted to the "special geography of the states," Mosquera presents the states of Magdalena and Bolívar as located "on the shores of the Atlantic" (286, 289).

63. Mosquera, *Compendio de geografía*, 287, 13.

64. Mosquera and Samper were members of prestigious international learned societies. Mosquera was honorary member of Paris's Society for Practical Agronomy, member of Brazil's Historical and Geographical Institute, and founding member of Denmark's Royal Society of Northern Antiques. Samper was a member of the Paris-based Geographical Society and Society of Ethnography. Mosquera, *Memoir*; Samper, *Ensayo sobre las revoluciones*.

65. Samper, *Ensayo aproximado*, 10, 12, 13, 19.

66. Samper, *Ensayo aproximado*, 4.

67. Samper, *Ensayo sobre las revoluciones*, xii. The essay "La confederación granadina y su población" appears as an appendix to *Ensayo sobre las revoluciones*.

68. Samper, *Ensayo sobre las revoluciones*, 286–287, 292.

69. Along with Mosquera and Samper, another politician-geographer, Felipe Pérez, who took over the task of finishing the work of the Chorographic Commission after Agustín Codazzi's death in 1859, published several geographical treatises—some of them national in scope, others related to specific provinces including the coastal departments of Bolívar and Magdalena—that advanced the decaribbeanization agenda by describing Colombia's "general limits" to the north as "the coasts running over the Atlantic" and locating all the country's northern islands, gulfs, bays, and peninsulas "in the Atlantic Ocean." Pérez, *Geografía general*, 1:124, 128, 131, 142, 335, 377–380. See also Pérez, *Jeografía física i política*.

70. [Acevedo Tejada], *Noticia sobre la geografía*; Cuervo, *Resumen de la jeografía*. I borrow the term "geographical literacy" from Martin Brückner, who defines it as "the basic competence to read maps and to read and write about the world in modern geographic terms." Because geographical texts, encyclopedias, and catechisms were the main vehicles through which U.S. citizens learned geography and acquired "geographical consciousness," Brückner understands geography as a "textual experience" through which Americans learned to be U.S. citizens. See Brückner, *The Geographic Revolution*, 3, 6, 145, 149–158.

71. [Acevedo Tejada], *Noticia sobre la geografía*, 4.

72. [Acevedo Tejada], *Noticia sobre la geografía*, 8, 11, 25, 29.

73. *Catecismo de geografía*, 9.

74. Pérez, *Compendio de jeografía*, 23.

75. Araujo, *Tratado de geografía física*, 51.

76. Goswami, *Producing India*, 132–153.

77. In a different geographic and temporal setting—Mexico in the 1890s—William Beezley developed a similar argument regarding the limits of imitation. Using sports and recreation practices as an analytical lens, Beezley argued that "simple imitation of U.S. and European sports" does not provide a valid explanation for the rise of organized sports in Porfirian Mexico. Selective imitation (one that incorporated cultural specificities), he demonstrated, better explains the process through which "Porfirian elites appropriated foreign recreational forms and made them uniquely Mexican." Beezley, *Judas at the Jockey Club*, 14, 65.

78. "Carta de un amigo," *Gaceta de Cartagena de Colombia*, Cartagena, June 26, 1831, AGNC, AHR, fondo 11, vol. 19.

79. Bolívar, "The Jamaica Letter," 23–26.

80. Cockburn to Watts, quoted in Vaughan, "Fracaso de una misión," 552.

81. For the rumor of a Colombian-Mexican expedition, see Helg, *Liberty and Equality*, 196; and Barcia, *The Great African Slave Revolt*, 1–3, 121–123.

82. Múnera, "El Caribe colombiano," 45–47; Bell Lemus, "El impacto económico"; Helg, *Liberty and Equality*, 211, 214.

83. Múnera, "El Caribe colombiano," 47.

84. Helg, *Liberty and Equality*; Lasso, *Myths of Harmony*.

85. For these and more biographical details, see Helg, *Liberty and Equality*, 196–198; and Lasso, *Myths of Harmony*, 116–117.

86. Bolívar to Santander, quoted in Helg, *Liberty and Equality*, 201.

87. Lasso, *Myths of Harmony*, 126.

88. Lasso, *Myths of Harmony*, 122.

89. Helg, *Liberty and Equality*, 207–209.

90. Both Lasso and Helg present evidence that demonstrates, if not necessarily an actual connection, the conviction of Colombian political elites of a connection between Jamaica's Christmas Rebellion and rumors of race war in Colombia's Caribbean provinces. See Lasso, *Myths of Harmony*, 133; and Helg, *Liberty and Equality*, 232.

91. For details of Nieto's early childhood years, political awakenings, and early political career, see Fals Borda, *Historia doble de la costa*, 32A–40A; and Lemaitre, *El general Juan José Nieto*, 11–14.

92. Calvo, quoted in Fals Borda, *Historia doble de la costa*, 51A; and Lemaitre, *El general Juan José Nieto*, 14.

93. Nieto to Francisco de Paula Santander, Cartagena, August 7, 1835, published as Nieto, "Una temprana argumentación," 13–26.

94. Cámara de la Provincia de Cartagena, *Informe de la comisión*.

95. McGraw, *The Work of Recognition*, 59.

96. Nieto's political and military career is described in detail in Fals Borda, *Historia doble de la costa*; and Lemaitre, *El general Juan José Nieto*. For brief biographical summaries, see Avelar, "Ingermina"; Cabrera, "Elementos de colonialidad," 71.

97. Nieto, "Una temprana argumentación," 18; and Nieto, "Bosquejo histórico," 115.

98. Nieto, *Geografía histórica*, 6.

99. Its publication date makes *Yngermina*, according to literary critic Raymond Williams, the first Colombian novel. Williams, *The Colombian Novel*, 93–100. Despite being recognized as the first Colombian novel, *Yngermina* has never been central to Colombia's literary canon. Marta Cabrera characterizes it as "totally peripheral within [Colombia's] literary canon." Idelber Avelar considers it "*uncanonizable*," because of the national vision it advances. He claims that "there are textual reasons to believe that *Ingermina* is a sort of 'national anti-allegory.'" Germán Espinosa called it "transcendental" because it paved the way for the emergence of the "novelistic genre . . . in Hispanic America" and considered Nieto one of Colombia's "literary precursors." Cabrera, "Elementos de colonialidad," 71; Avelar, "Ingermina," 126; Espinosa, "*Ingermina*," 357, 362.

100. Avelar, "Ingermina," 123.

101. Nieto, *Yngermina*, 1:v, 1:xvii, 1:xviii, 1:37, 1:47, 1:87, 2:58.

102. Doris Sommer has argued that nineteenth-century romantic novels—"foundational fictions"—were key constitutive elements of Latin America's nation-making process. "Romantic novels," she writes, "go hand in hand with patriotic

history in Latin America." Sommer, *Foundational Fictions*, 7. See also Earle, *The Return of the Native*, 117–129; and Beckman, *Capital Fictions*.

103. Cabrera, "Elementos de colonialidad," 74. For references to the civilized nature of the Andean Muiscas, see Langebaek, "Civilización y barbarie"; Earle, *The Return of the Native*, 111, 141–142, 166; and Mosquera, *Compendio de geografía*.

104. Mosquera, *Compendio de geografía*, 287; Samper, *Ensayo sobre las revoluciones*, 286–287, 292.

105. Nieto, *Geografía histórica*, 6.

106. Massey, *For Space*, 9.

107. Bolívar to Santander, quoted in Helg, "Simón Bolívar and the Spectre," 455; Bolívar to Hyslop, in Bolívar, *Cartas del Libertador: Tomo I*, 183.

108. Sanders, *The Vanguard of the Atlantic*.

109. Ferreira, *Cross-Cultural Exchange*, 242–248.

110. Gabaccia, "A Long Atlantic," 1. See also Sanders, *The Vanguard of the Atlantic*.

111. For the critique of the Atlantic world as largely a British Atlantic one, see Cañizares-Esguerra, *Puritan Conquistadors*, 218. See also Cañizares-Esguerra and Breen, "Hybrid Atlantics" and Bassi, "Beyond Compartmentalized Atlantics."

112. The new state of Atlantic was first created in 1905. Shortly afterward, in 1908, it was abolished, and then in 1910 it was reestablished permanently. "Ley número 17 de 1905"; "Ley número 21 de 1910."

Conclusion: Of Alternative Geographies and Plausible Futures

1. Putnam, "To Study the Fragments/Whole," 620.

2. See for example Wimmer and Schiller, "Methodological Nationalism and Beyond"; and Wimmer and Schiller, "Methodological Nationalism, the Social Sciences."

3. Wimmer and Schiller, "Methodological Nationalism, the Social Sciences," 576. Colmenares, "La 'Historia de la Revolución.'" For a more recent analysis of Restrepo's *Historia*—a history of his *History*—see Mejía, *La revolución en letras*.

4. Pratt, *Imperial Eyes*.

5. For a discussion of distance as "relative," "flexible," and "contextual," see Sellers-García, *Distance and Documents*, 1–5.

6. Thompson, *The Making of the English Working Class*, 12.

7. Echeverri, *Indian and Slave Royalists*; Sartorius, *Ever Faithful*, xi ("black and mulatto Cubans"); Sanders, *The Vanguard of the Atlantic*, 36 ("monarchy as the answer"); Landers, *Atlantic Creoles*, 233 ("monarchy was . . . the best option"); and Eller, *We Dream Together*. See also Brown, *The Struggle for Power* (for monarchical imaginaries); and Fitz, *Our Sister Republics* (for visions of hemispheric solidarity).

8. Soja, *Postmodern Geographies*, 28.

9. Trouillot considers two ways in which the Haitian Revolution was "unthinkable." Not only was it unthinkable "before [it] happened" (95), it also "entered

history with the particular characteristic of being unthinkable even as it happened" (73). Trouillot, *Silencing the Past*, 70–107.

10. Goswami, "Imaginary Futures," 1462.

Appendix I

1. For a more detailed methodological discussion of how to follow ships through the colonial archives, see Bassi, "The Space Between."

2. AGNC, AA-I, Aduanas, 22.

BIBLIOGRAPHY

Archives

All archives are cited using abbreviations. The name of the archive (e.g., AGNC or AGI) is usually followed by the name of a division within that archive (e.g., SC or Santa Fe). The next level corresponds to specific series within divisions (e.g., Aduanas, Milicias y Marina, or Gobierno). The numbers after a division or series correspond to specific *legajos*, boxes, volumes, or folders.

COLOMBIA

AGNC: Archivo General de la Nación, Bogotá

> AA-I: ARCHIVO ANEXO, GRUPO I
> Aduanas, 8, 16, 22, 33, 34, 41, 44, 47, 51
> Gobierno, 13
> Guerra y Marina, 44, 48, 61, 118, 130
> Historia, 3

> AHR: ARCHIVO HISTÓRICO RESTREPO
> Fondo XI, vol. 19

> REPÚBLICA
> Libros de Manuscritos y Leyes Originales, 34, 50

> SC: SECCIÓN COLONIA
> Aduanas, 2, 5, 17, 21, 22
> Milicias y Marina, 80, 81, 82, 112, 115
> Negocios Exteriores, 2
> Virreyes, 16

SPAIN

AGI: Archivo General de Indias, Seville

Estado, 12, 52, 53, 57, 60, 61

MP-Panamá, 182, 184Bis, 202Bis, 262

Santa Fe, 640, 641, 645, 651, 653, 655, 952, 954, 955, 956, 957, 959, 960, 1015, 1019, 1091, 1095, 1149

AGS: Archivo General de Simancas, Valladolid, Spain

SGU: Secretaría de Guerra, 6945, 6949, 7072, 7242

UNITED KINGDOM

TNA: The National Archives, London

CO: Colonial Office, 142/22–29, 137/142, 137/143

BT: Board of Trade, 5–4

Printed Primary Sources

[Acevedo Tejada, Pedro.] *Noticia sobre la geografía política de Colombia proporcionada para la primera enseñanza de los niños en este importante ramo de su educación.* London: Imprenta española de M. Calero, 1825.

"Acta de la legislatura de la provincia de Cartagena. 13 de octubre de 1815." In Gustavo Bell Lemus, *Cartagena de Indias: De la colonia a la república,* 68–73. Bogotá: Fundación Simón y Lola Guberek, 1991.

Allen, James. *Considerations on the Present State of the Intercourse between His Majesty's Sugar Colonies and the Dominions of the United States of America.* London, 1784.

Araujo, D. H. *Tratado de geografía física y política del estado de Bolívar destinado a la enseñanza.* [Cartagena?]: Imprenta de Ruiz e Hijo, 1871.

Arébalo, Antonio de. *La pacificación de la Provincia del Río del Hacha (1770–1776).* Bogotá: El Áncora Editores, 2004.

Arévalo, Antonio de. "Descripción o relación del Golfo de el Darién e Istmo del mismo nombre. . . ." In *Colección de documentos inéditos sobre la geografía y la historia de Colombia,* edited by Antonio B. Cuervo, 2:264–273. Bogotá: Casa Editorial de J. J. Pérez, 1892.

Arévalo, Antonio de. "Plan de operaciones que deveran executarse en la Provincia del Hacha contra los Yndios de ella." In *La Goajira,* edited by María Teresa Oliveros de Castro, 177–197. Mérida: Universidad de Los Andes, 1975.

Arguedas, Luis. "Diario de una expedición reservada a cargo del capitán de fragata Luis Arguedas." In *Colección de documentos inéditos sobre la geografía y la historia de Colombia,* edited by Antonio B. Cuervo, 1:372–429. Bogotá: Casa Editorial de J. J. Pérez, 1892.

Blanco, José A., ed. *Atlas histórico-geográfico: Colombia.* Bogotá: Archivo General de la Nación, 1992.

Bolívar, Simón. *Cartas del Libertador: Tomo I (1799–1817).* Caracas: Banco de Venezuela, Fundación Vicente Lecuna, 1968.

Bolívar, Simón. *Cartas del libertador: Tomo VI (1827–1828)*. Caracas: Banco de Venezuela, Fundación Vicente Lecuna, 1968.

Bolívar, Simón. "Decree for the Emancipation of the Slaves." In *The Bolivarian Revolution*, edited by Matthew Brown, 65–66. London: Verso, 2009.

Bolívar, Simón. "The Jamaica Letter: Response from a South American to a Gentleman from This Island." In *El Libertador: Writings of Simón Bolívar*, edited by David Bushnell, 12–30. New York: Oxford University Press, 2003.

Caballero y Góngora, Antonio. "Relación del estado del Nuevo Reino de Granada." In *Relaciones e informes de los gobernantes de la Nueva Granada*, edited by Germán Colmenares, 1:361–492. Bogotá: Ediciones Banco Popular, 1989.

Caldas, Francisco José de. "Del influjo del clima sobre los seres organizados." In *Semanario del Nuevo Reino de Granada*, edited by Francisco José de Caldas 1:136–196. Bogotá: Editorial Minerva, 1942.

Caldas, Francisco José de. "Estado de la geografía del Virreinato de Santafé de Bogotá, con relación a la economía y al comercio." In *Semanario del Nuevo Reino de Granada*, edited by Francisco José de Caldas, 1:15–54. Bogotá: Editorial Minerva, 1942.

Cámara de la Provincia de Cartagena. *Informe de la comisión en la representación del ciudadano Juan José Nieto sobre federación o aumento de poder de las Cámaras de Provincia*. Cartagena: Imprenta de los herederos de Juan A. Calvo, 1838.

Catecismo de geografía de la república de la Nueva Granada. Bogotá: Imprenta de J. A. Cualla, 1842.

Codazzi, Agustín. *Geografía física y política de la Confederación Granadina. Volumen VI. Estado del Istmo de Panamá. Provincias de Chiriquí, Veraguas, Azuero y Panamá (1854)*, edited by Camilo A. Domínguez Ossa et al. Bogotá: Universidad Nacional de Colombia, 2002.

"Convención de paz y vasallaje celebrada por los indios del Darién, con el excelentísmo señor virrey de Santa Fe, D. Antonio Caballero y Góngora." In *Efemérides y anales del Estado Soberano de Bolívar*, edited by Manuel Ezequiel Corrales, 163–176. Bogotá: Gobernación de Bolívar/Instituto Internacional de Estudios del Caribe, 1999.

Cortázar, Roberto, ed. *Correspondencia dirigida al General Francisco de Paula Santander*, vol. 2. Bogotá: Academia Nacional de la Historia, 1964.

Cruden, John. *An Address to the Loyal Part of the British Empire, and the Friends of Monarchy throughout the Globe*. London, 1785.

Cuervo, Antonio B. *Resumen de la jeografía histórica, política, estadísitica y descriptiva de la Nueva Granada para el uso de las escuelas primarias superiores*. Bogotá: Imprenta de Torres Amaya, 1852.

"The Definitive Treaty of Peace and Friendship between His Britannick Majesty, and the King of Spain. Signed at Versailles, the third of September, 1783." In *A Collection of All the Treaties of Peace, Alliance, and Commerce, between Great Britain and Other Powers, from the Treaty Signed at Munster in 1648, to the Treaties Signed at Paris in 1783*, 3:392–399. London: J Debrett, 1785.

Depons, François. *Travels in South America during the Years 1801, 1802, 1803, and 1804; Containing a Description of the Captain-Generalship of Caracas, and an Account of the Discovery. Conquest, Topography, Legislature, Commerce, Finance, and Natural Productions of the Country, with a View of the Manners and Customs of the Spaniards and the Native Indians.* 2 vols. London: Longman, Hurst, Rees, and Orme, 1807.

Ducoudray-Holstein, H. L. V. *Memoirs of Simón Bolívar, President Liberator of the Republic of Colombia and of His Principal Generals.* Boston: S. G. Goodrich & Co., 1829.

Edwards, Bryan. *The History, Civil and Commercial of the British West Indies.* 5 vols. London: T. Miller, 1819.

Edwards, Bryan. *Thoughts on the Late Proceedings of Government Respecting the Trade of the West India Islands with the United States of North America.* London: T. Cadell, 1784.

Equiano, Olaudah. *The Life of Olaudah Equiano, or Gustavus Vassa, the African.* Boston: Isaac Knapp, 1837.

Ezpeleta, Josef de. "Relación del gobierno del Exmo. Sor. Dn. Josef de Ezpeleta, etc., en este Nuevo Reino de Granada con expresión de su actual estado en los diversos ramos que abraza, de lo que queda por hacer y de lo que puede adelantarse en cada uno." In *Relaciones e informes de los gobernantes de la Nueva Granada,* edited by Germán Colmenares, 2:153–311. Bogotá: Biblioteca Banco Popular, 1989.

Fidalgo, Joaquín Francisco. *Derrotero y cartografía de la Expedición Fidalgo por el Caribe neogranadino, 1792–1801,* edited by Camilo Domínguez Ossa, Hernando Salcedo Fidalgo, and Luisa Martín-Meras Verdejo. Bogotá: Universidad Externado de Colombia, 2011.

Franco, José Luciano, ed. *Documentos para la historia de Haití en el Archivo Nacional de Cuba.* Havana: Archivo Nacional de Cuba, 1954.

García del Río, Juan. "Meditaciones colombianas." In *Ensayos costeños. De la colonia a la república: 1770–1890,* edited by Alfonso Múnera, 229–395. Bogotá: Colcultura, 1994.

García del Río, Juan. "Página de oro de la historia de Cartagena." In *Documentos para la historia de la Provincia de Cartagena de Indias, hoy Estado Soberano de Bolívar en la Unión Colombiana,* edited by Manuel Ezequiel Corrales, 2:230–245. Bogotá: Imprenta de Medardo Rivas, 1883.

Gil y Lemos, Francisco. "Relación de D. Francisco Gil y Lemos." In *Relaciones e informes de los gobernantes de la Nueva Granada,* edited by Germán Colmenares, 2:5–33. Bogotá: Biblioteca Banco Popular, 1989.

Guirior, Manuel. "Instrucción que deja a su sucesor en el mando el Virrey D. Manuel Guirior." In *Relaciones e informes de los gobernantes de la Nueva Granada,* edited by Germán Colmenares, 1:271–359. Bogotá: Biblioteca Banco Popular, 1989.

Humboldt, Alexander von. "Geografía de las plantas, o cuadro físico de los Andes equinocciales y de los países vecinos." In *Semanario del Nuevo Reino de Granada,* edited by Francisco José de Caldas, 2:21–162. Bogotá: Editorial Kelly, 1942.

Humboldt, Alexander von. *Personal Narrative of Travel through the Equinoccial Regions of America during the Years 1799–1804.* 3 vols. London: George Bell and Sons, 1894.

"Informe reservado del governador de Rio Hacha sobre el comercio que hacen los ingleses con los indios Guajiros." In *Materiales para el estudio de las relaciones inter-étnicas en La Guajira, siglo XVIII. Documentos y mapas,* edited by P. Josefina Moreno and Alberto Tarazona, 288–296. Caracas: Academia Nacional de la Historia, 1984.

Janvier, Louis Joseph. *Les constitutions d'Haïti, 1801–1885.* Paris: C. Marpon et E. Flammarion, 1886.

Julián, Antonio. *La perla de América, Provincia de Santa Marta.* Bogotá: Academia Colombiana de Historia, 1980.

"Ley número 17 de 1905." In *Diario Oficial* 12,328, Bogotá, April 15, 1905.

"Ley número 21 de 1910." In *Diario Oficial* 14,049, Bogotá, July 28, 1910.

Long, Edward. *A Free and Candid Review of a Tract Entitled "Observations on the Commerce of the American States."* London: T. and W. Lowndes, 1784.

Long, Edward. *The History of Jamaica, or, General Survey of the Antient and Present State of That Island.* 3 vols. London: T. Lowndes, 1774.

Mendinueta, Pedro. "Relación del estado del Nuevo Reino de Granada presentada por el Excmo. Sr. Virrey D. Pedro Mendinueta a su sucesor el Excmo. Sr. Don Antonio Amar y Borbón. Año de 1803." In *Relaciones e informes de los gobernantes de la Nueva Granada,* edited by Germán Colmenares, 3:5–191. Bogotá: Biblioteca Banco Popular, 1989.

Moll, Herman. *A System of Geography: Or, a New and Accurate Description of the Earth in All Its Empires, Kingdoms and States.* 2 vols. London: Timothy Childe, 1701.

Monty, Francisco Xavier. "Reconocimiento y exploración de la costa de Calidonia y el Golfo del Darién." In *Colección de documentos inéditos sobre la geografía y la historia de Colombia,* edited by Antonio B. Cuervo, 1:481–504. Bogotá: Casa Editorial de J. J. Pérez, 1892.

Morante, José Antonio, and Fabián Abances. "Exploración de la costa atlántica de Panamá." In *Colección de documentos inéditos sobre la geografía y la historia de Colombia,* edited by Antonio B. Cuervo, 1:465–480. Bogotá: Casa Editorial de J. J. Pérez, 1892.

Moreno y Escandón, Francisco Antonio. "Estado del Virreinato de Santa Fe, Nuevo Reino de Granada." In *Relaciones e informes de los gobernantes de la Nueva Granada,* edited by Germán Colmenares, 1:153–270. Bogotá: Biblioteca Banco Popular, 1989.

Moreno, P. Josefina, and Alberto Tarazona, eds. *Materiales para el estudio de las relaciones inter-étnicas en La Guajira, siglo XVIII. Documentos y mapas.* Caracas: Academia Nacional de la Historia, 1984.

Mosquera, Tomás Cipriano de. *Compendio de geografía general, política, física y especial de los Estados Unidos de Colombia.* London: H. C. Panzer, 1866.

Mosquera, Tomás Cipriano de. *Memoir on the Physical and Political Geography of New Granada.* New York: T. Dwight, 1853.

Mosquera, Tomás Cipriano de. *Memoria sobre la geografía física y política, de la Nueva Granada.* New York: S. W. Benedict, 1852.

Narváez y la Torre, Antonio. "Discurso del Mariscal de Campo de los Reales Exércitos D. Antonio de Narváez y la Torre sobre la utilidad de permitir el comercio libre de neutrales en este Reyno." In *Escritos de dos economistas coloniales: Don Antonio de Narváez y la Torre y don José Ignacio de Pombo,* edited by Sergio Elías Ortiz, 67–120. Bogotá: Banco de la República, 1965.

Narváez y la Torre, Antonio. "Provincia de Santa Marta y Río Hacha del Virreynato de Santa Fé" (1778). In *Ensayos costeños. De la colonia a la república: 1770–1890,* edited by Alfonso Múnera, 27–73. Bogotá: Colcultura, 1994.

Nieto, Juan José. "Bosquejo histórico de la revolución que regeneró al Estado de Bolívar." In *Selección de textos político-geográficos e históricos,* edited by Gustavo Bell Lemus, 47–115. Barranquilla: Ediciones Gobernación del Atlántico, 1993.

Nieto, Juan José. *Geografía histórica, estadística y local de la Provincia de Cartagena República de la Nueva Granada descrita por cantones.* Cartagena: Imprenta de Eduardo Hernández, 1839.

Nieto, Juan José. "Una temprana argumentación en favor del federalismo en la costa Caribe de la Nueva Granada." In *Selección de textos político-geográficos e históricos,* edited by Gustavo Bell Lemus, 13–26. Barranquilla: Ediciones Gobernación del Atlántico, 1993.

Nieto, Juan José. *Yngermina o la hija de Calamar: Novela histórica, o recuerdos de la conquista, 1533 a 1537. Con una breve noticia de los usos, costumbres i religión del pueblo de Calamar.* 2 vols. Kingston: Imprenta de Rafael J. de Cordova, 1844.

Nissen, Johan Peter. *Reminiscences of a 46 Years' Residence in the Island of St. Thomas, in the West Indies.* Nazareth, PA: Senseman and Co., 1838.

Nugent, Maria. *Lady Nugent's Journal: Jamaica One Hundred Years Ago,* edited by Frank Cundall. London: Adam and Charles Black, 1907.

Pérez, Felipe. *Compendio de jeografía para uso de las escuelas primarias de niños y niñas: Contiene la jeografía particular de los Estados Unidos de Colombia.* Bogotá: Imprenta de Echeverría Hermanos, 1865.

Pérez, Felipe. *Geografía general, física y política de los Estados Unidos de Colombia.* 2 vols. Bogotá: Imprenta de Echeverria Hermanos, 1883.

Pérez, Felipe. *Jeografía física i política del estado de Bolívar.* Bogotá: Imprenta de la Nación, 1863.

Pombo, José Ignacio de. *Comercio y contrabando en Cartagena de Indias.* Bogotá: Procultura, 1986.

Pombo, Lino de. "Reminiscencias del sitio de Cartagena." In *Documentos para la historia de la Provincia de Cartagena de Indias, hoy Estado Soberano de Bolívar en la Unión Colombiana,* edited by Manuel Ezequiel Corrales, 2:167–174. Bogotá: Imprenta de Medardo Rivas, 1883.

Pombo, Manuel Antonio, and José Joaquín Guerra, eds. *Constituciones de Colombia.* Bogotá: Imprenta de Echeverría Hermanos, 1892.

Rafter, M. *Memoirs of Gregor M'Gregor Comprising a Sketch of the Revolution in New Granada and Venezuela, with Biographical Notices of Generals Miranda, Bolívar, Morillo and Horé, and a Narrative of the Expeditions to Amelia Island, Porto Bello, and Rio de la Hache, Interspersed with Revolutionary Anecdotes.* London: J. J. Stockdale, 1820.

"Real Orden de la Junta Suprema Central Gubernativa del Reino organizando la representación de los dominios de las Indias en ella." In *Instrucciones para los diputados del Nuevo Reino de Granada y Venezuela ante la Junta Central Gubernativa de España y las Indias*, edited by Ángel Rafael Almarza Villalobos and Armando Martínez Garnica, 51–52. Bucaramanga: Universidad Industrial de Santander, 2008.

Restrepo, José Manuel. *Autobiografía: Apuntamientos sobre la emigración de 1816, e índices del "Diario Político."* Bogotá: Biblioteca de la Presidencia de Colombia, 1957.

Restrepo, José Manuel. *Historia de la revolución de la república de Colombia.* 10 vols. Medellín: Editorial Bedout, 1974.

Robinson, William Davis. *Memorias de la revolución mexicana: Incluyen un relato de la expedición del general Xavier Mina*, translated and with an introduction by Virginia Guedea. Mexico City: Universidad Nacional Autónoma de México, 2003.

Rodríguez Villa, Antonio. *El Teniente General don Pablo Morillo primer conde de Cartagena, marqués de la Puerta (1778–1837). Estudio biográfico documentado.* 4 vols. Madrid: Establecimiento Topográfico de Fortanet, 1908–1910.

Salazar, José María. "Memoria descriptiva del país de Santa Fe de Bogotá. . . ." In *Semanario del Nuevo Reino de Granada*, edited by Francisco José de Caldas, 2:193–230. Bogotá: Editorial Kelly, 1942.

Samper, José María. *Ensayo aproximado sobre la jeografía política i estadística de los ocho estados que compondrán el 15 de setiembre de 1857 la Federación Neo-Granadina.* Bogotá: Imprenta de "El Neo-Granadino," 1857.

Samper, José María. *Ensayo sobre las revoluciones políticas y la condición social de las repúblicas colombianas (Hispano-Americanas) con un apéndice sobre la orografía y la población de la confederación granadina.* Bogotá: Biblioteca Popular de la Cultura Colombiana, 1861.

Sarmiento, Domingo Faustino. *Facundo: Civilization and Barbarism.* Berkeley: University of California Press, 2004.

Scott, Michael. *Tom Cringle's Log.* Ithaca, NY: McBooks, 1999.

Sevilla, Rafael. *Memorias de un oficial del ejército español.* Madrid: Editorial América, n.d.

Sheffield, John Lord. *Observations on the Commerce of the American States.* London: J. Debrett, 1784.

Silvestre, Francisco. "Apuntes reservados particulares y generales del estado actual del Virreinato de Santafé de Bogotá, formado por un curioso y celoso del bien del Estado, que ha manejado los negocios del Reino muchos años, para auxiliar a la memoria en los casos ocurrentes y tener una idea sucinta de los pasados:

De modo que puedan formarse sobre ellos algunos cálculos y juicios políticos, que se dirijan, conociendo sus males públicos a ir aplicándoles oportuna y discretamente los remedios convenientes por los encargados de su Gobierno." In *Relaciones e informes de los gobernantes de la Nueva Granada*, edited by Germán Colmenares, 2:35–152. Bogotá: Biblioteca Banco Popular, 1989.

Smith, Adam. *An Inquiry into the Nature and Causes of the Wealth of Nations*. 3 vols. Edinburgh: Mundell, Doig, and Stevenson, 1809.

[Stephen, James.] *War in Disguise; or, the Frauds of the Neutral Flags*. London: C. Wittingham, 1806.

Torre Revollo, José. "Escritos hallados en poder del espía inglés Roberto Hodgson (1783)." *Boletín del Instituto de Investigaciones Históricas* 5 (July–September 1926): 76–100.

Torres Ramírez, Bibiano, and Javier Ortiz de la Tabla, eds. *Reglamento y aranceles reales para el comercio libre de España a Indias de 12 de octubre de 1778*. Seville: Consejo Superior de Investigaciones Científicas, 1978.

Turner, Frederick Jackson. "English Policy toward America." *American Historical Review* 7 (July 1902): 728–733.

[Walker, Alexander, and Francisco Antonio Zea]. *Colombia: Being a Geographical, Statistical, Agricultural, Commercial, and Political Account of That Country, Adapted for the General Reader, the Merchant, and the Colonist*. London: Baldwin, Cradock, and Joy, 1822.

[Walker, Alexander, and Francisco Antonio Zea]. *Colombia: Siendo una relación geográfica, topográfica, agricultural, comercial, política, &c. de aquel pays, adaptada para todo lector en general y para el comerciante y colono en particular*. London: Baldwin, Cradock and Joy, 1822.

Walton, William. *Present State of the Spanish Colonies, Including a Particular Report of Hispaniola, or the Spanish Part of Santo Domingo*. 2 vols. London: Longman, Hurst, Rees, Orme, and Brown, 1810.

Secondary Sources

Abello, Alberto, and Ernesto Bassi. "Un Caribe por fuera de la ruta de la plantación." In *Un Caribe sin Plantación*, edited by Alberto Abello, 11–43. San Andrés: Universidad Nacional de Colombia, 2006.

Adelman, Jeremy. *Sovereignty and Revolution in the Iberian Atlantic*. Princeton, NJ: Princeton University Press, 2006.

Adelman, Jeremy, and Stephen Aron. "From Borderlands to Borders: Empires, Nation-States, and the People in Between in North American History." *American Historical Review* 104, no. 3 (June 1999): 814–841.

Agnew, John. *Geopolitics: Re-Visioning World Politics*. London: Routledge, 1998.

Akerman, James R. "Introduction." In *The Imperial Map: Cartography and the Mastery of Empire*, edited by James R. Akerman, 1–9. Chicago: University of Chicago Press, 2009.

Alfonso Mola, Marina. "The Spanish Colonial Fleet." In *Atlantic History: History of the Atlantic System, 1580–1830*, edited by Horst Pietschmann, 365–374. Göttingen: Vendehoek and Ruprecht, 2002.

Allen, John, Doreen Massey, and Allan Cochrane. *Re-Thinking the Region: Spaces of Neo-Liberalism*. London: Routledge, 1998.

Anderson, Benedict. *Imagined Communities: Reflections on the Origin and Spread of Nationalism*. London: Verso, 1991.

Anderson, Benedict. *Under Three Flags: Anarchism and the Anti-Colonial Imagination*. London: Verso, 2005.

Anderson, Fred. *Crucible of War: The Seven Years' War and the Fate of Empire in British North America, 1754–1766*. New York: Alfred Knopf, 2000.

Anderson, Jennifer. *Mahogany: The Costs of Luxury in Early America*. Cambridge, MA: Harvard University Press, 2012.

Appadurai, Arjun. *The Future as Cultural Fact: Essays on the Global Condition*. London: Verso, 2013.

Appadurai, Arjun. "Patriotism and Its Futures." *Public Culture* 5, no. 3 (1993): 411–429.

Appelbaum, Nancy P. *Mapping the Country of Regions: The Chorographic Commission of Nineteenth-Century Colombia*. Chapel Hill: University of North Carolina Press, 2016.

Appelbaum, Nancy. *Muddied Waters: Race, Region, and Local History in Colombia, 1846–1948*. Durham, NC: Duke University Press, 2003.

Applegate, Celia. "A Europe of Regions: Reflections on the Historiography of Sub-National Places in Modern Times." *American Historical Review* 104, no. 4 (October 1999): 1157–1182.

Armitage, David. *The Ideological Origins of the British Empire*. Cambridge: Cambridge University Press, 2000.

Armytage, Frances. *The Free Port System in the British West Indies: A Study in Commercial Policy, 1766–1822*. London: Longmans, Green, 1953.

Avelar, Idelber. "Ingermina, de Juan José Nieto: Antagonismo y alegoría en los orígenes de la novela caribeña." *Revista de Estudios Sociales* 38 (January 2011): 120–127.

Baptist, Edward E. *The Half Has Never Been Told: Slavery and the Making of American Capitalism*. New York: Basic Books, 2014.

Barcia, Manuel. *The Great African Slave Revolt of 1825: Cuba and the Fight for Freedom in Matanzas*. Baton Rouge: Louisiana State University Press, 2012.

Barr, Juliana. "Geographies of Power: Mapping Indian Borders in the 'Borderlands' of the Early Southwest." *William and Mary Quarterly*, 3rd series, 68, no. 1 (January 2011): 5–46.

Barr, Juliana. *Peace Came in the Form of a Woman: Indians and Spaniards in the Texas Borderlands*. Chapel Hill: University of North Carolina Press, 2007.

Barr, Juliana, and Edward Countryman. "Introduction: Maps and Spaces, Paths to Connect, and Lines to Divide." In *Contested Spaces of Early America*, edited by Juliana Barr and Edward Countryman, 1–28. Philadelphia: University of Pennsylvania Press, 2014.

Barrera Monroy, Eduardo. *Mestizaje, comercio y resistencia: La Guajira durante la segunda mitad del siglo XVIII*. Bogotá: Instituto Colombiano de Antropología e Historia, 2000.

Barrera-Osorio, Antonio. *Experiencing Nature: The Spanish American Empire and the Early Scientific Revolution*. Austin: University of Texas Press, 2006.

Bassi, Ernesto. "Beyond Compartmentalized Atlantics: A Case for Embracing the Atlantic from Spanish American Shores." *History Compass* 12, no. 9 (2014): 704–716.

Bassi, Ernesto. "La importancia de ser Caribe: Reflexiones en torno a un mal chiste." *Aguaita* 21 (December 2009): 11–24.

Bassi, Ernesto. "Raza, clase y lealtades políticas durante las guerras de independencia en las provincias de Cartagena y Santa Marta." In *La región y sus orígenes*, edited by Gustavo Bell Lemus, 125–165. Bogotá: Nomos, 2007.

Bassi, Ernesto. "The Space Between." *The Appendix* 2, no. 4 (December 2014). http://theappendix.net/issues/2014/10/the-space-between.

Baugh, Daniel. *The Global Seven Years War, 1754–1763: Britain and France in a Great Power Contest*. New York: Longman, 2011.

Bayly, C. A. *Imperial Meridian: The British Empire and the World 1780–1830*. London: Longman, 1989.

Bayly, C. A. "The Second British Empire." In *The Oxford History of the British Empire*. Vol. 5, *Historiography*, edited by Robin W. Winks, 54–72. Oxford: Oxford University Press, 1999.

Beckert, Sven. *Empire of Cotton: A Global History*. New York: Alfred A. Knopf, 2014.

Beckman, Ericka. *Capital Fictions: The Literature of Latin America's Export Age*. Minneapolis: University of Minnesota Press, 2013.

Beezley, William. *Judas at the Jockey Club and Other Episodes of Porfirian Mexico*. Lincoln: University of Nebraska Press, 1987.

Bell Lemus, Gustavo. "Cartagena de Indias británica." In *Cartagena de Indias: De la colonia a la república*, 39–67. Bogotá: Fundación Simón y Lola Guberek, 1991.

Bell Lemus, Gustavo. "¿Costa atlántica? No: Costa Caribe." In *El Caribe en la nación colombiana*, edited by Alberto Abello, 123–143. Bogotá: Museo Nacional de Colombia, 2006.

Bell Lemus, Gustavo. "El impacto económico de la independencia en Cartagena, 1821–1830." In *Cartagena de Indias: De la colonia a la república*, 105–130. Bogotá: Fundación Simón y Lola Guberek, 1991.

Bell Lemus, Gustavo. "La conexión Jamaiquina y la Nueva Granada 1760–1840." In *Cartagena de Indias: De la colonia a la república*, 11–37. Bogotá: Fundación Simón y Lola Guberek, 1991.

Bender, Thomas. *A Nation among Nations: America's Place in World History*. New York: Hill and Wang, 2006.

Benítez-Rojo, Antonio. *The Repeating Island: The Caribbean and the Postmodern Perspective*. Durham, NC: Duke University Press, 1992.

Benton, Lauren. *A Search for Sovereignty: Law and Geography in European Empires*. Cambridge: Cambridge University Press, 2010.

Berlin, Ira. "From Creole to African: Atlantic Creoles and the Origins of African-American Society in Mainland North America." *William and Mary Quarterly* 53, no. 2 (April 1996): 251–288.

Berman, Marshall. *All That Is Solid Melts into Air: The Experience of Modernity*. New York: Simon and Schuster, 1982.

Berruezo León, María Teresa. *La lucha de Hispanoamérica por su independencia en Inglaterra, 1800–1830*. Madrid: Ediciones de Cultura Hispánica, 1989.

Berry, Stephen. *A Path in the Mighty Waters: Shipboard Life and Atlantic Crossings to the New World*. New Haven, CT: Yale University Press, 2015.

Blanchard, Peter. "An Institution Defended: Slavery and the English Invasions of Buenos Aires in 1806–1807." *Slavery and Abolition* 35, no. 2 (2014): 253–272.

Blanchard, Peter. *Under the Flags of Freedom: Slave Soldiers in the Wars of Independence in Spanish South America*. Pittsburgh: University of Pittsburgh Press, 2008.

Blaufarb, Rafe. "The Western Question: The Geopolitics of Latin American Independence." *American Historical Review* 112, no. 3 (June 2007): 742–763.

Bleichmar Daniela. *Visible Empire: Botanical Expeditions and Visual Culture in the Hispanic Enlightenment*. Chicago: University of Chicago Press, 2012.

Bolster, W. Jeffrey. *Black Jacks: African American Seamen in the Age of Sail*. Cambridge, MA: Harvard University Press, 1997.

Boucher, Philip P. *Cannibal Encounters: Europeans and Island Caribs, 1492–1763*. Baltimore: Johns Hopkins University Press, 1992.

Braudel, Fernand. *Civilization and Capitalism, 15th–18th Century*. Vol. 2, *The Wheels of Commerce*. New York: Harper and Row, 1982.

Brierre, Jean F. *Petión y Bolívar*. Buenos Aires: Ediciones Troquel, 1955.

Brown, Gordon S. *Toussaint's Clause: The Founding Fathers and the Haitian Revolution*. Jackson: University Press of Mississippi, 2005.

Brown, Matthew. *Adventuring through Spanish Colonies: Simón Bolívar, Foreign Mercenaries and the Birth of New Nations*. Liverpool: Liverpool University Press, 2006.

Brown, Matthew. "Introduction." In *Informal Empire in Latin America: Culture, Commerce and Capital*, edited by Matthew Brown, 1–22. Malden, MA: Blackwell, 2008.

Brown, Matthew. *The Struggle for Power in Post-Independence Colombia and Venezuela*. New York: Palgrave Macmillan, 2012.

Brückner, Martin. *The Geographic Revolution in Early America: Maps, Literacy, and National Identity*. Chapel Hill: University of North Carolina Press, 2006.

Bunzl, Martin. "Counterfactual History: A User's Guide." *American Historical Review* 109, no. 3 (June 2004): 845–858.

Burnard, Trevor. "Kingston, Jamaica: Crucible of Modernity." In *The Black Urban Atlantic in the Age of the Slave Trade*, edited by Jorge Cañizares-Esguerra, Matt D. Chils, and James Sidbury, 122–144. Philadelphia: University of Pennsylvania Press, 2013.

Burnett, D. Graham. *Masters of All They Surveyed: Exploration, Geography, and a British El Dorado*. Chicago: University of Chicago Press, 2000.

Bushnell, Amy Turner. "Gates, Patterns, and Peripheries: The Field of Frontier Latin America." In *Negotiated Empires: Centers and Peripheries in the Americas*, edited by Christine Daniels and Michael V. Kennedy, 15–28. New York: Routledge, 2002.

Bushnell, David. *The Making of Modern Colombia: A Nation in Spite of Itself*. Berkeley: University of California Press, 1993.

Cabrera, Marta. "Elementos de colonialidad y biopolítica en una historia caribeña (ficticia)." *Nómadas* 26 (April 2006): 70–79.

Canaparo, Claudio. *Geo-Epistemology: Latin America and the Location of Knowledge*. New York: Peter Lang, 2009.

Canaparo, Claudio. "Marconi and Other Artifices: Long-Range Technology and the Conquest of the Desert." In *Images of Power: Iconography, Culture and the State in Latin America*, edited by Jens Andermann and William Rowe, 241–254. New York: Berghahn, 2005.

Canaparo, Claudio. *Muerte y transfiguración de la cultura rioplatense: Breve tratado sobre el pensamiento del espacio en el Río de la Plata, 1830–1980*. Buenos Aires: Zibaldone Editores, 2005.

Cañizares-Esguerra, Jorge. " 'Enlightened Reform' in the Spanish Empire: An Overview." In *Enlightened Reform in Southern Europe and Its Atlantic Colonies, c. 1750–1830*, edited by Gabriel Paquette, 33–35. Burlington, VT: Ashgate, 2009.

Cañizares-Esguerra, Jorge. "Entangled Histories: Borderland Historiographies in New Clothes?" *American Historical Review* 112, no. 3 (June 2007): 787–799.

Cañizares-Esguerra, Jorge. *Nature, Empire, and Nation: Explorations in the History of Science in the Iberian World*. Stanford, CA: Stanford University Press, 2006.

Cañizares-Esguerra, Jorge. *Puritan Conquistadors: Iberianizing the Atlantic, 1550–1700*. Stanford, CA: Stanford University Press, 2006.

Cañizares-Esguerra, Jorge, and Benjamin Breen. "Hybrid Atlantics: Future Directions for the History of the Atlantic World." *History Compass* 11, no. 8 (2013): 597–609.

Carney, Judith A. *Black Rice: The African Origins of Rice Cultivation in the Americas*. Cambridge, MA: Harvard University Press, 2001.

Carney, Judith A., and Richard Nicholas Rosomoff. *In the Shadow of Slavery: Africa's Botanical Legacy in the Atlantic World*. Berkeley: University of California Press, 2009.

Carrington, Selwyn H. H. *The British West Indies during the American Revolution*. Providence, RI: Foris, 1988.

Carter, Paul. *The Road to Botany Bay: An Exploration of Landscape and History.* Minneapolis: University of Minnesota Press, 2010.

Castillero Calvo, Alfredo. *Conquista, evangelización y resistencia. ¿Triunfo o fracaso de la política indigenista?* Panama: Instituto Nacional de Cultura, 1995.

Chaterjee, Partha. *The Nation and Its Fragments: Colonial and Postcolonial Histories.* Princeton, NJ: Princeton University Press, 1993.

Chaunu, Pierre, and Huguette Chaunu. *Sevilla y América: Siglos XVI y SVII.* Seville: Universidad de Sevilla, 1983.

Childs, Matt. *The 1812 Aponte Rebellion in Cuba and the Struggle against Atlantic Slavery.* Chapel Hill: University of North Carolina Press, 2006.

Chust, Manuel, ed. *Doceañismos, constituciones e independencias: La Constitución de 1812 y América.* Madrid: Fundación Mapfre, 2006.

Clarke, Colin G. *Kingston, Jamaica: Urban Development and Social Change, 1692–2002.* Kingston: Ian Randle, 2006.

Clavin, Mathew J. *Toussaint Louverture and the American Civil War: The Promise and Peril of a Second Haitian Revolution.* Philadelphia: University of Pennsylvania Press, 2010.

Colley, Linda. *Britons: Forging the Nation, 1707–1813.* New Haven, CT: Yale University Press, 1992.

Collier, Simon. "Nationality, Nationalism, and Supranationalism in the Writings of Simón Bolívar." *Hispanic American Historical Review* 63, no. 1 (February 1983): 37–64.

Colmenares, Germán. "La 'Historia de la Revolución,' por José Manuel Restrepo: Una prisión historiográfica." In *La independencia: ensayos de historia social,* by Germán Colmenares, Zamira Díaz de Zuluaga, José Escorcia, and Francisco Zuluaga, 7–23. Bogotá: Instituto Colombiano de Cultura, 1986.

Conrad, Sebastian, and Prasenjit Duara. *Viewing Regionalisms from East Asia.* Washington, DC: American Historical Association, 2013.

Cooper, Frederick, and Rogers Brubaker. "Identity." In *Colonialism in Question: Theory, Knowledge, History,* by Frederick Cooper, 59–90. Berkeley: University of California Press, 2005.

Coronil, Fernando. "Beyond Occidentalism: Toward Nonimperial Geohistorical Categories." *Cultural Anthropology* 11, no. 1 (1996): 51–87.

Coronil, Fernando. "Foreword." In *Close Encounters of Empire: Writing the Cultural History of U.S.-Latin American Relations,* edited by Gilbert M. Joseph, Catherine C. Legrand, and Ricardo D. Salvatore, ix–xii. Durham, NC: Duke University Press, 1998.

Corpis, Duane J., and Ian Christopher Fletcher. "Editors' Introduction." In "Another World Was Possible: A Century of Movements," special issue, *Radical History Review* 92, no. 1 (spring 2005): 1–6.

Costello, Ray. *Black Salt: Seafarers of African Descent on British Ships.* Liverpool: Liverpool University Press, 2012.

Craib, Raymond B. *Cartographic Mexico: A History of State Fixations and Fugitive Landscapes.* Durham, NC: Duke University Press, 2004.

Craib, Raymond. "Cartography and Power in the Conquest and Creation of New Spain." *Latin American Research Review* 35, no. 1 (2000): 7–36.

Craton, Michael. *Testing the Chains: Resistance to Slavery in the British West Indies.* Ithaca, NY: Cornell University Press, 1982.

Cresswell, Tim. *On the Move: Mobility in the Modern World.* New York: Routledge, 2006.

Cresswell, Tim, and Peter Merriman. "Introduction: Geographies of Mobilities—Practices, Spaces, Subject." In *Geographies of Mobilities: Practices, Spaces, Subjects,* edited by Tim Cresswell and Peter Merriman, 1–15. Burlington, VT: Ashgate, 2011.

Cubides, Fernando. "Representaciones del territorio, de la nación y de la sociedad en el pensamiento colombiano del siglo XIX: Cartografía y geografía." In *Miguel Antonio Caro y la cultura de su época,* edited by Rubén Sierra Mejía, 319–343. Bogotá: Universidad Nacional de Colombia, 2002.

Cuño Bonito, Justo. *El retorno del rey: El restablecimiento del régimen colonial en Cartagena de Indias, 1815-1821.* Castellón: Universitat Jaume I, 2008.

Daniels, Christine, and Michael V. Kennedy, eds. *Negotiated Empires: Centers and Peripheries in the Americas, 1500-1820.* New York: Routledge, 2002.

Deas, Malcolm. *Del poder y la gramática y otros ensayos sobre historia, política y literatura colombianas.* Bogotá: Tercer Mundo Editores, 1993.

de Certeau, Michel. *The Practice of Everyday Life.* Berkeley: University of California Press, 1988.

de la Pedraja, René. "La Guajira en el siglo XIX: Indígenas, contrabando y carbón." In *El Caribe colombiano: Selección de textos históricos,* edited by Gustavo Bell Lemus, 1–38. Barranquilla: Ediciones Uninorte, 1988.

del Castillo, Lina. "Cartography in the Production (and Silencing) of Colombian Independence History, 1807-1827." In *Mapping the Transition from Colony to Nation,* edited by Jim Ackerman. Chicago: University of Chicago Press, forthcoming.

del Castillo, Lina. "La Gran Colombia de la Gran Bretaña: La importancia del lugar en la producción de imágenes nacionales, 1819-1830." *Araucaria: Revista Iberoamericana de Filosofía, Política y Humanidades* 12, no. 24 (2010): 124–149.

del Castillo Mathieu, Nicolás. *La llave de las Indias.* Bogotá: Ediciones El Tiempo, 1981.

DeLay, Brian. *War of a Thousand Deserts: Indian Raids and the U.S.-Mexican War.* New Haven, CT: Yale University Press, 2008.

Deloria, Philip. *Indians in Unexpected Places.* Lawrence: University Press of Kansas, 2004.

Dening, Greg. "Deep Times, Deep Spaces: Civilizing the Sea." In *Sea Changes: Historicizing the Ocean,* edited by Bernhard Klein and Gesa Mackenthun, 13–35. New York: Routledge, 2004.

Dening, Greg. *Islands and Beaches: Discourse on a Silent Land. Marquesas, 1774-1880.* Honolulu: University of Hawaii Press, 1980.

Díaz Angel, Sebastián, Santiago Muñoz Arbeláez, and Mauricio Nieto Olarte. *Ensamblando la nación: Cartografía y política en la historia de Colombia*. Bogotá: Uniandes, 2010.

Díaz Consuegra, Fabían. "La búsqueda de lo *Americano*: Matices del discurso apologético de Manuel del Socorro Rodríguez." In *Sociedad y cultura en la obra de Manuel del Socorro Rodríguez de la Victoria. Nueva Granada 1789–1819*, edited by Iván Vicente Padilla Chasing, 195–229. Bogotá: Universidad Nacional de Colombia, 2012.

Di Meglio, Gabriel. *¡Viva el bajo pueblo! La plebe urbana de Buenos Aires y la política de la revolución de mayo y el rosismo (1810–1829)*. Buenos Aires: Prometeo Libros, 2006.

Dodge, Bertha S. *Cotton: The Plant That Would Be King*. Austin: University of Texas Press, 1984.

Dominguez Ossa, Camilo. "Territorio e identidad nacional: 1760–1860." In *Museo, memoria y nación: Misión de los museos nacionales para los ciudadanos del futuro*, edited by Gonzalo Sánchez and María Emma Wills, 335–348. Bogotá: Ministerio de Cultura, 2000.

Donnell, E. J. *Chronological and Statistical History of Cotton*. New York: James Sutton and Co., 1872.

Drescher, Seymour. *Econocide: British Slavery in the Era of Abolition*. Chapel Hill: University of North Carolina Press, 2010.

Duarte French, Jaime. *Los tres Luises del Caribe: ¿Corsarios o libertadores?* Bogotá: El Áncora Editores, 1988.

Dubcovsky, Alejandra. "One Hundred Sixty-One Knots, Two Plates, and One Emperor: Creek Information Networks in the Era of the Yamasee War." *Ethnohistory* 59, no. 3 (summer 2012): 489–513.

Dubois, Laurent. *Avengers of the New World: The Story of the Haitian Revolution*. Cambridge, MA: Harvard University Press, 2004.

Dubois, Laurent. "An Enslaved Enlightenment: Rethinking the Intellectual History of the French Atlantic." *Social History* 31, no. 1 (February 2006): 1–14.

Dubois, Laurent. *Haiti: The Aftershocks of History*. New York: Metropolitan, 2012.

Dubois, Laurent. "Thinking Haiti's Nineteenth Century." *Small Axe* 44 (2014): 72–79.

Dull, Jonathan R. *The French Navy and the Seven Years' War*. Lincoln: University of Nebraska Press, 2005.

Duque Muñoz, Lucía. "Geografía y cartografía en la Nueva Granada (1840–1865): Producción, clasificación temática e intereses." *Anuario Colombiano de Historia Social y de la Cultura* 33 (2006): 11–30.

Duque Muñoz, Lucía. "Territorio nacional, cartografía y poder en la Nueva Granada a mediados del siglo XIX." *Amérique Latine Histoire et Mémoire. Les Cahiers* ALHIM 15 (2008). http://alhim.revues.org/2907.

DuVal, Kathleen. *The Native Ground: Indians and Colonists in the Heart of the Continent*. Philadelphia: University of Pennsylvania Press, 2006.

Dym, Jordana. *From Sovereign Villages to National States: City, State, and Federation in Central America, 1759–1839*. Albuquerque: University of New Mexico Press, 2006.

Earle, Rebecca. *The Return of the Native: Indians and Myth-Making in Spanish America, 1810–1930*. Durham, NC: Duke University Press, 2007.

Earle, Rebecca. "*Sobre Héroes y Tumbas*: National Symbols in Nineteenth-Century Spanish America." *Hispanic American Historical Review* 85, no. 3 (August 2005): 375–416.

Earle, Rebecca. *Spain and the Independence of Colombia*. Exeter: University of Exeter Press, 2000.

Echeverri, Marcela. *Indian and Slave Royalists in the Age of Revolution: Reform, Revolution, and Royalism in the Northern Andes, 1780–1825*. Cambridge: Cambridge University Press, 2016.

Edney, Matthew. *Mapping an Empire: The Geographical Construction of British India, 1765–1843*. Chicago: University of Chicago Press, 1997.

Edwards, Michael M. *The Growth of the British Cotton Trade, 1780–1815*. New York: A. M. Kelley, 1967.

Eller, Anne. *We Dream Together: Dominican Independence, Haiti, and the Fight for Caribbean Freedom*. Durham, NC: Duke University Press, 2016.

Ellison, Thomas. *The Cotton Trade of Great Britain, Including a History of the Liverpool Cotton Market and of the Liverpool Cotton Brokers' Association*. London: Effingham Wilson, Royal Exchange, 1886.

Epstein, James. *Scandal of Colonial Rule: Power and Subversion in the British Atlantic during the Age of Revolution*. Cambridge: Cambridge University Press, 2012.

Esdaile, Charles. "Latin America and the Anglo-Spanish Alliance against Napoleon, 1808–1814." *Bulletin of Hispanic Studies* 69, no. 1 (January 1992): 55–70.

Espinosa, Germán. "*Ingermina*: Avanzada en Hispanoamérica." In *Ensayos completos, 1989–2002*, 2:354–362. Medellín: Fondo Editorial Universidad EAFIT, 2002.

Ewell, Judith. "Bolívar's Atlantic World Diplomacy." In *Simón Bolívar: Essays on the Life and Legacy of the Liberator*, edited by David Bushnell and Lester D. Langley, 35–54. Lanham, MD: Rowman and Littlefield, 2008.

Fabel, Robin F. A. *Colonial Challenges: Britons, Native Americans, and Caribs, 1759–1775*. Gainesville: University Press of Florida, 2000.

Fals Borda, Orlando. *Historia doble de la costa*. Vol. 2, *El presidente Nieto*. Bogotá: Carlos Valencia Editores, 1981.

Farnie, Douglas A. *The English Cotton Industry and the World Market, 1815–1896*. Oxford: Clarendon, 1979.

Farnie, Douglas A., and David J. Jeremy, eds. *The Fibre That Changed the World: The Cotton Industry in International Perspective, 1600–1990s*. New York: Oxford University Press, 2004.

Ferreira, Roquinaldo. *Cross-Cultural Exchange in the Atlantic World: Angola and Brazil during the Era of the Slave Trade*. Cambridge: Cambridge University Press, 2012.

Ferrer, Ada. *Freedom's Mirror: Cuba and Haiti in the Age of Revolution*. Cambridge: Cambridge University Press, 2014.

Ferrer, Ada. "Haiti, Free Soil, and Antislavery in the Revolutionary Atlantic." *American Historical Review* 117, no. 1 (February 2012): 40–67.

Ferrer, Ada. "Speaking of Haiti: Slavery, Revolution, and Freedom in Cuban Slave Testimony." In *The World of the Haitian Revolution*, edited by David Geggus and Norman Fiering, 223–247. Bloomington: Indiana University Press, 2009.

Fick, Carolyn E. *The Making of Haiti: The Saint Domingue Revolution from Below*. Knoxville: University of Tennessee Press, 1990.

Fischer, Sibylle. "Bolívar in Haiti: Republicanism in the Revolutionary Atlantic." In *Haiti and the Americas*, edited by Carla Calargé, Raphael Dalleo, Luis Duno-Gottberg, and Clevis Headley, 25–52. Jackson: University Press of Mississippi, 2013.

Fisher, John. *Commercial Relations between Spain and Spanish America in the Era of Free Trade, 1778–1796*. Liverpool: Centre for Latin American Studies, University of Liverpool, 1985.

Fisher, John. *The Economic Aspects of Spanish Imperialism in America, 1492–1810*. Liverpool: Liverpool University Press, 1997.

Fitz, Caitlin. *Our Sister Republics: The United States in an Age of American Revolutions*. New York: Liveright, 2016.

Fortman, B. de Gaay. "The Colony of Curaçao under British Rule from 1807–1816." In *Dutch Authors on West Indian History: A Historiographical Selection*, edited by M. A. P. Meilink-Roelofsz, 282–298. The Hague: Martinus Nijhoff, 1982.

Frykman, Niklas. "Seamen on Late Eighteenth-Century European Warships." *International Review of Social History* 54 (2009): 67–93.

Gabaccia, Donna. "A Long Atlantic in a Wider World." *Atlantic Studies: Global Currents* 1, no. 1 (2004): 1–27.

Gaffield, Julia. *Haitian Connections in the Atlantic World: Recognition after Revolution*. Chapel Hill: University of North Carolina Press, 2015.

Gallagher, John, and Ronald Robinson. "The Imperialism of Free Trade." *Economic History Review* 6, no. 1 (1953): 1–15.

Gallup-Díaz, Ignacio. *The Door of the Seas and Key to the Universe: Indian Politics and Imperial Rivalry in the Darién, 1640–1750*. New York: Columbia University Press, 2001.

García, Claudia. "Ambivalencia de las representaciones coloniales: Líderes indios y zambos de la Costa de Mosquitos a fines del siglo XVIII." *Revista de Indias* 67, no. 241 (2007): 673–694.

García, Claudia. "Interacción étnica y diplomacia de fronteras en el reino miskitu a fines del siglo XVIII." *Anuario de Estudios Latinoamericanos* 56, no. 1 (1999): 95–121.

García-Baquero, Antonio. *Comercio colonial y guerras revolucionarias: La decadencia de Cádiz a raíz de la emancipación americana*. Seville: Escuela de Estudios Hispanoamericanos, 1972.

García de León Griego, Antonio. *El mar de los deseos: El Caribe hispano musical. Historia y contrapunto.* Mexico City: Siglo XXI Editores, 2002.

Garraway, Doris. *The Libertine Colony: Creolization in the Early French Caribbean.* Durham, NC: Duke University Press, 2005.

Garrido, Margarita. *Reclamos y representaciones: Variaciones sobre la política en el Nuevo Reino de Granada, 1770–1815.* Bogotá: Banco de la República, 1993.

Gaspar, David B., and David P. Geggus, eds. *A Turbulent Time: The French Revolution and the Greater Caribbean.* Bloomington: Indiana University Press, 1997.

Geggus, David P. *Haitian Revolutionary Studies.* Bloomington: Indiana University Press, 2002.

Geggus, David P., ed. *The Impact of the Haitian Revolution in the Atlantic World.* Columbia: University of South Carolina Press, 2001.

Geggus, David P. "Preface." In *The Impact of the Haitian Revolution in the Atlantic World*, edited by David P. Geggus, ix–xviii. Columbia: University of South Carolina Press, 2001.

Geggus, David P. *Slavery, War, and Revolution: The British Occupation of Saint Domingue, 1793–1798.* Oxford: Clarendon, 1982.

Geggus, David P., and Norman Fiering, eds. *The World of the Haitian Revolution.* Bloomington: Indiana University Press, 2009.

Gerbi, Antonello. *The Dispute for the New World: The History of a Polemic, 1750–1900.* Pittsburgh: University of Pittsburgh Press, 1973.

Gillis, John. *Islands of the Mind: How the Human Imagination Created the Atlantic World.* New York: Palgrave Macmillan, 2004.

Giovannetti, Jorge L. "Caribbean Studies as Practice: Insights from Border-Crossing Histories and Research." *Small Axe* 41 (2013): 74–87.

Girard, Philippe. *Haiti: The Tumultuous History—from Pearl of the Caribbean to Broken Nation.* New York: Palgrave Macmillan, 2010.

Giusti-Cordero, Juan. "Beyond Sugar Revolutions: Rethinking the Spanish Caribbean in the Seventeenth and Eighteenth Centuries." In *Empirical Futures: Anthropologists and Historians Engage the Work of Sidney W. Mintz*, edited by George Baca, Aisha Khan, and Stephan Palmié, 58–83. Chapel Hill: University of North Carolina Press, 2009.

Goebel, Michael. *Overlapping Geographies of Belonging: Migrations, Regions, and Nations in the Western South Atlantic.* Washington, DC: American Historical Association, 2013.

Gómez, Pablo F. "Bodies of Encounter: Health, Disease and Death in the Early Modern African Spanish Caribbean." PhD diss., Vanderbilt University, 2010.

Goswami, Manu. "Imaginary Futures and Colonial Internationalisms." *American Historical Review* 117, no. 5 (December 2012): 1461–1485.

Goswami, Manu. *Producing India: From Colonial Economy to National Space.* Chicago: University of Chicago Press, 2004.

Goucher, Candice. *Congotay! Congotay! A Global History of Caribbean Food.* Armonk, NY: M. E. Sharpe, 2014.

Gould, Eliga H. *Among the Powers of the Earth: The American Revolution and the Making of a New World Empire*. Cambridge, MA: Harvard University Press, 2012.

Gould, Eliga H. "Entangled Atlantic Histories: A Response from the Anglo-American Periphery." *American Historical Review* 112, no. 5 (December 2007): 1415–1422.

Gould, Eliga H. "Entangled Histories, Entangled Worlds: The English-Speaking Atlantic as Spanish Periphery." *American Historical Review* 112, no. 3 (June 2007): 764–786.

Gould, Eliga H. *The Persistence of Empire: British Political Culture in the Age of the American Revolution*. Chapel Hill: University of North Carolina Press, 2000.

Gould, Peter, and Rodney White. *Mental Maps*. London: Penguin, 1986.

Goveia, Elsa. *Slave Society in the British Leeward Islands at the End of the Eighteenth Century*. New Haven, CT: Yale University Press, 1965.

Grafenstein, Johanna von, ed. *El Golfo Caribe y sus puertos*. 2 vols. Mexico City: Instituto Mora, 2006.

Grafenstein, Johanna von. *Haiti*. Guadalajara: Universidad de Guadalajara, 1988.

Grafenstein, Johanna von. *Nueva España en el Circuncaribe, 1779–1808: Revolución, competencia imperial y vínculos intercoloniales*. Mexico City: Universidad Nacional Autónoma de México, 1997.

Grahn, Lance R. "Guajiro Culture and Capuchin Evangelization: Missionary Failure on the Riohacha Frontier." In *The New Latin American Mission History*, edited by Erick Langer and Robert H. Jackson, 130–156. Lincoln: University of Nebraska Press, 1995.

Grahn, Lance R. *The Political Economy of Smuggling: Regional Informal Economies in Early Bourbon New Granada*. Boulder, CO: Westview, 1997.

Grandin, Greg. *The Empire of Necessity: Slavery, Freedom, and Deception in the New World*. New York: Metropolitan, 2014.

Greer, Allan. "National, Transnational, and Hypernational Historiographies: New France Meets Early American History." *Canadian Historical Review* 91, no. 4 (2010): 695–724.

Grummond, Jane Lucas de. *Renato Beluche: Smuggler, Privateer, and Patriot, 1780–1860*. Baton Rouge: Louisiana State University Press, 1983.

Guillén, Nicolás. "Un son para niños antillanos." In *Antología mayor*, 145. Mexico City: Editorial Diógenes, 1972.

Gupta, Akhil. "The Song of the Nonaligned World: Transnational Identities and the Reinscription of Space in Late Capitalism." *Cultural Anthropology* 7, no. 1 (February 1992): 63–79.

Guterl, Matthew Pratt. *American Mediterranean: Southern Slaveholders in the Age of Emancipation*. Cambridge, MA: Harvard University Press, 2008.

Gutiérrez Ardila, Daniel. "Colombia y Haití: Historia de un desencuentro." *Secuencia* 81 (September–December 2011): 67–93.

Gutiérrez Ardila, Daniel. *Un nuevo reino: Geografía política, pactismo y diplomacia durante el interregno en Nueva Granada, 1808–1816*. Bogotá: Universidad Externado de Colombia, 2010.

Hämäläinen, Pekka. *The Comanche Empire*. New Haven, CT: Yale University Press, 2008.

Hämäläinen, Pekka, and Samuel Truett. "On Borderlands." *Journal of American History* 98, no. 2 (September 2011): 338–361.

Hancock, David. *Oceans of Wine: Madeira and the Emergence of American Trade and Taste*. New Haven, CT: Yale University Press, 2009.

Haring, Clarence. *Trade and Navigation between Spain and the Indies in the Time of the Hapsburgs*. Cambridge, MA: Harvard University Press, 1918.

Harley, J. B. "New England Cartography and the Native Americans." In *The New Nature of Maps: Essays in the History of Cartography*, edited by Paul Laxton, 169–195. Baltimore: Johns Hopkins University Press, 2001.

Harley, J. B. "Power and Legitimation in the English Geographical Atlases of the Eighteenth Century." In *The New Nature of Maps: Essays in the History of Cartography*, edited by Paul Laxton, 109–147. Baltimore: Johns Hopkins University Press, 2001.

Harley, J. B. "Rereading the Maps of the Columbian Encounter." *Annals of the Association of American Geographers* 82, no. 3 (September 1992): 522–542.

Harlow, Vincent. *The Founding of the Second British Empire, 1763–1793*. 2 vols. London: Longmans, Green, 1952.

Hart, Francis Russell. *The Disaster of Darien: The Story of the Scots Settlements and the Causes of Its Failure, 1699–1701*. Boston: Houghton Mifflin, 1929.

Hartog, Johan. *Biografía del Almirante Luis Brión*. Caracas: Academia Nacional de la Historia, 1983.

Hau'ofa, Epeli. "Our Sea of Islands." In *We Are the Ocean: Selected Works*, 27–40. Honolulu: University of Hawaii Press, 2008.

Hawthorn, Geoffrey. *Plausible Worlds: Possibility and Understanding in History and the Social Sciences*. Cambridge: Cambridge University Press, 1991.

Head, David. *Privateers of the Americas: Spanish American Privateering from the United States in the Early Republic*. Athens: University of Georgia Press, 2015.

Helg, Aline. "A Fragmented Majority: Free 'of All Colors,' Indians, and Slaves in Caribbean Colombia during the Haitian Revolution." In *The Impact of the Haitian Revolution in the Atlantic World*, edited by David P. Geggus, 157–175. Columbia: University of South Carolina Press, 2001.

Helg, Aline. *Liberty and Equality in Caribbean Colombia*. Chapel Hill: University of North Carolina Press, 2004.

Helg, Aline. "Simón Bolívar and the Spectre of *Pardocracia*: José Padilla in Post-Independence Cartagena." *Journal of Latin American Studies* 35 (August 2003): 447–471.

Helms, Mary W. "Miskito Slaving and Culture Contact: Ethnicity and Opportunity in an Expanding Population." *Journal of Anthropological Research* 39, no. 2 (summer 1983): 179–197.

Herrera, Marta. *Ordenar para controlar: Ordenamiento espacial y control político en las llanuras del Caribe y en los Andes centrales neogranadinos, siglo XVIII*. Bogotá: Instituto Colombiano de Antropología e Historia, 2002.

Hoffnung-Garskof, Jesse. *A Tale of Two Cities: Santo Domingo and New York after 1950*. Princeton, NJ: Princeton University Press, 2008.

Horton, John, and Peter Kraftl. *Cultural Geographies: An Introduction*. London: Routledge, 2014.

Howe, James. *A People Who Would Not Kneel: Panama, the United States and the San Blas Kuna*. Washington, DC: Smithsonian Institution Press, 1998.

Hulme, Peter. *Colonial Encounters: Europe and the Native Caribbean, 1492–1797*. London: Methuen, 1986.

Hulme, Peter. "The Rhetoric of Description: The Amerindians of the Caribbean within Modern European Discourse." *Caribbean Studies* 23, no. 3–4 (1990): 35–49.

Jaksic, Iván. *Andrés Bello: Scholarship and Nation-Building in Nineteenth-Century Latin America*. Cambridge: Cambridge University Press, 2001.

James, Winston. *Holding Aloft the Banner of Ethiopia: Caribbean Radicalism in Early Twentieth-Century America*. London: Verso, 1998.

Jarvis, Michael J. *In the Eye of All Trade: Bermuda, Bermudians, and the Maritime Atlantic World, 1680–1783*. Chapel Hill: University of North Carolina Press, 2010.

Jasanoff, Maya. *Edge of Empire: Lives, Culture, and Conquest in the East, 1750–1850*. New York: Vintage Books, 2006.

Jasanoff, Maya. *Liberty's Exiles: American Loyalists in the Revolutionary World*. New York: Alfred Knopf, 2011.

Johnson, Lyman L. *Workshop of Revolution: Plebeian Buenos Aires and the Atlantic World*. Durham, NC: Duke University Press, 2011.

Johnson, Sara. *The Fear of French Negroes: Transcolonial Collaboration in the Revolutionary Americas*. Berkeley: University of California Press, 2012.

Johnson, Sherry. *Climate and Catastrophe in Cuba and the Atlantic World in the Age of Revolution*. Chapel Hill: University of North Carolina Press, 2011.

Johnson, Walter. *River of Dark Dreams: Slavery and Empire in the Cotton Kingdom*. Cambridge, MA: Harvard University Press, 2013.

Joseph, Gilbert, and Daniel Nugent, eds. *Everyday Forms of State Formation: Revolution and the Negotiation of Rule in Modern Mexico*. Durham, NC: Duke University Press, 1994.

Kaufmann, William. *British Policy and the Independence of Latin America, 1804–1828*. New Haven, CT: Yale University Press, 1951.

Klein, Herbert S. *The Atlantic Slave Trade*. Cambridge: Cambridge University Press, 1999.

Knight, Alan. "Britain and Latin America." In *The Oxford History of the British Empire*. Vol. 3, *The Nineteenth Century*, edited by Andrew Porter, 122–145. Oxford: Oxford University Press, 1999.

Knight, Franklin W. *The Caribbean: The Genesis of a Fragmented Nationalism*. New York: Oxford University Press, 1978.

Knight, Franklin W. *Slave Society in Cuba during the Nineteenth Century*. Madison: University of Wisconsin Press, 1970.

Knight, Franklin W., and Peggy K. Liss, eds. *Atlantic Port Cities: Economy, Culture, and Society in the Atlantic World, 1650–1850*. Knoxville: University of Tennessee Press, 1991.

Koselleck, Reinhart. *Futures Pasts: On the Semantics of Historical Time*. New York: Columbia University Press, 2004.

Kuethe, Allan J. "The Pacification Campaign on the Riohacha Frontier, 1772–1779." *Hispanic American Historical Review* 50, no. 3 (August 1970): 467–481.

Kupperman, Karen Ordahl. *Providence Island, 1630–1641: The Other Puritan Colony*. Cambridge: Cambridge University Press, 1993.

Landers, Jane. "The African Landscape of Seventeenth-Century Cartagena and Its Hinterlands." In *The Black Urban Atlantic in the Age of the Slave Trade*, edited by Jorge Cañizares-Esguerra, Matt D. Chils, and James Sidbury, 147–162. Philadelphia: University of Pennsylvania Press, 2013.

Landers, Jane G. *Atlantic Creoles in the Age of Revolutions*. Cambridge, MA: Harvard University Press, 2010.

Lane, Kris. *Pillaging the Empire: Piracy in the Americas, 1500–1750*. Armonk, NY: M. E. Sharpe, 1998.

Langebaek, Carl Henrik. "Civilización y barbarie: El indio en la literatura criolla en Colombia y Venezuela después de la independencia." *Revista de Estudios Sociales* 26 (April 2007): 46–57.

Langley, Lester D. *Simón Bolívar: Venezuelan Rebel, American Revolutionary*. Lanham, MD: Rowman and Littlefield, 2009.

Larson, Brooke. *Trials of Nation Making: Liberalism, Race, and Ethnicity in the Andes, 1810–1910*. Cambridge: Cambridge University Press, 2004.

Lasso, Marixa. *Myths of Harmony: Race and Republicanism during the Age of Revolution. Colombia, 1795–1831*. Pittsburgh: University of Pittsburgh Press, 2007.

Lefebvre, Henry. *The Production of Space*. Oxford: Blackwell, 1991.

Lemaitre, Eduardo. *El general Juan José Nieto y su época*. Bogotá: Carlos Valencia Editores, 1983.

Lemire, Beverly. *Cotton*. Oxford: Berg, 2011.

Lewis, Martin W. "Dividing the Ocean Sea." *Geographical Review* 89, no. 2 (April 1999): 188–214.

Lewis, Martin W., and Kären Wigen. "A Maritime Response to the Crisis in Area Studies." *Geographical Review* 89, no. 2 (April 1999): 161–168.

Liévano Aguirre, Indalecio. *Los grandes conflictos sociales y económicos de nuestra historia*. Bogotá: Intermedio Editores, 2002.

Linebaugh, Peter, and Marcus Rediker. *The Many-Headed Hydra: Sailors, Slaves, Commoners, and the Hidden History of the Revolutionary Atlantic*. Boston: Beacon, 2000.

Lynch, John. "British Policy and Spanish America, 1783–1808." *Journal of Latin American Studies* 1 (May 1969): 1–30.

Lynch, John. "The Institutional Framework of Colonial Spanish America." *Journal of Latin American Studies* 24, Quincentenary Supplement: The Colonial and

Post Colonial Experience. Five Centuries of Spanish and Portuguese America (1992): 69–81.

Lynch, John. *Simón Bolívar: A Life*. New Haven, CT: Yale University Press, 2006.

Madariaga, Salvador de. *Bolívar*. New York: Pellegrini and Cudahy, 1952.

Maingot, Anthony P. "Haiti and the Terrified Consciousness of the Caribbean." In *Ethnicity in the Caribbean: Essays in Honor of Harry Hoetink*, edited by Gert Oostindie, 53–80. London: Macmillan Education, 1996.

Manning, Patrick. *Navigating World History: Historians Create a Global Past*. New York: Palgrave Macmillan, 2003.

Mapp, Paul W. *The Elusive West and the Contest for Empire, 1713–1763*. Chapel Hill: University of North Carolina Press, 2011.

Markovits, Claude, Jacques Pouchepadass, and Sanjay Subrahmanyam. "Introduction: Circulation and Society under Colonial Rule." In *Society and Circulation: Mobile People and Itinerant Cultures in South Asia, 1750–1850*, edited by Claude Markovits, Jacques Pouchepadass, and Sanjay Subrahmanyam, 1–22. Delhi: Permanent Black, 2003.

Marshall, P. J. "The First British Empire." In *The Oxford History of the British Empire*. Vol. 5, *Historiography*, edited by Robin W. Winks, 576–595. Oxford: Oxford University Press, 1999.

Marshall, P. J. *The Making and Unmaking of Empires: Britain, India, and America c. 1750–1783*. Oxford: Oxford University Press, 2005.

Marshall, P. J. *Remaking the British Atlantic: The United States and the British Empire after American Independence*. Oxford: Oxford University Press, 2012.

Martínez, Fréderic. *El nacionalismo cosmopolita: La referencia europea en la construcción nacional en Colombia, 1845–1900*. Bogotá: Banco de la República/ Instituto Francés de Estudios Andinos, 2001.

Martínez Garnica, Armando. "La independencia del Nuevo Reino de Granada: Estado de la representación histórica." In *Debates sobre las independencias iberoamericanas*, edited by Manuel Chust and José Antonio Serrano, 201–220. Madrid: AHILA-Iberoamericana, 2007.

Marx, Karl. *The Eighteenth Brumaire of Louis Bonaparte*. Accessed June 4, 2014. http://www.marxists.org/archive/marx/works/1852/18th-brumaire/ch01.htm.

Massey, Doreen. *For Space*. London: Sage, 2005.

Masur, Gerhard. *Simon Bolivar*. Albuquerque: University of New Mexico Press, 1969.

McFarlane, Anthony. *The British in the Americas, 1480–1815*. New York: Longman, 1994.

McFarlane, Anthony. "Building Political Order: The 'First Republic' in New Granada, 1810–1815." In *In Search of a New Order: Essays on the Politics and Society of Nineteenth-Century Latin America*, edited by Eduardo Posada-Carbó, 8–33. London: Institute of Latin American Studies, 1998.

McFarlane, Anthony. *Colombia before Independence: Economy, Society and Politics under Bourbon Rule*. Cambridge: Cambridge University Press, 1993.

McFarlane, Anthony. "El comercio exterior del virreinato de la Nueva Granada: Conflictos en la política económica de los Borbones (1783–1789)." *Anuario Colombiano de Historia Social y de la Cultura* 6–7 (1971–1972): 69–118.

McGraw, Jason. *The Work of Recognition: Caribbean Colombia and the Postemancipation Struggle for Citizenship*. Chapel Hill: University of North Carolina Press, 2014.

McKittrick, Katherine. *Demonic Grounds: Black Women and the Cartographies of Struggle*. Minneapolis: University of Minnesota, 2006.

McLynn, Frank. *1759: The Year Britain Became Master of the World*. New York: Atlantic Monthly Press, 2004.

McNeill, J. R. *Mosquito Empires: Ecology and War in the Greater Caribbean, 1620–1914*. Cambridge: Cambridge University Press, 2010.

Mejía, Sergio. *La revolución en letras: La Historia de la Revolución en Colombia de José Manuel Restrepo (1781–1863)*. Bogotá: Universidad de Los Andes, 2007.

Merriman, Peter. *Mobility, Space and Culture*. London: Routledge, 2012.

Mignolo, Walter. *The Darker Side of the Renaissance: Literacy, Territoriality, and Colonization*. Ann Arbor: University of Michigan Press, 1995.

Miller, Rory. "Informal Empire in Latin America." In *The Oxford History of the British Empire*. Vol. 5, *Historiography*, edited by Robin W. Winks, 437–449. Oxford: Oxford University Press, 1999.

Millett, Nathaniel. *The Maroons of Prospect Bluff and Their Quest for Freedom in the Atlantic World*. Gainesville: University Press of Florida, 2013.

Milobar, David. "Conservative Ideology, Metropolitan Government, and the Reform of Quebec, 1782–1791." *International History Review* 12 (February 1990): 45–64.

Mintz, Sidney. "The Caribbean as Socio-Cultural Area." In *Peoples and Cultures of the Caribbean*, edited by Michael M. Horowitz, 17–46. Garden City, NY: Natural History Press, 1971.

Mitchell, Laura J. *Belongings: Property, Family, and Identity in Colonial South Africa. An Exploration of Frontiers, 1725–c. 1830*. New York: Columbia University Press, 2008.

Mongey, Vanessa. "A Tale of Two Brothers: Haiti's Other Revolutions." *The Americas* 69, no. 1 (July 2012): 37–60.

Moreno Chuquén, Liz Karine. "Manuel del Socorro Rodríguez: Entre la Colonialidad y la Modernidad." In *Sociedad y cultura en la obra de Manuel del Socorro Rodríguez de la Victoria. Nueva Granada 1789–1819*, edited by Iván Vicente Padilla Chasing, 163–193. Bogotá: Universidad Nacional de Colombia, 2012.

Moya, José. "Introduction: Latin America—the Limitations and Meaning of a Historical Category." In *The Oxford Handbook of Latin American History*, edited by José Moya, 1–24. Oxford: Oxford University Press, 2011.

Moya Pons, Frank. *History of the Caribbean: Plantations, Trade, and War in the Atlantic World*. Princeton, NJ: Marcus Wiener, 2007.

Mulcahy, Matthew. *Hurricanes and Society in the British Greater Caribbean, 1624–1783*. Baltimore: Johns Hopkins University Press, 2006.

Mundy, Barbara. *The Mapping of New Spain: Indigenous Cartography and the Maps of the Relaciones Geográficas*. Chicago: University of Chicago Press, 1996.

Múnera, Alfonso. "El Caribe colombiano en la república andina: Identidad y autonomía política en el siglo XIX." *Boletín Cultural y Bibliográfico* 33, no. 41 (1996): 29–49.

Múnera, Alfonso. *El fracaso de la nación: Región, clase y raza en el Caribe colombiano (1717–1821)*. Bogotá: Banco de la República/El Áncora Editores, 1998.

Múnera, Alfonso. "José Ignacio de Pombo y Francisco José de Caldas: Pobladores de las tinieblas." In *Fronteras Imaginadas: La construcción de las razas y de la geografía en el siglo XIX colombiano*, 45–88. Bogotá: Editorial Planeta, 2005.

Mutis, Álvaro. *La última escala del tramp steamer*. Bogotá: Arango Editores, 1989.

Naylor, Robert A. *Penny Ante Imperialism. The Mosquito Shore and the Bay of Honduras, 1600–1914: A Case Study in British Informal Empire*. London: Associated University Presses, 1989.

Newton, Melanie. "Geographies of the Indigenous: Hemispheric Perspectives on the Early Modern Lesser Antilles." Paper presented at the research workshop "Placing Histories, Historicizing Geographies: A Cross-Disciplinary Dialogue on the Relations between Geography and History," University of Toronto, Toronto, March 25–26, 2013.

Nieto Olarte, Mauricio. "Caldas, la geografía y la política." In *La obra cartográfica de Francisco José de Caldas*, edited by Mauricio Nieto Olarte, 23–51. Bogotá: Uniandes, 2006.

Nieto Olarte, Mauricio, ed. *La obra cartográfica de Francisco José de Caldas*. Bogotá: Uniandes, 2006.

Nieto Olarte, Mauricio. *Orden natural y orden social: Ciencia y política en el Semanario del Nuevo Reyno de Granada*. Bogotá: Uniandes, 2009.

Norton, Marcy. *Sacred Gifts, Profane Pleasures: A History of Tobacco and Chocolate in the Atlantic World*. Ithaca, NY: Cornell University Press, 2008.

Ocampo López, Javier. *La patria boba*. Bogotá: Panamericana Editores, 1998.

Offen, Karl. "British Logwood Extraction from the Mosquitia: The Origin of a Myth." *Hispanic American Historical Review* 80, no. 1 (February 2000): 113–136.

Offen, Karl. "Creating Mosquitia: Mapping Amerindian Spatial Practices in Eastern Central America, 1629–1779." *Journal of Historical Geography* 33 (2007): 254–282.

Offen, Karl. "Puritan Bioprospecting in Central America and the West Indies." *Itinerario* 35, no. 1 (April 2011): 15–48.

Offen, Karl. "Race and Place in Colonial Mosquitia, 1600–1787." In *Blacks and Blackness in Central America: Between Race and Place*, edited by Lowell Gudmundson and Justin Wolfe, 92–129. Durham, NC: Duke University Press, 2010.

Offen, Karl. "The Sambo and Tawira Miskitu: The Colonial Origins and Geography of Intra-Miskitu Differentiation in Eastern Nicaragua and Honduras." *Ethnohistory* 49, no. 2 (spring 2002): 319–372.

O'Shaughnessy, Andrew Jackson. *An Empire Divided: The American Revolution and the British Caribbean*. Philadelphia: University of Pennsylvania Press, 2000.

Ó Tuathail, Gearóid. *Critical Geopolitics: The Politics of Writing Global Space*. Minneapolis: University of Minnesota Press, 1996.

Ó Tuathail, Gearóid. "General Introduction: Thinking Critically about Geopolitics." In *The Geopolitics Reader*, edited by Gearóid Ó Tuathail, Simon Dalby, and Paul Routledge, 1–14. London: Routledge, 2006.

Padilla Chasing, Iván Vicente. "Despotismo ilustrado y contrarrevolución en el *Papel Periódico de la Ciudad de Santafé de Bogotá*." In *Sociedad y cultura en la obra de Manuel del Socorro Rodríguez de la Victoria. Nueva Granada 1789–1819*, edited by Iván Vicente Padilla Chasing, 45–92. Bogotá: Universidad Nacional de Colombia, 2012.

Palacios, Marco. "La Regeneración ante el espejo liberal y su importancia en el siglo XX." In *Miguel Antonio Caro y la cultura de su época*, edited by Rubén Sierra Mejía, 261–278. Bogotá: Universidad Nacional de Colombia, 2002.

Pantaleão, Olga. *A penetracão comercial da Inglaterra na America Espanhola de 1713 a 1783*. São Paulo: Universidade de São Paulo, 1946.

Paquette, Gabriel. *Enlightenment, Governance, and Reform in Spain and Its Empire, 1759–1808*. New York: Palgrave Macmillan, 2008.

Pares, Richard. *War and Trade in the West Indies, 1739–1763*. London: Frank Cass, 1963.

Parmenter, Jon. *The Edge of the Woods: Iroquoia, 1534–1701*. East Lansing: Michigan State University Press, 2010.

Parry, J. H. *Trade and Dominion: The European Overseas Empires in the Eighteenth Century*. New York: Praeger, 1971.

Pearce, Adrian. *British Trade with Spanish America, 1763–1808*. Liverpool: Liverpool University Press, 2007.

Pérez Morales, Edgardo. *El gran diablo hecho barco: Corsarios, esclavos y revolución en Cartagena y el Gran Caribe, 1791–1817*. Bucaramanga: Universidad Industrial de Santander, 2012.

Polo Acuña, José. *Etnicidad, conflicto social y cultura fronteriza en La Guajira (1700–1850)*. Bogotá: Ediciones Uniandes, 2005.

Polo Acuña, José. *Indígenas, poderes y mediaciones en la Guajira en la transición de la colonia a la república (1750–1850)*. Bogotá: Universidad de Los Andes, 2012.

Popkin, Jeremy D. *You Are All Free: The Haitian Revolution and the Abolition of Slavery*. Cambridge: Cambridge University Press, 2010.

Prado, Fabrício. *Edge of Empire: Atlantic Networks and Revolution in Bourbon Río de la Plata*. Berkeley: University of California Press, 2015.

Pratt, Mary Louise. *Imperial Eyes: Travel Writing and Transculturation*. New York: Routledge, 1992.

Prokopow, Michael John. "'To the Torrid Zones': The Fortunes and Misfortunes of American Loyalists in the Anglo-Caribbean Basin, 1774–1801." PhD diss., Harvard University, 1996.

Putnam, Lara. *Radical Moves: Caribbean Migrants and the Politics of Race in the Jazz Age*. Chapel Hill: University of North Carolina Press, 2013.

Putnam, Lara. "To Study the Fragments/Whole: Microhistory and the Atlantic World." *Journal of Social History* 39, no. 3 (spring 2006): 615–630.

Racine, Karen. *Francisco de Miranda: A Transatlantic Life in the Age of Revolution.* Wilmington, DE: Scholarly Resources, 2003.

Rediker, Marcus. *Between the Devil and the Deep Blue Sea: Merchant Seamen, Pirates, and the Anglo-American Maritime World, 1700–1750.* Cambridge: Cambridge University Press, 1987.

Rediker, Marcus. *Outlaws of the Atlantic: Sailors, Pirates, and Motley Crews in the Age of Sail.* Boston: Beacon, 2014.

Rediker, Marcus. *Villains of All Nations: Atlantic Pirates in the Golden Age.* Boston: Beacon, 2004.

Reid, Anthony. *Southeast Asia in the Age of Commerce, 1450–1680.* 2 vols. New Haven, CT: Yale University Press, 1988–1993.

Reis, João José, and Flávio dos Santos Gomes. "Repercussions of the Haitian Revolution in Brazil, 1791–1850." In *The World of the Haitian Revolution,* edited by David P. Geggus and Norman Fiering, 284–313. Bloomington: Indiana University Press, 2009.

Resendez, Andrés. *Changing National Identities at the Frontier: Texas and New Mexico, 1800–1850.* Cambridge: Cambridge University Press, 2005.

Richter, Daniel K. *Facing East from Indian Country: A Native History of Early America.* Cambridge, MA: Harvard University Press, 2003.

Riello, Giorgio. *Cotton: The Fabric That Made the Modern World.* Cambridge: Cambridge University Press, 2013.

Riello, Giorgio, and Prasannan Parthasarathi, eds. *The Spinning World: A Global History of Textiles, 1200–1850.* New York: Oxford University Press, 2009.

Ripoll, María Teresa. "El comercio ilícito, un vicio de difícil curación cuando se contrae. Una visión no moralista del contrabando intercolonial." In *El Caribe en la nación colombiana,* edited by Alberto Abello Vives, 150–170. Bogotá: Museo Nacional de Colombia/Observatorio del Caribe Colombiano, 2006.

Rippy, J. Fred, and E. R. Brann. "Alexander von Humboldt and Simón Bolívar." *American Historical Review* 52, no. 4 (July 1947): 697–703.

Robson, Martin. *Britain, Portugal and South America in the Napoleonic Wars: Alliances and Diplomacy in Economic Maritime Conflict.* London: I. B. Tauris, 2011.

Rodríguez, Moisés Enrique. *Freedom's Mercenaries: British Volunteers in the Wars of Independence of Latin America.* Vol. 1, *Northern South America.* Lanham, MD: Hamilton, 2006.

Rodríguez O., Jaime E. *The Independence of Spanish America.* Cambridge: Cambridge University Press, 1998.

Rodríguez O., Jaime E. *"We Are Now the True Spaniards": Sovereignty, Revolution, Independence, and the Emergence of the Federal Republic of Mexico, 1808–1824.* Stanford, CA: Stanford University Press, 2012.

Rupert, Linda. "Contraband Trade and the Shaping of Colonial Societies in Curaçao and Tierra Firme." *Itinerario* 30, no. 3 (November 2006): 35–54.

Rupert, Linda. *Creolization and Contraband: Curaçao in the Early Modern Atlantic World.* Athens: University of Georgia Press, 2012.

Rushforth, Brett. *Bonds of Alliance: Indigenous and Atlantic Slaveries in New France.* Chapel Hill: University of North Carolina Press, 2012.

Rydjord, John. "British Mediation between Spain and Her Colonies: 1811–1813." *Hispanic American Historical Review* 21, no. 1 (February 1941): 29–50.

Saether, Steiner. *Identidades e independencia en Santa Marta y Riohacha, 1750–1850.* Bogotá: Instituto Colombiano de Antropología e Historia, 2005.

Safford, Frank, and Marco Palacios. *Colombia: Fragmented Land, Divided Society.* New York: Oxford University Press, 2002.

Safier, Neil. *Measuring the New World: Enlightenment Science and South America.* Chicago: University of Chicago Press, 2008.

Sahlins, Peter. *Boundaries: The Making of France and Spain in the Pyrenees.* Berkeley: University of California Press, 1989.

Said, Edward. *Culture and Imperialism.* New York: Knopf, 1993.

Sánchez, Efraín. *Gobierno y geografía: Agustín Codazzi y la Comisión Corográfica de la Nueva Granada.* Bogotá: Banco de la República/El Áncora Editores, 1998.

Sanders, James. *The Vanguard of the Atlantic: Creating Modernity, Nation, and Democracy in Nineteenth-Century Latin America.* Durham, NC: Duke University Press, 2014.

Sartorius, David. *Ever Faithful: Race, Loyalty, and the Ends of Empire in Spanish Cuba.* Durham, NC: Duke University Press, 2014.

Schiebinger, Londa. *Plants and Empire: Colonial Bioprospecting in the Atlantic World.* Cambridge, MA: Harvard University Press, 2004.

Schmidt-Nowara, Christopher, and Josep M. Fradera, eds. *Slavery and Antislavery in Spain's Atlantic Empire.* New York: Berghahn, 2013.

Schneider, Elena. *The Occupation of Havana: Slavery, War, and Empire in the Eighteenth Century.* Chapel Hill: University of North Carolina Press, forthcoming.

Schoen, Brian. *The Fragile Fabric of Union: Cotton, Federal Politics, and the Global Origins of the Civil War.* Baltimore: Johns Hopkins University Press, 2009.

Schwartz, Stuart. *Sea of Storms: A History of Hurricanes in the Greater Caribbean from Columbus to Katrina.* Princeton, NJ: Princeton University Press, 2015.

Scott, James C. *The Weapons of the Weak: Everyday Forms of Peasant Resistance.* New Haven, CT: Yale University Press, 1986.

Scott, Julius. "The Common Wind: Currents of Afro-American Communication in the Era of the Haitian Revolution." PhD diss., Duke University, 1986.

Scott, Rebecca J. *Degrees of Freedom: Louisiana and Cuba after Slavery.* Cambridge, MA: Harvard University Press, 2005.

Scott, Rebecca J., and Jean M. Hébrard. *Freedom Papers: An Atlantic Odyssey in the Age of Emancipation.* Cambridge, MA: Harvard University Press, 2012.

Seed, Patricia. *Ceremonies of Possession in Europe's Conquest of the New World, 1492–1640.* Cambridge: Cambridge University Press, 1995.

Seigel, Micol. *Uneven Encounters: Making Race and Nation in Brazil and the United States.* Durham, NC: Duke University Press, 2009.

Sellers-García, Sylvia. *Distance and Documents at the Spanish Empire's Periphery.* Stanford, CA: Stanford University Press, 2014.

Semmel, Bernard. *The Rise of Free Trade Imperialism: Classical Political Economy, the Empire of Free Trade and Imperialism, 1750–1850.* Cambridge: Cambridge University Press, 1970.

Serje, Margarita. *El revés de la nación: Territorios salvajes, fronteras y tierras de nadie.* Bogotá: Uniandes, 2005.

Serrato Gómez, Andrés Felipe. "Un ilustrado ante la Revolución francesa: Manuel del Socorro Rodríguez como sujeto histórico." In *Sociedad y cultura en la obra de Manuel del Socorro Rodríguez de la Victoria: Nueva Granada 1789–1819,* edited by Iván Vicente Padilla Chasing, 127–161. Bogotá: Universidad Nacional de Colombia, 2012.

Silva, Renán. *Los ilustrados de Nueva Granada, 1760–1808: Una comunidad de interpretación.* Medellín: Banco de la República/Fondo Editorial EAFIT, 2002.

Singleton, John. "The Lancashire Cotton Industry, the Royal Navy, and the British Empire, c. 1700–c. 1960." In *The Fibre That Changed the World: The Cotton Industry in International Perspective, 1600–1990s,* edited by Douglas A. Farnie and David J. Jeremy, 57–83. New York: Oxford University Press, 2004.

Smith, Neil. *Uneven Development: Nature, Capital, and the Production of Space.* New York: Blackwell, 1984.

Smith, Neil, and Anne Godlewska. "Introduction." In *Geography and Empire,* edited by Neil Smith and Anne Godlewska, 1–8. Oxford: Blackwell, 1994.

Soja, Edward. *Postmodern Geographies: The Reassertion of Space in Critical Social Theory.* London: Verso, 1989.

Solano Alonso, Jairo. *El Caribe colombiano en la formación de la nación: El médico y prócer José Fernández Madrid.* Barranquilla: Ediciones Universidad Simón Bolívar, 2012.

Sommer, Doris. *Foundational Fictions: The National Romances of Latin America.* Berkeley: University of California Press, 1991.

Soto Arango, Diana. *Francisco Antonio Zea: Un criollo ilustrado.* Madrid: Ediciones Doce Calles, 2000.

Soto Arango, Diana. *Mutis: Educador de la élite neogranadina.* Tunja: Universidad Pedagógica y Tecnológica de Colombia, 2005.

Sourdís, Adelaida. *Cartagena de Indias durante la primera república.* Bogotá: Banco de la República, 1988.

Souto Mantecón, Matilde. *Mar abierto: La política y el comercio del Consulado de Veracruz en el ocaso del sistema imperial.* Mexico City: El Colegio de México/Instituto de Investigaciones Dr. José María Luis Mora, 2001.

Stein, Barbara, and Stanley Stein. *Apogee of Empire: Spain and New Spain in the Age of Charles III, 1759–1789.* Baltimore: Johns Hopkins University Press, 2003.

Stein, Barbara, and Stanley Stein. *Silver, Trade, and War: Spain and America in the Making of Early Modern Europe.* Baltimore: Johns Hopkins University Press, 2000.

Steinberg, Philip E. "Of Other Seas: Metaphors and Materialities in Maritime Regions." *Atlantic Studies: Global Currents* 10, no. 2 (2013): 156–169.

Stern, Philip J., and Carl Wennerlind, eds. *Mercantilism Reimagined: Political Economy in Early Modern Britain and Its Empire.* Oxford: Oxford University Press, 2014.

Stinchcombe, Arthur L. "Class Conflict and Diplomacy: Haitian Isolation in the 19th-Century World System." *Sociological Perspectives* 37, no. 1 (spring 1994): 1–23.

Stoler, Ann L. *Carnal Knowledge and Imperial Power: Race and the Intimate in Colonial Rule.* Berkeley: University of California Press, 2002.

Studnicki-Gizbert, Daviken. *A Nation upon the Ocean Sea: Portugal's Atlantic Diaspora and the Crisis of the Spanish Empire, 1492–1640.* Oxford: Oxford University Press, 2007.

Sued Badillo, Jalil. "The Island Caribs: New Approaches to the Question of Ethnicity in the Early Colonial Caribbean." In *Wolves from the Sea: Readings in the Anthropology of the Native Caribbean,* edited by Neil L. Whitehead, 61–89. Leiden: KITLV Press, 1995.

Sweet, James H. *Domingos Álvares, African Healing, and the Intellectual History of the Atlantic World.* Chapel Hill: University of North Carolina Press, 2012.

Tagliacozzo, Eric. *Secret Trades, Porous Borders: Smuggling and States along a Southeast Asian Frontier, 1865–1915.* New Haven, CT: Yale University Press, 2005.

Taylor, Alan. *American Colonies.* New York: Viking, 2001.

Taylor, Alan. *The Civil War of 1812: American Citizens, British Subjects, Irish Rebels, and Indian Allies.* New York: Alfred A. Knopf, 2010.

Taylor, Alan. "Colonial North America." *History Compass* 1, no. 1 (2003): 1–3.

Taylor, Alan. *The Divided Ground: Indians, Settlers, and the Northern Borderlands of the American Revolution.* New York: Vintage, 2006.

Thibaud, Clément. *Repúblicas en armas: Los ejércitos bolivarianos en la guerra de independencia en Colombia y Venezuela.* Bogotá: Editorial Planeta, 2003.

Thompson, E. P. *The Making of the English Working Class.* New York: Vintage Books, 1966.

Thomson, J. K. J. *A Distinctive Industrialization: Cotton in Barcelona, 1728–1832.* Cambridge: Cambridge University Press, 1992.

Thongchai Winichakul. *Siam Mapped: A History of the Geo-Body of a Nation.* Honolulu: University of Hawaii Press, 1994.

Tomich, Dale. "The Wealth of Empire: Francisco Arrango y Parreño, Political Economy, and the Second Slavery in Cuba." *Comparative Studies in Society and History* 45, no. 1 (January 2003): 4–28.

Trouillot, Michel-Rolph. *Silencing the Past: Power and the Production of History.* Boston: Beacon, 1995.

Tuan, Yi-Fu. "Images and Mental Maps." *Annals of the Association of American Geographers* 65, no. 2 (June 1975): 205–212.

Tuan, Yi-Fu. "Space and Place: Humanistic Perspective." *Philosophy in Geography* 20 (1979): 387–427.

Van Young, Eric. "Doing Regional History: A Theoretical Discussion and Some Mexican Cases." In *Writing Mexican History*, 167–197. Stanford, CA: Stanford University Press, 2012.

Vaughan, Edgard. "Fracaso de una misión: La historia de Alejandro Cockburn, primer enviado extraordinario y ministro plenipotenciario británico en Colombia, 1826–1827." *Boletín de Historia y Antigüedades* 52, no. 609–611 (1965): 529–566.

Vaughan, Megan. "Slavery and Colonial Identity in Eighteenth-Century Mauritius." *Transactions of the Royal Historical Society* 8 (1998): 189–214.

Verna, Paul. *Bolívar y los emigrados patriotas en el Caribe (Trinidad, Curazao, San Thomas, Jamaica, Haití)*. Caracas: Instituto Nacional de Cooperación Educativa, 1983.

Verna, Paul. *Petión y Bolívar: Cuarenta años (1790–1830) de relaciones haitiano-venezolanas y su aporte a la emancipación de Hispanoamérica*. Caracas, 1969.

Verna, Paul. *Robert Sutherland: Un amigo de Bolívar en Haití*. Caracas: Fundación John Boulton, 1966.

Vickers, Daniel. *Young Men and the Sea: Yankee Seafarers in the Age of Sail*. New Haven, CT: Yale University Press, 2005.

Vidal, Antonino. *Cartagena de Indias y la región histórica del Caribe, 1580–1640*. Seville: Consejo Superior de Investigaciones Científicas/Universidad de Sevilla, 2002.

Vidal, Antonino, and Jorge Elías Caro, eds. *Ciudades portuarias en la gran cuenca del Caribe: Visión histórica*. Barranquilla: Ediciones Uninorte, 2010.

Wadell, D. A. G. *Gran Bretaña y la independencia de Venezuela y Colombia*. Caracas: Ministerio de Educación, 1983.

Walcott, Derek. "The Sea Is History." In *The Star-Apple Kingdom*, 25–28. New York: Farrar, Straus, and Giroux, 1979.

Ward, J. R. "The British West Indies in the Age of Abolition, 1748–1815." In *The Oxford History of the British Empire*. Vol. 2, *The Eighteenth Century*, edited by P. J. Marshall, 415–439. Oxford: Oxford University Press, 1998.

Warren, Harris Gaylord. "The Origin of General Mina's Invasion of Mexico." *Southwestern Historical Review* 42, no. 1 (July 1938): 1–20.

Weber, David J. *Bárbaros: Spaniards and Their Savages in the Age of Enlightenment*. New Haven, CT: Yale University Press, 2005.

Weber, David J. "Bourbons and Bárbaros: Center and Periphery in the Reshaping of Spanish Indian Policy." In *Negotiated Empires: Centers and Peripheries in the Americas, 1500–1820*, edited by Christine Daniels and Michael V. Kennedy, 79–103. New York: Routledge, 2002.

Wheat, David. "The First Great Waves: African Provenance Zones for the Transatlantic Slave Trade to Cartagena de Indias, 1570–1640." *Journal of African History* 52, no. 1 (March 2011): 1–22.

White, Ashli. *Encountering Revolution: Haiti and the Making of the Early Republic*. Baltimore: Johns Hopkins University Press, 2010.

White, Richard. *The Middle Ground: Indians, Empires, and Republics in the Great Lakes Region, 1650–1815*. Cambridge: Cambridge University Press, 1991.

White, Richard. "What Is Spatial History?" Working Paper, Spatial History Project, Stanford University, February 2010. Accessed June 9, 2014. http://www.stanford .edu/group/spatialhistory/cgi-bin/site/pub.php?id=29.

Whitehead, Neil L. "Introduction: The Island Carib as Anthropological Icon." In *Wolves from the Sea: Readings in the Anthropology of the Native Caribbean*, edited by Neil L. Whitehead, 9–22. Leiden: KITLV Press, 1995.

Wigen, Karen, and Michael Lewis. *The Myth of Continents: A Critique of Metageography*. Berkeley: University of California Press, 1997.

Williams, Eric. *Capitalism and Slavery*. Chapel Hill: University of North Carolina Press, 1994.

Williams, Raymond. *Marxism and Literature*. Oxford: Oxford University Press, 1977.

Williams, Raymond L. *The Colombian Novel, 1844–1987*. Austin: University of Texas Press, 1991.

Wilson, Kathleen. "Introduction: Histories, Empires, Modernity." In *A New Imperial History: Culture, Identity and Modernity in Britain and the Empire, 1660–1840*, edited by Kathleen Wilson, 1–26. Cambridge: Cambridge University Press, 2004.

Wilson, Kathleen. *The Island Race: Englishness, Empire and Gender in the Eighteenth Century*. New York: Routledge, 2003.

Wimmer, Andreas, and Nina Glick Schiller. "Methodological Nationalism and Beyond: Nation-State Building, Migration and the Social Sciences." *Global Networks* 2, no. 4 (2002): 301–334.

Wimmer, Andreas, and Nina Glick Schiller. "Methodological Nationalism, the Social Sciences, and the Study of Migration: An Essay in Historical Epistemology." *International Migration Review* 37, no. 3 (fall 2003): 576–610.

Witgen, Michael. *An Infinity of Nations: How the Native New World Shaped Early North America*. Philadelphia: University of Pennsylvania Press, 2012.

Wulf, Andrea. *The Invention of Nature: Alexander von Humboldt's New World*. New York: Alfred A. Knopf, 2015.

Wunder, John R., and Pekka Hämäläinen. "Of Lethal Places and Lethal Essays." *American Historical Review* 104, no. 4 (October 1999): 1229–1234.

Young, Elliott. *Alien Nation: Chinese Migration in the Americas from the Coolie Era through World War II*. Chapel Hill: University of North Carolina Press, 2014.

Young, Elliott. "Regions." In *Palgrave Dictionary of Transnational History*, edited by Akira Iriye and Pierre-Yves Saunier, 882–887. New York: Palgrave, 2009.

Zahra, Tara. "Imagined Noncommunities: National Indifference as Category of Analysis." *Slavic Review* 69, no. 1 (spring 2010): 93–119.

Websites

Banco de la República, Actividad Cultural, Biografías, http://www.banrepcultural .org/blaavirtual/biografias/a

Banco de la República, Cartografía Histórica, http://www.banrepcultural.org
/blaavirtual/cartografia
Biblioteca Nacional de Colombia, Ministerio de Cultura, Mapoteca Digital, http://
www.bibliotecanacional.gov.co/content/mapas-de-colombia
David Rumsey Map Collection, http://www.davidrumsey.com
Razón Cartográfica, http://razoncartografica.com/mapoteca/
Trans-Atlantic Slave Trade Database, http://www.slavevoyages.org/assessment
/estimates

INDEX

Aballe, Josef, 61

Acevedo Tejada, Pedro, 190

Acosta, Joaquín, 178–80, 185, 291n52, 292n55

Afro-American communities: Bolívar's disassociation from, 167–69; communication in the Caribbean among, 57; geopolitics in Caribbean and, 109–12

Age of Revolutions: geographical transformation during, 5–6, 208, 211–12; insurgency in Caribbean region and, 143–45

Age of Sail, mobility and, 8–9

Agnew, John, 11–14

agricultural produce: transatlantic trade in Cartagena and, 37–42; transport from Cartagena to Spain of, 33–34

Alcoy, Antonio de, 103

Alexandre (vessel), 46, 222

Allen, James, 122–23, 125–26, 274n50

Allen, John, 7, 246n24

Altagracia (schooner), 66–74, 80–81

Amable (schooner), 62

Amador, Juan de Dios, 1–2

Amar y Borbón, Antonio, 46

American Revolution, 5–6, 14; British Empire and, 118–20, 139–41; Caribbean trade and, 27–31, 53–54, 121–27; European geopolitics and, 146–47; geopolitics and, 115–18, 128–34, 208; legacy in Caribbean trade of, 139–41; Spanish entrance into, 30–31, 114

Ana Maria (vessel), 42, 219

Ancízar, Manuel, 178–91, 289n38

Andean-Atlantic nation: as Atlantic process, 201–3; Caribbean counternarrative to, 191–201; *patria boba* ideology and, 172–74

Anderson, Benedict, 11–12

Anglo-Spanish War of 1796, 33, 35, 38–40, 53–54, 60–61, 135, 138–39, 146–47

animal exports, 33–34; transatlantic trade in Cartagena and, 37–42

Annette (schooner), 45, 258n116

Antepara, José María de, 176

Appadurai, Arjun, 12, 247n54

aqueous territory: Greater Caribbean free trade area as, 75–81, 263n66; indigenous groups in, 85–88; transimperial geography and, 7–11

Araujo, D. H., 186, 191

Arcano Sublime de la Filantropía, 176

area studies, critique of, 5, 8–11

Arévalo, Antonio de, 89–95, 100, 104, 267n27

Arkwright, Richard, 136

Armytage, Francis, 40, 41, 250n7

Arosemena, Pablo, 153

Arrowsmith, J., 184

Assembly of United Loyalists, 128–29

Astigárraga, José de, 55–56, 255n63

Atencio, Pedro, 61

Atlantic creoles, 17, 87–88, 112–13, 211

Atlantic region: Andean-Atlantic nation building in context of, 201–3; New Granada ports and trade in, 31–52; politician-geographers' mapping of, 179–91; transimperial geography in, 14–16; twentieth-century geopolitics and, 203. *See also* Andean-Atlantic nation

Aury, Louis, 69, 159, 161

Babal, Pedro, 70

Badger (cutter), 164

Baron, José, 70

Barr, Juliana, 266n13, 271n100

Battle of Boyacá, 172

Beckford, William, 122–23

Beezley, William, 293n77

Bell Lemus, Gustavo, 1–2, 42, 185, 289n37, 291n51

Bella Narcisa, 42, 219

Bello, Andrés, 175–76

Benítez-Rojo, Antonio, 10, 252n24

Benton, Lauren, 88

Berlin, Ira, 17, 87, 249n76

Bermúdez, Miguel Francisco, 110, 159, 164

Bernardo (Cuna chief), 85–86, 95, 101, 207, 212

Blaufarb, Rafe, 146

Bliz, Manuel, 46

Blommart, Juan, 114–15, 128

Bolívar, Simón: Caribbean expeditions of, 18–19, 142–43, 166–69, 248n58; Enlightenment education of, 167–68, 175–78, 287n12, 287n14; in Haiti, 158–66, 285n112; insurgency in Caribbean and, 143–45, 151–58, 170–71, 197, 208, 210–12; Jamaica Letter by, 152, 192–93; military victories of, 172–74; murder attempt against, 281n43; Padilla and, 194, 196; *pardos* (pardocracia) and, 168–69, 194, 196, 202–3, 285n125; Pétion and, 157–69, 283n75; Les Cayes expedition of, 158–66

Bonaparte, Joseph, 147–48

Bonpland, Aimé, 287n6

border-crossing: sailors' accounts of, 65–74; Spanish commercial shipping and, 24–27; in transimperial Caribbean, 6–11; region making and, 6–11, 72, 75–82, 205–8

Borregio, Josef, 23, 49

Bourbon Family Compact, 27–31, 251n13

Bowles, William Augustus, 128–29, 133–34, 140, 208, 212, 275n66

Braudel, Fernand, 47

Brazil, sailors from, 70

Breen, Benjamin, 14

Briceño, Pedro, 159

Brierre, Jean F., 142

Brion, Louis, 159, 164

British Empire: American Revolution and Caribbean trade of, 121–27, 139–41, 210–12, 278n117; Bolívar and, 151–58, 166–69, 175–76; Caribbean colonization and, 18–19, 127–34; Cartagena and, 1–6, 114–15; colonial cartography of, 184; cotton cultivation and, 135–39; counter-narrative of Caribbean and, 191–201; insurgency in Caribbean and, 145, 170–71; in Latin America, 118–20; maritime Indians interaction with, 96–106, 107–12; Napoleonic Wars and, 146–51; neutrality in Spanish America of, 148–58, 166–69; occupation of Spanish colonies by, 133, 154–58, 279n11; sailors from, 70; Seven Years' War and ascendancy of, 27–31; transatlantic trade and dominance of, 26–27, 42–47, 52–54, 61, 134–39, 252n20; West India Planters and Merchants and, 121–27

British-Spanish alliance, 152–58

British West Indies, impact of American Revolution on, 121–27

Brooks, John, 114–15, 272n2

Brückner, Martin, 290n70

Bruno, Pedro, 164

Buadas, José, 164

Buenos Aires, British occupation of, 133, 279n11

Buffon, comte de (Georges-Louis Leclerc), 177–78

bullion, transatlantic trade in Cartagena and, 33–34, 38–42, 46–47, 256n71

Burnard, Trevor, 257n102

Burnett, D. Graham, 289n34

Caballero y Góngora, Antonio: American Revolution and, 114, 116, 129, 132–34; Caribbean colonization and, 18; cotton cultivation and, 134–39; foreign neutrals in New Granada and, 62; geopolitics in Caribbean and, 77; maritime Indians and, 101; trans-Caribbean trade policies and, 35–36

Cádiz Constitution, 148, 280n20

Caldas, Francisco José de, 172, 174, 176–78, 181–91, 288n17, 299n44

Calvo, Bartolomé, 197

Campbell, Archibald, 119

Canaparo, Claudio, 75

Cañizares-Esguerra, Jorge, 14

Capitalism and Slavery (Williams), 118

Caporinche (Wayuu chief), 95, 207, 212

Capuchin missionaries, 102–3

Carabaño, Fernando, 159

Carabaño, Miguel, 159

Caribbean: cotton trade in, 136–39; frequency of voyages by trading vessels in, 50–52; geopolitics in, 11–14, 115–18; history of Colombia and, 2–3; interimperial trade in, 16, 47–52; New Granada ports and trade in, 31–34, 42–47; peddler vessels and trade in, 47–52; sailors' role in configuration of trade in, 65–74; sea captains and transimperial configuration of, 58–65; transimperial geography in, 6–11; wartime shipping and trade in, 27–31

Caridad (schooner), 70

Carleton, Guy, 123

Carmelita (schooner), 58–65

Carmen (schooner), 58–65

Carmona, Francisco, 199

Carrera, Antonio de la, 136

Carrera de Indias, 252n24

Carrington, Selwyn, 121

Carta del Departamento del Ismo, 183–91

Carta del Departamento del Magdalena, 183–91

Cartagena: British Empire and, 1–6, 114–15, 128, 154–55; civil war in, 1–6, 40–41, 45, 193; contraband trade in, 97; cotton exports from, 134–39; frequency of trading voyages to, 50; independence of, 256n93; indigenous groups in, 85–86; insurgency in, 144–45, 194–201; sailors from, 65, 80–81; slave trade in, 36–37; Spanish commercial shipping and, 23–27; transatlantic trade and, 31–42, 44–47, 53–54, 60–61

Carter, Paul, 179

cartography: European cartography, 88–95, 289n34; geopolitics and, 77–81, 263n66; of politician-geographers, 179–91, 201–4; of protest, 183–91; in transimperial Caribbean, 88–95, 266n13

Castillo, Pablo del (Golden Hat) (Cuna chief), 95

Cavero, Ignacio, 64, 197

Caymani, Isidro Josef, 63

Central America, British presence in, 129–30

Chagres: Spanish commercial shipping and, 23–27; transatlantic trade and, 42–47

Chatterjee, Partha, 11–12

Cheque, Francisco, 95

Childs, Matt, 96

Chorographic Commission, 186, 293n69

Christophe, Henry, 150, 279n6

Clarke, Alured, 119

climatology, *criollos ilustrados* embrace of, 177–78

Cochrane, Allan, 7, 246n24

Cocinas (indigenous group), 92–95

Cockburn, Alexander, 192–93

Codazzi, Agustín, 180, 186, 289n38, 293n69

Cohn, Bernard, 247n41

Colegio Nuestra Señora del Rosario, 175

Colegio San Bartolomé, 175

Colley, Linda, 111–12

Colmenares, Germán, 204–5

Colombia, Republic of: Caribbean trade and creation of, 16, 53–54, 253n37; cartography and nation formation in, 179–91,

Colombia, Republic of (*continued*) 209–12; counternarrative of Caribbean and creation of, 192–201; indigenous groups in, 86–88; *patria boba* ideology in, 172–74; patriotic narrative of, 1–6; politician-geographers and, 201–3; Reconquista period in, 142; scientific exploration and formation of, 174–78; Spanish commercial shipping and, 24–27; terminology concerning, 286n3; territories included in, 243n4; twentieth-century geopolitics and, 203

Colombia tomado de Humboldt y de otras varias autoridades recientes (Colombia taken from Humboldt and several other recent authorities), 183–91

colonialism: Caribbean free trade and, 2–6, 26–27, 31, 39–42, 53–54, 251n19; cartography of indigenous groups and, 90–95; foreign population influx into Caribbean region and, 10; Haitian Revolution impact on, 169–71; maritime Indians' resistance to, 96–106; politician-geographers' resistance to, 180–91; sailors as information vectors during, 57

Columbus, Christopher, 191

comercio libre y protegido (free and protected trade), 16; in Cartagena, 32–42; hidden ports of New Granada and, 26–27; historical development of, 250n1; impact of war on, 27–31; weight of vessels in, 47

commodities: New Granada trade in, 44–47; shipping to Cartagena of, 33–42

communication networks: geopolitics and maritime Indians use of, 108–12; Haitian insurgency and, 163–66; of maritime Indians, 96–106; transimperial geography and, 17

Compendio de geografía general, política, física y especial de los Estados Unidos de Colombia (1866) (Mosquera), 187

Compendio de jeografía (Pérez), 186, 190–91

Concepción, voyage of, 23–27, 80, 256n71

Condamine, Charles-Marie de la, 287n7

Considerations on the Present State (Allen), 274n50

contemporaneous plurality, Caribbean geopolitics and, 245n18

contraband: maritime Indians' trade in, 97–106, 268n51; peddler vessel traffic in, 47–52; transatlantic trade in Cartagena and, 34–42; as "undertrading," 250n8

convoy system (*sistema de flotas*), 29–31, 252n24

Core, Gaspar, 70

Cornwallis (Lord), 119, 128

Coronil, Fernando, 7

Corrales, Pedro, 58–65, 236

corsair insurgents, 143–45; Haitian Revolution and, 164–66; sailors as, 66–74, 261n33

Corsica, sailors from, 70

Cort, Juan, 70

Cortes (Spanish assembly), 148, 280n20, 280n23

cosmopolitanism: in Haiti, 283n79; of maritime Indians, 17, 86–113; Spanish-indigenous interaction and, 95, 106

cotton: British economic dominance in Caribbean and, 134–39; transatlantic trade in Cartagena and, 38–42, 46–47

Craib, Raymond, 179

Cresswell, Tim, 8

criollos ilustrados (enlightened creoles), 19; Andean-Atlantic nation and, 173–78, 201–3, 288n22; Bolívar as, 167–68; Haitian Revolution impact on, 169–71

Crompton, Samuel, 136

Cruden, John, 114, 128–29, 133–34, 140, 208, 210, 212, 275n66

Cruz de Herazo, Juan, 61

Cuba: British occupation of during Seven Years' War, 28–31; slavery in, 4–6, 96, 245n16; transimperialism in, 14–15

Cuervo, Antonio, 186, 190

Cuna Indians, 85–88, 92–95; mobility and cosmopolitanism of, 95–106, 207–12; Spanish terminology for, 265n1

Cuna-Spanish peace treaty, 93–96, 100–101, 105–6; European geopolitics and, 107–12

López, Cecilio (Wayuu cacique), 111
López Méndez, Luis, 175
Louisiana, Spanish comercio libre policy and, 30–31
Louis XVIII (King), 159
Louverture, Toussaint, 163
Lozano, Jorge Tadeo, 176, 288n17
Lugan (vessel), 49
Luite Bets (schooner), 64
Luque, Andrés de, 110

MacGregor, Gregor, 159, 165
Malaspina, Alessandro, 287n7
Malta, sailors from, 70
Margeran, Francisco, 61
Marinero Alegre (schooner), 45
Mariño, Santiago, 159
maritime history: Indians in, 85–113, 207–12; sailors as resource in, 55–56, 75–81
Marshall, P. J., 273n30, 278n117
Martinez, José, 61
Martínez, Nicolás, 58–65
Martinique, British acquisition of, 53
Marx, Karl, 11
Massey, Doreen, 5–7, 202, 246n24
McFarlane, Anthony, 34, 42, 149
McKittrick, Katherine, 1
McNeill, J. R., 10
Medina Galindo, Josef, 90–91, 98–99, 111
Memoria sobre la geografía física de la Nueva Granada (Mosquera), 186–87
Mendinueta, Pedro, 105, 109, 111
Menéndez de Avilés, Pedro, 252n24
mental maps, 248n58; geopolitics and, 12–14; political imaginaries, 208–12
mercantilism: American Revolution geopolitics and, 122–27; British Caribbean colonization and, 127–34; trade between Spain and Cartagena and, 34–42
mercenaries, 143–45
Merriman, Peter, 8
methodological nationalism, 204–5
Mexico: cultural practices in, 293n77; insurgency in, 165–66
Mier, Fray Servando Teresa de, 176

Miguel, Francisco, 70
military adventurers, 18; in the British Caribbean, 127–34, 275n57; legacy in Caribbean trade of, 139–41
military technology, maritime Indians acquisition of, 97–106
Mina, Francisco Xavier, 159, 165
minor ports (New Granada): British free trade system and, 54; commercial shipping and, 23–27; Spanish comercio libre policy and, 30–31; transatlantic trade and, 42–47
Mintz, Sidney, 9–10, 247n51
Miranda, Francisco de, 114, 175–76, 202, 287nn13–14
Miskito Indians, 86, 95, 99–100; European geopolitics and, 108–12, 131
missionary activities, incorporation of maritime Indians through, 102–6, 269n70
Miyares, Fernando, 110
mobility: of maritime Indians, 99–106, 246n33, 265n5; of sailors, 72–81; transimperial geography and, 8–11
Moñino, José, 34
Montalvo, Francisco de, 163, 264n72
Monteros, Salvador de los, 58–65, 77–78, 237
Montevideo, British attacks on, 133
Montilla, Mariano, 159, 194, 196
Mora, Pablo Francisco, 61
Moreno y Escandón, Francisco, 97, 101–2
Morillo, Pablo, 1, 142, 150–51, 154–56, 163–66, 193–94, 256n93
Mosquera, Tomás Cipriano de, 180, 185–91, 199, 201, 289n38, 291n42, 292n64
Mosquito Coast: American Revolution geopolitics and, 18, 115–18; British presence in, 127–34
mulatos: maritime Indians' interaction with, 107–12; as sailors, 70–71
Múnera, Alfonso, 185, 193, 289n37, 291n51
Muskogee (independent Creek state), 128–29
mutinies, incidence in Caribbean of, 72–74
Mutis, José Celestino, 174, 176

Scott, James, 101, 269n64
Scott, Julius, 56–57
Scott, Michael, 43, 250n7
sea captains: creation of transimperial geography and, 56–74; itineraries of, 235–37; professional career trajectories of, 58–65; region making role of, 81–82
Sebastián (Cuna chief), 85–86, 95
Sederman, Samuel, 70–72
Semanario del Nuevo Reino de Granada, 176–78
Seven Years' War, 4–6, 14; Caribbean trade and, 27–31, 250n7
Sheffield (Lord), 122–27
ship flags, geopolitics and display of, 80–81, 275n59
ship inspections (*visitas de entrada*), 63–65
ships: in Cartagena, 32–42; cosmopolitan composition of crews on, 69–74; destinations of, 224, 226–28; hidden ports of New Granada and, 23–27; impact of war on, 27–31; Indian participation in, 96; interimperial trade and growth of, 16; itineraries of Spanish schooners, 217–22; between Jamaica and New Granada's ports, 42–47; methodological approach to, 213–15; ports of origin for, 223, 225–28; routes of vessels crossing Greater Caribbean, 213–15; ship inspections (*visitas de entrada*), 63–65; slave trade and, 36–37; typical cargoes for transatlantic trade, 44–47; vessel size and, 47–52. *See also* peddler vessels
Siam Mapped, 179
situados, transfer in Caribbean of, 4–6
slavery: abolition of, 245n16; American Revolution geopolitics and, 129, 273n53; in Caribbean history, 4–6; geopolitics and, 13–14; legalization of, 28–31; maritime Indians' practice of, 99–106, 111–12; sailors' contact with slaves and, 57, 67–76, 261n39; transatlantic trade and, 36–42; transimperialism and, 14–15; in United States, 8–9, 246n37
Smith, Adam, 251n16

Smith, Neil, 7, 107
Society of Ethnography (Paris), 188
Society of West India Planters and Merchants, 121–27
Soja, Edward, 6
Soledad (vessel), 46, 217
Sommer, Doris, 294n102
Sosa, Manuel, 61
Soublette, Carlos, 159
space, human construction of, 6–7, 245n21
Spain: American Revolution geopolitics and, 114–18, 126–28, 130–34; British Caribbean and, 127–34; Caribbean trade and, 32–47, 53–54, 253n34; cartography of New Granada and, 90–95, 290n44; cotton cultivation in New Granada and, 134–39; European geopolitics and, 107–12; insurgency in Caribbean against, 143–45, 280n20; invasion of Venezuela by, 142; maritime Indians' resistance to, 95–106, 208–12; Napoleonic invasion of, 40–41, 146–51; sailors from, 70–71; Seven Years' War and decline of, 28–31; warships from, 70–74
Stirling, Charles, 149, 154
Stoler, Ann, 9, 247n41
structures of feelings, 6, 245n19
Studnicki-Gizbert, Daviken, 263n66
"Summer Islands" (Bermuda and Bahamas), American Revolution geopolitics and, 126–27
Sutherland, Robert, 160–61, 164, 166

Tagliacozzo, Eric, 250n8
technological development, cotton cultivation and, 135–36
territorial autonomy: for maritime Indians, 102–6; nation-building and, 179, 289n32
Tertulia del Buen Gusto, 176
Tertulia Eutropélica, 176
tertulias (literary societies), 175–78
Thailand, geo-body of, 179
Thibaud, Clément, 161
Thompson, E. P., 211

Wilson, Kathleen, 117, 272n16
Woodford, Ralph, 156

Ximénez, Manuel, 70

Yngermina, o la hija de Calamar (Nieto), 200–201, 294n99

Yucatán, Spanish comercio libre policy and, 30–31

Zea, Francisco Antonio, 159, 175–76, 183–91, 288n17, 290n47, 291n50, 292n55
Zejudo, Anastasio, 64